WARNE IN WISDEN

An Anthology

EDITED BY

Richard Whitehead

WISDEN
Bloomsbury Publishing Plc
50 Bedford Square, London, WC1B 3DP, UK
29 Earlsfort Terrace, Dublin 2, Ireland

BLOOMSBURY, WISDEN and the wood-engraving device are trademarks of
Bloomsbury Publishing Plc

First published in Great Britain in 2023

This edition published in 2023

Copyright © John Wisden & Co 2023

Richard Whitehead has asserted his right under the Copyright, Designs and
Patents Act, 1988, to be identified as Editor of this work.

www.wisdenalmanack.com
www.wisdenrecords.com
Follow Wisden on Twitter @WisdenAlmanack
and on Facebook at Wisden Sports

A catalogue record for this book is available from the British Library.

Library of Congress Cataloguing-in-Publication data has been applied for.

ISBN: HB: 978-1-3994-0773-1
ePub: 978-1-3994-0772-4
ePDF: 978-1-3994-0774-8

2 4 6 8 10 9 7 5 3 1

Typeset in Minion by Deanta Global Publishing Services, Chennai, India
Printed and bound in Great Britain by CPI Group (UK) Ltd, Croydon CR0 4YY

To find out more about our authors and books visit www.wisdenalmanack.com
and sign up for our newsletters.

Foreword

By Ian Healy

It was well before we first played together that I heard about a young Victorian leggie. The Queensland coaching director, Toot Byron, called me into his office to show me a video of Shane Warne on an Australia Under-19 tour of the Caribbean. He was quite chunky, had a very round-arm action, and as the footage was grainy and shot from a distance, alarms didn't immediately begin ringing for me. However, I had never been called into the coaching director's office before, so I trusted that this was big.

Within two years I was playing with the round-armed kid for an Australian XI in Hobart against the summer's touring team, West Indies. The initial hype of the Under-19 coaches was fully justified – he acted and played well above his years.

Two years after that, it was Rod Marsh and Terry Jenner ringing me from the Australian Academy. My new role as Australia wicketkeeper was to look out for several specifics in Shane's bowling which would keep him focused on the crucial parts of his action, enabling him to bowl consistently well. "Spin up" was our catch cry which ensured the important bowling basics were completed.

Warney's total trust in T. J. and in their mutually great relationship provided a wonderful focus when things weren't too good. Yes that's correct, there were hard times when his drift wasn't happening or the wickets weren't coming and the arm was tired. T. J. was never far away.

Shane's ability to flick the ball vigorously out of his fingers, yet still land it where he wanted, 18 metres or so down the pitch, was his greatest quality. Such total commitment to spinning the ball hard created drift into a right-hander, followed by ripping spin. This had traditionally yielded plenty of bad balls from leggies, usually one every two overs, but with Warney it would be one every hour.

Most batsmen could read him, probably even defend against him, but scoring fluently from his bowling was rare. Even in his rookie year, it felt like he was an old timer who had been through it all before.

Beautifully landed, inswinging, big-spinning leg-breaks were first unearthed on a tour of New Zealand prior to the 1993 Ashes. A couple of months later, Mike Gatting would find out what we all now knew was possible!

Back then, in quite a macho dressing-room, our best player was also the most vulnerable. He regularly checked in with us after good or not-so-good days, asking, "Was that OK?" That is rare and something that astounded us. "Yes Warney, three for 68 from 32 overs was great mate," we'd say.

He became Australia's first cricket superstar, dealing with big endorsements, promotional initiatives and, later, the arrival of the internet, which could be used for good but bring on some stress as well. Donald Bradman and Dennis Lillee spring to mind as possible rivals to be regarded as our first superstar, but in their eras there was less exposure in India, sponsors weren't clamouring for attention so often, media requests were limited and there was no worldwide web. The Don and Dennis played in much simpler times. Maintaining incredible performances while your world swirls around you is what the legends master, whether they are the first global superstar or not.

Let me have a go at defining him as a person before I outline my thoughts of him on the field and then in our post-career years together in the commentary box.

He was always close to his immediate family, Brigitte, Keith and Jason – his mum, dad and brother – who were always fun to have on tour or in the change-rooms after play. Shane was always a people person, had a presence in any room he was in, and considered others – better than most. That was his charisma, felt by kids and adults, male and female, of all ages.

We loved the hilarious yarns he used to tell: about his early employment for a bedding company, delivering mattresses with colleagues who spent hours together in the cabin of a van. Or dropping jam from a piping-hot donut on to his white T-shirt while watching the footy.

Warney was the most generous professional I ever met. Autograph and photo time never ended, or time spent helping me understand his bowling, or introducing us to his high-profile friends such as businessman Lloyd Williams or Kerry and James Packer.

Shane regularly found it difficult to balance the different aspects of his life. He had to move between a self-centred cricket life, finding time for the many who wanted it (and many who had paid for it), while finding some solace of normal life in the real world. He was a major player in all these facets – his dependent cricket team, sponsors, friends and, biggest of all, in the lives of his beloved three children, Brooke, Jackson and Summer.

On the field there was a physiological side to his genius. His hands were built for leg-spin, with thick, strong fingers and arms. His mind had an impressive match-toughness. There was rarely any obvious evidence of physical fitness, but in searing temperatures, he could bowl very long spells without a decline in standards. Amazing.

His passion for the hardest craft in cricket was blatantly obvious. He developed the versatility to change plans within an over, knowing what to bowl to different batsmen, left- and right-handers, top-order sweepers or Asian hitters. His accuracy was his number one quality, he knew what batsmen didn't want.

For Shane nothing was left to chance. As is often the case, the greatest risk-takers are the most well prepared performers. Everything he encountered in the middle had been considered in advance and plans devised, which was always a delight. He made all of us better.

He did polarise people who didn't know him personally. A cricketing genius, with some relationship flaws, created many and varied opinions among fans and the media. He endured the stress of bad opinions in public life, yet still maintained high on-field performances and team relationships. This was another of his remarkable abilities.

Shane Keith Warne was our modern superstar, with a great respect for tradition. He was a bowling genius who coped with incredibly high expectations better than anyone I know, even though he constantly battled insecurities like the rest of us mere mortals.

His love of the game had him constantly discussing and debating best 11s, worst 11s, best red-haired 11, best left-handed 11 ad nauseam. *Wisden* might have been a good nickname for him and my feeling is that he'd be very happy to have his career mapped out by this pillar of cricket. He had joined MCC's World Cricket Committee, and no one was better qualified to discuss changes to playing conditions and to the laws. He was a high-quality thinker on the game, who was willing to be accountable for reforms. In fact, he loved it.

Commentating alongside Warney was also full-on. It highlighted his cricket brain, he strategised as if he was out there, he argued if you disagreed and it continued over dinner. These were the same instincts he displayed as a player, fully committed to winning, with great ability. Several times in his playing days he was well managed by Allan Border and Mark Taylor, who kept him on track.

I hope you can tell, I feel the following pages will be entertaining, thrilling, mind-boggling, authentic and caring – just like Warney.

BOWLED SHANE!

Ian Healy

Ian Healy kept wicket to Shane Warne in 74 Test matches and 68 one-day internationals. In Tests, they combined for 83 dismissals (47 catches and 36 stumpings).

Introduction

By Richard Whitehead

It would be fair to say Shane Warne made an inauspicious start to life in the pages of *Wisden*. In the 1992 Almanack report of his first-class debut, for Victoria against Western Australia in February 1991, he did not warrant a mention. The following year, in his review of the Sheffield Shield, John MacKinnon wrote a brief and unflattering summary of his season. "...expectation exceeded fulfilment," he concluded, referring to Warne's less-than-spectacular Test debut against India and modest 12 wickets in the Shield.

Seven years later, Warne was named as one of *Wisden*'s Cricketers of the Century – it was quite a transformation. The story of how he did it, while simultaneously becoming the most controversial and colourful figure in the game, is told on these pages. It's some tale.

This anthology also goes beyond that hectic first phase of his career, exploring his stellar comebacks, first from shoulder surgery and then a drugs ban, and his barely less frantic years after retiring from Test cricket. It concludes in the shock and all-consuming sadness of his sudden death in March 2022.

From Muhammad Ali to Diego Maradona and Tiger Woods to Michael Jordan, the greatest stars in sport transcend the pursuits that made them famous. Shane Warne certainly fell into that category. From the moment he revealed his extraordinary gifts to the wider world in the Ashes series of 1993, he became the most luminescent performer in cricket history, his charisma outshining the greats of the past such as Don Bradman or Garry Sobers as well as contemporaries such as Sachin Tendulkar and Brian Lara.

This selection of writing about Warne has been chosen not just from the pages of *Wisden Cricketers' Almanack*, but also its Australian counterpart, the magazines *Wisden Cricket Monthly*, *The Wisden Cricketer* and *Wisden Asia Cricket*, and the quarterly *Wisden* publication *The Nightwatchman*.

The following abbreviations have been used to indicate the source of the content:

Wisden – *Wisden Cricketers' Almanack*

Wisden Australia – *Wisden Cricketers' Almanack Australia*

WCM – *Wisden Cricket Monthly*

TWC – *The Wisden Cricketer*

WAC – *Wisden Asia Cricket*

TN – *The Nightwatchman*

Contents

PART ONE

The Rising
1991–1998

The Rising:
1991–1998

"Until he came along, many feared wrist-spin was a lost art, gone the way of the dinosaurs, who vanished years ago when Planet Earth failed to duck a cosmic bumper"
Ashley Mallett, *Wisden* 1997

At first sight, Old Trafford on the afternoon of Friday June 4 1993 was an unlikely place for the birth of a sporting legend. It may have been the second day of an Ashes series – that most storied of sporting rivalries – but what was then a slightly ramshackle ground was less than full, and the Manchester weather was grey and overcast at the end of a damp, cheerless week.

Then Australia captain Allan Border threw the ball to Shane Warne and the world of cricket was sent spinning on its axis.

It had been far from certain that Warne, the 23-year-old leg-spinner from Victoria, would play in his first Ashes Test. In *The Daily Telegraph*, Christopher Martin-Jenkins cast doubt on his selection and Alan Lee, his broadsheet rival in *The Times,* agreed that Australia would play only one slow bowler and that off-spinner Tim May might well be favoured. But Warne was selected, and as he stood at the end of his mark waiting to bowl to Mike Gatting, England's No. 3 and one of the team's best players of spin, there was a sense of curiosity rather than fevered expectation.

The whole world knows what happened next. Warne bowled Gatting with an astonishing delivery that drifted, pitched outside leg stump and fizzed across the bewildered batsman to hit the top of off. "Gatting has absolutely no idea what has happened to it," said Richie Benaud on TV commentary. Then, after a magisterial Benaud pause, and as the cameras showed a bemused Gatting trudging off, he added: "Still doesn't know." The Ball of the Century is now so celebrated that it has its own Wikipedia page, though at the time "The Ball from Hell" was often the more popular sobriquet. "I got a bit lucky there with the first one," Warne told Australian TV viewers that evening.

Luck had little to do it. "Sporting skill elevated to fine art," wrote Robin Marlar in *The Sunday Times* while deploying the words "ball of the century" for perhaps the first time. Whatever you chose to call it, the delivery that bamboozled Gatting and entranced Benaud launched the most spectacular, publicised and controversial career in cricket since ... well, since anyone you care to mention.

Little more than six years after that startling Manchester moment, a distinguished panel of 100 players, journalists and broadcasters voted Warne one of *Wisden*'s five Cricketers of the Century, joining Jack Hobbs, Don Bradman, Garry Sobers and Viv Richards. It was a remarkable accolade – but such had been Warne's mastery of his craft and impact on the game that there were few quibbles.

To English cricket lovers in the summer of 1993, it was almost as if Warne had landed from outer space. "We hadn't heard a lot about him," Gatting admitted. "We're not particularly worried," said England manager Keith Fletcher after Warne ended his first day of Ashes bowling with three for 51. "He won't turn it so much elsewhere." England may have been unprepared but this was Warne's 12th Test, and he had already begun to leave behind the memory of a chastening debut in which he'd taken one for 150 against India at Sydney in January 1992.

By the end of that year, he'd underlined his potential with a match-winning seven for 52 against West Indies at Melbourne. A few weeks before the Australians left for England, he took seven wickets in the match against New Zealand at Christchurch. Martin Crowe, the New Zealand batsman, said he was the best leg-spinner he had seen. In *Wisden Cricket Monthly*, editor David Frith wrote a prescient pre-tour profile which acknowledged his emerging skill and noted that Warne's "lifestyle has got him into most of Australia's colourful women's magazines".

While Fletcher tried to play down the significance of Warne's sensational start at Old Trafford, his opposite number Bobby Simpson did not. "He's the best leg-spinner at 23 I've ever seen," he said. "Even better than Richie Benaud." By the end of a series which brought 34 wickets at 25 (while conceding less than two runs an over), few were doubting the wisdom of Simpson's words – a stratospheric career had been launched. He was a shoo-in as a *Wisden* Cricketer of the Year in 1994 and was celebrated equally for dusting off one of the game's ancient arts and simultaneously sporting a look and exhibiting an attitude likely to draw younger people to the game. As Almanack editor Matthew Engel wrote, he "... single-handedly did a huge amount to switch cricket back into a game where the batsman's fear is of mental torture rather than physical."

By the time the teams met again in Australia in the winter of 1994-95, Warne's hold over the England batsmen was complete. This time he took 27 wickets at 20, including 11 in the match at Brisbane and a hat-trick at Melbourne. Moreover, he achieved a fame that went beyond cricket. As Gideon Haigh wrote in his award-winning book *On Warne* "...he became Australia's best-known sportsman; perhaps even the most recognised Australian." In the middle of the series, Frith wrote an editorial that asked "Is he the greatest?" Given Frith's standing as a historian, this was a significant moment.

While Warne seemed to relish his celebrity status, it had its downsides. For a start, it brought scrutiny of his behaviour off the field, while the focus on the way he conducted himself on it remained intense. At Johannesburg in March 1994, his "celebration" after dismissing South Africa's Andrew Hudson was so unhinged that Jack Bannister, reporting for the Almanack, feared it might spill over into physical violence. "It's probably one of the things I most regret in my life," Warne admitted later.

And there were physical pressures, too. Bowling leg-spin puts an unusual strain on a body. In 1996, he was forced to have an operation on his spinning finger – the third on his right hand – prompting fears that he might be burnt out after a few short years at the top. Two years later, after a tour of India on which he struggled to impose his usual mastery, he underwent an operation on his right shoulder. There was a very real chance he would not recover sufficiently to bowl again, and Australia feared the worst. "Nothing in sport is ever quite as strong as it seems," wrote Peter Roebuck in the first edition of the Australian *Wisden*.

RICHARD WHITEHEAD

1991

The King in the North   Scott Oliver, *WCM*, September 2019

On June 4, 1993, not long before tea on the second day of the Ashes curtain-raiser at Old Trafford, the cricketing world's collective jaw was lowered when a young blond leg-spinner's first delivery in Ashes cricket fizzed, curved and then ripped along such an improbable flight path that England's best player of spin, Mike Gatting, had to seek confirmation from the umpire that the ball that he'd seen (or not seen) rag past the outside edge of his bat, had in fact hit the stumps.

It was soon anointed the 'Ball of the Century', and cricket would never be the same again. Just two short years earlier, however, and only 30 miles up the road, the same S. K. Warne was being booed from the field after his home debut for Accrington in the Lancashire League. "Send 'im back!" bellowed some members. "Go 'ome, pro," foghorned a few more. Tough crowd! (But then, previous pros had included Wes Hall, Eddie Barlow and Bobby Simpson, while Graeme Fowler and David 'Bumble' Lloyd were homegrown stars.)

Warne had just had his off stump sent cartwheeling, first ball, by Ramsbottom's Steve 'Dasher' Dearden, this after an earlier spell of 16-1-82-2 during which Jack Simpson (father of Middlesex's John) had swept him to distraction. "The very first ball he bowled at me pitched outside leg stump," Simpson recalls, "and I was looking to help it on its way, but I absolutely nailed it and it went for four. He came down the wicket, saying: 'What's your f****** game, sweeping leg-spin?' I said: 'If you keep bowling there, I'll keep sweeping you.'"

The previous week, on debut at Burnley, where an eight-year-old Jimmy Anderson was helping operate the scoreboard, Warne had recorded tidy figures of 15-3-34-2 but had then been run out for two. "The committee called me," Warne recalled in his autobiography, *No Spin*, "and said, 'Listen, the pro never gets run out. You have to learn to turn your back on the bloke and burn him.' I argued back, saying the run out was just one of those things and that I wasn't going to be burning anyone. 'No way,' they said, 'the pro doesn't get run out.' End of story."

It was all a bit of a culture shock and certainly far removed from his first experience of English club cricket, two years earlier, when, with his heart still belonging to Australian Rules football, he had played for the now defunct Imperial CC in Bristol, tagging along with a friend, Ricky Gough, and sleeping in the pavilion. "I was 19 years old and began to hang out with a bunch of great guys who loved a beer and taught me how to drink a pint," Warne wrote. "I was 79 kilograms on the scales when I left Oz and I came back 99 kilos. I learned to drink, play cricket and, well, a few other things about life too! It was competitive enough for me to have to pull a finger out or be the Aussie pro who made a goose of himself."

He had stayed home for the following southern hemisphere winter, and only learned of the Accrington offer when his bowling mentor Terry Jenner introduced him to the agent and ex-Test player Neil Hawke, a former pro at both Nelson and East Lancashire. Hawke explained that Accrington's first choice, Shaun Young, the

Tasmanian all-rounder, had sustained a serious shoulder injury and they needed a last-minute replacement, so Warne took the plunge.

"I kind of wanted to go back to Bristol," he writes, "but I was on a fiver a week there for painting the fences. At Accrington I was offered between £1,500 and £2,000 – plus car, airfare and accommodation. I thought, 'Wow, I've got to do this.' So I used to drive miles up and down the motorway to get on the piss with the boys in Bristol through the night and then, too often, arrive back at Accy the next morning worse for wear."

This home-from-homesickness and long-distance carousing may have explained Warne's early struggles, for after the Burnley and Ramsbottom losses he sent down 11-0-40-0 in defeat to East Lancs, whose pro, Warne's fellow Victorian and soon to be Australia teammate, Paul Reiffel, struck an unbeaten 70 while Phil Mooney castled him for two to leave his batting average sitting at 1.33, while his bowling average was a portly 39.

Even so, skipper Andy Barker is adamant that Warne's extracurricular behaviour was nothing particularly untoward and only once impinged upon his cricket, when he turned up late for the start of a game, had to be admonished and never repeated the infraction. Indeed, aside from lauding his competitiveness and generosity, his Accrington teammates attest to his enthusiasm and diligence at training, where he introduced professional drills and the then-novelty of stretching. He could invariably be found bowling for hours on end in the nets, even on non-training days, with a group of Aussie professionals located in the north-west.

He may not have been entirely the model pro in other areas of his life, however, with Barker recalling how "he was a lot chubbier then. He was carrying a bit of timber. He used to live off McDonald's. And his terrace house wasn't the cleanest or tidiest place you've ever seen. I wouldn't have fancied a cup of tea there. It was like *Men Behaving Badly*."

Warne's indifferent start to the season moved Barker to take morale-boosting action. "I decided to take him out to a local nightspot, Martholme Grange. Strippers and chicken in a basket. He was a bit down. You could see it in his face. He was only 21 years old, trying to be a professional in a team with a lot of guys who were older than him, which isn't easy, whoever you are. We were in transition – we'd lost five or six players, and 'Bumble' had retired – but because we'd always been there challenging for the league there was a lot of pressure on him from the members. It was the first time we'd seen him relaxed. We all had a few drinks and said: our season starts now."

Things began to improve the very next weekend – personally, at least, as Warne returned 15-3-38-4 against Colin Miller's Rawtenstall and scored 34 (he was stumped, charging at Keith Roscoe). But it was the following day that finally got his season jumping. The Worsley Cup first-round match against Ramsbottom has entered Lancashire League folklore, with Accrington defending a middling score of 166 and the opposition having reached 107 for two in reply, with 18 overs left, when the game was interrupted by rain and had to be finished off on the Monday evening. Inspired by Warne's 19-7-46-5 – which included a final over that began with 10 to defend and went: leg-bye, two missed stumpings, slogged six, stumping, dot – Accrington got home by two runs.

However, it would be a further month before they won their first game in the league, the return fixture against East Lancs, who would finish the season in second place. Warne picked up 4-45, another step in placating his detractors among the membership, another step in his understanding of the culture, as he explains in *No Spin*. "I hadn't realised how important this Lancashire League cricket was – it was more important than Test cricket in their world. The supporters got there really early and I remember thinking, 'Whoa, look at this lot!' There were loads of people setting up their barbecues and stuff – there were people everywhere… The rules were simple: if you didn't perform they bagged you! Or worse, they didn't even bother to talk to you."

Despite the uptick in performance, Warne would have to wait until after the summer equinox for his first league 'Michelle' five-for (and the fabled 'collection hat', which Warne habitually put back behind the bar for team drinks), taking 6-63 at Rishton, whose own Australian leg-spinning pro, Peter Sleep, nevertheless edged the head-to-head (taking 6-24 and scoring 60) as he would in the return fixture, with 100* and 4-32 to Warne's 4-58. Sleep wouldn't be the only gnarled old pro of the leagues to school the young tyro on these alien northern pitches, with Bacup's West Indian all-rounder Roger Harper also having the better of things.

It had taken Warne a while to get to grips with conditions – on the field, at least, for Shane was no stranger to the town's main nightspot, Lar-de-dars, reputed to be the country's first million-pound nightclub (tipple: daiquiri and lemonade) – but Barker never lost faith and knew, beyond the stats, that he had a gem on his hands. The problem, he says, was that diabolical close-catching and even worse wicketkeeping failed to support Warne's emergent genius.

"We dropped about 30 catches off him, and the amount of missed stumpings was unbelievable. It was also The Season of Byes and I ended up virtually putting a longstop in. We had one of the top keepers in the league at the time, Billy Rawstron, and Shane was making him look as though he'd never kept before. We tried a code for when he bowled his variations. He used to scratch his backside, tie his shoelace, all sorts. It was no use. He ended up throwing his gloves down and said: 'I can't pick him!' He was quite agitated. It was painful."

Warne duly followed his six-for at Rishton with 5-35 against Ramsbottom, for whom Jack Simpson once again made a half-century to become one of only two amateur players to get twin fifties against Warne that summer. The other was Nelson's Ian Clarkson, an insurance salesman who scored 69 and 50, both not out, ably assisted by yet another Aussie pro, Joe Scuderi, who made 121 and 52, also both unbeaten.

Clarkson admits he couldn't pick him: "Joe told me I'd spot the googly because he drops his arm. His first googly, I never saw it. It was like a snake. But if he tossed it up I couldn't resist. We became quite friendly and he got us tickets for Old Trafford, the day he bowled the Gatting ball."

Accrington would only win two more games before Warne's early departure for an Australia A tour of Zimbabwe, and ended up just one spot above the wooden spoon, having come fourth and second the previous two years. Barker felt this was less a reflection of Warne's contribution – 73 wickets at 15.43 and sixth in the wicket charts despite missing the last three games – and more 'a squad in transition'. He was unequivocal when consulted about retaining the leggie for the following season. "I said he'd benefit enormously from having a year under his belt and that he'd play for Australia within 12 months, and people in the committee room laughed at me."

As it transpired, Warne wouldn't have been available. On the second day of the following year, four months and a day after his Accrington farewell, he made a Test debut at the SCG and after that… well, it's rumoured to have gone fairly well.

WORDS ON WARNE

"Yes he misbehaved and he was a bit over the top sometimes but he wasn't bad at all. Whenever he was in any difficulties he'd always call me up. That included things like boils on his bum or car breakdowns."

Peter Barratt, Accrington CC – *TWC*, September 2010

1991-92

Cricket in Australia   John MacKinnon, *Wisden* 1993

Shane Warne became the new leg-spinning hope, thanks to some promising returns in Zimbabwe, and dismissing mostly tailenders for the Australian XI against the West Indies. Again expectation exceeded fulfilment, but Warne demonstrated control if not variety; that may come with experience.

1992-93

Sri Lanka v Australia, Colombo (SSC)   Mike Coward, *Wisden* 1994
(First Test, August 17-22)

A final total of 471 set Sri Lanka 181 in 58 overs and gave the visitors just a little optimism. Then, after De Silva's fateful error, Matthews returned four for 76 and with Warne, who claimed three in 13 balls without conceding a run, he engineered an improbable victory.

Australia v West Indies, Melbourne   Tony Cozier, *Wisden* 1994
(Second Test, December 26-30)

While Simmons and his captain, Richardson, were attacking in a second-wicket partnership of 134 on the final morning West Indies threatened a remarkable victory, but a target of 359 on a worn pitch was an enormous one. Once Warne, in his fifth Test, bowled Richardson with a top-spinner just before lunch, the effort disintegrated.

The last nine wickets fell for 76 and by tea Australia were 1-0 up in the series. Warne was the destroyer with seven wickets, three from the North End and his last four, for three runs, from the South.

WORDS ON WARNE

"You have to remember there are a lot of spinners who come in and take a lot of wickets in one match and then you never hear of them again. I don't think our batsmen are afraid of him. We respect him as a Test player but he's not a worry."

Richie Richardson, West Indies captain – *WCM*, February 1993

New Zealand v Australia, Christchurch   Patrick Smithers, *Wisden* 1994
(First Test, February 25-28)

The Australian bowlers had no trouble finding their line. McDermott dismissed Greatbatch and Jones before stumps on the second day, and Hughes removed Crowe, sparring indecisively at a lifter, during a splendid spell early on the third. Picking up Crowe twice in the match was a considerable service. But no one made the New Zealanders more uncomfortable than Warne. Wright and Rutherford poked and prodded at his leg-spin with such suspicion that his first seven overs did not yield a run. Warne bowled unchanged in each innings, 22 overs in the first and 26 in the second, for match figures of seven wickets for 86.

New Zealand v Australia, Auckland   Patrick Smithers, *Wisden* 1994
(Third Test, March 12-16)

The impression that Eden Park was a swing bowler's paradise was reinforced next day by Steve Waugh, whose potent out-swinger had Crowe caught at first slip attempting to turn the ball to leg. Unfortunately, that resulted in Border holding back Warne – other than a maiden before lunch – until the last hour of the day, when New Zealand led by 39. Once again Warne changed a game's direction, taking four wickets for eight from 15 overs. Collectively the New Zealand batsmen had struck their best form of the series, but had little to show for it: the top five reached 20, but none passed Rutherford's 43, which ended when he danced recklessly down the pitch to Warne's second delivery.

New Zealand v Australia in 1992-93   Patrick Smithers, *Wisden* 1994

The cricket throughout the tour was engaging, not for any sustained excellence, but for the intensity of the struggle. The man who did more than any other to entertain was Shane Warne, who somehow managed to combine that quality with a consistency not matched by any other player. After helping bowl Australia to victory in the

Christchurch Test, he was unfortunate not to have more time in Wellington or more runs to defend in Auckland. His 17 wickets at 15.05 broke Dennis Lillee's record of 15 for the most by an Australian on a Test tour of New Zealand and equalled Craig McDermott's record for Australia against New Zealand in either country. Incredibly for a wrist-spinner, he conceded an average of only 1.61 runs per over.

THE ASHES, 1993

The 1993 Australians   David Frith, *WCM*, May 1993

Regular spin is in the hands of the sole South Australian, Tim May, the off-spinner who toured in 1989 without playing in a Test, and Shane Warne, the blond leg-spinner whose lifestyle has got him into most of Australia's colourful women's magazines. Warne, 23, chosen by Australia's cricket writers as Young Cricketer of the Year, already knows what it is like to spin his country to victory (seven for 52 v West Indies, Melbourne), and his big-spinning leg-break, well-concealed googly and nasty "flipper" may be aimed at spiking England's big guns, Hick and Smith. His target is 20 wickets for the series, and he wants them to come when they are most needed.

Worcestershire v Australians, Worcester   Chris Moore, *Wisden* 1994
(May 5-7)

Worcestershire's recovery owed everything to Hick's 187, including 132 in boundaries. He reached his 69th century, on the fifth anniversary of his 405 against Somerset, off 136 balls and won hands down his first confrontation with Warne, off whom he scored 96 from 77 balls. However, Warne appeared entirely unruffled by the experience and close observation suggested his main concern was to give Hick as little idea as possible of his tricks and variations.

CLASSIC TEST 1

England v Australia, Manchester   Patrick Murphy, *Wisden* 1994
(First Test)
June 3, 4, 5, 6, 7 – Australia won by 179 runs. Toss: England.
Debuts: A. R. Caddick, P. M. Such; B. P. Julian, M. J. Slater

An enthralling match of splendid individual achievements was won by Australia with 9.4 overs to spare. A rarity among modern Tests in England, it was shaped by slow bowling and finally decided by leg-spin. Warne, the 23-year-old Victorian, returned match figures of eight for 137, the best in England by an Australian leg-spinner since W. J. O'Reilly took ten for 122 at Leeds in 1938. One particular delivery from Warne set the tone for the series. His first ball in an Ashes contest pitched outside leg stump

England v Australia, Manchester, 1993

AUSTRALIA	First innings		Second innings	
M. A. Taylor c and b Such	124	–	lbw b Such	9
M. J. Slater c Stewart b DeFreitas	58	–	c Caddick b Such	27
D. C. Boon c Lewis b Such	21	–	c Gatting b DeFreitas	93
M. E. Waugh c and·b Tufnell	6	–	b Tufnell	64
*A. R. Border st Stewart b Such	17	–	c and b Caddick	31
S. R. Waugh b Such	3	–	not out	78
†I. A. Healy c Such b Tufnell	12	–	not out	102
B. P. Julian c Gatting b Such	0			
M. G. Hughes c DeFreitas b Such	2			
S. K. Warne not out	15			
C. J. McDermott run out (Lewis/Stewart)	8			
B 8, lb 8, nb 7	23		B 6, lb 14, w 8	28

1/128 (2) 2/183 (3) 3/221 (4) **289** 1/23 (1) **(5 wkts dec.) 432**
4/225 (1) 5/232 (6) 6/260 (5) 2/46 (2) 3/155 (4)
7/264 (8) 8/266 (9) 9/267 (7) 10/289 (11) 4/234 (5) 5/252 (3)

First innings—Caddick 15–4–38–0; DeFreitas 23–8–46–1; Lewis 13–2–44–0; Such 33.3–9–67–6;
Tufnell 28–5–78–2.
Second innings—Caddick 20–3–79–1; DeFreitas 24–1–80–1; Such 31–6–78–2; Tufnell 37–4–112–1;
Hick 9–1–20–0; Lewis 9–0–43–0.

ENGLAND	First innings		Second innings	
*G. A. Gooch c Julian b Warne	65	–	handled the ball	133
M. A. Atherton c Healy b Hughes	19	–	c Taylor b Warne	25
M. W. Gatting b Warne	4	–	b Hughes	23
R. A. Smith c Taylor b Warne	4	–	b Warne	18
G. A. Hick c Border b Hughes	34	–	c Healy b Hughes	22
†A. J. Stewart b Julian	27	–	c Healy b Warne	11
C. C. Lewis c Boon b Hughes	9	–	c Taylor b Warne	43
P. A. J. DeFreitas lbw b Julian	5	–	lbw b Julian	7
A. R. Caddick c Healy b Warne	7	–	c Warne b Hughes	25
P. M. Such not out	14	–	c Border b Hughes	9
P. C. R. Tufnell c Healy b Hughes	1	–	not out	0
B 6, lb 10, nb 5	21		Lb 11, w 1, nb 4	16

1/71 (2) 2/80 (3) 3/84 (4) **210** 1/73 (2) 2/133 (3) **332**
4/123 (1) 5/148 (5) 6/168 (7) 3/171 (4) 4/223 (1)
7/178 (8) 8/183 (6) 9/203 (9) 10/210 (11) 5/230 (5) 6/238 (6) 7/260 (8)
8/299 (7) 9/331 (9) 10/332 (10)

First innings—McDermott 18–2–50–0; Hughes 20.5–5–59–4; Julian 11–2–30–2; Warne 24–10–51–4;
Border 1–0–4–0.
Second innings—McDermott 30–9–76–0; Hughes 27.2–4–92–4; Warne 49–26–86–4; Julian 14–1–67–1.

Umpires: H. D. Bird and K. E. Palmer.   Referee: Mansur Ali Khan.

and hit the top of Gatting's off stump. Gatting looked understandably bewildered as he dragged himself off the field. Thereafter only Gooch played Warne with conviction: never, perhaps, has one delivery cast so long a shadow over a game, or a series. Warne also produced a stunning catch at backward square leg to dismiss Caddick in the tense final stages as England tried to salvage a draw. He was rightly named Man of the Match.

No time was lost in the Test but a succession of wet days beforehand had hampered the preparations of the groundstaff. The soft pitch was not planned but it allowed the spinners to hold unexpected sway on the first two days, and improved the cricket. It ought to have given England the advantage since they fielded two spinners to Australia's one. There was more confusion, though, about England's seam attack. Alan Igglesden was prevented from adding to his solitary cap when he sustained a groin strain in the indoor school the day before the game. DeFreitas was summoned from Lancashire's match and then picked ahead of Ilott, who had been in the original 12. DeFreitas did little to justify his selection.

Such, however, found himself bowling before Thursday lunchtime and shared the first day's honours with Taylor – who made another impressive start to an Ashes series – and Slater. The opening pair, both from the New South Wales town of Wagga Wagga, began with a stand of 128 but then Australia lost three wickets for 11 in the final hour, including Steve Waugh, who was bowled off stump trying to drive – a classic off-spinner's dismissal. On the second day, Such moved on to take six for 67 and his cool and control compared favourably with the palpable lack of confidence shown by Tufnell.

With Australia out for 289 and Gooch and Atherton resuming their sequence of reassuring opening partnerships, England briefly looked like a team ready to compete for the Ashes. Then Atherton was out, Warne came on for the 28th over, bowled what became known as "The Ball from Hell" and the series really began. Gatting's departure was followed by that of Smith, caught at slip, and Gooch, who hit a full-toss to mid-on. By the close England had eight down and Keith Fletcher, the England manager, was saying he had never seen a Test pitch in England turn so much.

The third day began with another flurry of wickets. Such came on to bowl the ninth over of the Australian innings and with his fifth ball had Taylor lbw, sweeping. But Boon then batted with his customary pragmatism while Mark Waugh unleashed a series of glittering strokes. The cricket was more attritional after Waugh was out but Australia were just as sure-footed: Steve Waugh and Healy batted England out of the match with an unbroken stand of 180 in 164 minutes. Healy became the first Australian to make his maiden first-class century in a Test since H. Graham, exactly a hundred years earlier, at Lord's. England looked depressingly pallid in the field during this partnership. With the pitch drying out and the spinners negated by the lack of bounce, there was little attempt to wrest the initiative.

The declaration came at 3pm and England were left to score 512 in a day and a half. Gooch and Atherton again batted securely, with the captain notably authoritative. Then Gatting played with freedom until he was bowled off his pads from the last ball of the day by the indefatigable Hughes, a due reward for his willingness to vary his line and length. Gooch was understandably more circumspect on the final morning and – although Smith was tormented and then bowled by Warne – he reached his 18th Test hundred and England had the chance of a draw. Yet half an hour after lunch Gooch became the fifth cricketer, and the first Englishman, to be dismissed handled the ball in a Test as he instinctively flicked out with a glove at a ball dropping on to his stumps. Umpire Bird had no hesitation in giving Gooch out, with the moral victory, if not the wicket, going to Hughes for extracting extra bounce on an increasingly lifeless pitch.

Although the first ten English batsmen all batted for at least half an hour in the second innings, none could match the technical skill and authority of Gooch. For a time Caddick and Such threatened an unlikely stalemate but brilliant catches by Warne and Border completed their downfall. The Australians embarked on some typically committed celebrations.

Man of the Match: S. K. Warne. **Attendance:** 55,788.

WORDS ON WARNE

"The first turning point was Warne's first delivery, which left not only the batsman but the whole ground dumbfounded. What a delight it has been to see leg-spin re-emerge as an art in Test cricket – like a bloom among the stinging nettles that have been those attacks consisting of four fast bowlers. Real cricket lovers will remember 'Gatting b Warne 4' for a very, very long time."

Bob Willis, former England captain – WCM, July 1993

England v Australia, Lord's Vic Marks, *Wisden* 1994
(Second Test, June 17-21)

The Australian spinners, who shared 15 wickets in the match, patiently removed the middle order. Warne then took the last two wickets in consecutive balls by bowling Such and Tufnell around their legs, a suitably humiliating end for England. For the Australians there was enough time to spruce themselves up before meeting the Queen who, optimistically, had maintained the tradition of visiting Lord's at tea-time on the Monday, even though, with Sunday play, it was now the final day.

Combined Universities v Australians, Oxford Paton Fenton, *Wisden* 1994
(June 23-25)

The headlines were stolen by the maiden century of the Cambridge fresher Russell Cake, playing only because John Crawley was at his graduation ceremony. He hit 19 fours in 237 balls and claimed he could read Warne.

England v Australia, Nottingham David Frith, *WCM*, August 1993
(Third Test, July 1-6)

While Lathwell stood fast, puzzling over Warne, Smith grabbed every scoring opportunity. Missed low down by Steve Waugh at backward point when 24, he mixed perfect cover-drives with ferocious pulls and thrashing hits off May full tosses. When Healy let four byes through off a giant Warne leg-break, one suspected it was merely a propaganda exercise, particularly when he did it again four overs later. But two balls after he had reached a 69-ball fifty, Smith was sunk by another leg-spinner from which he just failed to drop his bat. It marked a grim final hour for England, Lathwell (33 in 34 overs) falling without a stroke to Warne's top-spinner and Stewart going lbw to Hughes, a ball which might just have touched leg stump. Thus, in nine overs, England's inadequacy was exposed yet again, this time in such a manner as to crush most of the last lingering hopes of regaining the Ashes.

England v Australia, Birmingham David Frith, *WCM*, September 1993
(Fifth Test, August 5-9)

While there was a certain relief at seeing Smith put out of his misery, the reservations about the likelihood that the ball would have hit the off stump which were felt by most TV scrutineers were not shared by umpire Hampshire. Nor did he hesitate when Stewart, well forward to a leg-break, was deemed to be lbw. Maynard failed again, given caught behind for 10, and Gooch was bowled round his pads by another grotesque leg-spinner from Warne which gripped in the rough. It was less like the killer ball which was Warne's first in Ashes Tests and which bowled Gatting at Old Trafford than the one with which Benaud bowled May (P. B. H.) at that ground 1961 to push England towards a defeat which was – in contrast to this 1993 reverse – quite unexpected.

Wisden Cricket Monthly, July 1993

Had May then thrust his defensive pad as far out as Gooch did now, he would have survived: which underlines the degree of turn earned by Shane Keith Warne's strong fingers and wrist.

The Australians in England 1993 John Thicknesse, *Wisden* 1994

Although Warne had two startling analyses to his credit in his 11 previous Tests, seven for 52 against West Indies and four for eight against New Zealand, his reputation before the tour was more that of a beach-boy than a budding Test-winner. His shock of dyed blond hair, earring and blobs of white sun-block on the tip of his nose and lower lip lent his appearance a deceptive air of amiability, which an expression of wide-eyed innocence enhanced. However, his incessant niggling of umpires and truculent questioning of unfavourable decisions made it obvious that the sunny exterior hid a graceless streak, which stopped him earning the unqualified respect of his opponents. In his hitherto unexplored method of attack, founded on ferociously spun leg-breaks, as often as not angled a foot or more outside the leg stump from round the wicket, he left no doubt that Australia had uncovered not only a match-winner of singular inventiveness but a cricketer crowds would flock to see.

Thanks to TV, Warne's first ball in Ashes cricket, which bowled Mike Gatting, may become the most famous ever bowled. It was flighted down the line of middle and leg, the fierceness of the spin causing it to swerve almost a foot in its last split-seconds in the air, so that it pitched six inches outside the leg-stump. From there, it spun viciously past Gatting's half-formed forward stroke to hit the off-stump within two inches of the top. Had Gatting been in half an hour longer, or ever faced Warne before, he might have got a pad to it. As it was the ball was unplayable and, by impressing the bowler's capacities on England, it had a profound impact on the series. Of Warne's subsequent 33 wickets, only two came from deliveries that seemed to turn as far – 18 inches or more – and in each case the spin was accentuated by the ball being delivered round the wicket. Gooch was the victim on both occasions, caught at slip for 120 in the second innings of the Third Test, and bowled behind his legs for 48 in the second innings of the Fifth. Nothing better illustrated England's problems than the fact that one of the most experienced batsmen in the world could be bowled in a way when all he was attempting was to block the ball's progress with his pads.

Warne bowled half as many overs again as any other bowler, without showing signs of tiring, even in his frequent two-hour spells. Of leg-spinners, only Arthur Mailey, with 36 in 1920-21 (in five Tests) has taken more wickets in an Ashes series than Warne's 34.

The Summer of Shane Rob Smyth, *WCM*, August 2019

The story of Shane Warne's debut Ashes series is usually told in one ball. It has its own Wikipedia page, its own song (*Jiggery Pokery* by the Duckworth Lewis Method) and its own mythology. But while the theatre and symbolism of that delivery to Mike Gatting are unimprovable, the full story of Warne's 1993 Ashes is a little more Homeric. It is told in 2,639 deliveries – the most ever bowled in a Test series, during which he made himself at home in England's subconscious.

If the 'Ball of the Century' was a killer lead single, the album that followed was full of subtler classics. It revealed a bit more with each listen: variety, intelligence, aura and much else besides. Some mystery spinners are one-hit wonders; by the end of the 1993 Ashes, when Australia had won 4-1 and Warne had 34 wickets at 25.79 in six Tests, it was clear England were dealing with a potential all-time great.

"I faced some of the fastest bowlers in history," says Robin Smith. "But Warnie was the one bowler who really intimidated me. Give me Sylvester Clarke on a dodgy pitch over Warnie any day of the week. Clarke might knock me out; Warnie would just get me out."

Smith, and England, were neither forewarned nor forearmed. "My memories are that we knew very little about him beforehand," says Mike Atherton, one of only three England batsmen to play all six Tests that summer. "It was different then – there wasn't the dissemination of information there is now, and I can't remember any footage being made available. There certainly wasn't a sense of threat about Warne before the series."

There were a few reasons for that. Warne had a modest Test record, averaging 31 after 11 games, although he'd had a good Australian summer against West Indies and especially New Zealand. It rained so much before the First Test at Old Trafford that the England players – and Warne himself – thought Australia might prefer the finger-spinner Tim May. And in a tour game at Worcester a month earlier, Graeme Hick had butchered Warne while making 187, including a burst of four sixes in 10 balls. There was one unknown caveat: Allan Border had told Warne to bowl nothing but leg-spinners and keep his variations under wraps.

One ball changed everything. The story of Warne's delivery to Mike Gatting has been told a million times, which makes it harder to remember how it was received at the time. Although it went into folklore, its immediate impact was not necessarily as dramatic as legend has it. "The notion that suddenly this ball destabilised the dressing-room is complete nonsense," says Atherton. "It was obviously a brilliant delivery and a startling moment, but I can't remember whispers going round the dressing-room after that. As always in a dressing-room, you look up, he's out, and you get on with things."

Hick has a similar memory. "It had obviously drifted and spun a lot, but I wouldn't say there was any great buzz about it," he says. "A ball like that makes you realise what a person can do, so you have to work out a plan to counteract it when it's your turn."

This was long before YouTube, so most people – even those involved in the match – only saw the ball a few times on TV. At the end of that second day, the England coach Keith Fletcher partly attributed Warne's success to a "rogue" pitch. "Warne is a good bowler but we are not particularly worried about him," he said. "He won't turn it so much elsewhere." It's easy to snigger now, although at the time many good judges agreed with Fletcher that they had never seen an English pitch turn as much.

What nobody knew is that Warne could turn it viciously on anything, especially from outside leg stump. He redefined bowling round the wicket, making it an angle of attack, and made batsmen fear the blind spot behind them. He finished the Lord's Test by bowling Peter Such and Phil Tufnell behind their legs, and did the same to Graham Gooch at Edgbaston. Warne imparted so many revolutions on the ball that prodigious turn – and the accompanying drift – were his biggest weapons. Graham Thorpe, who with Gooch was the only England batsman to make a century in the series, says he has never seen anyone drift the ball like Warne in his early years.

"At that stage, his shoulder was fine," says Atherton. "He bowled the genuine flipper, which he kind of put away afterwards, and the googly as well. He had all the tricks."

Some struggled to read his variations. Others didn't even know what they were. When Matthew Maynard was bowled by Warne's flipper at The Oval, he could barely have been more surprised if he'd seen a five-legged cat. It was the first time he'd received the delivery – not just from Warne, but from anyone. "There was no feel for leg-spin in the English game," says Atherton. "That was a real advantage for him." England had faced Mushtaq Ahmed and Anil Kumble in the previous year, but Warne was a very different kind of leg-spinner. Few people had any frame of reference. In his *Daily Express* column, after the second day of the Old Trafford Test, Ray Illingworth was taken back to the 1940s. "Warne," he said, "reminds me of Bruce Dooland – some compliment."

It helped that England were such good hosts. They could barely have been more accommodating to Warne had they introduced a fag break every hour. Thorpe, brought in for the Third Test, was the only left-hander they picked all series, and 33 of Warne's 34 wickets were right-handers. The pitches also turned throughout the summer. The off-spinner Tim May played the last five Tests and took 21 wickets at 28. Gooch, Atherton and Smith all use the same word to describe May – "underrated" – while Thorpe, as a left-hander, found him a tougher challenge than Warne in that series.

May and Warne each had a cricket IQ that was Mensa level. Atherton and Stewart both describe Warne as the smartest bowler they ever faced. And though he had to rely on his wiles less in 1993 than later in his career when his shoulder became an issue, there were still signs of his ability to set a batsman up.

The most famous example came in the Fifth Test at Edgbaston, when Warne took a wicket that gave him even more satisfaction than the Gatting ball. "For me," he said, "the biggest thrill is the deception." At the end of the third day, in the bar with his captain Border, Warne outlined a plan to bowl Gooch round his legs. Border was unsure but told Warne to try it. The next day, it happened exactly as Warne said it would. The first thing he did was run to Border, joyously shouting, "I told you!"

Warne says Gooch is the greatest England batsman he bowled to, just ahead of Kevin Pietersen. In the 1993 series he called him 'Mr Gooch' – a mark of respect, he said, but one which Gooch thought was overdone and at least partly sarcastic. Either way, the mutual respect was sincere, and both loved facing each other. Warne got Gooch five times in 1993, more than any other batsman, but Gooch's 673 runs were the most on either side.

For the England batsmen, runs against Warne were a badge of honour. "I always enjoyed playing against Warnie," says Atherton. "I always found him a pretty straight-up competitor, as I did with a lot of their players, actually. He had a few words on the field but he was the kind of guy that, if you played well, would look you in the eye and say, 'Well played.'"

Later in his career, as his shoulder deteriorated, Warne became more accomplished at sledging batsmen out. In 1993, that wasn't really the case. There were, inevitably, a few reminders that Australia were sponsored by XXXX – Maynard was told to "take that f***ing shot back to Wales" when he padded up to the flipper – but for the most part he didn't need to get his mouth dirty. Besides, he had people to do that for him. Ian Healy, the wicketkeeper, was Warne's *consigliere*, who tried to unsettle batsmen with sly, dry comments.

At Edgbaston, when Thorpe was left with only Such and Mark Ilott, he played a defensive stroke off Warne. Healy observed to his teammates that Thorpe was "playing for red ink". The accusation was a red rag. "F**k this," thought Thorpe. "I'm not playing for myself. I'll show you." And he did, by charging down the wicket and deleting that red ink. *Thorpe stumped and sledged Healy b Warne 60.*

That was the only time Thorpe was dismissed by Warne in the series. He felt reasonably comfortable against him – but he knew, at that stage, he could not dominate him. Warne confounded every English assumption about leg-spin bowling, but perhaps the most problematic was the fact he bowled hardly any bad balls. He went for 1.99 an over during the series and bowled a frankly ludicrous 178 maidens, more than twice as many as in any other series throughout his career. It was the slowest torture.

England were relatively good at surviving against Warne – his strike rate in the series was 78, compared to his career strike rate of 57 – but that was often the extent of their ambition. "He was so accurate that he gave you nothing," says Smith. "There was a drip effect until it all became too much."

Atherton played beautifully for much of the series, making six fifties, but did not reach three figures. An unfortunate slip at Lord's when on 99 was only one reason for that. "I never felt as though I was dominating, and that's why I would often get out between 50 and 100," he says. "It took me quite a while to get those runs, and that was because of Warne and May. They had constant control."

When Warne did bowl a bad delivery, his force of personality sometimes turned it into a wicket-taking ball. Gooch cuffed a long hop to mid-wicket at Old Trafford; Stewart slapped a full toss to cover at Trent Bridge. "He was a once-in-a-lifetime cricketer," said Stewart. "*He* controlled *me*."

He also controlled Smith, who suffered a crisis of confidence and method. In the first innings at Old Trafford, he edged a beautiful delivery – as good as the Gatting ball, in Richie Benaud's opinion – to slip. But he played with hard hands and was criticised accordingly. In the second innings he softened his hands against Warne – and watched in horror as a defensive shot span back onto the stumps.

Smith was reluctant to ask for help, lest it show weakness, but Atherton picked the brains of Gooch, who played majestically for most of the series. "Goochie was a great player, and in his golden period," says Atherton. "Informally, I would certainly chat to him and that's how it was done then – peer-to-peer rather than the coaches giving you information."

Some of the batsmen could not cope – mentally, technically or both. There were a number of embarrassing dismissals, either because the batsman offered no stroke or, in Gatting's case, didn't know they were out. Smith was dismantled, averaging 28 in the series before he was dropped for the final Test. "He just got inside my head," says Smith. "He tormented me with demons that didn't even exist. He barely said a word but the way he looked at me really unsettled me – it was superior and knowing, as if he'd already decided exactly how and when he was going to put me out of my misery."

Smith was Hampshire captain when Warne joined the county in 2000, and they became best friends. On the first day of training, Warne bowled to him in the nets. "He got me out three times in about six deliveries," says Smith. "As captain, I ordered him to bugger off, because I wanted to come out of the nets feeling upbeat about my game. It was only then – seven years after I faced him in the Ashes – that I realised just how big a hold he had over me."

Notes by the Editor   Matthew Engel, *Wisden* 1994

Shortly after lunch on the first day of the Edgbaston Test in 1993, Shane Warne was bowling leg-breaks to Alec Stewart, who had momentarily discarded both his helmet and his faded baseball cap in favour of a real, old-fashioned, three lions of England version. As he pushed forward, he looked the image of his father at the crease. Behind the stumps, there was Ian Healy wearing his baggy cap and air of ageless Australian aggression. And there was Warne, bowling beautifully with a method thought to have been relegated to the museum.

For a moment the years seemed to roll away. The detail of the cricket was suspended; the game was overtaken by the timelessness of the scene. It was summer in England and all was well. Then, of course, Stewart got out and everything became secondary to the fact that we were being licked again. Of England's national traumas, more later.

In a number of respects cricket had a very good year in 1993. In England, India and Australia, crowds showed they would respond to the thrill of an exciting Test series, as well as to the gimcrack appeal of one-day cricket. Warne was the most talked-about player of the year and single-handedly did a huge amount to switch cricket back into a game where the batsman's fear is of mental torture rather than physical.

Five Cricketers of the Year   Vic Marks, *Wisden* 1994

When Martin Crowe announced just before the 1993 Ashes series that Shane Warne was the best leg-spinner in the world, few alarm bells clanged in England. Such a declaration could be interpreted as an attempt to restore the confidence of Kiwi batsmen, notoriously vulnerable against spin, who had just been undermined by Warne. Moreover, no Australian wrist-spinner had made a significant impact in an English Test series since the days of Grimmett and O'Reilly between the wars. England, it was assumed, had to quell McDermott and Hughes to have a chance of retrieving the Ashes.

Such a complacent misconception was dispelled at Old Trafford by Warne's first delivery in Test cricket in England. It was bowled to Mike Gatting, an acknowledged master of spin. Warne does not indulge in low-risk looseners, and that first ball was flicked vigorously out of the back of the hand. It set off on the line of Gatting's pads and then dipped in the air further towards the leg side until it was 18 inches adrift of the stumps; by this time Gatting was beginning to lose interest, until the ball bounced, turned and fizzed across his ample frame to clip the off bail. Gatting remained rooted at the crease for several seconds – in disbelief rather than dissent – before trudging off to the pavilion like a man betrayed. Now the Englishmen knew that Crowe's assessment was more than propaganda.

Throughout six Tests they could never master Warne. He bowled 439.5 overs in the series, took 34 wickets – surpassing Grimmett's 29 in the five Tests of 1930 – and also managed to concede under two runs per over, thereby flouting the tradition of profligate wrist-spinners buying their wickets. Some English batsmen were completely mesmerised; Robin Smith, England's banker in the middle order, was unable to detect any of his variations and had to be dropped. The admirable Gooch could obviously distinguish the googly from the leg-spinner, yet Warne still disposed of him five times in the series. Once Gooch carelessly clubbed a full toss to mid-on, but otherwise he was dismissed while playing the appropriate defensive stroke, the surest indication that Warne has a special talent.

Ominously for Test batsmen of the 1990s, Warne is not yet the complete wrist-spinner. His googly is not so penetrating or well-disguised as Mushtaq Ahmed's, which is one reason why he employs it so infrequently. His flipper is lethal if it is on target, but it often zooms down the leg side. But he is the most prodigious spinner of the ball of the last three decades, a gift which causes deceptive in-swing as well as excessive turn. He is also remarkably accurate, but if ever his control is threatened, he can regroup by bowling around the wicket to the right-handed batsman, thereby restricting him to just one scoring stroke, a risky sweep. Hence in the Ashes series his captain, Border, was able to use him as both shock and stock bowler.

Warne's success in 1993 was a triumph for the Australian selectors as well as his own resolve. They might easily have discarded him as a liability early in his career. SHANE KEITH WARNE, born in a smart bayside suburb of Melbourne on September 13, 1969, did not display many of the hallmarks of his predecessors – Grimmett, O'Reilly and Benaud – in his youth. Bleached blond hair, a stud in his ear plus a fondness for good life, which caused his waistline to expand with alarming speed, and an aversion to discipline, which in 1990 led to his departure under a cloud from the Australian Cricket Academy in Adelaide, do not reflect the perfect credentials for the modern Australian Test cricketer. Yet selectors trusted their judgment.

They pitched him into two Test matches against India in January 1992, after just four Sheffield Shield appearances, in which he had taken eight wickets. He had shown form on tour in Zimbabwe and against the West Indians. None the less, his state captain Simon O'Donnell expressed public reservations. Warne took one for 228 against the Indians and the gamble seemed to have backfired. Warne was then invited by Rod Marsh to return to the Academy, where he was coached by another reformed larrikin, Terry Jenner. Warne was now prepared to make the sort of sacrifices that impress Australians: he gave up beer, trained hard, lost 28 pounds and was rewarded by selection for the tour to Sri Lanka in August 1992.

In Colombo, having yielded 107 runs from 22 wicketless overs in the first innings of the opening Test, Warne took three for 11 from 5.1 overs in the second as Australia conjured a dramatic victory. His victims were only tailenders, but it was a start. That Border entrusted him with the ball at all at such a crucial moment did wonders for his confidence. His seven for 52 against West Indies at Melbourne in December 1992 was an isolated success in that series but confirmed his match-winning potential. But his efforts in New Zealand (17 wickets in three matches) and in last summer's Ashes series have established Warne as an integral cog, perhaps *the* integral cog, of the Australian team.

On a broader scale he has triggered a mini-renaissance in the art of wrist-spin bowling. In the summer of 1993 young village cricketers could be spied on the outfield, no longer seeking to emulate Curtly Ambrose or Merv Hughes, but attempting to ape the more subtle skills of Warne. For that we should all be grateful.

1993-94

Australian Diary   Trevor Grant, *WCM*, December 1993

From the moment Shane Warne opened his 1993 Ashes campaign with that unplayable delivery which rattled the off stump of a bemused Mike Gatting at Old Trafford, the young Australian's career had changed forever. People no longer *hoped* he would take wickets; they *expected* him to do so.

Warne managed to live up to these expectations, thanks to his burgeoning talent and the unbelievably timid approach of the England batsmen. But even despite his stunning Ashes haul of 34 wickets at 25.79 apiece, it was always going to be an immensely difficult task to come anywhere near the level of performance now demanded of him.

Apart from the fact that the pitches here were going to be less responsive to his turn, the Australian batsmen who are less inclined to be mortified by the sight of a wrist-spinner were always going to make life tougher. As Queensland batsman Stuart Law observed to the Melbourne *Herald-Sun*: "I think he'll find it a different game. Shield batsmen are more aggressive, more prepared to take risks. The English were scared stiff of him most of the time."

Law was speaking from first-hand knowledge, the day after sharing a stand of 148 from 175 balls with Dirk Wellham which gave Queensland a handsome first up victory in the Mercantile Mutual one-day series. Law, who made an unbeaten 107, led the attack on Warne, who returned figures of 0 for 60 from his 10 overs. In the upbeat atmosphere of the limited-overs format, the Queenslanders went after Warne, happily dancing down the track, hitting against the spin and lofting him over the infield at every opportunity.

To his credit, he hit back in the next match, taking four for 119 from a marathon 43 overs in the first innings in Victoria's opening Sheffield Shield match, against South Australia at Adelaide. It was a most welcome sign of Warne's ever-growing maturity, and his four top-order wickets played the decisive role in restricting a potentially massive SA total after Paul Nobes marked his return from Victoria with 141, sharing a stand of 232 for the second wicket with Jamie Brayshaw (134).

After the South Australians, looking assured and threatening for the first time in many seasons, cleaned up by nine wickets, Victoria hit back the following day with a win in the sides' limited-overs encounter.

Once again Warne showed that he's very quick on the uptake, bowling far better than in the first one-dayer. He finished with the respectable figures of 0 for 24 from his 10 overs, far better than his seam-bowling colleagues managed. After the match, new Victorian captain Dean Jones gave some insight into the difficulties confronting Warne, when he said he had been trying too hard: "He just has to bowl some dot-balls, and not try to get a wicket every ball," Jones remarked.

Warne himself is well aware that he will not be able to rely on batsmen self-destructing, as the lemming-like English did. With the batsmen sure to attack him more on the truer, bouncier Australian pitches, he will have to revert to the leg-spinner's more traditional role of wheedling out batsmen with subtle variation in flight. But he's not about to be overwhelmed by the spotlight which hovers over his every move, as we saw by his announcement, at the official media launch of the Australian season, that he has been working on a couple of new deliveries to fling at the New Zealanders and South Africans.

Teasing the audience as he would a batsman newly-arrived at the crease, the Victorian would say only that he began experimenting in secret a couple of weeks before the end of the Ashes tour, and has been honing the 'secret weapons' in the nets after discussions with his old mentor from the Australian Cricket Academy Terry Jenner and Australian coach Bob Simpson. 'I don't want to let the secret out, but it could be pretty interesting this summer,' he said, leaving his audience drooling in anticipation.

Warne would give only one clue. The delivery is a possible variation on his wrong'un, and rather than trying to increase the massive turn from leg which scuttled the likes of Gatting and Gooch, he was working on a ball that did the opposite. "I've been working on a couple of different wrong'uns and a few other things. There might even be one that goes straight!"

Australia v New Zealand, Hobart   Greg Baum, *Wisden* 1995
(Second Test, November 26-29)

New Zealand went in just before 4pm on the second day and in less than ten playing hours were all out twice – each time for 161, and still 23 runs shy of the original follow-on target. Both innings had the same pattern. McDermott began by dismissing Greatbatch, Mark Waugh took a high-order wicket and Warne and May rolled up the rest like an old carpet. May, mostly through his heavily disguised arm-ball, took five wickets in an innings for the third time in Tests, all in 1993. Warne reciprocated with six for 31, giving him 63 Test wickets in a calendar year – already more than any spinner in history.

Australia v New Zealand, Brisbane

Greg Baum, *Wisden* 1995

(Third Test, December 3-7)

Young bolstered New Zealand's second innings with a poised half-century, but Warne, after having Jones caught at mid-wicket from a limp pull, bowled Young with a ball that spun prodigiously around his outstretched front pad. Like Gatting and Gooch before him, Young had discovered that elementary defence was not enough.

The New Zealanders in Australia 1993-94

Greg Baum, *Wisden* 1995

New Zealand's batsmen were no more conversant with Shane Warne's leg-spin than they had been earlier in the year and his 18 wickets eclipsed the Australian Test record against New Zealand (17, shared by himself and McDermott).

Australia v South Africa, Sydney

Steven Lynch, *WCM*, February 1994

(Second Test, January 2-6)

The breakthrough brought in Cullinan, who broke his duck for the series with two fours off Warne. However, he made a tactical error in smiling at the leg-spinner, who unleashed a flipper which shot into his stumps. Warne's verbal send-off to the "batsman who smiled" was less savoury than the delicious delivery itself, but the Victorian was now launched on a spell which transformed his figures and delighted the 32,681 crowd – the largest for a Sydney Test since the 1982-83 Ashes series.

Warne next did for Rhodes with another flipper, then ended Kirsten's 218-minute resistance with another, which seemed to swing away from the left-hander: Healy completed the stumping as Kirsten – whose 67 was his first Test fifty – did the splits. Richardson was smartly caught one-handed by Taylor at slip off the perfect leg-break (Warne's 50th wicket of the Australian first-class season), and just before tea Wessels drove back a full toss and Warne snapped up the low catch.

After the interval (147 for seven) Matthews gave a simple catch to slip, giving Warne five for five in 22 balls. Soon Symcox was gone too, bowled behind his legs by a prodigious leg-break. Warne, with seven for 56, led the team off. Only Jack Saunders (seven for 34, 1902-03) has bettered Warne's figures in Australia–South Africa Tests. It was two years to the day since Warne's undistinguished Test debut (one for 150) against India at the SCG.

South Africa v Australia, Johannesburg

Jack Bannister, *Wisden* 1995

(First Test, March 4-8)

The pitch was cracked, but proved home forecasts right and those from the Australian camp wrong, by lasting the five days and not offering inordinate turn to the spinners. None the less it seemed curious that Border did not bowl Warne until the 49th over of the first innings and the 44th of the second, which is thought to have put him in the temper that led to his disgraceful – and almost unprecedented – outburst when he finally came on and dismissed Hudson. Rarely on a cricket field has physical violence seemed so close.

South Africa v Australia, Cape Town　　　　　　Mike Coward, *WCM*, May 1994
(Second Test, March 17-21)

… Warne and Hughes were much quieter. But while Warne was able to lift himself above the maelstrom of the Wanderers, Hughes had a dreadful time on a vastly improved but slow pitch which broke his heart and spirit. He failed to take a wicket from 25 overs and, to bring another scowl to his formidable countenance, he returned a primary.

Conversely Warne, with his father in town and looking over his shoulder, showed some maturity and toiled manfully – and again, it must be said, without much luck – for 77 overs for the splendid match analysis of 6 for 116. Certainly there were clear signs that the South Africans had determined a policy not to play shots at all against him.

In a revealing interview, Warne suggested he had been possessed by demons in Johannesburg. To the undisguised relief of the Establishment everywhere, Warne exorcised those demons at Newlands and provided wonderful support for Steve Waugh…

1994-95

Pakistan v Australia, Lahore　　　　　　Mike Coward, *Wisden* 1996
(Third Test, November 1-5)

But again the belligerent Malik matched his wits with the bowlers, for a further three hours and ten minutes – after two hours' stubborn resistance on the fourth day – and scored another hundred. Along the way he cajoled Sohail into forgetting the stiff neck which forced him to wear a brace the previous afternoon, so persuasively that Sohail completed a century at No. 7, adding 196 in 215 minutes with Malik to dash Australian hopes. Not even Warne could break through, although he battled manfully for three for 104 and match figures of nine for 240, from a colossal 71.5 overs; fears were expressed for his right shoulder under such a heavy workload.

THE ASHES, 1994-95

CLASSIC TEST 2

Australia v England, Brisbane   John Thicknesse, *Wisden* 1996
(First Test)
November 25, 26, 27, 28, 29 – Australia won by 184 runs. Toss: Australia

Yet another display of exceptional all-round cricket took Australia to victory by the now-familiar crushing margin. Warne, who had held England's batsmen spellbound from the moment he bowled Gatting at Old Trafford in 1993, was again the executioner, taking three for 39 and eight for 71 – his best analysis in first-class cricket. It was not until the final innings, though, that he commandeered the spotlight. During the first three days, it was the combined efforts of Slater, Taylor, Mark Waugh, McDermott and Healy which forced the tourists into a position from which there was little prospect of escape.

England suffered a severe setback when Malcolm went down with chicken-pox three days before the game, and one of even greater significance when Atherton lost the toss on Brisbane's driest and most closely shaven pitch for an Ashes Test in more than 20 years. It was a formality that Australia would bat. Indeed, it was so obvious that there would be more help for spinners the longer the game lasted that Taylor chose to bat again with a lead of 259, rather than enforce the follow-on, after England, through pitiful batting against McDermott, were dismissed for 167 on the third day. It was a mistake because it allowed England the opportunity to regain a little self-respect, but it did no lasting damage.

The ball swung on the first morning. But when an erratic start by DeFreitas and McCague allowed Slater and Taylor to score 26 off four overs by doing nothing more than punish leg-side balls and off-side long-hops, the initiative was won and lost in 20 minutes. In the 33rd over Slater was responsible for Taylor's run-out, failing to respond to a call for a sharp single to mid-off. But the mistake increased his resolution. He scored a dashing 112 out of 182 with Mark Waugh, and was on course to pass 200 in the day when, 36 minutes from the close, he failed to clear mid-off against Gooch. Slater faced 244 balls and scored a hundred in fours.

Australia lost six for 97 on the second day; Mark Waugh, who faced 215 balls as he completed his third century against England, was ninth out when a ball from Gough inexplicably reared shoulder-high and carried to the covers from a fend-off. But then England's disintegration began: Stewart was caught at the wicket off a wide out-swinger in what might otherwise have been the last over of McDermott's new-ball spell; Hick soon followed, caught behind, mishooking; only while Atherton and Thorpe were adding 47 did England briefly promise to recover. All that subsequently redeemed a supine effort were 234 minutes of orthodox defence by Atherton and a huge swept six by Gooch off Warne, during a calculated attempt to hit the spinners off their length. But Gooch perished after half an hour, another catch for Healy, off a soaring top edge when May's drift from round the wicket undermined a sweep.

Australia v England, Brisbane, 1994

AUSTRALIA	First innings		Second innings
M. J. Slater c Gatting b Gooch	176	– (2) lbw b Gough	45
*M. A. Taylor run out (Gough/Rhodes)	59	– (1) c Stewart b Tufnell	58
D. C. Boon b Gough	3	– b Tufnell	28
M. E. Waugh c Stewart b Gough	140	– b Tufnell	15
M. G. Bevan c Hick b Gough	7	– c Rhodes b DeFreitas	21
S. K. Warne c Rhodes b Gough	2	– (8) c sub (C. White) b DeFreitas	0
S. R. Waugh c Hick b DeFreitas	19	– (6) c sub (C. White) b Tufnell	7
†I. A. Healy c Hick b DeFreitas	7	– (7) not out	45
C. J. McDermott c Gough b McCague	2	– c Rhodes b Gough	6
T. B. A. May not out	3	– not out	9
G. D. McGrath c Gough b McCague	0		
B 5, lb 2, nb 1	8	B 2, lb 9, w 2, nb 1	14

1/99 (2) 2/126 (3) 3/308 (1)   426   1/109 (2)   (8 wkts dec.) 248
4/326 (5) 5/352 (6) 6/379 (7)   2/117 (1) 3/139 (4)
7/407 (8) 8/419 (9) 9/425 (4) 10/426 (11)   4/174 (5) 5/183 (6)
     6/190 (3) 7/191 (8) 8/201 (9)

First innings—DeFreitas 31–8–102–2; McCague 19.2–4–96–2; Gough 32–7–107–4; Tufnell 25–3–72–0; Hick 4–0–22–0; Gooch 9–2–20–1.
Second innings—DeFreitas 22–1–74–2; Gough 23–3–78–2; Tufnell 38–10–79–4; Gooch 3–2–5–0; Hick 2–1–1–0.

ENGLAND	First innings		Second innings
*M. A. Atherton c Healy b McDermott	54	– lbw b Warne	23
A. J. Stewart c Healy b McDermott	16	– b Warne	33
G. A. Hick c Healy b McDermott	3	– c Healy b Warne	80
G. P. Thorpe c and b Warne	28	– b Warne	67
G. A. Gooch c Healy b May	20	– c Healy b Warne	56
M. W. Gatting lbw b McDermott	10	– c Healy b McDermott	13
M. J. McCague b McDermott	1	– (10) lbw b Warne	0
†S. J. Rhodes lbw b McDermott	4	– (7) c Healy b McDermott	2
P. A. J. DeFreitas c Healy b Warne	7	– (8) b Warne	11
D. Gough not out	17	– (9) c M. E. Waugh b Warne	10
P. C. R. Tufnell c Taylor b Warne	0	– not out	2
Lb 1, nb 6	7	B 9, lb 5, nb 12	26

1/22 (2) 2/35 (3) 3/82 (4)   167   1/50 (2) 2/59 (1)   323
4/105 (5) 5/131 (6) 6/133 (7)   3/219 (4) 4/220 (3)
7/140 (1) 8/147 (9) 9/151 (8) 10/167 (11)   5/250 (6) 6/280 (7) 7/309 (5)
     8/310 (8) 9/310 (10) 10/323 (9)

First innings—McDermott 19–3–53–6; McGrath 10–2–40–0; May 17–3–34–1; Warne 21.2–7–39–3.
Second innings—McDermott 23–4–90–2; McGrath 19–4–61–0; Warne 50.2–22–71–8; May 35–16–59–0;
M. E. Waugh 7–1–17–0; Bevan 3–0–11–0.

Umpires: C. J. Mitchley and S. G. Randell.   Third umpire: P. D. Parker.
Referee: J. R. Reid.

Batting again before lunch on the third day, Australia began their second innings with a stand of 109 in 28 overs from Taylor and Slater. But frustrated by Tufnell's accuracy over the wicket, into the rough, they lost eight for 92 before Healy pushed the lead beyond 500. Taylor's declaration left his bowlers 11 hours to win the match and England, improbably, 508 runs.

There was a possibility of Australia winning inside four days when, in Warne's second and third overs, Stewart was bowled by an undetected flipper midway through a pull and Atherton played back to a full-length leg-break and was lbw. Hick and Thorpe spared England that embarrassment, doggedly adding 152 in four hours to the close. On the last day, however, Warne was irresistible. In action from the start with May and – in contrast to the fourth day – bowling mainly round the wicket, he pinned Thorpe to defence for half an hour before beating him with a yorker. The 160 Thorpe added with Hick in 275 minutes was England's highest stand in eight Ashes Tests. England's chance of survival ended there, however: in Warne's next over, Hick was caught at the wicket via pad, chest and back of bat. Gooch hit ten fours in scoring 56, but he became the last of Healy's nine victims (equalling the Australian Test record) and the first wicket of Warne's final spell, in which he captured the last four wickets to bring his figures on the final day to six for 27 off 25.2 overs. They truly told the story of Warne's brilliance.

Man of the Match: S. K. Warne. **Attendance:** 46,022.

WORDS ON WARNE

"The difference, of course, is the Surfie of Slow Bowling, Shane Warne. He resembles a billiard player: the Victor Lindrum of leg-spin. He imparts 57 varieties of side and bottom on the ball, attacking the batsman from every angle and using the rough like side-cushions. His astonishing accuracy limits the opposition to less than two runs an over and his aggression is volubly and physically daunting."

Frank Tyson, former England bowler – WCM, January 1995

Is He The Greatest? – Editorial   David Frith, *WCM*, January 1995

Some years ago, public opinion on who was the greatest bowler that cricket had ever seen was divided simply between England's S. F. Barnes and Australia's Bill O'Reilly. It is no longer that straightforward.

Over the past 40 years, further names have suggested themselves. No more competent off-spinner ever lived than England's Jim Laker. Australia's fast bowlers Ray Lindwall, Dennis Lillee and Jeff Thomson often looked unplayable. From West Indies have come fast men galore, the thoroughbred Michael Holding and the awkward beanpole Curtly Ambrose being the pick of the bunch. Another skilled paceman who customarily gave batsmen little hope of long life was New Zealand's

Richard Hadlee; while from the subcontinent came the crippled genius Chandrasekhar, with his fizzing, bucking googlies and leg-breaks, and Pakistan's ace trickster Abdul Qadir, with pacemen Wasim Akram and Waqar Younis doing things with fast cricket balls which have seldom if ever been done before.

Statistics inevitably come into it, but there is more to it than that: otherwise Kapil Dev, the Test leader, would be top of the list or Wilfred Rhodes, with his supreme tally of 4,187 first-class wickets.

That bowlers win matches is a maxim repeatedly demonstrated. At the Gabba on November 29, Shane Warne completed an Australian victory over England which was initially shaped by McDermott, a bowler of a different temperament and technique. "Wizard" Warne once again came into his own in the later stages of a match, when the pitch was uneven from the constant pounding and scraping of the bowlers throughout four days. Much of Warne's damage was launched from around the wicket, leaving the batsman no sensible alternative but to block the delivery with pad or body. It was therefore, in a sense, *negative* leg-spin bowling, which is almost a contradiction in terms. Warne's spiritual ancestor, Arthur Mailey, attacked non-stop, tossing the ball high from over the wicket, dipping it with topspin, turning it this way and that, chuckling as he was belted for six lighting up with his Irish grin as his over-confident opponent met his demise.

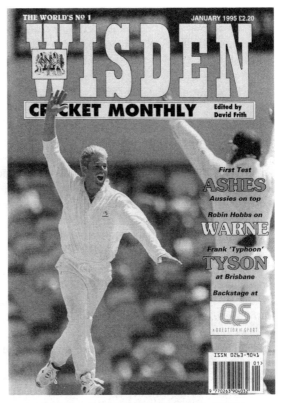

Wisden Cricket Monthly, January 1995

Warne, like Mailey, believes that laughter is permissible on the Test cricket field, and that is an endearing characteristic. But he is less inclined to "buy" his wickets. There is more of O'Reilly about him, a belligerence more usually associated with the fast men. Mailey, Grimmett, O'Reilly, Benaud – none of them would have turned into a screaming madman as Warne did in Johannesburg last March after his dismissal of Hudson. But Warne deeply regrets "cracking" in public, has apologised repeatedly, and asks how many times does he have to be "hung" for his deranged exhibition.

Reputation restored, the Wizard now looks capable of taking at least 40 wickets in the 1994-95 series against England. He continues to spin the ball extravagant distances, with the widest range of variations known to man, all controlled with extraordinary accuracy. Importantly, he is supported by a highly skilled wicketkeeper in Ian Healy and a crowd of close fielders who miss hardly anything. At times, one's sympathy for the batsman as he seeks to live in this hostile environment is heartfelt.

Warne bowled 50.2 overs in England's second innings at Brisbane, and was as bright as a button at the conclusion. His eight for 71 removed another by the name of Keith from the top of the best-bowling table in Ashes Tests in that city; Keith Miller, who turned 75 during the match, and to judge from the verdicts of Len Hutton and other batsmen, merits inclusion among the luminaries listed above.

It seems, therefore, that Shane Keith Warne is close to being as lethal a bowler as any that cricket has seen. At Brisbane, he slipped past O'Reilly's total of 144 Test wickets, and it is food for thought that at the Wizard's age (25 years 77 days), the Tiger had not yet made his Test debut. At the rate at which Tests are played now, Warne could end up with 100 caps, and that might bring him 500 wickets. How many Tests might he win for Australia in that time? He has taken 61 wickets in nine Tests this year, following 72 in 1993.

The lip-cream gleams whiter than white; the creamy yellow hair spikes up in disciplined rebellion; the blue-green eyes sparkle in unison with the diamond ear-stud; the personal pride and joy ooze boyishly. The challenge to England – indeed, to the world – is to find broader pads, broader bats even, and some kind of strategy (apart from winning the toss) which so far remains undiscovered. Even Ambrose needs rest after 10 overs. Warne, it seems, cannot be worn down.

News Register   *WCM,* January 1995

Lloyd's of London have put a value of £1 million on Shane Warne's spinning fingers. A broker said they were a "national treasure". Warne had no immediate plans to take out digital insurance.

Australia v England, Melbourne   John Thicknesse, *Wisden* 1996
(Second Test, December 24-29)

DeFreitas, Gough and Malcolm formed Warne's hat-trick, his first in any cricket. All were victims of leg-breaks, DeFreitas lbw on the back foot to one that skidded through, Gough well taken at the wicket off one that turned and bounced and Malcolm brilliantly caught off his gloves by Boon, who dived two feet to his right to scoop up a fast low half-chance.

England in Australia   John Thicknesse, *Wisden* 1996

Australia looked unbeatable in the first two Tests, when it seemed Taylor had only to throw Warne the ball for wickets to start tumbling. His figures in Brisbane and Melbourne were 112.2-43-190-20, including, in the Second Test, his first hat-trick. In the New Year, however, his workload increased when off-spinner Tim May was dropped, and inevitably it took its toll: in the last three Tests Warne's seven wickets cost 51.28 apiece. By Perth, rather than touring New Zealand and the Caribbean, Warne looked in need of a holiday to rest his bowling shoulder.

WORDS ON WARNE

"England look at last to have come to terms with the Shane Warne factor. Admittedly Warne was not at the peak of his form – there were persistent reports of a shoulder injury – but in any case he was always unlikely to be able to continue to bowl out Test batsmen on good pitches to the degree that he had been. Leg-spinners should be able to account for the tailenders and the occasional top-line batsman but not whole sides."

Greg Chappell, former Australia captain – WCM, March 1995

Warne The Wizard   Robin Hobbs, *WCM*, January 1995

Certain sporting moments stick in the memory for ever, and I'm sure that all those who were present at Old Trafford in 1993 will never forget Shane Warne's first ball in a Test in England. In the words of Desmond Lynam, "How did he do that?"

Mike Gatting, one of the best players of spin in the country, was like a rabbit transfixed by a weasel. A dipping leg-break, spun from a high, cocked wrist, pitched just outside leg stump, and turned about 18 inches to hit the top of the off stump. Gatting stood rooted to the spot, and disbelief showed on his face when he shuffled off to the pavilion. Warne had arrived.

In 1930, Clarrie Grimmett, the most successful wrist-spinner to visit these shores from Australia, had taken 29 wickets in five Tests. By the time the sun set at The Oval at the end of August 1993, Warne had taken 34 wickets in six Tests – but if it hadn't been for the confidence shown in him by the Australian selectors, Warne's talent could have been lost for ever, for he started indifferently at Test level in 1991-92.

After a handful of Sheffield Shield matches for Victoria, Warne was pitched into the Test arena against India at Sydney and was hit for 150 from 45 overs, taking only one wicket. At Adelaide, he failed to take a wicket while conceding 78 runs, and was then dropped from the national side.

I'm convinced that had he been English he would never have been seen at the top level again, but with help and encouragement from three ex-Australian leg-spinners – Jim Higgs, Kerry O'Keeffe and Terry Jenner – a much fitter, trimmed down Shane Warne was selected to tour Sri Lanka. It proved to be the turning point of the young man's career. Mauled to the tune of 107 runs in 22 overs, Warne must have been wondering if he would ever take another Test wicket... but, thrown the ball by Allan Border with Sri Lanka coasting in their second innings, Warne came up trumps – three wickets for none in 13 balls and Australia won a famous victory by just 16 runs.

The blond leg-spinner has not looked back since then. In the next two series, against West Indies and New Zealand, world-renowned players like Richie Richardson and Martin Crowe struggled to come to terms with his subtle variations. Indeed, just before the 1993 Ashes series Crowe opined that Warne was the best leg-spinner in the world. Nobody in England took much notice: we had heard it all before. Richie Benaud had little success here, other than in one memorable Test on his third tour in 1961; John Gleeson took 12 wickets in the 1968 series, but never looked like running through England, and the three H's – Holland, Hohns and Higgs, all of whom were leg-spinners of high pedigree at home – struggled to come to terms with the much slower English pitches. Surely Warne was just another name on this list? How wrong we were!

So how *does* he do it? Warne has a very economical run-up and a classic side-on delivery: bad balls are a rarity. Highly frugal, he can and does bowl for hours on end – his new captain Mark Taylor has said it is most difficult to take the ball from him. He never seems to tire, wheeling away over after over, often bowling around the wicket into the rough outside leg stump. Some call this negative bowling: I would disagree, as so few present-day batsmen have the technique to cope with this form of attack. For many, the only shot they have to offer is the infernal sweep, which is very dangerous against the turning ball.

As his Brisbane triumph showed, Shane Warne will be playing a major role in the current Ashes series, and should be a thorn in the side of England and the other Test-playing countries for years to come. He really is a jewel in the crown in my eyes. How nice it was in 1993 to see boys everywhere trying to emulate Shane Warne instead of just another fast bowler.

Rumours abound that he was offered lucrative terms to play county cricket. He may have been right to reject the overtures. Look at Mushtaq Ahmed: so successful for Somerset, he has been dropped for Pakistan's tour of South Africa.

During the recent short series in Pakistan, Warne met and swapped theories with the wily old Pakistan leg-spinner Abdul Qadir, and the results of their meeting are awaited with interest. It has been suggested that one new Warne variation will see the ball spinning backwards after pitching. If that's the case, at least the English batsmen are unlikely to be out bowled!

WORDS ON WARNE

"I wonder what he will be doing in 10 years' time, at the ripe old age of 35, when most spinners are near full maturity? I cannot hazard a guess, because how can he improve any more?"

Keith Stackpole, former Australia opener – WCM, January 1995

1994-95

New Zealand v Australia, Auckland Terry Power, *Wisden* 1996
(Centenary Tournament, February 19)

The match was marred first by spectators throwing rubbish at Warne and then by Rutherford's remark that New Zealand Cricket had announced the injured Crowe's chances of playing as 50-50 only to boost the attendance.

West Indian Board President's XI v Australians Robert Craddock, *Wisden* 1996
(St Lucia, March 25-28)

Warne sat alone outside the dressing-room, staring coldly into the distance, after a third-day mauling left him with figures of two for 84 at six an over. He was thumped unmercifully by the robust Dave Joseph and none of his colleagues looked Test primed.

The Australians in the West Indies 1994-95 Robert Craddock, *Wisden* 1996

For once, Australia did not have to saddle up Shane Warne as a stock and shock bowler rolled into one. In fact, he was neither. Averaging barely 34 overs a Test, he took 15 wickets at 27.06; unlike the cement-footed batsmen of England and South Africa, the West Indians viciously attacked his bad balls... and some of his good ones.

Bribery Allegation Shock *WCM*, April 1995

The cricket world was stunned in February by accusations of match-rigging and bribery by certain Pakistan players current and past. The accusations came from Australian players, and after initial consideration the International Cricket Council asked the Board of Control for Cricket in Pakistan to conduct a full investigation.

February 12: It is revealed that the ICC have been asked by the Australian Cricket Board to look into claims by spin bowlers Shane Warne and Tim May that they were offered £35,000 to "throw" the Karachi Test match last September/October (Pakistan won by one wicket) and the Lahore Test in early November (drawn). It was believed that big-money gamblers in India were behind the approach. Australian manager Col Egar says his players told the propositioner to "p*** off".

February 15: Salim Malik, on the eve of a Test in Zimbabwe, is named as the alleged maker of the offers to Warne and May, a claim the Pakistan captain vehemently denies.

March 7: Captain Salim Malik is suspended from playing and given seven days to reply to the charges.

1995-96

Australia v Pakistan, Brisbane　　　　　　　　　David Hopps, *Wisden* 1997
(First Test, November 9-13)

After Warne's match-rigging allegations against Salim Malik, dramatic necessity dictated that the pair should confront each other at the Gabba. Warne dismissed Malik for nought, fourth ball, which was as satisfying in itself for Australia as the entire lop-sided result, achieved with more than five sessions to spare. On the first day Malik had made a splendid diving catch at midwicket to dismiss Australia's captain Taylor, and had needed six stitches in split webbing on his left hand. By the time he walked out to bat at No. 8 in Pakistan's second innings, to sporadic abuse, with overwhelming defeat beckoning and his hand heavily strapped, all Australia had cast Warne in the role of avenging angel. Malik offered a hesitant leading edge against a slightly turning top-spinner and McDermott plunged to hold a low catch at mid-off.

The fielders' temperate reaction was testimony to Taylor's positive influence, but Warne, understandably, could not resist commenting after the match. "It showed that there is justice in the game," he said. Warne's match figures of 44-19-77-11 took his record in three Tests at the Gabba, a traditional haven for seam bowling, to 30 wickets at 10.40. Brisbane's extra bounce enabled him to make full use of flight and dip as well as turn. At times, by his own high standards, he did not bowl uncommonly well, but he did not need to, such was his psychological hold over the batsmen.

Australia v Pakistan, Sydney　　　　　　　　　David Frith, *WCM*, January 1996
(Third Test, November 30-December 4)

Only 19 runs accrued in that tense final hour, and when it came to the final ball of the day, Healy and Warne met in mid-pitch for a tactical chat that can have done nothing to soothe Basit Ali's nerves. The final delivery, from around the wicket, pitched wide, spun a mile, shot between the wretched batsman's legs, and struck the leg stump. It was such a ball that gave several England batsmen nightmares in 1993.

The Pakistanis in Australia and New Zealand 1995-96　　　David Hopps, *Wisden* 1997

Leg-spinner Shane Warne, Malik's principal accuser, had received lengthy counselling before the Brisbane Test, and he was beset by other off-field problems. A picture of him smoking during a press conference was used by one newspaper to whip up a health storm, and he also started court action over the publication of private wedding pictures. Warne did not look his usual exuberant self, but such impressions were misleading – his match figures of 11 for 77 at the Gabba were the best by an Australian against Pakistan and no one played him comfortably.

In building their reputation as the best Test team in the world, Australia had had one nagging doubt in the back of their minds. Since he was dropped after his first four undistinguished Tests, Warne's leg-spin had brought 183 wickets at 21.47 each. What would happen if he was missing? They discovered the answer, briefly at least, in the Second Test at the Bellerive Oval when Warne broke a toe while batting on the first day. Warne's big toe became the talk of Australia, but a national crisis was averted; Hobart's chilly, overcast conditions meant a three-man attack could cope.

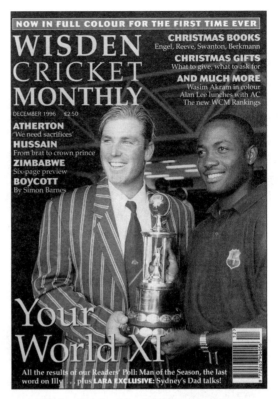

Wisden Cricket Monthly, December 1996

Australia v Sri Lanka, Perth

Steven Lynch, *WCM*, February 1996

(First Test, December 8-11)

The fourth day was a frustrating one for Warne, who took his 199th Test wicket early on when de Silva was caught at cover by the diving Ponting, but the 200th scalp was elusive, and arrived only in the closing minutes when left-hander Vaas swung him vertically to be caught by Healy. The 200 came up in his 42nd Test: only four bowlers (including Waqar Younis, who reached 200 next day) have done it in fewer matches, the record being held by another Australian leg-spinner Clarrie Grimmett, who reached 200 wickets in his 36th Test.

News Register

WCM, January 1996

Australian leg-spinner Shane Warne has begun legal proceedings against a company of film developers whose employee apparently retained negatives from Warne's September wedding in Melbourne and provided prints for publication by *Woman's Day* magazine. Warne and wife Simone are seeking damages of $A150,000. Exclusive rights to photographs of the wedding had been granted elsewhere, though special permission had been granted for a guest to take private pictures.

Australia v West Indies, Mohali
(World Cup semi-final, March 14)

Steven Lynch, *WCM*, April 1996

Almost inevitably the architect of West Indies' downfall was the matchless Warne, who dismissed stand-in opener Browne with his first ball and accounted for Gibson, Adams and Bishop in a crucial final spell of three for six as panic mounted.

Australia v Sri Lanka, Lahore
(World Cup Final, March 17)

David Frith, *WCM*, April 1996

In the aftermath, Mark Taylor bravely summoned all the diplomacy and sportsmanship he could find in his battered soul, and soon the vanquished Australians, still clad in their canary-gold outfits, were whisked away with police escort, Shane Warne sitting at the front of the bus, puffing at a cigarette, features uncharacteristically strained.

News Register

WCM, June 1996

There wasn't a bookmaker in sight at Lahore racecourse recently when Shane Warne, a four-year-old bay colt ridden by 15-year-old M. Rehan, romped home to win the Pakistan derby by two lengths from Nice Bird.

News Register

WCM, July 1996

Master leg-spinner Shane Warne has undergone an operation to repair ligament damage in his spinning finger, and hopes to be back to full fitness soon after a course of physiotherapy.

1996-97

The Burnout Factor

Alan Lee, *WCM*, October 1996

The burnout factor is also being explored in Australia, where the physical condition of Shane Warne has been giving rise to concern. Warne has just registered his 27th birthday. I hesitate to say he celebrated it, because he will presently relish no reminders of advancing age. Warne, who suffered severe pain when bowling in the World Cup, underwent surgery in May for tendon damage to his spinning finger – the third on his right hand – after being advised by American specialists that it could and should produce a full recovery. Three months passed before he was permitted to start bowling leg-breaks again, and he said recently: "I'm on a strict diet of no more than 12 leg-breaks a day, but it feels great to get back to it. In the early days after the operation I was worried about how it was going and whether I would ever bowl again."

Cricket can ill-afford to lose a gem like Warne, the most skilful and refreshing bowler of the last decade, but a glance at his workload is all that is necessary to know the risk. Warne has been playing Test cricket for five years and has already played 44 matches, taking 207 wickets. Richie Benaud, the last great Australian leg-spinner, took an additional 41 wickets in 19 more Tests – but they were spread over 12 years rather than five.

Warne was hoping to be fit for Australia's one-off Test in Delhi this month. Thereafter, his programme within nine months involves five Tests at home against West Indies, three in South Africa and then six in England. It may not just be his spinning finger that hurts after that lot.

Australia v West Indies, Brisbane Alan Lee, *WCM*, January 1997
(First Test, November 22-26)

Hasty conclusions were drawn and the whispers included word that Taylor and Geoff Marsh, the new coach, would not endure as a partnership and that Ian Healy would soon be replaced as both wicketkeeper and vice-captain. The batting, so the gossip went, was no longer what it was and the pace bowling relied too much on Glenn McGrath, who was struggling for fitness and refusing to respond to his physiotherapist's advice. Oh yes, and Shane Warne was probably finished.

This last rumour attracted more attention than any. No surprise in that, for Warne is an Australian icon, a revolutionary of modern Test cricket. The state of his spinning finger, six months after serious surgery, became a national obsession and even Warne himself, though lean, fit and optimistic, could not be entirely confident he could retain and sustain those magical powers.

Brisbane did not put all the fears to rest, but it was no mean comeback. Warne, understandably tentative at first, offered less variation and more waywardness than usual, but this is to judge by high standards. Come the second innings, he was bowling with the old intensity and much of the old accuracy. He got through 68 overs in the game and was fit to begin another three days later.

Australia v West Indies, Sydney Greg Baum, *Wisden* 1998
(Second Test, November 29-December 3)

Meanwhile, the elfin Chanderpaul struck back with such abandon that Warne had to be removed from the attack. He reached 50 from just 38 balls and, with Hooper, put on 117 in a bare 95 minutes. That rate of scoring might have delivered victory. But Warne returned and, on the stroke of lunch, conjured a ball that, had it held its line, would have gone to slip; instead, it rounded wickedly on Chanderpaul and cannoned from his pad into his stumps.

Australia v West Indies, Adelaide   Mark Ray, *WCM*, March 1997
(Fourth Test, January 25-28)

McGrath began Australia's campaign with a fine early spell, but it was Warne who destroyed West Indies' chances with the key wickets of Shivnarine Chanderpaul and Brian Lara. Chanderpaul was beautifully caught at slip by Taylor after Warne delivered a sliding ball from wide of the crease across the in-form left-hander. Lara, with four consecutive single-figure scores in the previous two Tests, fell victim to ego when he tried to loft the first ball he faced from Warne over midwicket.

Australia v West Indies, Perth   Greg Baum, *Wisden* 1998
(Fifth Test, February 1-3)

Lara came in at 43 for two; when he left, West Indies were in the lead and he had made a century such as only he can make. For him, the cracks closed up and the bounce evened out, or so it seemed. His innings grew like a symphony, two hours for the first fifty, just over an hour for the second, and then a crescendo as he hit Warne for 26 in 14 balls.

...

Even Taylor seemed to lose his captaincy bearings, bowling Warne for only two overs in a session at the height of the Lara–Samuels stand. Eventually, Warne was to dismiss both, half an hour apart, but Hooper's silky fifty helped to stretch the lead to 141.

Australia v West Indies, Sydney   Robert Craddock, *Wisden* 1998
(Carlton & United Series, December 8)

For most of the summer, West Indies' tail disappeared quicker than that of a field mouse scurrying behind a barn door. Here, they lost their last six for 19 off the final 37 balls of another limp innings. Five of them went to Warne, who mesmerised the bottom order in 15 balls to transform nought for 29 into a career-best five for 33. Twice he bowled for hat-tricks.

Australia v Pakistan, Sydney   Robert Craddock, *Wisden* 1998
(Carlton & United Series, January 1)

Warne, who took four for 37, did his best to launch a salvage operation but was like a lone frogman trying to raise the *Titanic*. Surprisingly, he received the match award ahead of Aamir Sohail, who scored 52, took two spectacular catches, one off his own bowling, and bowled Blewett. Two policewomen, who danced the Macarena when the band played the tune during the interval, delighted spectators but were given a warning by their superiors.

Australia v West Indies, Perth

Robert Craddock, *Wisden* 1998

(Carlton & United Series, January 12)

Lara simply took the breath away, scoring 90 off 110, including 40 off 24 balls at the death. Rarely had Warne received such a battering: his last three overs went for 31 after he bowled the first seven into a difficult breeze for just 15. With an improbable 66 needed off 42 balls, Lara, who started poorly, switched on the afterburners to smack Warne over the mid-on and mid-off fences.

The Australians in South Africa 1996-97

Jack Bannister, *Wisden* 1998

Warne's 11 wickets came at an average of 25.63, but he conceded barely two an over; his stock bowling in totally unsuitable conditions in the Second Test showed he is more than a great wrist-spinner, or even a great slow bowler. He is simply a great bowler.

1997

A Spin Doctor Writes

Ashley Mallett, *Wisden* 1997

The genius of Shane Warne has led to a surge of interest in spin bowling. Warne keeps his method simple – walk-up start, eyes focused, wrist cocked and an enormous surge of power through the crease. Until he came along, many feared wrist-spin was a lost art, gone the way of the dinosaurs, who vanished years ago when Planet Earth failed to duck a cosmic bumper.

...

Then came Warne. He bowled the leg-break with over-spin, the flipper and the top-spinner; he did not need to bowl the wrong'un too often. Instead of the googly against the left-hander beating the bat by a fair margin, his top-spinner took the edge. Smart. Above all, he was accurate. During the bleak years for spin, the idea was that finger-spinners were more accurate and could be trusted. Turn to history and you will find that many of the most accurate bowlers of all time were leg-spinners: Grimmett, Wright, O'Reilly, Barnes, Gupte, Benaud, Kumble, Warne.

The wrist-spinner can sometimes get away with a shortish delivery, anyway, because of the work he achieves on the ball, given that he is using a combination of fingers, wrist and arm. The ball bounces high and often tucks the batsman up. The delivery might cost him one run whereas an orthodox spinner's short one would not usually have steepling bounce and would get the full treatment. And when the ball is wet, the wrist-spinner has a decided advantage. Offies hold the ball very tightly, with fingers widely spaced across the seam; that makes purchase very difficult.

THE ASHES, 1997

The 1997 Australians Bob Woolmer, *WCM*, June 1997

No superlatives are too strong for this supreme leg-spinner. In South Africa he probably wasn't at his most effective, partly thanks to two very green wickets. However, he bowled some extraordinary deliveries that turned in spite of the unhelpful surfaces. His injuries may have affected his confidence a little, and during the tour he worked hard with his mentor, Terry Jenner, to put things right. Warne has the ability to strangle one end up, even when he isn't taking wickets, and so he can give the seam bowlers a rest – a capacity that is used brilliantly by Taylor. He has a wide range of variations including the flipper (of which he has two or three), the sliding inswinger, the vicious bouncing leg-break, the one that doesn't turn and of course the googly. Underestimate him at your peril.

England v Australia, Birmingham Scyld Berry, *WCM*, July 1997
(First Test, June 5-8)

Thorpe's left-handedness, and Butcher's at the start, kept the Australian line as disrupted as their length and Warne must hate Thorpe as O'Reilly did Leyland for his unflowery effectiveness. Thorpe did not seem to read everything out of Warne's hand, but that did not stop him sweeping and cutting, and it was a flipper which he may have read off the pitch that Thorpe punched for his hundred. On the third morning Ealham cracked on, the Australians so resigned to an enormous deficit that they did not call on Warne and McGrath.

CLASSIC TEST 3

England v Australia, Manchester Ken Casellas, *Wisden* 1998
(Third Test)
July 3, 4, 5, 6, 7 – Australia won by 268 runs. Toss: Australia. Test debut: D. W. Headley

The slumbering giant, aroused by the unaccustomed situation of trailing in a Test series, awoke, flexed its not inconsiderable muscle and demolished the opposition with brutal efficiency. Australia's emphatic triumph put them back on track after a stuttering start and weeks of depressing grey skies and rain. Suddenly, the weather resembled something vaguely like summer, but England's first defeat in eight Tests dampened the optimism springing from their resounding victories in the one-day series and the First Test. The contest had high achievement and occasional drama, but, from the moment Steve Waugh put his stamp on it, the whip hand was held by Australia. Waugh became the first batsman to score twin Ashes hundreds for 50 years;

backed up by Warne, who convincingly returned to his best form, he well and truly wrested the initiative from England.

Australia had reinforced McGrath's intimidating pace with Gillespie, who replaced Kasprowicz after proving his recovery from a hamstring strain. England gave Dean Headley a historic debut: he was the third generation of his family to play Test cricket, following his grandfather George and his father Ron, who both represented West Indies. Malcolm was dropped, and Tufnell and the Gloucestershire left-armer Mike Smith were also omitted from a squad of 14.

Headley was straight into the action, striking Taylor on the helmet as he ducked into a bouncer in his opening over. England had hardly concealed their joy when Taylor chose to bat on a moist, green pitch with bare patches at either end. It seemed a foolish gamble; it proved a brave and calculated decision – one made easier for a captain with Warne's genius at his disposal. But Taylor was the first sufferer. Headley pressed home the advantage in his third over, squaring him up with a fiery delivery which was edged to first slip. Taylor's headache worsened as Australia declined to 42 for three. That was when Steve Waugh entered the fray, but he got little support from the middle order. The total was a miserable 160 for seven when Reiffel joined him, just before tea.

Their luck changed, shortly after a break for bad light, when Reiffel was dropped on 13 by Stewart, off Headley. This could be construed as the turning point of the entire season. Reiffel contributed 31 to a tremendously important stand of 70 before he finally fell next morning, to Gough's trademark in-swinging yorker. By then, Waugh had completed a century of enormous skill and character. With his lucky red handkerchief poking from his trouser pocket like a matador's cap, he faced the charging attack for four hours, and later called it his finest Test innings. When he was ninth out, edging Gough's delivery on to his middle stump, he had seen Australia to 235, an admirable total in testing conditions. Headley ensured it went no higher with his fourth wicket, thanks to Stewart, whose sixth catch equalled England's record for an innings against Australia; later, he added two more to break the record for a match. His opposite number, Healy, soon retaliated. A brilliant leg-side stumping off a full toss from Bevan removed Butcher and provided Healy's 100th dismissal in 25 England-Australia Tests. Only Rod Marsh (148 in 42 games) and Alan Knott (105 in 34) had previously reached this landmark.

Healy's 99th victim had been Atherton, who, for the third time in three Tests, went cheaply in the first innings to McGrath. This time, he gloved a seemingly erratic leg-side delivery. But Butcher, possibly sensing his last chance to justify his place, and his brother-in-law Stewart steered England serenely to 74. Then Warne made his first telling impact and sent shivers of apprehension through the home camp. Recalling his ball from hell to dismiss Mike Gatting here four years earlier, he bowled a sharply spinning leg-break; Stewart, nonplussed, jabbed desperately and jerked his head back to see Taylor fling himself sideways at slip and snaffle a superb low catch. Now Warne was ready to put Australia in charge, and he had just the pitch to encourage him. The green demon of the previous day had been transformed into a brown strip, already scarred by footmarks. Flighting the ball cleverly and getting some vicious spin, he dismissed Thorpe, Hussain and Crawley for one run in a magical spell of

England v Australia, Manchester, 1997

AUSTRALIA	*First innings*		*Second innings*	
*M. A. Taylor c Thorpe b Headley	2	–	(2) c Butcher b Headley	1
M. T. G. Elliott c Stewart b Headley	40	–	(1) c Butcher b Headley	11
G. S. Blewett b Gough	8	–	c Hussain b Croft	19
M. E. Waugh c Stewart b Ealham	12	–	b Ealham	55
S. R. Waugh b Gough	108	–	c Stewart b Headley	116
M. G. Bevan c Stewart b Headley	7	–	c Atherton b Headley	0
†I. A. Healy c Stewart b Caddick	9	–	c Butcher b Croft	47
S. K. Warne c Stewart b Ealham	3	–	c Stewart b Caddick	53
P. R. Reiffel b Gough	31	–	not out	45
J. N. Gillespie c Stewart b Headley	0	–	not out	28
G. D. McGrath not out	0			
B 8, lb 4, nb 3	15		B 1, lb 13, nb 6	20

1/9 (1) 2/22 (3) 3/42 (4)　　　　　　235　　1/5 (2)　　　　　　　(8 wkts dec.) 395
4/85 (2) 5/113 (6) 6/150 (7)　　　　　　　　2/33 (3) 3/39 (1)
7/160 (8) 8/230 (9) 9/235 (5) 10/235 (10)　　4/131 (4) 5/132 (6)
　　　　　　　　　　　　　　　　　　　　6/210 (7) 7/298 (8) 8/333 (5)

First innings—Gough 21–7–52–3; Headley 27.3–4–72–4; Caddick 14–2–52–1; Ealham 11–2–34–2; Croft 4–0–13–0.
Second innings—Gough 20–3–62–0; Headley 29–4–104–4; Croft 39–12–105–2; Ealham 13–3–41–1; Caddick 21–0–69–1.

ENGLAND	*First innings*		*Second innings*	
M. A. Butcher st Healy b Bevan	51	–	c McGrath b Gillespie	28
*M. A. Atherton c Healy b McGrath	5	–	lbw b Gillespie	21
†A. J. Stewart c Taylor b Warne	30	–	b Warne	1
N. Hussain c Healy b Warne	13	–	lbw b Gillespie	1
G. P. Thorpe c Taylor b Warne	3	–	c Healy b Warne	7
J. P. Crawley c Healy b Warne	4	–	hit wkt b McGrath	83
M. A. Ealham not out	24	–	c Healy b McGrath	9
R. D. B. Croft c S. R. Waugh b McGrath	7	–	c Reiffel b McGrath	7
D. Gough lbw b Warne	1	–	b McGrath	6
A. R. Caddick c M. E. Waugh b Warne	15	–	c Gillespie b Warne	17
D. W. Headley b McGrath	0	–	not out	0
B 4, lb 3, nb 2	9		B 14, lb 4, w 1, nb 1	20

1/8 (2) 2/74 (3) 3/94 (1)　　　　　　162　　1/44 (2) 2/45 (3)　　　　　　200
4/101 (5) 5/110 (4) 6/111 (6)　　　　　　　　3/50 (4) 4/55 (1)
7/122 (8) 8/123 (9) 9/161 (10) 10/162 (11)　　5/84 (5) 6/158 (7) 7/170 (8)
　　　　　　　　　　　　　　　　　　　　8/177 (6) 9/188 (9) 10/200 (10)

First innings—McGrath 23.4–9–40–3; Reiffel 9–3–14–0; Warne 30–14–48–6; Gillespie 14–3–39–0; Bevan 8–3–14–1.
Second innings—McGrath 21–4–46–4; Gillespie 12–4–31–3; Reiffel 2–0–8–0; Warne 30.4–8–63–3; Bevan 8–2–34–0.

Umpires: G. Sharp and S. Venkataraghavan.　　Third umpire: J. H. Hampshire.
Referee: R. S. Madugalle.

26 balls, as the baffled Englishmen slumped to 111 for six with barely a whimper. He and McGrath mopped up the final two wickets in 22 balls of the third morning, and England were all out for 162. Warne finished with six for 48 from 30 overs, his first haul of five or more since he took seven for 23 against Pakistan at Brisbane in November 1995.

Australia led by 73, but Headley and Croft removed their top three for 39 by the 14th over. Controversy enveloped the second wicket: Hussain, at slip, lunged forward as Blewett drove at Croft, and the ball bounced out of his right hand before he clasped it with his left. Umpire Venkataraghavan was unsure whether the edge had carried and consulted George Sharp before giving Blewett out. But the Waughs combined to guide Australia into safer waters. Mark played a sublime two-hour 55, with seven fours and a six, while the flint-eyed Steve, often wincing in pain as he snatched a badly bruised right hand away from his bat, held firm for more than six hours. In that time, he became the third Australian to score a century in each innings against England in 288 Tests, and the first right-hander, joining Warren Bardsley, at The Oval in 1909, and Arthur Morris, at Adelaide in 1946-47. Though Bevan failed again, the lower order did themselves proud. Taylor finally declared 20 minutes after Sunday lunch.

He left England a theoretical target of 469 in a minimum of 141 overs – 63 more than any Test team had made to win. The pressure was overwhelming and England buckled. Butcher and Atherton opened aggressively, Atherton hooking Gillespie for six; the angry bowler struck back by trapping him lbw as he snapped up three for five in 19 balls. Warne and McGrath completed the rout. On bowling Stewart, Warne became the third Australian bowler, after Dennis Lillee and Craig McDermott, to take 250 Test wickets, in his 55th match; his legend was further enhanced when Healy put on a helmet, complete with grille, to keep to him. Only Crawley resisted, but he emulated Atherton at Lord's by treading on his wicket when in sight of a century. England were all out for 200 at 12.30 on the final day. Australia's champagne celebrations were in stark contrast to the glum atmosphere in the home camp; the series was level at 1-1, but the momentum now was all one-way.

Man of the Match: S. R. Waugh. **Attendance:** 87,829.

Australia Man By Man   Matthew Engel, *WCM*, August 1997

Shane Warne set England back almost to the point they were at Melbourne at Christmas 1994. If Warne had said then he had perfected a delivery that could do the hokey-cokey, England would have started worrying about it. Now at least they could call in a hokey-cokey expert to give the players technical advice. Off the pitch he was probably not that unplayable. But England were so petrified by what the ball might do out of the rough it hardly mattered. His last spell, culminating in the match-winning dismissal of Caddick, was his least effective of the game. This might be a harbinger of something. But, then again, probably not. Oh yes, he batted very well too.

England v Australia, Leeds   Steven Lynch, *WCM*, September 1997
(Fourth Test, July 24-28)

The Australians said they had no quibble with the actual decision to switch pitches, although they must have noticed that the original, with its bare ends, would have been Warne-friendly. The new one turned out to be Gillespie-friendly, McGrath-friendly and Reiffel-friendly, so they didn't lose much.

Somerset v Australians, Taunton   Eric Hill, *Wisden* 1998
(August 1-4)

The tourists' only scheduled four-day match was terminated by rain after two days. Those days attracted large crowds, a small number of whom were ejected by the police for abusing Warne.

England v Australia, Nottingham   Peter Johnson, *Wisden* 1998
(Fifth Test, August 7-10)

Australia's 427 left them virtually fireproof. Yet they were singed by Stewart's 87. He made the runs with his old, instinctive timing off only 107 balls, hitting 14 fours. He and Atherton had reached 106 in 27 overs and were promising England an honourable retreat when Warne turned in another of his hugely influential spells, removing both of them, plus Hussain, in 40 deliveries.

...

Australia claimed the extra half-hour at 173 for eight and one of the more lifeless and misguided England innings of a dark decade passed quietly into history with seven balls to spare. Warne led Australia's cavortings in front of the pavilion as they claimed the Ashes for the fifth time in a row.

News Register   *WCM*, December 1997

After months of negotiation Shane Warne eventually decided not to play county cricket in 1998, preferring to stay at home to spend more time with his wife and baby daughter. Figures as high as £450,000 for a two-year contract had been mentioned – but the three counties which had been competing for his services soon settled on alternatives. Northants and Sussex signed up Warne's Australian team-mates Paul Reiffel and Michael Bevan, while Notts went for Paul Strang, the Zimbabwean leg-spinner who played for Kent in 1997 while Carl Hooper was unavailable.

1997-98

Australia v New Zealand, Perth   Steven Lynch, *WCM*, January 1998
(Second Test, November 20-23)

Mark Taylor took three catches off Shane Warne in the First Test at Brisbane. This gave him 40 catches off Warne in 57 matches together, beating the previous Test record for a bowler/fielder combination – Garry Sobers's 39 catches off Lance Gibbs, in 60 matches.

News Register   *WCM*, February 1998

Shane Warne has been asked to watch his weight by national coach Geoff Marsh. "He is bowling well but I'd like to make sure he was a little bit fitter," Marsh told *The Australian* newspaper. "It's something we've asked him to watch and that's all we can do." Warne subsequently made a promotional appearance at Madame Tussaud's in Melbourne, and was asked by a reporter whether he preferred his own shape, or that of the waxwork. That was too much for the great leg-spinner who walked out.

Australia v South Africa, Melbourne   Mark Ray, *Wisden Australia* 1998
(First Test, December 26-30)

The lasting image from this Test match is that of Shane Warne ripping another leg-break past an uncertain South African bat – and past the stumps as well – on a tense fifth day. Warne bowled 86 overs in the match and 35 on that last day as Australia tried to dismiss South Africa to win the game.

The main obstacle to Warne and an Australian victory was Jacques Kallis. Despite an average to that point of 14 from nine Test innings, Kallis showed impressive maturity and a defensive technique far superior to his team-mates in making an excellent 101. Most batsmen who try to defend against Warne fall soon enough, the merest flaws eventually exposed by the great leg-spinner. Kallis showed it could be done, placing his front foot in the right position and often cleverly withdrawing his bat at the last instant as another fizzing leg-break snapped across him.

Australia v South Africa, Sydney   Steven Lynch, *Wisden* 1999
(Second Test, January 2-5)

Four years earlier, Warne had taken 12 wickets against South Africa at Sydney, but still lost, as Australia were beaten by five runs after collapsing for 111. There was no mistake this time, though: Warne took 11 wickets, including his 300th in Tests, six years to the day after his first: Ravi Shastri on January 5, 1992. This time the landmark victim was Kallis, bemused by a perfect top-spinner which dipped through his forward lunge. "A quality ball for a quality batsman," Taylor called it. Warne was back to his best here after the disappointments of the First Test: the ball which removed Richardson in the first innings was a near-replica of the famous one which did for Mike Gatting at Old Trafford in 1993. And, with the close fielders backing him up well, another South African escape act proved impossible.

Australia v New Zealand, Sydney Robert Craddock, *Wisden* 1999
(Carlton & United Series, January 14)

Playing without either Waugh twin for the first time in 11 years (Steve had a pulled muscle, Mark a virus), Australia were led to a convincing victory by Warne. Dozens of flash bulbs went off in the crowd when he bowled his first ball as captain, in the 21st over...

Australia v South Africa, Melbourne Robert Craddock, *Wisden* 1999
(Carlton & United Series, January 23)

Earlier, South Africa had chosen to bat and pulled a surprise by opening with Cullinan, an attempt to short-circuit his problems with Warne. The plan worked for a while as he thumped 26 off 22 balls. But Warne dismissed him for the 11th time when a pumped-up Cullinan roared out of his crease on a death-or-glory mission and was stumped.

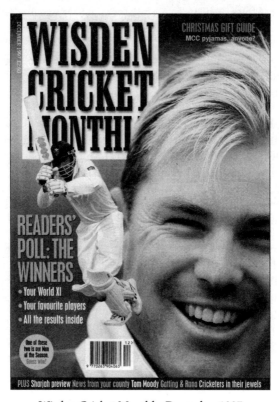

Wisden Cricket Monthly, December 1997

Vendetta: Warne v Cullinan
Mark Ray, *WCM*, March 1998

At least for the foreseeable future, South African batsman Daryll Cullinan has lost his personal feud with Shane Warne. The two have been public enemies since their first meeting at Melbourne in December 1993, and have carried on a high-profile vendetta spiced with sledging and counter-sledging. And amid all this public flexing of muscles and vocal cords is a cricket story: of one highly rated batsman's destruction at the hands of a master bowler.

Back in Melbourne a few weeks ago, Cullinan was clean-bowled by Warne on the tense final day of the First Test. It was the fourth time Warne had dismissed Cullinan in seven Tests and the tenth time in international cricket. Cullinan was left out for the Second and Third Tests. His international career was in jeopardy because of persistent failures against Australia, in particular a humiliating weakness against Warne.

The antipathy between Cullinan and Warne began in the first overs of the first Test between the two countries following South Africa's long years of isolation.

Play in that First Test at Melbourne on Boxing Day 1993 did not start until 5pm because of rain, but as soon as it did Cullinan made his presence felt. Standing at first slip, he set to sledging the Australian batsmen. The Australians have never denied that they regularly sledge the opposition, so they had no complaints about copping some of their own. Except that they thought Cullinan seemed to have rather a lot to say for someone in only his fifth Test.

Cullinan had arrived in Australia with quite a reputation. Just before the tour to Australia he had made 337 not out for Transvaal against Northern Transvaal, a record for South African domestic cricket. Soon after, he made his first Test century, in Colombo. Yet years before that Cullinan had attracted notice. He made his first-class debut and his first hundred at 16, replacing the legendary Graeme Pollock as the youngest South African to make a first-class century.

Soon, that reputation seemed to become a burden. It is noteworthy that Cullinan has been unpopular with the Australians while the rest of the South Africans are quite friendly with Warne and company.

On that first Boxing Day, as well as sledging like a grizzled veteran, Cullinan started dropping catches in the slips. When his turn came to bat, he was out first ball, caught Border bowled McDermott. The Australians' first impressions of Daryll Cullinan were of someone who had too much to say and too little to back it.

A few days later, the Second Test began in Sydney and Cullinan faced Shane Warne for the first time in a Test. Cullinan had faced Warne in the one-day series and been bowled for a duck in a game at Melbourne. In the Sydney Test, he pulled a short ball from Warne for four and smiled in satisfaction at the bowler. He might not have smiled had he known that Warne often sets up a batsman for the flipper by deliberately giving him short one.

The ball after the boundary, Warne duly sent down a flipper and clean-bowled Cullinan. Warne then gave him a send-off in return for that smile, a gesture which drew criticism of Warne and attention to the developing duel. Warne then took Cullinan's wicket in the second innings of the same Test, caught by Steve Waugh for three.

Warne, like many great bowlers before him, has a keen sense of the dramas of cricket and did not miss a chance to promote the idea of a personal duel between him and Cullinan. He let it be widely known that he would not mind bowling to Cullinan for a living. The momentum was building and it was all behind Warne. Cullinan failed twice in the Third Test at Adelaide for series scores of nought, nine, two, ten and five. He was dropped the return series in South Africa which followed after. Round one to Warne.

Before this season's Sydney Test, South African coach Bob Woolmer said that the alleged duel between Cullinan and Warne was a media invention. Yet between the 1994 series and the return bout in South Africa early last year, Cullinan spoke on occasions about his battle with the great spinner. In October 1996, he gave an interview to a Johannesburg paper and said: "After this season I think I'll know within myself, can I or can't I handle him... All I can say is, 'Yes, I do believe, and I am confident I can come up against Warne and acquit myself better.' It's pointless my saying I have no worries. I can only be confident in myself and the result will be there to see. I'm determined to settle the score with him."

Cullinan was not talking about Glenn McGrath or Craig McDermott. Even then, he knew a personal duel was developing. In that interview he went on to express his ambition to be his country's top batsman and "one best in the world".

"I welcome that pressure," he said. "I want that pressure." Just as well, as there was never any doubt the Australians would apply it.

Cullinan's preoccupation with one bowler is typical of a player under intense pressure and scrutiny. The pressure from Terry Alderman in 1989 in England so affected Graham Gooch that he stood down from the Fifth Test. Geoff Lawson took Gooch's wicket three times in the same series and David Gower's seven times, yet the Alderman–Gooch confrontation is the one that is remembered.

In 1987-88, Dean Jones had a bet with Martin Crowe who would score the most runs in the Test series. Richard Hadlee heard about the bet and decided that Jones would not win it. The great fast bowler then took Jones's wicket three times for six runs in the three Tests.

The lesson is surely that if you are going to start something with a great player, you have to be prepared for a very tough contest and to cop the consequences.

Yet Cullinan still tries to get on the metaphorical front foot to Warne. Each time this season that Warne has come out to bat against South Africa, the loudest voice abusing him has been Cullinan's.

Warne has no complaints. "I've never been one to complain about being sledged because I dish it out," he said. "But I've heard a few whispers that he has not been too happy with the verbals he's been receiving. In Test cricket, if you can't cop it, don't dish it out. The thing that has been happening between us has been good for the fans. They were right into it in Melbourne [at the First Test]. For me to have a psychological advantage over a batsman is enjoyable and it's good for the Australian team. He's an important player. He bats at No. 4. He's a good striker of the ball and he's made 300 in a first-class game. If you have an advantage over someone like that, you don't give that advantage away.

"I admit I get a buzz out of it, but so does the Australian public and the other guys in the Australian team. The South Africans don't, but they will if he makes a big score against us one day. If he does, he'll probably wrap his bat around my head. Hopefully he will never make that big score. It's our job to stop him."

Cullinan says that most players from both teams sledge each other, but that it will probably not get out of hand as there is enough mutual respect between the two sides.

"As for Boxing Day in 1993, that sort of cricket talk goes on all the time and I wasn't the only one talking. There are guys in our team who say a lot more than I do. Quite frankly, they give it and we give it back. That's cricket. What's the big deal?"

Warne regularly receives a solid dose of sledging from Brian McMillan, yet they respect and like each other and occasionally enjoy a night out together. Cullinan has never made an effort to sit beside Warne after a day's play and hold a conversation. He might have been surprised by the welcome he would receive. Warne regards those dressing-room meetings as an important part of the game.

By sledging Warne and refusing to meet his foe, Cullinan has surely fanned the flames of this duel. Even South African team management on this tour advised Cullinan to go easy on the sledging, but he refused.

Cullinan says he's not the sort of person to seek out opponents after a day's play. "Some time I'll probably have a chat to him, but at this stage I don't know. If he wants to have a chat with me or have a beer me, he's welcome, but I've never really been one for that sort of thing. It's not personal though."

It seems that both players have become somewhat obsessed with each other as the years have passed. But to suggest that the Australian media are at fault is to say the South African selectors have dropped Cullinan after learning the opinions of the local media.

In the one-day game at Sydney on December 4, Cullinan had a rare pleasure: brought on to bowl his occasional off-breaks, he had Warne lbw. He took the opportunity to say to Warne, "Go and deflate yourself, balloon." Cullinan is said to have been annoyed Gary Kirsten mentioned the incident in his newspaper column back home. Cullinan says that Warne returned the favour so heavily in the second innings of the Melbourne Test that he went beyond gamesmanship and was unnecessarily personal.

"I've never had a problem with the other Australians nor with Shane until the second innings in Melbourne," Cullinan said. "I think he overstepped the mark there. He doesn't need to do that. He's a great cricketer and I'm not even averaging 40 in Test cricket. He'd have so much respect if he didn't go to that level. He ridiculed Paul Adams in South Africa [in 1997] and he had a full go at Andrew Hudson [in 1994]. He doesn't need to do that because he's the best spin bowler ever. That's why I have some reservations. I don't know how much respect I have for him as a person."

The result of this has been to add greatly to the pressures on Cullinan whenever he faces Warne. Each meeting is now a major public confrontation, with all the pressure focused on the batsman and the crowd roaring in anticipation. Even Cullinan called it a no-win situation for him. After all, a bowler can be hit for four one ball and dismiss the batsman with the next. For a batsman, failure is always only a ball away and there is no escape except through making runs.

Most times Cullinan has walked out to bat Warne has asked him not to get out before he has had a bowl at him. One way or another Cullinan has fallen for the bait.

It even got to the stage that when New Zealand's Chris Harris bowled a leg-break at Cullinan during a recent one-day game, keeper Adam Parore could be heard on the TV microphone saying: "Bowled Shane."

Yet there are other ways of handling Warne and sledging. During his fine, match-saving century at Melbourne, Jacques Kallis not only played forward whenever possible but also showed so little reaction to Australian sledging that one frustrated fieldsman finally asked: "Are you f*** deaf or what?"

Kallis's attitude was the perfect counter to sledging, and you can bet that the Australians did not waste any more breath on him.

For all the sledging and the public nature of this one-on-one confrontation, cricket technique has still been important. When, in the second innings at Melbourne, Cullinan ignored a team plan, devised before this tour by the great Graeme Pollock, to play Warne off the front foot as often as possible, he was bowled by the sort of ball which Hansie Cronje and Kallis had been playing comfortably off the front foot. The dismissal proved that Cullinan had learned little about playing Warne. Most cricketers know that, when in doubt against a good spinner, play well forward.

In Cullinan's defence, that dismissal came during his first tilt at Warne since the series in South Africa in February and March last year when Warne dismissed him only once, for a duck in the First Test at Johannesburg. But then Warne did not always get the chance to bowl to Cullinan in that series, such was the dominance of pace. And the innings at Melbourne was also against a Warne who has all but lost his most dangerous weapon, the flipper. He could be forgiven for thinking that against Cullinan he no longer needs it.

Cullinan's attempt to become South Africa's best batsman appears to have failed because of his own shortcomings – technical and temperamental – as much as the attentions of a high-class bowler. Had Cullinan been prepared at Melbourne to follow the team plan and push forward to Warne, he might have managed his second double-figure score in Tests in Australia. He might even have been given another chance in the Test at Sydney. Had he followed team advice not to sledge so much, he might have eased the pressure on himself from his own leaders as well as, ultimately, easing some of the verbals he was copping.

Whether Cullinan can make it back to the South Africa side after his latest setback remains to be seen. One thing is for certain, Warne and the Australians will be waiting next time. No wonder we call it Test cricket.

WORDS ON WARNE

"Look, Warne cleaned up a lot of batsmen in that era, I was just one of them. He was too good for me. Full stop."

Daryll Cullinan, South Africa batsman – *TWC*, August 2008

News Register WCM, April 1998

Shane Warne has been rested from the four-match one-day series in New Zealand which followed the Adelaide Test against South Africa, where he was suffering from fatigue and a sore shoulder. Warne returned for the three-Test tour of India which followed.

Mumbai v Australians, Mumbai (Brabourne) Mike Coward, *Wisden Australia* 1998
(February 24-26)

This match ignited a theme of desperation for Australia, which lasted the entire tour. Sachin Tendulkar's magnificent 204 – his first first-class double century – won him membership of the Mumbai Cricket Club and a psychological advantage over Australia's bowlers that he never relinquished. The home side started with a game plan to intimidate their greatest threat, Shane Warne. He went for 111 off 16 wicketless overs in one of the greatest maulings of his career. Tendulkar came at him early with a six over midwicket and proceeded to hit boundaries to all parts of the Brabourne Stadium.

India v Australia, Chennai Dicky Rutnagur, *Wisden* 1999
(First Test, March 6-10)

The head-to-head contest between Sachin Tendulkar and Shane Warne was the key to this opening encounter. Warne's quick conquest of Tendulkar in the first innings gave Australia the initial advantage. But Tendulkar retaliated so devastatingly in the second, scoring 155 not out, that India were able to declare with a lead of 347, and 105 overs to bowl Australia out on a spinners' pitch. They had three men out overnight and won in comfort on the final afternoon.

On the first day, Tendulkar had been as much a victim of Warne's guile as of his own daring. He drove his first ball with scorching power past the bowler. But the fifth dipped as he rushed forward, and turned to take the edge of his flailing bat; Taylor completed a marvellous slip catch. In the second innings, however, when Tendulkar scored his third and highest century in seven Tests against Australia, he was as severe on Warne as on the rest. Warne followed up his first-innings four for 85 with a deflating one for 122. Tendulkar's belligerence was awesome and his shot-placement enthralling.

India v Australia, Bengaluru Dicky Rutnagur, *Wisden* 1999
(Third Test, March 25-28)

Warne's dismissal of Dravid – which made him Test cricket's most successful spinner, carrying him past Lance Gibbs's 309 wickets – was a classic. The ball drifted and dipped on to leg stump, then spun away to hit off. Minutes earlier, he had bowled Sidhu, and he added Mongia through a magnificent catch at cover by Ponting.

The Australians in India 1997-98 Dicky Rutnagur, *Wisden* 1999

Pre-series hype concentrated on the head-to-head contest between India's batting champion, Sachin Tendulkar, and Warne, the greatest contemporary bowler. The two jousted five times during the Tests and only once was Warne the winner. Of the Indian bowlers savaged by Don Bradman in the first-ever series between the two countries, in 1947-48, a handful survive: watching Tendulkar blasting away at Warne *et al* might have left them with a sense that vengeance had come at last. The 446 runs Tendulkar scored in the series, at a strike-rate of 80.65 per hundred balls received and a Bradmanesque average 111.50, were the product of sheer genius. The Australians had been given a warning of the storm to come in their opening fixture against Mumbai, when Tendulkar made 204 not out from 192 balls. Warne's ten wickets in the series cost 54 runs apiece; his career average previously was 23.81. The Indians, using their feet, played him expertly. But the limitations of the pace department and the inexperience of

© Nick Newman

his fellow spinner, Gavin Robertson (ironically, Australia's main wicket-taker), thrust on him the colossal burden of holding the fort as well as attacking. And the figures were unkind: there were times when he bowled really well, though at a slower pace than usual and without trying to turn his leg-break extravagantly.

1998

Ashes Campaign Starts Early Mark Ray, *WCM*, June 1998

The first shots in the 1998-99 Ashes campaign were fired as early as the beginning of May. On the day that England unveiled their two captains, Australia announced that despite the players' misgivings, Mark Taylor would continue as Tests-only captain, with Steve Waugh taking charge of the one-day team. A couple of days later came a piece of news that could affect the Ashes result more than any captaincy choice. Shane Warne emerged from surgery in Melbourne to reveal that his shoulder was much more damaged than was first thought. He will definitely miss the tour of Pakistan starting in October, may well sit out the whole Ashes series as well, and is even doubtful for the tour of West Indies next February.

Doctors involved in the operation told Warne that had he played a few more games on the recent tour of India, his shoulder would probably have fallen apart completely and his phenomenal playing career would have come to an end.

It had been general knowledge in cricket circles that Warne had been bowling in pain, but no one realised how severe it was. His doctors said they were amazed that he was able to bowl at all in the final one-day games of the winter. He had suffered a torn rotator cuff and torn cartilage in his right shoulder. It had been hurting for two years but the damage was exacerbated by a fall in the field in a one-day game in India, when the shoulder landed on the ball.

"It's disappointing news," Warne told me after speaking to both Taylor, Waugh, Australian team physio Errol Alcott, the ACB and the Victorian Cricket Association. "It is worse than we had hoped but I just have to do all the right things from now on to get it right and get back on the field. If I do have to put most of my life on hold, then I'll do that, but it's not going to be easy, especially on my wife and baby daughter."

In 67 Tests, Warne has taken 313 wickets, more than any other spinner – in India he overtook Lance Gibbs (309). In three Ashes series, he has 85 wickets in 17 Tests, at 23.57 apiece. Still only 28, he remains upbeat despite having his shoulder in a sling for four to six weeks. "The doctors told me that if the rehabilitation goes well the shoulder will eventually be better than brand new, so there's no reason why I couldn't have another five years playing for Australia if my form is good enough."

PART TWO

Star Turn
1999–2003

Star Turn:
1999–2003

"In the semi-final and final of the World Cup, Warne dragged himself out of a brief form slump, rose above homesickness and an emotional depression that had him thinking of retirement and, yet again, performed like a champion"
Mark Ray, *Wisden Cricket Monthly*, July 1999

Getting back on the field was one thing, recalibrating the weaponry in his formidable arsenal was quite another. There were many who wondered if Shane Warne could be the same bowler again after the operation to repair his damaged right shoulder – even Warne himself admitted to doubts – although it was clear he would fully commit his extraordinary willpower to the task. And at Sydney in the final Test of the 1998-99 Ashes series, there he was, out there again, taking a wicket in his first over, copping abuse from the Barmy Army – it was as if he had never been away.

Well almost. Warne took just two wickets in the match – dismissing Mark Butcher in both innings – but he was upstaged by Stuart MacGill, a leg-spinner who had made his debut a year earlier and who had proved a more-than-adequate stand-in during Warne's absence. MacGill took 12 wickets at the SCG, his constant threat in marked contrast to the innocuous nature of much of Warne's bowling. "There was no swerve yesterday and no huge turn either. Nor was the flipper coming out right," wrote Mike Selvey gloomily in *The Guardian.*

And there was something else. When he came out to bat on the opening day, Warne was booed by some of the crowd. That was a taste of the public reaction to revelations that he and batsman Mark Waugh had accepted money for providing information to an Indian bookmaker in Colombo in September 1994. The offence had been hushed up by the Australian Cricket Board. Though this was not in the same league as match-fixing, the players had clearly made a significant error of judgement.

"They were not spring chickens but experienced travellers who had been offered a gift horse and omitted to inspect its mouth, nostrils, feet and bloodline," wrote Peter Roebuck in *Wisden Australia*. Warne always maintained he had thought the gift was a present from an admirer and that he was innocent of any wrongdoing. In any case, he'd lost the money in a casino within hours of receiving it.

But it was the first significant blemish on Warne's reputation and perhaps the first time he was alerted to the downsides of being the most famous cricketer on the planet. The revelations, coming at the same time as he strove to return from serious injury, were an unwanted landmark in his career. And his comeback was proving arduous. In four Sheffield Shield matches for Victoria before his Test recall, he took eight wickets at 65. After a particularly undistinguished performance against New South Wales, he sought reassurance about his bowling from Test colleagues Steve and Mark Waugh and Michael Slater. All three offered soothing words – but then each of them had scored centuries in the match.

Matters came to a head in the Caribbean on a tour that followed the Ashes. After two expensive wickets in the first three Tests, Warne was dropped for the fourth match in Antigua. What perhaps made it worse was that, as vice-captain, he attended the selection meeting where the decision was taken. Moreover, the move came at the express wish of captain Steve Waugh, who went against coach Geoff Marsh and former captain Allan Border, who was consulted despite not being on the tour committee. Warne was shattered. His relationship with Waugh, until then a trusted ally, never recovered. "I always believe the art of captaincy is to support your players and back them every time," Warne wrote in *No Spin*, his final autobiography. "He didn't, it's history, but I never found it easy with him after that."

Such was the relentless nature of international cricket that soon after that traumatic trip, Australia were in England trying to regain the World Cup. Their tournament did not begin well until, facing elimination, they embarked on a run of five successive wins that carried them to a semi-final against favourites South Africa at Edgbaston. The match was an epic – one of the greatest one-day internationals in history – but Australia progressed to the final (the game was tied, but they had finished higher than South Africa in the second-stage table) only after a Herculean individual performance by Warne. He took four for 29, launching Australia's thrilling counter-thrust, by bowling Herschelle Gibbs with a delivery that evoked memories of the Gatting ball six years earlier. He won the match award and picked up another at Lord's as Australia strolled to victory in the final. "With those two games, Warne swept himself back into the hearts of his teammates, and his countrymen," wrote Simon Wilde in *Shane Warne: Portrait of a Flawed Genius*. Indisputably, he was back.

A year later there was perhaps an even greater honour. In preparation for its 2000 edition, *Wisden* asked a distinguished panel of former players, writers and historians to name their five Cricketers of the Century. With 27 votes, Warne was the only still-active player in the five, joined by his fellow Australian Sir Donald Bradman (who polled 100 votes), Sir Garry Sobers, Sir Jack Hobbs and Sir Viv Richards. He may have been the only one lacking a knighthood, but Warne was thrilled. "It's hard for me to wrap my head around it," he said. The comments of Crawford White, the octogenarian former *Daily Express* cricket correspondent who had seen Bill O'Reilly between the wars, were especially telling. "I don't think O'Reilly caught the imagination quite as much as this lad."

The breakneck nature of Warne's life could be dizzying. At Auckland in March 2000, he overtook Dennis Lillee as Australia's leading Test wicket-taker. A few weeks later he flew into a chilly English spring for his first season of county cricket with Hampshire. It was a disappointing summer for a serial winner such as Warne, but he generated more interest in county cricket than any overseas signing since Sobers in 1968. At Portsmouth in July, he fought a memorable duel with the India batsman Rahul Dravid, who was playing for Kent. On a sunny midweek afternoon on an English outground, here was a close-up glimpse of the intensity of Test cricket.

But Warne's fame now went well beyond cricket. He made the tabloid front pages when he admitted leaving lewd messages on the mobile phone of a nurse he had met in a Leicester nightclub. "Celebrity – I hate that word," he said in an interview with the Australian journalist Jana Wendt, although there was no doubt he had courted fame.

More unwelcome attention was to follow, and again it would call his future into question. On the eve of Australia's World Cup defence in South Africa in February 2003, a drugs test revealed Warne had taken a banned diuretic. He insisted they were slimming tablets given to him by his mother to help him lose weight before a press conference. He was banned for a year – the speculation about his future started all over again.

RW

1998

The South Africans in England Shane Warne, *WCM*, June 1998

Daryll Cullinan
No one questions his ability. He hits the ball crisply, has a full range of shots and plays fast bowling quite well. It is his temperament that is fragile, and obviously he struggles against spin. On the mental side of the game, he is prone to playing the man not the ball. He can be upset under pressure by a few comments and some tight bowling...

News Register *WCM*, September 1998

Shane Warne has admitted that his career might be over after his recent shoulder operation. "There is a slim chance of that," he said in Melbourne. "It's a bit daunting to think that you may never play again. The thing is, no other leg-spinner has had the operation. It puts some people out for 18 months and some never return." Warne, who has taken 313 Test wickets, definitely misses Australia's tour of Pakistan, and is very doubtful for this winter's Ashes series.

News Register *WCM*, October 1998

Shane Warne hopes he may be fit to play in the coming Ashes series after all. Doctors found that his shoulder had full rotation after his recent operation. Warne is aiming to be fit for the First Test at Brisbane, which starts on November 20.

News Register *WCM*, October 1998

Sachin Tendulkar and Shane Warne went toe-to-toe again recently. This time the duelling was at an auction of Bradman memorabilia at a black-tie dinner for 1,300 in Adelaide on August 27 to mark Sir Donald's 90th birthday. The pair swapped bids for a signed photo of him. Tendulkar won with a bid of $A4,000. A framed signed photograph of the Don and Tendulkar sold for $A22,000.

1998-99

News Register *WCM*, January 1999

Shane Warne has promised to quit smoking on January 1 as part of a deal with a Sydney pharmaceutical company.

News Register	*WCM*, January 1999

Shane Warne was found guilty of breaching the ACB's code of conduct for comments made about an lbw decision after captaining Victoria in a Shield game against Western Australia. Referring to the dismissal of Victoria's Graeme Vimpani, Warne said: "Everyone in the ground knew he hit it, bar the umpire."

Bookiegate	Mark Ray, *WCM*, February 1999

If you were a rich and ruthless bookmaker wanting to fix a cricket match, who would be your main targets? Players – or umpires? With an umpire on your payroll, you will control key events when you need to.

Nobody has yet accused an umpire of match-fixing. But if only half of the rumours spreading through the cricket world are true, the ICC's new independent watchdog, the Code of Conduct Commission, will need to investigate the roles played by umpires and officials in the bribery scandal which has rocked the game in the past four years.

Certainly in Australia there are now suspicions that the cover-up ordered by the ACB in February 1995, when it fined Shane Warne and Mark Waugh for selling information to an Indian bookmaker, may have been even greater than was first thought. Some important documents relating to two key events may be incomplete or even missing – the events being the fining process, and the allegations made by Warne, Waugh and Tim May in 1994 against Pakistan's Salim Malik, namely that he offered them money to bowl badly in a Test match.

The handling of the affair by ACB officials has been included in the terms of reference of an enquiry which ACB was forced to initiate after embarrassing revelations of the fines and the subsequent cover-up. The enquiry, conducted by lawyer Rob O'Regan, has already begun calling witnesses. It has the power to call all 25 players who are under contract to the ACB: they must and will appear. The ACB has also sent invitations to former officials and to every player who has represented Australia since 1992, the year Dean Jones refused a bookie's offer for money in return for team information during a tour to Sri Lanka.

Already two ACB officials who imposed the fines on Waugh and Warne, the then chief executive Graham Halbish and chairman Alan Crompton, have said they will appear. O'Regan could end up interviewing up to 60 people. It will be surprising if there are not further revelations.

Editor's Notebook	Tim de Lisle, *WCM*, February 1999

Anyone getting on their high horse needs to be clear about one thing: we are dealing with three distinct, if interlocking, crimes and misdemeanours. The first is match-fixing. This is the gravest of the three – although I cling to the view, expressed here two months ago, that future transgressions should be punished severely, while past ones are treated more leniently. The second is selling information to bookmakers.

Mark Waugh and Shane Warne – and perhaps three other wearers of the Baggy Green – behaved in a way that was naive and stupid, as they admitted. It was also cheap and tawdry. But it wasn't treacherous or corrupt. The ACB's decision to allow them to be captain and vice-captain of the one-day side is surprising, but not wrong (except perhaps on cricket grounds: by making Warne captain, the selectors squeezed out Stuart MacGill, just when he was the bowler England least wanted to face).

The third crime or misdemeanour is covering things up. Here the ACB was plainly culpable – in fact self-defeatingly so. These things come out in the end – they used not but they do now. The modern world, that mysterious realm with which cricket administration occasionally intersects, believes in disclosure, and has means at its disposal (ranging from newspaper chequebooks to the internet) to make the men in blazers shudder. Imagine if the fines story had come out a year later. Warne might well have just succeeded Mark Taylor as Test captain. The effect would have been even more dramatic. A cover-up is a time bomb, and this one would have had the unusual property of becoming more explosive the longer it ticked. Warne would have been forced to resign.

As it is, he is now in an interesting moral position: he can still be captain of Australia, but cannot write for the London *Daily Mirror*, which kept up the great tradition of ethical posturing by the red-top tabloids. Warne keeps pointing that what he did was far from match-fixing, and that's fair enough He looks as if he is telling the truth. It was striking how, when hauled up before the Pakistani enquiry in Melbourne, Warne related that his relationship with "John" the bookmaker had begun when he lost a four-figure sum at a Colombo casino. When the ACB owned up to the whole affair in December, nothing was said about casinos. Did the Board advise its star player to keep quiet about his gambling? If so, the cover-up was continuing. And perhaps it still is now. Warne and Waugh have lost a bit of lustre, but the ACB has lost credibility, which is worse.

Notes by the Editor   Matthew Engel, *Wisden* 1999

On a couple of occasions last November, *The Times*, a newspaper which made its reputation by not exaggerating, said cricket faced its worst crisis in 20 years – the Kerry Packer schism being the benchmark for modern cricketing crises. The paper was right, but not in the way it intended. The supposed worst crisis was the bizarre industrial dispute in which the West Indian players refused to start their tour of South Africa and instead holed up in a London hotel for a week. It was settled soon enough.

At the time, the real crisis was being ignored. Justice Qayyum, a Pakistani judge, was in Lahore conducting his investigation into the tangled skein of allegations about gambling and match-fixing. But elsewhere in the cricket world, no one was listening.

A month later, the Australian Cricket Board was finally forced to admit something it had known, and covered up, since February 1995. Mark Waugh and Shane Warne, who had made the original allegations of attempted match-fixing against the former Pakistan captain Salim Malik, had themselves accepted thousands of dollars from an Indian bookmaker for providing apparently innocuous information.

Of itself, what Waugh and Warne did was only borderline-reprehensible. My own hunch is that it was a sting that went wrong: the bookmaker, using old spymasters' techniques, tried to draw them into a web of deceit from which there could be no escape, but was too unsubtle. The Waugh–Warne case is just a small but rocky outcrop of the mountain range of corruption that almost certainly still lies shrouded in the mists elsewhere.

But its emergence at last galvanised public opinion, and – on the face of it – the administrators. Suddenly, the Australian Cricket Board announced that it would hold an investigation. So did the International Cricket Council. Unfortunately, said ICC chairman Jagmohan Dalmiya, the very fabric of the great game is being damaged. Yet both bodies had known about Waugh and Warne for four years, since the ACB had informed ICC officials (but no one else) at the time. The fabric, apparently, was damaged only when the public found out.

Notes Peter Roebuck, *Wisden Australia* 1999

Clearly the players behaved badly and deserved the ignominy that fell upon them. They had been greedy and indiscriminate. They were not spring chickens but experienced travellers who had been offered a gift horse and omitted to inspect its mouth, nostrils, feet and bloodline. Spectators booed the pair at the next few appearances and later gave the Sri Lankans the same treatment. Barracking has long been part of the Australian cricket scene and sometimes it has gone too far. But booing is another matter and it seemed unsportsmanlike.

The condemnation of the players also went too far. They did not perform below their best in any match or attempt to undermine their team. Only later, when the match-rigging scandal came to light, did they understand the risks they had taken. A rule is needed that cricketers must not gamble on their own sport or take money from any bookmaker, and it must be ruthlessly applied in case grey areas are exploited by the cunning.

Ashes Preview Allan Donald, *WCM*, December 1998

Shane Warne

Our captain, Hansie Cronje, plays him as well as any one because he can pick him. But picking him is only part of the problem, otherwise finger-spinners would never get a wicket. Warne is the best spinner in living memory, because he has so many variations and is unique in that he can bowl over and around the wicket to left- and right-handers alike as an attacking option. He is almost impossible for right-handers to sweep when he bowls around the wicket, because he spins it so much that he creates an angle that makes it difficult to control the stroke.

As for left-handers, most leggies go around the wicket to exploit the rough, but Warne can do that from over. The biggest question he has to answer after his operation is whether he is still capable of getting big turn.

He can be a dangerous batsman, but in four series we've kept him quiet so well that he's only got 120 runs against us in 19 innings, at an average of seven. He loves to play square of the wicket both sides, and either makes room to cut or steps right back across to hoick to leg. We've done him with pace 12 times, but Symcox and Adams have also got him out. There's no best advice for batsmen, but bowlers must not give him any width.

Allan Donald faced Shane Warne in 14 Test matches between 1993 and 2002.

Australia v England, Sydney   Tanya Aldred, *WCM*, February 1999

(Fifth Test, January 2-5)

Like Botham before him, much of Warne's magic lies on his reputation. His haul of eight wickets at 65 in four Shield matches hardly demanded a recall. But he'd said he was ready which was good enough for the selectors. That wicket in his first over was a formality.

It was good to have him back. All peroxide barnet and glinting ear-stud, he indulged in his old tricks, winking at Gough after his hat-trick, and colluding in mind games with Healy. He had to suffer a rendition of "You fat bastard" from the Barmy Army, but is living proof, along with Lehmann and Taylor, that being a bit portly doesn't do an Australian cricketer any harm.

He was not back to his best. The famous flipper let him down, and he was comprehensively out-hauled by the young pretender. But, as Taylor said, the 12:2 wicket ratio was unjust. And although Taylor bowled MacGill first, he opened with the old firm of Warne and McGrath on the last day, when the pressure was really on.

The rivalry between the two should now be enthralling. MacGill now has 47 wickets in eight Tests. At the same stage, Warne had 13. Would both be taken to West Indies?

Cricket in Australia   John MacKinnon, *Wisden* 2000

Shane Warne's return from his shoulder operation was something of a world event, but eight wickets at more than 65 each suggested that his rehabilitation might require patience. However, his contest with Michael Slater and the Waugh brothers on a slow Sydney pitch that took spin was Shield cricket at its best, though the match ended in a high-scoring draw.

Australia v England, Melbourne   Robert Craddock, *Wisden* 2000

(Carlton & United Series, January 15)

Australian captain Warne probably saved the game when he came on to the field at Stewart's request to calm drunken spectators who had tossed golf and billiard balls at English outfielders. He playfully put on Waugh's helmet before approaching the trouble-makers. Play resumed after a five-minute halt. Warne controlled the match equally effectively, and Waugh and Ponting coasted to victory in the 40th over.

Australia v England, Adelaide　　　　　　　　　Robert Craddock, *Wisden* 2000
(Carlton & United Series, January 26)

Australia's 239 for eight had looked vulnerable on a sound pitch, although Waugh's stellar form produced his sixth successive half-century. But England seemed distracted after their dust-up with Sri Lanka earlier in the week. Warne captained Australia well, using eight bowlers and taking three for 39, probably his best bowling of the summer: walking to the press conference, he whispered to a friend: "Chalk up one for the fat leg-spinner."

Australia v England, Sydney　　　　　　　　　Robert Craddock, *Wisden* 2000
(Carlton & United Series, February 10)

England were 198 for four in the 43rd over, needing only 35 from 47 balls, when Hussain took a huge bite at Warne, who had been baiting him, charged down the pitch and was stumped. (This almost cost him a place in the World Cup: he was omitted from the original squad after much criticism of this one shot and only included when Atherton was injured.)

Carlton & United Series 1998-99　　　　　　　Robert Craddock, *Wisden* 2000

But there was a big plus for Australia in the inspired captaincy of Shane Warne, which saw them to victory in their last seven games. Deputising for the injured Steve Waugh, Warne's attacking field placings stopped singles and created pressure. He rallied his troops like a football coach, with plenty of backslaps and good communication. Warne leads the busiest life of all Australian cricketers, yet when any of his players had a problem, he instantly called them to his room for a chat.

WORDS ON WARNE

"He reinvented the art of spin bowling, a facet of the game that had been dying. Through his efforts and his momentous success, he triggered an overall reappraisal in the value of having a spin bowler in a Test line-up."

Mark Taylor, former Australia captain – WCM, June 1999

The Australians in the West Indies 1998-99　　　Malcolm Knox, *Wisden Australia* 1999

Shane Warne's poor form, yielding him four wickets in four Tests after his return from shoulder surgery, forced him out of the team for the Fourth Test, and his leg-spinning partner Stuart MacGill did not enjoy the success he might have expected. Vice-captain Warne, who voted against his omission, was arguably the most successful Test cricketer ever to be dropped at this stage of his career. To his credit, he rebuilt his game during the limited-overs series and emerged as its outstanding bowler.

1999

World One-Day XI Allan Donald, *WCM*, May 1999

Shane Warne
He has to be my main spinner. It's all been said before but he's one of the greatest slow bowlers in history. He might not be quite back to his best, but he showed against England in the winter's one-day series what a match-winner he is. He doesn't compromise in one-day cricket, and still gives it a rip. He can turn it on anything and is difficult to slog because of his control. Also, he thinks about the game, as he showed against England when he won a couple of games from nowhere with his tactics. On his day he is simply the best, and he is also a useful batter.

Wisden Cricket Monthly, May 1999

CLASSIC ONE-DAY INTERNATIONAL

Australia v South Africa, Birmingham　　　　　Simon Briggs, *WCM*, July 1999
(World Cup semi-final)
June 17 – Tied. Toss: South Africa

It was always going to take something special to dispose of these indomitable South Africans. And one-day games don't come any more special than this. Steve Waugh, who has more than 260 of them under his belt, said: "It was the best game of cricket I've ever played' – though he might not have been so sanguine if his team had gone out on net run rate.

The result could not have been crueller for South Africa, who have endured more than their share of disappointment in England lately. Victory was within their grasp when Klusener squared up to Fleming in the 50th over, needing nine to win, and lanced the first two balls through the off-side ring for four. Just one to win off four, but the next ball cramped Klusener for room, and as Donald, the last man, backed up, Lehmann missed a chance to run him out from mid-on.

Eleven gum-chomping Australians were clustered around the square, and a seed of doubt had been planted in Donald's mind. Now Fleming produced his trademark yorker. Klusener met it with the bottom corner of the bat and, as the ball rolled tantalisingly past the bowler's stumps, he charged in true Zulu fashion. But Donald never heard the call. Coming round from mid-off, Mark Waugh dived and flicked the ball to Fleming, who rolled it, Trevor Chappell-style, to Gilchrist. Donald was run out by almost 10 yards, the match was tied, and Australia were in the final thanks to their higher Super Six position.

"You can't blame Allan or Lance," said a dejected Cronje afterwards, and he was right. If anyone could be blamed, it was South Africa's top four, who cracked under the weight of expectation yet again. The bowling had been better than ever: honorary Brummies Donald and Pollock shared nine wickets between them, and Kallis shrugged off a stomach strain to bowl his most economical spell of the tournament.

But pressure alone is rarely enough against Australia. Even at 68 for four, Steve Waugh and Bevan were confident enough to bed themselves in taking only six runs off eight overs. Bevan had mislaid his famous placement, but Waugh gave Klusener a dose of his own medicine, stretching the stand to 90 before Pollock produced a priceless double strike: Waugh and Moody in the same over. Australia's 213 was the same score that they had failed to defend against New Zealand – surely a bad omen. At lunch, they were 7-2, South Africa 6-1 on.

For once, McGrath's gun-barrel was less than straight, and Gibbs and Kirsten reached 48 without loss. But cometh the hour, cometh the fat man. Warne didn't just bowl a spell, he wove one, dismissing both openers and Cronje in eight runless balls.

The ball that bowled Gibbs was up there with Warne's most miraculous moments, pitching outside leg and hitting the top of off. After that, no one dared attack anything that landed near the footholds. The aura of a great player was at work, mesmerising both the South Africans and the crowd, and Cullinan soon became another victim in all but name.

If Australia had possessed an attacking fifth bowler, there might have been no way back. As it was, Waugh shuffled his brother, Moody and Reiffel around for 15 overs without taking a wicket. Kallis and Rhodes plundered 84 in reasonable time, and the

Australia v South Africa, Birmingham, 1999

Australia

†A. C. Gilchrist c Donald b Kallis	20		D. W. Fleming b Donald		0
M. E. Waugh c Boucher b Pollock	0		G. D. McGrath not out		0
R. T. Ponting c Kirsten b Donald	37		B 1, lb 6, w 3, nb 6		16
D. S. Lehmann c Boucher b Donald	1				
*S. R. Waugh c Boucher b Pollock	56		1/3 (2) 2/54 (3)	(49.2 overs)	213
M. G. Bevan c Boucher b Pollock	65		3/58 (4) 4/68 (1)		
T. M. Moody lbw b Pollock	0		5/158 (5) 6/158 (7)		
S. K. Warne c Cronje b Pollock	18		7/207 (8) 8/207 (9)		
P. R. Reiffel b Donald	0		9/207 (10) 10/213 (6)	15 overs: 61-3	

Pollock 9.2–1–36–5; Elworthy 10–0–59–0; Kallis 10–2–27–1; Donald 10–1–32–4; Klusener 9–1–50–0; Cronje 1–0–2–0.

South Africa

G. Kirsten b Warne	18		A. A. Donald run out		0
H. H. Gibbs b Warne	30		(Waugh/Fleming/Gilchrist)		
D. J. Cullinan run out (Bevan)	6		Lb 1, w 5		6
*W. J. Cronje c M. E. Waugh b Warne	0				
J. H. Kallis c S. R. Waugh b Warne	53		1/48 (2) 2/53 (1)	(49.4 overs)	213
J. N. Rhodes c Bevan b Reiffel	43		3/53 (4) 4/61 (3)		
S. M. Pollock b Fleming	20		5/145 (6) 6/175 (5)		
L. Klusener not out	31		7/183 (7) 8/196 (9)		
†M. V. Boucher b McGrath	5		9/198 (10) 10/213 (11)	15 overs: 53-3	
S. Elworthy run out (Reiffel/McGrath)	1				

McGrath 10–0–51–1; Fleming 8.4–1–40–1; Reiffel 8–0–28–1; Warne 10–4–29–4; M. E. Waugh 8–0–37–0; Moody 5–0–27–0.

Umpires: D. R. Shepherd and S. Venkataraghavan.   Third umpire: S. A. Bucknor.
Referee: R. Subba Row.

equation had come down to 61 from 48 balls by the time Warne returned. His last over cost 15, one more than his previous nine combined: first Kallis was dropped at long-off by Reiffel, at three runs, then Pollock turned into Tendulkar, with an on drive for six and a cover carve for four. But Warne's balloon wasn't burst yet. His penultimate delivery lured Kallis into an ugly stroke, an inside-out poke to short extra.

South Africa had left it to Klusener yet again, and why not? With no deep midwicket posted, he played merry hell with the bowling, smashing 23 from his first 12 balls, and surviving a chance to the man at long-on, who palmed a skimming drive over the rope for six. Infamy beckoned for the fielder, the unfortunate Reiffel once again, but that extraordinary last over offered a reprieve. As Alex Ferguson might have said: "Cricket ... bloody hell."

Man of the Match: S. K. Warne. **Attendance:** 19,639.

Australia v Pakistan, Lord's   Hugh Chevallier, *Wisden* 2000
(World Cup final, June 20)

With Pakistan faltering at 69 for three after 21 overs, Waugh brought on Warne. It was, literally, the turning point of the match.

Warne produced an astounding delivery to dismiss Ijaz, who had hung around doggedly for 22. The ball pitched on or just outside leg and hit off. It was not quite the famous Gatting ball, nor even the one that dismissed Gibbs in the semi-final, but it sent shockwaves through the lower order. Pakistan tried to get out of trouble with all guns blazing. But for every ball that ricocheted off the boards, another landed in Australian hands. Luck was against them, too: a ball from Reiffel clipped Inzamam's pad on its way to Gilchrist. The Australians went up in appeal; umpire Shepherd's finger in judgment. An incredulous Inzamam plodded off at funereal pace. When Wasim holed out, Warne had claimed four wickets for the second game running, taking his tally to 20, a World Cup record shared with Geoff Allott of New Zealand. McGrath brought the innings to a swift end when Ponting held a superlative catch at third slip in the 39th over. The target was just 133.

A Matter of Emotion   Mark Ray, *WCM*, July 1999

A few years ago, Greg Chappell said that the thing that would most likely shorten Shane Warne's career was not the collapse of his shoulder or spinning finger but that of his emotional wellbeing. Chappell thought that Warne put the same emotional effort into his bowling as the last great Australian bowler, Dennis Lillee.

Because Warne is a spinner not a fast bowler, some people assume that life in the middle is easier for him than it was for Lillee. Yet the similarities are numerous.

Just as Lillee overcame a crippling back injury to continue his great career, Warne has overcome two career-threatening operations – the first on his spinning finger, the second and more serious on his bowling shoulder.

Warne, like Lillee, is an aggressive, wicket-taking bowler. Like Lillee, he tries hard to assert his dominance over opponents. To do so, Warne resorts to similar theatrics. Think of the way he appeals or celebrates a big wicket or glares down the pitch at a bemused batsman. To dominate his opponents Warne, as Lillee did, tries to dominate the field as well, to ensure that the attention of spectators, television viewers and opponents falls on him rather than on his opponents. Out in the middle Warne plays a game within the game and, in the heat of the contest, he sometimes overacts, just as Lillee did. Yet deep down that posturing and bravado is there as much to overcome Warne's insecurities as to inspire team-mates and intimidate opponents.

Match-winning cricketers are performers who must produce the goods day in day out, but especially on big occasions. It is acceptable for a rock star, an actor or an opera singer to be precious and to overact, yet many people object to gifted cricketers psyching themselves up in the same way. We cannot have it both ways and nor can they. There is a price to pay for that emotional effort. Even Don Bradman paid for his genius with bouts of ill-health.

Under all that pressure to maintain the high standards their genius imposes on them, players like Warne and Lillee – Ian Botham also – occasionally step over the line and find themselves in trouble with administrators and the public. Occasionally they lose control of those highly strung emotions.

In the semi-final and final of the World Cup, Warne dragged himself out of a brief form slump, rose above homesickness and an emotional depression that had him thinking of retirement and, yet again, performed like a champion. Lillee would have done the same. Warne argued that he was not in a form slump. Perhaps he was right, but in saying that, he was also fighting his own uncertainties. That he rose above those problems proves that he is a truly great performer.

News Register   *WCM*, July 1999

Shane Warne has been allowed to keep the A$200,000 Nicorette paid him to stop smoking, even though he was pictured with a cigarette at the end of the recent West Indies tour. "It is possible that ex-smokers relapse, particularly in stressful situations," said a company spokesman.

1999-2000

Sri Lanka v Australia, Kandy   Mark Ray, *WCM*, November 1999
(First Test, September 9-11)

With Sri Lanka 139 for three, Mahela Jayawardene swept Colin Miller high into a gap at square leg. Jayawardene had been making a habit of mishitting into gaps, and this one resulted in an awful collision between Steve Waugh, running back from square leg, and [Jason] Gillespie, hurtling in from the deep. Waugh's nose was crushed when it hit the shoulder of Gillespie, whose right leg was broken as his body snapped over with the force of the impact. Gillespie was carried off while Waugh, blood spurting from his nose, walked off under a towel.

Suddenly Shane Warne was captaining Australia in a Test match under extreme circumstances. A TV close-up showed him taking a deep breath before calling on his team-mates to rally. In the background an ambulance siren wailed. Shortly afterwards a military helicopter, with Waugh and Gillespie on board, flew over the beautiful Asgiriya ground before heading off to Colombo.

Warne took five for 52, his first five-wicket haul since January 1998. After those two match-winning efforts in the World Cup semi and final, he showed he could still do it in a Test match as well. The great leg-spinner seems to be returning to his best after three years which have included operations on his spinning finger and bowling shoulder.

Australia v Pakistan, Hobart　　　　　　　　　　Peter Deeley, *Wisden* 2001
(Second Test, November 18-22)

Saqlain's six for 46 were his best Test figures, while Gilchrist provided him with his 100th wicket in his 23rd Test. Waqar Younis contributed two wickets and brought memories flooding back when Ponting shouldered arms to a trademark in-swinger timed at 90mph.

Warne produced something special himself on the third day, pitching in the rough outside the left-handed Saeed Anwar's off stump and hitting leg.

The Pakistanis in Australia 1999-2000　　　　　Peter Deeley, *Wisden* 2001

Australia played the series without Jason Gillespie, still recovering from the injury sustained in Sri Lanka in September when he collided with Steve Waugh. In his place they gave two Tests to Queensland's Scott Muller, but he was clearly not up to standard. Certainly not in the opinion of a Channel 9 cameraman, whose "Can't bowl, can't throw" jibe in Hobart, caught on a sound-effects microphone, caused a furore when it was made public during the Perth Test and mistakenly attributed to Shane Warne.

Cricket and the Media　　　　　　Gideon Haigh, *Wisden Australia* 2000-01

Footage of Australian dressing-room rapture showed one conspicuous party-pooper: Queenslander Scott Muller, who had unaccountably been informed of his omission from the next Test before the finish. He would shortly be unhappier still. On Wednesday November 23, apparently after an anonymous tip-off, Channel Ten's *The Panel* screened a snatch of the Test in which a duff return by fine-leg Muller elicited from somewhere the *sotto voce* remark: "Can't bowl, can't throw."

It is still hard to believe anyone gave a tuppeny damn about this, but they did. The *Australian* led the charge – and charge it was – with a report by Malcolm Conn headed "Slur reveals crack in team spirit". It began: "Shane Warne is furious that his name has been linked to an on-field slur against team-mate Scott Muller [and] made it clear privately yesterday that he would take legal action if there was any attempt to suggest he had spoken in a derogatory manner about the recently dropped Queensland fast bowler." Muller commented miserably: "I've gone from being the happiest bloke going round two weeks ago to being rissoled completely."

Channel Nine weighed in after a check of its pitch microphones, Simon O'Donnell solemnly reading a statement on that day's *Cricket Show*: "We can confirm that it is definitely not from a player on either side." Others protested that so what, wasn't it a man's game? Geoff Lawson wrote in the *Sun-Herald*: "'Can't bowl, can't throw.' If only I had a rupee for every time someone has said that to me." Mike Whitney chimed in on Channel Seven's *At the Wicket*: "I've been told many times: 'Get down to fine-leg. You can't bowl and you can't throw.'" (The New South Wales Eleven of the mid-80s was clearly a tough school; or perhaps Lawson and Whitney used to sledge one another.)

75

But the *Australian* wouldn't be placated, Chip Le Grand's lengthy weekend feature contending: "The affable Queenslander is out of the Test team in Perth, and everyone in the country who can distinguish bat from balls knows that one of his team-mates thinks he shouldn't have been there in the first place."

But wait, there's more. On Sunday November 28, Muller, bowling successfully for Queensland against India, confided loudly to the C7 pitch microphone: "That's six for the game, Warnie." Say that again? Never mind, we'll replay it every five minutes for the next week. The story regathered momentum.

Even then, however, what should have killed Mullergate had been printed, The *Age* and *Herald-Sun* reporting that "sources close to Nine" had identified the culprit as a cameraman who had been picked up on a boundary effects mike. And a week after *The Panel* had screened the footage, Nine's *A Current Affair* came good with a body. Host Mike Munro introduced first Warne, who denied his involvement, then cameraman Joe Previtera, who confessed his: "Unfortunately I did say it. I didn't actually mean it. It's one of those things that comes out."

But wait, there's still more. The *Australian* wasn't to be fooled by this, admittedly corny, spectacle. It knew better. Jonathon Este's report on the Munro-Warne-Previtera trialogue railed: "Are the cricketing public really convinced that what they saw last night on the Nine Network's *A Current Affair...* was not a put-up job designed to protect their investment in star spin bowler Shane Warne who is under contract to the network?"

The newspaper even retained a "linguistic expert" to compare the voice on the tape to Warne's. But it came up with nothing. The ABC examined recordings from its own pitch mikes during the game. And it, too, found diddly-squat. All the Australian had, in fact, was the slaggee's unswerving belief in Warne as slaggor. Conn reported that Muller "was told by someone who was intimately involved in the Hobart Test that it was Warne who had said it". Muller himself told the *Sun-Herald*'s Alex Brown: "I'll let the public make up their own minds about this; but, put it this way, I chose not to watch."

But wait, there's even more (more's the pity). On December 9, Labor loose cannon Mark Latham used parliamentary privilege to inveigh against Nine, Warne and the whole sporting-industrial complex: "Fantastic excuses were invented to preserve Channel Nine's commercial interest in Mr Warne." When Warne was compelled to hold another press conference in Adelaide, it was difficult to disagree with the *Age*'s Mark Ray: "Warne has been the victim of a campaign by one newspaper and various other people within and without the cricket world who simply do not like him."

This was a story interesting only in terms of what it revealed about the media, its obsession with spurious conflict, and with itself. It was not a happy interlude in Australian cricket journalism. Just how unhappy, indeed, was revealed in a Garry Linnell profile of Warne in the *Bulletin* of January 11. Linnell revealed that, during the Perth Test, Conn had called the *Age*'s Martin Blake "a goose" for believing in Warne's innocence, and that Blake had in retaliation placed Conn in a headlock. Linnell reported: "Don't ever call me a goose, Blake muttered, before slowly relaxing his grip." Violence? In the press box? Guess that's just cricket reflecting its society again.

WORDS ON WARNE

"Facing him at his best has been the biggest test of my international career – and scoring runs off him has been the biggest thrill."

Nasser Hussain, former England captain – WCM, June 1999

Australia v India, Adelaide　　　　　　　　　Dicky Rutnagur, *Wisden* 2001
(First Test, December 10-14)

With Ganguly also at ease and free with his strokes, particularly the square cut, India added 92 in 22 overs before Tendulkar, having scored his last 49 off 64 balls, was adjudged caught at short leg off Warne. The videotape proved him unlucky. However, Warne's dismissal of Ganguly, 14 runs later, was a masterpiece. He drew the left-hander out to scotch the menace of a ball pitched into the rough outside his off stump, beat him with a googly and had him stumped. The lower order struggled manfully, but India were left with a deficit of 156.

The Indians in Australia 1999-2000　　　　　　Dicky Rutnagur, *Wisden* 2001

Eight wickets at 41.87 apiece do no justice to Shane Warne's part in a series in which the fast bowlers were the main destroyers. On an easy pitch in Adelaide, however, he took six wickets and in the first innings skimmed off the cream of India's batting: Dravid, Tendulkar and Ganguly. He again bowled superbly in the Second Test and, although his reward was merely two wickets, struck the mortal blow by dismissing Tendulkar in the second innings.

CLASSIC TEST 4

New Zealand v Australia, Auckland　　　　　Don Cameron, *WCM*, May 2000
(First Test)
March 11, 12, 13, 14, 15 – Australia won by 62 runs. Toss: Australia. Debut: D. L. Vettori

Steve Waugh, who cherishes the drama, tension and character of cricket, managed a little Hitchcock-style suspense of his own as Shane Warne closed on the Australian wicket-taking record. Warne needed five to overtake Dennis Lillee's old mark of 355, and the early moments of this Test suggested it would only be a matter of time before he got them. But Waugh managed to spin out the drama to the last ball of the match.

Eden Park has a history of providing Test pitches that are just a bit different. As recently as last season, when buckets of glue were rolled into what looked like a crumbling surface, the South Africans found themselves playing on a strip of unsympathetic motorway.

The latest curiosity had too much moisture at the start. This allowed the ball to grip, and occasionally to take a strange, looping bounce. After Waugh chose to bat, Langer was the first to twig that all batsmen would be on borrowed time on this spinner's heaven. He cracked 46 from 47 balls, then Mark Waugh ambled pleasantly to 72 while his team-mates fell about him. Vettori bowled superbly after taking some early hammer from Langer.

When New Zealand batted, Warne took three of the wickets he needed as Australia claimed an important lead of 51. The Kiwis regained some ground by picking up five wickets for 114 by the end of the second day.

Vettori, only just 21, gave another classic display of finger-spin, to finish with seven for 87 and 12 wickets in the match. Only Richard Hadlee, with 15 for 123 at Brisbane in 1985-86, had done better for New Zealand. Vettori's wickets included his 100th, in his 29th Test: he supplanted Saqlain Mushtaq as the youngest spinner to reach this landmark.

Chasing 281, New Zealand suffered their usual bad start, but recovered thanks to forthright batting from McMillan and Astle. But then Warne struck, with a waspishly sharp leg-break to bowl Astle round his legs, which made it 121 for five. That left Warne level with Lillee, but now he went through a surprising wicketless period while utility man Miller made inroads with his off-spin. Once McMillan was caught, after blasting 11 fours and two sixes, an Australian victory became inevitable.

But the bowlers doing the damage were Miller and Lee. Would Warne have to wait for the record? Waugh had told Warne he would bring him back at the right-handers while Miller bowled at the lefties. Miller duly removed the last of those (Vettori), and back hustled Warne with one wicket to go. Last man Wiseman clubbed two fours. Then up looped another leg-spinner, and he swung hugely. Ball missed bat, but as Wiseman whirled around, it hit his glove, forearm and his shoulder, and then lobbed gently back to Gilchrist.

So Warne's record-breaking wicket was not claimed with a spectacular catch or the bails flying, but rather with this ungainly sequence. "It didn't look great, did it?" he said afterwards. "But I'll take it."

In fact the quality of after-match comment was far higher than the batsmanship on such a one-sided pitch, on which Vettori and Wiseman shared 17 wickets, Warne and Miller 11. For a start, there was Warne on the record: "I did not bowl very well because of the record. I was trying too hard. Now relax and bowl properly."

Steve Waugh said of Warne: "His success has been great for cricket – he has turned the game around in Australia. He may have been born with that talent, he has worked hard. As a cricketer he has got the whole package."

Waugh paid generous tribute to his opponents: "They have got more steel now. They are a pretty tough side, they're getting like the South Africans – they don't want to take a back step." And he praised Vettori for "great" performance. "It might not be apparent from sidelines, but he has got so many variations of flight and pace."

Man of the Match: D. L. Vettori. **Attendance:** 9,250.

New Zealand v Australia, Auckland, 2000

AUSTRALIA	First innings			Second innings	
M. J. Slater b Cairns	5	–	(2) c Horne b Cairns		6
G. S. Blewett c Astle b Wiseman	17	–	(1) c Spearman b Vettori		8
J. L. Langer st Parore b Wiseman	46	–	c Astle b Vettori		47
M. E. Waugh not out	72	–	c Parore b Vettori		25
*S. R. Waugh c Spearman b Vettori	17	–	c and b Wiseman		10
D. R. Martyn c Astle b Vettori	17	–	b Vettori		36
†A. C. Gilchrist lbw b Wiseman	7	–	c Fleming b Vettori		59
S. K. Warne c Fleming b Vettori	7	–	c Wiseman b Vettori		12
B. Lee c Parore b Vettori	6	–	not out		6
C. R. Miller b Cairns	0	–	st Parore b Vettori		8
G. D. McGrath c Spearman b Vettori	8	–	lbw b Wiseman		1
B 7, lb 4, nb 1	12		B 7, lb 4		11
	214				229

1/10 (1) 2/77 (3) 3/78 (2)   214
4/114 (5) 5/138 (6) 6/161 (7)
7/184 (8) 8/192 (9) 9/193 (10) 10/214 (11)

1/7 (2) 2/46 (1)   229
3/67 (3) 4/81 (5)
5/107 (4) 6/174 (6) 7/202 (8)
8/214 (7) 9/226 (10) 10/229 (11)

First innings—Cairns 18-0-71-2; Doull 14-6-21-0; Vettori 25-8-62-5; Wiseman 14-3-49-3.
Second innings—Cairns 4-1-13-1; Wiseman 33.5-6-110-2; Vettori 35-11-87-7; Doull 5-1-8-0.

NEW ZEALAND	First innings			Second innings	
M. J. Horne c Blewett b McGrath	3	–	c Langer b Miller		11
C. M. Spearman c Martyn b Lee	12	–	lbw b McGrath		4
M. S. Sinclair lbw b Warne	8	–	lbw b Miller		6
P. J. Wiseman b Lee	1	–	(11) c Gilchrist b Warne		9
*S. P. Fleming st Gilchrist b Miller	21	–	(4) c Gilchrist b Miller		8
N. J. Astle c M. E. Waugh b Warne	31	–	(5) b Warne		35
C. D. McMillan lbw b Warne	6	–	(6) c Warne b Lee		78
C. L. Cairns c Gilchrist b McGrath	35	–	(7) c S. R. Waugh b Miller		20
†A. C. Parore c Gilchrist b McGrath	11	–	(8) c S. R. Waugh b Lee		26
D. L. Vettori not out	15	–	(9) c Warne b Miller		0
S. B. Doull c Lee b McGrath	12	–	(10) not out		5
B 4, lb 1, nb 3	8		B 7, lb 7, nb 2		16
	163				218

1/4 (1) 2/25 (3) 3/25 (2)   163
4/26 (4) 5/80 (6) 6/80 (5)
7/102 (7) 8/134 (8) 9/143 (9) 10/163 (11)

1/15 (1) 2/25 (3)   218
3/25 (2) 4/43 (4)
5/121 (5) 6/151 (7) 7/195 (8)
8/204 (6) 9/204 (9) 10/218 (11)

First innings—McGrath 11.1-2-33-4; Miller 22-8-38-1; Warne 22-4-68-3; Lee 7-4-19-2.
Second innings—McGrath 23-8-33-1; Lee 12-4-36-2; Miller 18-5-55-5; Warne 20.3-5-80-2.

Umpires: B. F. Bowden and S. Venkataraghavan.   Third umpire: D. B. Cowie.
Referee: M. H. Denness.

WORDS ON WARNE

"It's up to Warney now, but he could take 500 Test wickets if he has the motivation and he keeps up the fitness levels. He makes those decisions, no one else."

Steve Waugh, Australia captain – *Wisden* 2001

2000

Five Cricketers of the Century

Greg Baum, *Wisden* 2000

There are three elements to Shane Warne's greatness – skill, novelty and drama – and all were manifest in the one great delivery that made his name, at Old Trafford in 1993.

The delivery was exceptionally skilful. It began its flight innocently so as to lull Mike Gatting, drifted to leg, pitched in the batsman's blind spot, then rounded on him fiercely and bent back off stump. It was at once pinpoint in its accuracy and prodigious in its spin, qualities that had always been thought to be irreconcilable. Later that summer, John Woodcock would write that it was doubtful if there had ever been a bowler who could aim the ball as precisely and turn it as far as Warne. This is a sentiment that has echoed down the seasons.

The delivery was something different. West Indies and their battery of pace bowlers had set the agency for 20 years; spin, particularly wrist-spin, had become nearly defunct, but suddenly here it was again in more irresistible form than ever before.

Most of all, the Gatting ball was not just early in his spell, but his very first delivery – in the match, in the series, in Ashes cricket. That gave the ball a sense of theatre, and Warne a name for showmanship, that has grown at each new threshold of his startling career, and at its peak made him nearly mystical. In the modern era, only Ian Botham could compare.

The triumph of Shane Keith Warne is of the rarest kind, of both substance and style together. At his best, he has the ruthlessness of a clinician and the flourish of a performer, and his bowling is simultaneously a technical and dramatic masterpiece. It was not enough for him to take a hat-trick; it had to be in an Ashes Test on the MCG. It was not enough for him to take 300 wickets; the 300th had to be accompanied by lightning and apocalyptic thunderclaps at the climax of another consummate and match-winning performance against South Africa at the SCG.

Thus in 1993 a theme was established for Warne's career: extraordinary performances, extraordinary production values. He was the cricketer of and for his times. Australia's finest moments, but also their worst, their most controversial, most splendid, most dramatic, most sordid, have all revolved around Warne. From the wretchedness of the bookmakers' scandal to the glory of the World Cup triumph, from the agony of a one-wicket defeat in Pakistan in 1994-95 to the ecstasy of a come-from-behind Ashes win in 1997, he was always the central character.

By cold statistics, Warne had not had such a profound influence on Australian cricket in his time as Dennis Lillee in his. Australia were already on the rise when Warne joined the team and, when they had their crowning moment, in the Caribbean in 1994-95, he was good, but not dominant. He takes fewer wickets per match than Lillee at a more profligate average. Moreover, Australia can and do win matches without him. But Warne's impact can never be understated. When he was first picked, cricket was under the tyranny of fast bowling and aching for another dimension. Soon enough, the world came to know that a man could take Test wickets by seduction as well as extortion.

And the legend grew, moment by moment, coup by coup, performance by performance. He made fools of good players, short work of fools. Australia's method was indestructibly simple: bat first, bowl last, win quickly. Always it was the stage that invigorated him as much as the challenge. For Victoria, who play in empty stadia, he averages more than 40. But for Australia, he has taken more than 350 wickets and, although projections for him to take 600 now seem fanciful, he is already by some margin the most successful spinner in Test history.

At length, intimations came of Warne's mortality. Wear, tear and public glare took a toll. Variously, the fitness of his finger, shoulder, stomach, ethics and manners for Test cricket were called into question, but not until recently, when he returned too hastily from shoulder surgery, was his capability doubted.

Physically, undoubtedly, his powers have declined, but not his hold on opponents. So it was that on the biggest stage of all, at the climax of the World Cup, at a moment when Australia looked impossibly behind, he came again. The only caveat on making him one of the cricketers of the 20th century is that he may yet figure in deliberations for the 21st.

MY FAMOUS FIVE – JOHN WAITE *WCM*, January 2000

"I've never seen any spin bowler like him. I played a few times against Richie Benaud, he was a marvellous bowler, but Warne is even better. I have never seen any spin bowler do the things he can do. And he is just so good for cricket. So many fast bowlers just run in 40 yards and thud the ball into the wicketkeeper's gloves, but there is always something different happening when Warne is on. I never leave the television when he is bowling."

John Waite won 50 caps for South Africa between 1951 and 1965.

How They Were Chosen
Matthew Engel, *Wisden* 2000

Perhaps the biggest surprise is the identity of the player in fourth place. There were people among our hundred frightened to make a judgement on players they had not seen, which might have given present-day players an advantage. With perfect knowledge, maybe there would have been more votes for some of the early players, for Barnes, say, or Victor Trumper. But there are always former players who scorn the moderns, and perhaps an equal number of ballot papers reflected this factor. In any case, the votes for Shane Warne came from across the globe and across the generations. If anyone doubts his status, listen to Crawford White, 88 last year and the former cricket correspondent of the *Daily Express*, who watched both Warne and Bill O'Reilly. "O'Reilly didn't rip the ball through like Warne does," said White. "And I don't think he caught the imagination quite as much as this lad."

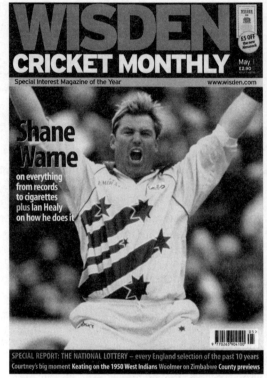

Wisden Cricket Monthly, May 2000

Just a Regular Superstar   Gideon Haigh, *WCM*, May 2000

"Why don't we all love Warnie?" read a headline in Sydney shortly after Shane Warne became Australia's leading wicket-taker at Eden Park last month. A fair question, really. For the past year or Shane Warne's public image has fluctuated like sterling when George Soros is about, trouble trailing him everywhere.

He might have surged back to stardom in a World Cup-winning team. He might been the only present-day player picked in Australia's Team of the Century, and broken Dennis Lillee's Test-wickets record. But he has also been stained by a fine for accepting money from an Indian bookmaker, suffered the indignity of omission from the Test team in West Indies, and been accused of sledging a team-mate, and losing his temper with teenage fans.

I've interviewed Warne several times in the past, but visiting his hotel I'm still genuinely curious about how I might find him. Will he be the Warne of old? Or will he have developed a touch of the Howard Hugheses, immured in his suite, fearful of the outside world, surrounded by food tasters and telephone sanitisers?

My answer comes swiftly. He's filming when I arrive, as part of a deal with a pay-TV network, but he catches my eye between takes, smiles broadly and gives a thumbs up. He might be a 30-year-old father of two these days, but Warne's charm remains that of your boyish kid brother: cheerful, spontaneous, surprisingly infectious.

When he bowls into his hotel room later, he looks fit, trim and sharp. His manager, Austin Robertson, has asked him to wear a suit ("Time to get Warnie out of the T-shirt and shorts") and it's a smart, all-black number. Apart from that, Warne is Warnie. What did you think of the Team of the Century? What's that you're reading? Did you see that show on TV the other night? Smoke? Thanks Shane, don't mind if I do.

Interviewing cricketers can be disheartening: a push-and-poke game on a flat wicket. But Warne talks as he bowls. He can serve up a stock ball, but more often you push forward without knowing exactly what's coming. It's fun. Entertaining. Why don't we all love Warnie? It may be more to do with us than it is with him.

Gideon Haigh: does the record, and featuring in the Team of the Century, alter the way you see yourself?
Shane Warne: I don't think so. You weigh up your career when you finish. That's when you think about the teams you played in, the games you played, times off the field, and also your own standing in the game. At the moment, it's actually quite hard to get my head around being the only current player in the Team of the Century, especially when I'm playing with so many great players.

Yet you have regularly been forced to take stock. Injuries and wear and tear have meant you're a very different bowler from the one who started. How many different Shane Warnes do you think there've been?
The first one was just a raw bloke who didn't know what he was doing. Knew how to spin a leg-break. Didn't know too much else. Then I started adding in a few other deliveries – wrong'un, top-spinner, flipper – but still didn't really know when to bowl them.

After about four or five years, I think I did gradually work out what to bowl when. Those three things – the why, when and how – are experience. In the past, I basically bowled massive leg-breaks, beat the bat a lot and eventually got a batsman to nick them. Then after the finger operation in '96, I had to come to terms with the fact that every time I tried that big leg-break there'd be a huge pain through my finger and arm. I had to get used to using the big leg-break occasionally, bringing the batsman forward a little bit more each time, then bowling it. After the finger operation, too, the feel was different. I remember bowling one to Terry Jenner and saying: "Aww, that was shit." He said: "What are you talking about, that's the best one you've bowled." I said: "Well why does it feel so different?"

After the shoulder operation, there was probably a fourth model, too, because I needed to get the confidence back. Looking back, I don't think I came back too early, but I should probably have played some more state cricket first. The Sydney Test [v England, January 1999] and the West Indies tour, I felt I was bowling OK, but I couldn't get the big bag or feel like I was at my best.

You were bowling well in one-day cricket.
Yeah, but that's only ten overs at a time. Looking back, I probably should have come back through the one-dayers, maybe missed the Tests in the West Indies. When you've got to do it in Test cricket – bowl 20-25-30 overs, and back it up the next day – you start waking up and saying to yourself: "Gee, bit stiff and sore today. Wonder if it's going to go again." You don't go out there and just rip 'em.

Does that mean that, in hindsight, you feel the selectors were right to leave you out at St John's?
No, not really. No, I still don't agree with it. I was one of the selectors and everyone wrote that I was pleading and begging for my position. I wouldn't ever beg for my spot. But I didn't agree.

What was the chat like around the table?
There was Steve, Geoff Marsh, myself and Allan Border, who was leading a tour group over there. And Steve and Geoff were keen for Stewy [MacGill] to play.

The rationale being?
That he was bowling better than me at the time. And I said: "I don't think either of us is bowling as well as we can. And when the pressure's been on in the past, I've done well. I don't think this'll be any different. This could be a situation where I bowl really well and it'll be a turning point." They said: "We're down in the series and we can't afford to take that risk." The general talk was that we needed to win this game and that this was the best team for that job. I said: "Fine, but I don't agree with it." And copped it. I think that, if we'd been winning, I'd have played. But we were losing and it was Stephen's first series and that made a difference.

You picked a bad time to try and give up smoking.
In hindsight, I couldn't have picked a worse one. But it was still something I wanted to give up, because of the kids, and the Nicorettes actually worked well for a while. When I got dropped, though, I just thought: "Bugger this." When you're vulnerable, you back to your bad habits. I had a smoke one night when I was pissed, a tourist took a photo, and sold it to the Mirror Group. And there were the headlines, you know: "Warnie back on the smokes." But I'm glad I had a go, and even now I'm not smoking anywhere near as many as I was. I was 50-a-day smoker, now I'm down to 20-25, so I've cut down and I would still like to give up.

Did being dropped affect your relationship with Steve Waugh?
Steve and I have always been good friends. In 1991 we toured Zimbabwe together when he was out of the Test side, and we got on well from the start. When I was in and out of the Victorian side, I spoke to him a lot, about maybe coming to NSW. In fact, we were basically all organised in that I was going to work nearby and play for his club. But our relationship at the time [of Warne's omission] was a bit uncomfortable for both of us. It hard for me, and it wasn't easy on him. He said at the team meeting that night: "It's the hardest decision I've had to make."

If the West Indies tour had finished there, would you have playing international cricket?
Well... if I was only playing one-day cricket and not Test cricket, I don't think I would have wanted to go on. As I said at the time, I don't think that just playing one form of the game would have been enough for me. That'll sound selfish. But I think that if you're playing for Australia, and you're not good enough to play in one form of the game, and you've been playing for a long time, it gets a bit tough.

Reading Steve's book on the World Cup, *No Regrets*, there's a hint awkwardness between you. That as a result of what happened the West Indies, you might still have been a little hurt, and maybe Steve didn't know how to approach you.
It was uncomfortable. It wasn't easy. I had a chat him before the first one-dayer. I wasn't happy with a few things. He wasn't happy with a few things. We had a chat and sorted things out.

Steve wrote that after the Zimbabwe match [at Lord's, June 9] you took a walk in the park together and you "informed the boys" that you were "going to retire".
I didn't get everyone together and say I was going to retire, but I was thinking about it. It was our recovery day, and there was Steve, Swampy and myself, and we had a walk in the park. I'd been away a long time, my son had just been born, I was missing home, and I was just copping it from every direction – the crowd, the media, everyone. Hookesy [David Hookes of 3AW Radio] had just come out and said that I'd never play Test cricket again, that there was more stuff to come out about the bookmaker thing. I said: "Jeez, this is ridiculous. I've had a gutful. You can all stick it up your arse. That's it. This is the last time."

Steve wrote that he thinks it was the tickertape parades when the team came home with the World Cup that persuaded you to keep going.
It was probably more the last three games. I wasn't sure if it was the man upstairs saying: "This is a good time to get out. Man of the Match in the semi and final," or whether it was more like, "Pull your head in. You've still got a lot to offer. And this is what it's about: winning games for Australia, getting some wickets along the way, and enjoying representing your country." Sitting back thinking about it, I wanted to keep playing. In fact, I couldn't imagine not playing. When I went to Sri Lanka [last August], I thought: "Well, I'm just going to keep my nose clean. Concentrate on playing good cricket, being vice-captain, helping Tugga out."
　　The other thing that's probably changed my outlook is turning 30, having a family, the two kids. Cricket was the most important thing in my life: I think my family is now. I want to go out now and simply enjoy my cricket, without worrying about all the stuff that goes with it. Of which there is so much. If that means my career finishes tomorrow, then so be it. But I think I've got more to offer: this summer, I've probably bowled better than at any time since my shoulder op.

Did you feel some irony in the parades? You'd been written off.
That's just Australians, though. If someone's down and out, they want to see them succeed. But if someone has too much success, they decide he's a bit arrogant or cocky.

What does a decade's exposure to those extremes of rapturous acclaim and harsh criticism do to you?
I'm a bit more guarded. I remember ages ago, when things were happening that I wanted to share with people, friends, suddenly there was a bit of jealousy there. And you start to notice that and think: "OK. I thought they'd be happy for me. I'll shut up." In reality, you're lucky if you have a few close friends that you share everything with, and I've got those friends. Besides that I've got "friends" that I probably don't share much with.

How are the media relations at the moment?
OK. Not too good. I'd actually like to mingle with the media more. I'd like to have played in the 1970s, when the media was more cricket-related. Unfortunately, that's society, the way it is now, people want to know the other stuff. People go: "Yeah, we saw the cricket yesterday. What about what he did last night? What car does he drive? Where does he live?"

And your relations with Roland Perry [author of two Warne biographies]?
I actually met him for the first time yesterday. He said: "Hello, I'm Roland Perry." I said: "Hi." And that was it. I think I've had five books done on me: two by him, one by Jack Pollard, one by Ken Piesse, one by me. It's frustrating to have all these people write about your life when they really have no idea what you're like.

Have you read any of those books?
I got to page 60 of Ken Piesse's book, and it wasn't accurate. Garbage. I read a little bit of Roland Perry's first one, and that wasn't accurate, so I didn't bother with the next one. And Jack Pollard's was neither here nor there.

Yet you have relationships with Channel 9 and Foxtel, and plan a role in the media industry. Isn't that a bit like a cop who spends so long round criminals that he thinks he might like to become one?
I see my role at Channel 9 as being a future thing. At the moment, I'm learning how it works, presenting, reading, commenting, doing commercials, rather than being a media person. The media relations I've got at the moment, it's just that a few people don't like me personally. Without really knowing me. But it affects what they're writing, because they're not really looking at what's going on in the field. The Scott Muller thing [a voice was heard on TV when Muller fired in a wayward throw, saying "Can't bowl, can't field"] – people just wanted that to be me. I could give them all the evidence in the world and they still wouldn't have believed me.

Your relationship with Channel 9 probably played a part in that.
Obviously. People thought there was a cover-up. The funny thing is it would have simpler for me to confess to something I hadn't done. And even if I had said it, I wouldn't have felt all that bad owning up to it. I would just have said: "Sorry Scotty. Heat of the moment." Because we've all said far worse things on the cricket field. What really hurt was being doubted. Someone had admitted to saying it. There was video evidence that showed my lips not moving. There was nothing on the stump mikes. A voice specialist said it wasn't my voice. But people just wanted it to be me.

Do you think any of it was a hangover from the match-fixing scandal? That the bookie stuff suggested to people that there were things that happen in cricket that never come out because they get hushed up?
You might be right. But it wasn't Mark and I that covered up the bookie stuff. The Board took the decision that it was in the best interests of Australian cricket, to protect the players and the game, for that not to become public.

Don't you think it was a mistake, though, not to tell the enquiry in Pakistan that this action had been taken?
I'd rather not go into what should and shouldn't have been done.

What I mean is, I can understand the short-term expedient of not making the information public at the time. But surely, when there was an enquiry trying to get to the bottom of payments to players by bookmaking interests, then that's precisely the sort of thing that should have been volunteered.
Probably. But I was never in Pakistan. And when I was called on to testify in Melbourne, I told them exactly what had happened. Just as I'd told the ACB at the time I was asked.

In hindsight, perhaps the oddest thing about the scenario is what it says about the world you're in. Very few people get offered $US5000 in a casino with, apparently, no strings attached. And I think that was the subtext of the criticism you copped: people saying "How can someone accept a cash gift like that and not twig that something will be expected in return?" Did it remind you how unusual it is, the life that you lead?
I remember AB telling me stories about Sharjah in the mid-80s when players were being given gold nuggets. Just recently in Sharjah, Tendulkar scored 150 and got two Mercedes-Benzes. And when we're overseas, we get offered things all the time, like diamonds at cheap rates.

I was 24, pretty wrapped up in the experience of being an Australian cricketer, and there's this guy offering me $US5000, saying: "I bet on cricket. I've made a lot of money from backing Australia. Please accept this as a token of my appreciation." That's how I took it: "Thanks very much, buddy." Took it down the casino. Lost it again. If that money had been offered to me in Australia, I'd have thought: "What does this bloke want?" But because it happened overseas, I didn't really think about it.

Does the attention you've had in the last year make any difference to how you regard the Australian captaincy? Given that the attention on you would probably be squared, even cubed.
If I got offered the captaincy, I'd say yes. Of course, I think I'd do a good job. But if my time doesn't arise, so be it. Steve's doing a great job at the moment. And a lot depends on how much longer he plays for. If he does play on for a while, then you're probably better off giving the job to someone younger than me.

In terms of retirement, do you want to do a Paul Reiffel or an Ian Healy?
I'll keep playing for as long as I enjoy it. If I stop enjoying it in 2005, so be it. 2001, so be it. I reckon you know when your time's up. I'm not someone who dwells in the past. I get more excited talking about the future.

Isn't it more difficult when you're actually on the spot making the decision? Ian Healy's no fool, but obviously found the choice hard. Had you been a selector, would you have picked him at Brisbane?
Gee, that's hard. (Laughs) I can't answer that. I'd get in trouble whatever I said.

Theoretically, though, do you think there's scope for sentimentality in selection policy?
A fair bit of responsibility falls on the player to choose his moment. Players shouldn't hang round just for the sake of it. Once someone's time's up, their time's up. You shouldn't keep playing just because you've got nothing better to do. That's something I won't do.

Bowled, Shane
Ian Healy, *WCM*, May 2000

Down I'd go into my crouch early enough to watch Warnie's visible cues, but not long enough to get leg-lock. I'd position myself outside the off stump so that the batsman couldn't obscure my view easily, and I'd go through my cues. Every ball, my mind says: "Watch the ball, move, stay down."

There's Warne's slow walk in, the build-up of energy through the crease, and the release. The flipper would have been detected two strides earlier, and this is not it. Leg-spinner coming, last seen leaving the hand, but how much will it turn? Looks like he's just rolled it out rather than ripping it, but it's heading straight for the big hole outside leg stump.

"Stay down and move late," I keep telling my legs. This could do anything off the pitch, and by then it will be behind the batsman. Must ignore the batsman as he will only further distract me as I strive to isolate the ball. It should slide down leg, but will it? That's the dilemma, and I must wait and watch before deciding to move low and strong. Gloves low and relaxed enough to give with the ball, and in it goes cleanly. Pat yourself on the back, take a deep breath or two and settle in for your second delivery of a captivating 30-over spell.

How great it was to witness the hustling, bustling blond ball of body language, systematically glueing batsmen's feet to the crease, as they realised that what they had in mind for that innings simply wasn't going to work. Last-day survival plans became impossible, by even the world's best players, when Warnie spun his magic. On-field genius aside, he has the team's fortunes at heart, which further inspires peers of all experience levels.

I was lucky enough to have the best seat in the house as the man who recently became Australia's greatest wicket-taker dismantled opposition batting line-ups and changed the face of world cricket.

Shane Warne is not just Australia's most successful bowler, but the most successful spin bowler in Test history.

COUNTY DUTY, 2000

Hampshire in 1999
Pat Symes, *Wisden* 2000

Hampshire grabbed the headlines in the last week of what had been a largely unspectacular summer. While the team were ensuring a place in the first division of the County Championship for 2000, with a two-run win at Derby so controversial it sparked an unsuccessful complaint from Warwickshire about collusion, an announcement was made which stopped the entire cricket world in its tracks. Hampshire had signed Shane Warne.

The club said it was financially the largest contract ever awarded over a single season by any county: estimates of £150,000 for one summer's work were not denied. Soon afterwards, there was confirmation of another big-money signing in Alan Mullally, Leicestershire's Test bowler, as Hampshire began the task of building a side worthy of the new stadium taking shape on the northern outskirts of Southampton. Hampshire were to vacate the County Ground, their home for more than a century, at the end of 2000, when Nigel Gray's square – much-loved (especially by batsmen) – would disappear under housing.

Considering the outlay for Warne and Mullally (there were also rumours about Andrew Flintoff, ended when he came to terms with Lancashire), the financing of the move to the new ground remained a problem.

Essex v Hampshire, Chelmsford   Nigel Fuller, *Wisden* 2001
(Benson and Hedges Cup, April 19)

Warne's introduction to county cricket, a day after flying in from South Africa, included being clobbered into the backyard of neighbouring flats, much to the delight of some 3,000 spectators. The striker was Irani, whose half-century, along with another 40-something from Peters, put Essex on track.

Hampshire v Warwickshire, Southampton   Pat Symes, *Wisden* 2001
(National League Division Two, May 1)

A serious injury to Donald overshadowed Warne's home debut before a crowd of some 3,000. The car park was full an hour and a half before the start. Donald, having effectively won the match earlier with a hostile spell of three in eight balls, broke two ribs when he stepped back into advertising boards in an attempt to catch Warne off Smith at long-on. He was taken from the field by stretcher and then by ambulance to hospital. Warne did eventually perish to a catch at long-on.

Hampshire v Somerset, Southampton   Pat Symes, *Wisden* 2001
(County Championship Division One, May 3-5)

Shane Warne recorded the first pair of his career, out third ball in each innings. His contribution to a match Hampshire lost before tea on the third day was a solitary wicket – and even then the replays suggested Holloway had not touched the ball.

Yorkshire v Hampshire, Leeds   David Warner, *Wisden* 2001
(County Championship Division One, May 12-14)

It was another depressing game for Warne, who took only two wickets and bagged a pair for the second match running as Yorkshire completed victory on the third morning.

Leicestershire v Hampshire, Leicester   Neville Foulger, *Wisden* 2001

(County Championship Division One, May 17-20)

This clash between the world's best wrist-spinners – Warne and Kumble – never lived up to expectations, mainly because of the weather. Rain and bad light chopped 66 overs from the second day and 42 from the third, when there were six stoppages. Neither side could gain much momentum, though Warne was nearer his best after a disappointing start to his Hampshire career, and was clearly delighted to end a run of four successive ducks.

Surrey   Kate Laven, *WCM*, June 2000

The excitement over Shane Warne's arrival hasn't been confined to fans and the media. Players, especially others spinners, are relishing the chance to see him at work, and then seek him out for a yarn afterwards.

Ian Salisbury is no exception. Now starting his 12th county season, he's keen to see how Warne does in English conditions. "Everyone perceives him as this great legend – which obviously he is – but he is a normal bloke like the rest of us," says Salisbury. "I'll be fascinated to talk about the differences between Australian and English cricket, how he finds the balls and the temperatures here.

"It's great he's here, and it's especially good for cricket. It should get the kids excited about leg-spin – and judging by the numbers who turned out to see him at The Oval, he has already captured people's imaginations. We are very different bowlers – I would love to be more like him. He's the very best there is."

But Salisbury, who has won 12 England caps, has a minor Warne-ing of his own: "Everyone is expecting him to take masses of wickets, but I don't think he'll take as many as people think – though he'll still get loads."

News Register   *WCM*, August 2000

Shane Warne feared he might lose the national vice-captaincy after admitting "dirty talk" over the phone with a nurse he met in a Leicester nightclub. Donna Smith told a tabloid newspaper that Warne had left lewd messages on her answerphone. The matter was discussed when Warne met Malcolm Speed, the ACB chief executive, who was in London for an ICC meeting.

Hampshire v Kent, Portsmouth   Pat Symes, *Wisden* 2001

(County Championship Division One, July 19-22)

After 112 years of visiting Portsmouth, Hampshire bade their Championship farewell to the United Services Ground with a defeat. The slow, dry pitch had clearly been prepared with Warne in mind, and his battle with Dravid proved crucial: Dravid's mastery in both innings tipped the balance. Playing Warne in soft-handed defence or effortless, wristy attack he hit his first Championship century, batting almost six hours for 137.

...

Most effective of the spinners was Patel, the Kent left-armer, who took nine wickets in the match. For Hampshire, Udal claimed six, Warne just four.

Eyewitness: Hampshire v Kent, Portsmouth

Simon Lister and Nagraj Gollapudi, *TWC*, June 2009

Matthew Fleming (Kent captain)

We had several young batsmen who were underperforming spectacularly. They all had shockers. For our coach, John Wright, it proved to be his nadir. We usually started batting from about four or five wickets down.

Rahul Dravid (Kent batsman)

I almost didn't play. My little pinky on the right hand was dislocated in the previous game against Derbyshire. I did not field in the slips for a month and a half but on the morning of the game I knocked a few balls and, although it was sore, I decided it was fine to bat. If the game had been a day earlier, I probably wouldn't have played.

Fleming

The US ground was really big thing for me because of my Army career, my Combined Services games. I really wanted to do well there.

Min Patel (Kent spinner)

Rahul was a class act. What you learned about him pretty quickly is that whether it was a Test match, a county game or a knock-about in the back garden, he absolutely loved batting for hours and hours and hated giving his wicket away.

Shane Warne (Hampshire spinner)

Even in my final year at the club, members would still ask me about this game at Portsmouth.

Adrian Aymes (Hampshire wicketkeeper)

There was a great excitement around the place when people knew Shane was coming. And when you're out there with him, face to face, you appreciated him even more. He always tried and you could see especially on flat pitches he'd work even harder.

This pitch was not flat. It was a turner from day one.

Dravid

It was a bit drier than you would normally expect in a county game but it wasn't a vicious turner. If anything it was two-paced. You could play the shots if you got settled down, yet there was purchase for spinners.

Hampshire won the toss and decided to bat. That meant Warne would be bowling last. First, though, he helped his side to get to 320 with the second highest score [69].

Fleming
He slapped it, carved it, a very difficult man to bowl to. Certainly he was not a man who was ever troubled by self-doubt. I got him out [in the second innings], I definitely remember that. He certainly wasn't caught at slip, but I'll claim it as a master-plan.

Late in the day Kent began their innings. Within four overs Warne was given the ball. He took a wicket with his second delivery.

Aymes
The funniest thing was the look in the batsman's eyes. Warne was a spinner but it was exactly the same look I remember when teams played Hampshire and they'd see Malcolm Marshall polishing the ball at the top of his run.

Warne
Sometimes batsmen play the man rather than the ball. In other words, they might treat a shortish delivery as a flipper when really it's a rank long-hop that deserves to be planted over midwicket.

When the nightwatchman, four balls later, treated a shortish delivery as a flipper and was lbw, Dravid came to the wicket. Kent were 15 for 2.

Patel
It was spinning already but it was slow spin, so Warney wasn't ripping it past Rahul's outside edge. He could get forward or back very quickly and play it off the pitch.

John Hampshire (umpire)
Dravid mostly played Warney with a straight bat. That's the first thing to say. In other words, he was playing against the spin.

Warne
I thought I was bowling pretty well but Dravid just picked up the length quicker than anybody else in the match and used his footwork to go all the way forward or all the way back.

No more wickets fell that evening. Dravid and David Fulton scored 16 runs between them to leave Kent on 31 for 2 at the end of the first day. After a night's sleep the contest between spinner and batsmen would get under way for real.

Aymes
Warne had the slow legger, the quicker one, the flipper and less often the googly because he'd had his shoulder operated on. The problems came when he went around the wicket into the rough. Then, he could bowl a leg-break which would go the other way if it hit the down part of a crater.

Dravid
I was looking to play him as I would in India: wait for the bad balls and probably play a few more shots than I would do normally.

Aymes

I could see it out of the hand and keepers will always tell you that the best bowlers put it in the right place. It's the lesser bowlers who have you throwing yourself down the leg side. Mind you, the first ball he ever bowled me was a flipper, against Leicestershire. For whatever reason it came out wrong and squirted down the leg side. The batsman fell out of the crease and I managed to get the bails off. A leg-side stumping first ball. Well, I felt like retiring there and then. "What's all this fuss about Ian Healy taking a year to read you?" I said to Warney in the middle.

Hampshire

As an umpire, you always have to be switched on but this was like umpiring a Test match. It was that good. You had to keep your wits about you and at the same time a small part of your mind was simply admiring the skill.

Warne

Most Indian batsmen pick the length very quickly, even when it is flighted above the eyeline. Dravid moved into position very early but Tendulkar moved quicker.

The Australian spinner began his day's work. Some runs came and some wickets fell. Warne was in for a long spell but Dravid wouldn't be beaten. Tanya Aldred was reporting on the game for The Guardian. "White wristband, gold necklace, white Adam Ant sun cream stripes and a surprisingly slight figure. Twirl, turn step, step, step, step, step, step-skip, skip-unfurl. Then it was hands on hips or a squat down on his haunches, first finger and thumb drawn to his nose in anguish. At times he spun it two inches, sometimes two feet, sometimes it went straight on... but he could not faze the Indian batsman." As Dravid batted on, Warne even tried to bounce him.

Aymes

He never gave me the signal but of course, if you saw two fingers across the seam, you were pretty certain it wasn't going to be the leggie. Actually, I remember Warney beat the bat time after time but Rahul was a class player. He played everything he had to and, when he miscalculated, he was clever enough to miss it. He played it ever so late but, when he did connect, it was with such quick hands.

Others were less skilful. 98 for 4, 99 for 5, 153 for 6. But Dravid stayed.

Fleming

He did this thing that no one else in the game at the time did. He played Warne by getting his front leg out of the way, towards the off side. So he played with his bat only. Certainly in England, everyone else played Warne by leading with bat and pad together, and that of course got them into trouble.

Patel

Yeah. He'd get his bat a good yard in front of his leg. You see Pietersen do it nowadays but we didn't back then. So what it did of course was rule out the bat-pad catch which is a massive mode of dismissal for the leggy.

Hampshire
I should imagine if there was a wagon-wheel of the innings, it would show that many of his scoring shots went between the bowler and straight midwicket.

Warne
His shot selection and timing were brilliant. He is not a stocky man and when you see him display that kind of lightness on his feet, you wonder whether he could have been a ballroom dancer.

Fleming
It was a spectacular lesson to us all. He never swept and had staggering powers of patience.

Patel
It's not often a world-class leg-spinner gives a right-hander a long-on, a deep midwicket and a deep backward square leg.

When Dravid reached his hundred, even Warne's toddler son applauded.

Warne
I remember my little lad Jackson being there – he was only a year old but even he managed to totter up and clap when Dravid got to his century. It was about the only thing that made me smile that day.

Warne would not even have the satisfaction of Dravid's wicket when he was out for 137 to a part-time spinner.

Aymes
Giles White got him. Dravid got a full bat on it but it spun back. "Should have brought him on ages ago instead of Warney," we all joked as we watched Dravid walk away.

Dravid was ninth man out. Soon the Kent innings was over for 252. But for their overseas player, the match would have been over too.

Fleming
It was a batting master class and I think even Shane was pleased to be there. Of course we were all mesmerised by Warne. To us he was a magician. To Dravid, he was just another slow bowler.

Hampshire had the advantage but soon lost it in their second innings. The possibility that the pitch had been prepared for spin was working against them. Kent's slow left-armer, Patel, was bowling well.

Fleming
He had the extremely annoying habit of trying to bowl an unplayable ball six times an over. The other thing was that he never knew who he got out, had no idea who he was

playing against. He just bowled and took wickets. That said, Min was easily the best left-arm spinner in the country. He really was excellent.

Patel

Well, I wouldn't disagree. At the time I would back myself to out-bowl any English finger spinner. I felt in pretty good rhythm that season. And the way I looked at it I was in a no-lose situation: I was the opposition spinner on a turning deck against the best spin bowler in the world. Everyone expected me to be out-bowled.

Patel had taken four Hampshire wickets in the first innings. Now he was on his way to another five. One of them was special.

Patel

Now, I didn't have a doosra but I had been working pretty fiendishly on a chinaman in the nets, you know a left-armer's leg-break. It wasn't a thing of beauty and when I bowled it my action was like: "Beware! This man is about to bowl a leg-spinner!" But this one landed right in the business area.

Dimitri Mascarenhas was facing and was delaying Kent's progress.

Patel

Whether or not Dimi knew it was coming, he couldn't stop it. That was the breakthrough wicket. My only chinaman dismissal in first-class cricket!

Thanks to Patel, Kent had bowled out Hampshire for 136. They needed 205 to win, batting last on a worn pitch against the world's best spinner.

Hampshire

It was a spiteful pitch by now. Shane was bowling at my end round the wicket into the rough and, as I recall, I don't think he had a shout.

That's because Dravid was batting again. The wickets that did fall went to Shaun Udal. But not Dravid's, even though Warne was trying hard.

Fleming

It could never be just another game when Shane Warne was on one side and Rahul Dravid was on the other and they were playing on a wearing wicket. We were watching something special.

Patel

This was one of the great innings against a spin bowler on a dry wicket. But it wasn't at Eden Gardens or the MCG, it was at an old ground in Portsmouth and I was watching it happen.

For every problem that Warne set, Dravid worked out the answer. He was not out on 73 when the winning run was scored. Kent had beaten Hampshire by 6 wickets.

Fleming
He was the sort of man who, when he came in at the end of a long innings, would talk through the five occasions that he had played and missed.

Patel
Warney had played enough and was bright enough to know when he'd been beaten by a better man.

Warne
Spectators told me afterwards it was the most captivating game they had seen in county cricket.

Hampshire
That's right. It was the finest exhibition of county cricket that I saw. Pure magic. Cricket at its best. An intriguing match.

Dravid
Obviously there is a huge amount of personal satisfaction when you score runs against one the greats. This was the biggest contribution I made for Kent. The batting revolved around me and you enjoy that sort of thing, especially when you come in as a pro and you want to do well.

Fleming
You could not imagine a greater ambassador for cricket in India. He was a sensational man.

Patel
I drove a lot with Rahul, or rather he was my passenger, so immediately I was impressed by his bravery. Not many people shared a lift, so I put him down as a legend and of course he already was back home in India. It was his humility, I remember, and he just loved talking cricket.

Fleming
Shane was well known for being a good loser but then could afford to be. He didn't lose that often. He said we all played well but really his congratulations were 75 per cent for Rahul and 25 per cent for the rest of us.

Patel
The difference between Kent and Hampshire this time? We had Dravid and they didn't.

Hampshire v Essex, Southampton   Pat Symes, *Wisden* 2001
(National League Division Two, July 30)

Having set Essex back with a superb one-handed slip catch to dismiss Stuart Law, Warne put Hampshire on track for their first win of the season at Northlands

Road – in any competition – with bowling of high quality. Only Peters blocked his path, finally stumped off the last delivery. Though Warne was subsequently out first ball, it did not matter. Hampshire always had wickets and overs to spare.

Kent v Hampshire, Canterbury	Andrew Gidley, *Wisden* 2001
(County Championship Division One, August 22-25)	

On the first morning, Warne touched down at 6 a.m. after a 26-hour flight from Melbourne, then removed Ed Smith with his fifth ball…

Hampshire v Nottinghamshire, Southampton	Pat Symes, *Wisden* 2001
(National League Division Two, September 17)	

A Royal Marine bugler played "Sunset" on the players' balcony as chairman Brian Ford ceremoniously lowered the Hampshire flag at the end of 115 years at Northlands Road. Warne threw his kit to eager fans below, and there were tears among a 2,500 crowd. For Hampshire to celebrate the occasion with a win, Udal needed to hit the final ball, from Tolley, for four; typical of their season, he missed it.

Hampshire	David Foot, *WCM*, November 2000

You only had to eavesdrop on officials around the counties to realise the marketability of Zimbabwe's sparky all-rounder Neil Johnson. Hampshire, now minus Shane Warne, are at the top of the queue for his services. Whether Warne ever returns to Hampshire remains uncertain – budgetary considerations will no doubt come into the discussions, and Hampshire with all the commitments that come with a new ground, aren't exactly flush these days.

Hampshire in 2000	Pat Symes, *Wisden* 2001

Hampshire had not had many seasons, if any, quite as revolutionary or extraordinary as the one they experienced in 2000. From the moment Shane Warne touched down in the dawn of a wet April morning – to unprecedented publicity as the club's overseas player – through to the emotion-charged last day at Northlands Road in the gloom of a September evening, this was a summer never to be forgotten.

On the field, little went right, despite Warne's presence and the international-calibre bowling of Alan Mullally, who between them cost Hampshire more than £200,000 in salaries.

2000-01

Positive Spin: The Record-Breaking Shane Warne   Richie Benaud, *Wisden Australia* 2000-01

Among the many extraordinary things about Shane Warne, now Australia's leading Test wicket-taker, perhaps most remarkable is that he managed to play international cricket again after two critical and essential operations: to his spinning finger and his shoulder. Other cricketers have had injuries and recovered from them, but generally they were batsmen or pace bowlers. Inspiration and dedication is needed at these times. Warne's inspiration was Dennis Lillee who, 23 years earlier, went through hell mentally and physically to surmount severe back problems just to get back on the field for Australia. Now other injured players in Australia, like Jason Gillespie or Damien Fleming, can look to Warne's example, so that even when told they might never make it back, they should not despair.

Warne's injuries were indisputably career-threatening. Two components an over-the-wrist spinner must have in perfect working order are his spinning finger and the rotator cuff of his shoulder. Each tiny part needs to work like well-oiled machinery; anything less, and the rusty arm, shoulder movement and body pivot conspire against the greatest effort.

It is a popular theory that the back-cracking, hip wrenching, knee-twisting golf swing is one of the most awkward movements performed by sports players. Yet Peter Thomson, in his memorable Rusack's Hotel interview with Henry Longhurst at St Andrews, managed to simplify it to three elements: put the club head in the correct position behind the ball, take the club head away and then hit the ball on the forward swing with the club face back in its original position. "Keep it simple" was his dictum. Over-the-wrist spinning is a little like that; you must keep it simple, as Warne does, and has done, on his way to becoming the greatest leg-spinner of his kind I have ever seen. O'Reilly and Grimmett, the other two great Australian spin bowlers, were different from each other and certainly different from Warne. That they didn't take as many wickets as Warne was because, in those days, Australia didn't play as many Tests; but it is noteworthy that when all three of them had played 27 Tests, covering the period of O'Reilly's Test career, the figures were Grimmett 147, O'Reilly 144 and Warne 124. Grimmett's figures of 216 wickets at the end of his career is the most ever taken at that point of any bowler's career, fast or slow, so Warne is in very good company.

At times in recent history the discipline of leg-spin has been threatened by administrative lethargy, fast bowling domination and the shortened version of the game. The pet theory for quite a number of summers in limited-overs matches was that pacemen, all-rounders and quickish, flat, off-spinners, are the only bowlers of interest to a captain and selectors. This assumed, however, that batsmen would suddenly and dramatically have improved their techniques against over-the-wrist spin and off-spinners who had the gift of being able to flight the ball and spin it at the same time. It was loose thinking, and good bowlers of any type have proved able to hold their own in the game. Warne has been one of those and his bowling in limited-overs internationals has often been outstanding, although it is unlikely that aspect would have had a great deal of influence on his being chosen as one of *Wisden Cricketers' Almanack's* Five Cricketers of the Century. The fact that he was elected was a proper indication of the extraordinary impact he has had on the game of cricket in the relatively short time he has played.

Generally, bowlers come in pairs. Certainly this is often the case with fast bowlers; Gregory and McDonald, Lindwall and Miller, Lillee and Thomson for Australia; Trueman and Statham, Tyson with Statham and in the West Indies, two pairs playing at once.

O'Reilly and Grimmett formed the outstanding Australian pairing of spin bowlers. Then in Australia in the late 1950s, there was a different type of pairing involving Davidson and me. From the time we first bowled together as the main bowlers in the Australian team at the Wanderers in Johannesburg, we took 333 wickets. We thought that was pretty good until recently we looked at the modern-day pairing of Glenn McGrath and Warne. In fewer than 60 Tests they have played together, they have taken 589 wickets for Australia. This is an astonishing statistic and it illuminates two things: that you need a partner at the other end; and that Australia might have problems in the near future when that combination breaks up. Steve Waugh will be hoping he retains the services of these two great bowlers for as long as possible. They have formed one of the most important, and for opposition batsmen, devastating combinations in the history of the game. Coincidentally, Warne and McGrath each took 288 wickets in their first 62 Tests for Australia.

Warne on his way towards 400 Test wickets has bowled out teams, thought out batsmen, made captains happy and cost opposition players their places in future teams. He has lifted Australia on many occasions in the shortened game, most notably in the World Cup of 1999, but also in the previous one when the semi-final was played against West Indies at Mohali. It was after that match I saw his swollen blood-filled spinning finger and wondered how he had been able to bowl at all, let alone bring Australia back from a brink where West Indies had needed only 37 with eight wickets in hand.

Warne has always desperately wanted to play for Australia. That was so when he played first for Victoria, then when he made his Test debut at the SCG, after the World Cup in India, Pakistan and Sri Lanka and after his shoulder operation. His chances of recovery from that shoulder operation were considered minimal. As always media people spent most of their waking moments, day and night, trying to find something new to say about the issue. There has never been any shortage of media feeding frenzies with anything Warne does, but he will be remembered, in the long term, more for the things he has done for Australian cricket, especially how he changed the accent of youngsters, so they chiefly wanted to bowl spin rather than pace.

When *Wisden's* greatest five for the past 100 years were named early in 2000, there were many great players who missed selection. Those chosen from the past, Bradman, Hobbs, Richards and Sobers, certainly qualify as great players. Warne is still playing and is a giant of the game.

News Register

WCM, December 2000

Shane Warne broke the third finger of his bowling hand attempting to catch Mark Waugh during Victoria's Pura Cup match against NSW in Melbourne on October 26. Initial reports suggested he could miss all five Tests against West Indies.

Australia v West Indies, Melbourne

Wisden 2002

(Carlton Series, January 11)

Warne's return after injury was notable only for a police warning when he kicked some tennis balls back into a rowdy crowd. He was told this could incite the spectators further; as it was, there were 34 arrests.

Australia v Zimbabwe, Sydney

Ian Jessup, *Wisden Australia* 2001-02

(Carlton Series, January 28)

When [Stuart] Carlisle hit Shane Warne for two sixes, as the Zimbabwean reached 100 in the 22nd over, Warne responded with an obscenity which the television microphones inadvertently broadcast live around the world. Channel Nine later apologised for the incident.

Foul Play

Tim de Lisle, *WCM*, March 2001

Shane Warne added another record to his collection when he was caught on a stump microphone calling Zimbabwe's Stuart Carlisle above a "f***ing arsey c****" during the one-dayer at the SCG on January 28. This now goes down as the most foul-mouthed quotation in cricket history, narrowly surpassing the line uttered by umpire Shakoor Rana to Mike Gatting – "f***ing cheating c****." Pushed down to third place is John Emburey's response to an inquiry about his suspect back: "The fackin' facker's fackin' facked." Warne's outburst was wrong not so much because it was foul-mouthed, but because it was beneath him. A great player was bowling to an ordinary one. If he needed to resort to bad-mouthing him, then he had failed. A glower would have been more eloquent, and more elegant. Just ask Curtly.

Australia v West Indies, Sydney

Ian Jessup, *Wisden Australia* 2001-02

(Carlton Series, February 7)

The other highlight for the dwindling crowd came with West Indies on nine for 113 when Shane Warne dropped a skied catch off his own bowling that he should have left for Damien Fleming at mid-on. Not only did he miss the ball by some margin, he also fell flat on his back. He was given an identical chance by Sylvester Joseph a few balls later and this time held it, despite a collision with Fleming.

Can Warne Get His Magic Back? Peter Hanlon, *WCM*, March 2001

Shane Warne's shortened summer was given neat bookend during Australia's drubbing of West Indies in the first one-day final at the SCG. Off the last ball of Warne's ninth over, Sylvester Joseph top-edged a sweep that sailed high in the direction of Damien Fleming. Warne trotted towards mid-on, called "mine", and didn't lay hand on it.

At least this time he was able to laugh. Back in October, after Mark Waugh had offered similar yet far easier chance to Warne at first slip in the opening state game of the season, his mood was more solemn.

When you've taken 366 Test wickets, your spinning finger is fairly important tool. Think David Beckham's right leg, Michael Schumacher's eyes, George Dubya Bush's atlas. Having a cricket ball land on the end of it and then inserting screw in same are not recommended practice.

Any doubts about Warne's recovery from the mangling of spinning finger were answered when the Australian selectors picked him to tour India and left Stuart MacGill at home. Another question, however, remains: can Warne, fit again and itching for return date with nemesis Sachin Tendulkar, be the bowler he used to be.

Warne himself has spoken so recent weeks of a return to "my golden years" that he's started to sound like Geoff Boycott. As wicketkeeper to every delivery Warne has for Victoria, Darren Berry is well placed to speak about Warne's recovery from a second major operation to his key digit in four years. Not to mention how he's wearing after surgery on his right shoulder two summers ago and a knee clean-out in September.

"After he had the op four years ago, I didn't think he was spinning the ball as hard as before," Berry says. Mindful of the privilege of having a front row seat at the show, he adds: "But he was still a great bowler.

"Since this one, having kept to him in Perth [Warne's first class return against Western Australia in the new year] and in the nets, there seems to be some real energy back in his bowling, some real fizz on the ball."

Warne's nine wickets at the spin-unfriendly WACA won him Simon Katich's endorsement that he is "still the king". At times in the tri-series against the Windies and Zimbabwe he tried to rip the ball too hard, dragged it down short and was punished. But other spells were sprinkled with the gold he loves so much.

And something a little different, just to keep them thinking: with the encouragement of coach John Buchanan, Warne now hurls down the occasional bouncer. "It's not illegal," he says, "so why not?"

Warne is also delivering more wrong'uns, a variation that has rarely interested him in the past. One theory is that his mentor, Terry Jenner, told Warne that if he wants to prolong his career he should shelve the flipper, which puts maximum strain on his shoulder. But then everyone has a theory about Warne.

His life has been ever the soap opera, the latest instalment coming when his opinion of Stuart Carlisle was broadcast to the nation via a stump microphone. The Australians despise having all of TV land eavesdropping on their every word, and in a single breath Warne presented the strongest of arguments for their removal. His profanity-per-word count was three-for-three.

It has also been pointed out that he's cheese toastie or two over the limit, which hardly seems relevant anymore; he's been lighter, but he's been heavier too. As always, the only act that matters is being played out on the field. Warne's return to the game has had one constant: when he has had the ball in his hand, it been compulsory viewing.

And now for a return to India. Culinary concerns aside, Berry believes Warne can't wait. "He's desperately keen to take Tendulkar on. He's conquered most, but Tendulkar's the one he really wants to take down."

The cards are again to fall for him. In a happening that should attract the attention of Mulder and Scully, Sylvester Joseph played exactly the same shot once more that night in Sydney, off the second ball Warne's last over. The ball have landed on the same square inch of turf. Again, Fleming ran in, Warne wandered back. Again, it was Fleming's catch. Again, they almost collided. This time, Warne caught it.

The Australians in India 2000-01   Dicky Rutnagur, *Wisden* 2002

Shane Warne, his level of fitness criticised by coach John Buchanan after the defeat at Eden Gardens, could provide only the odd good spell. The Indians played him with such comfort, and sometimes even disdain, that Waugh did not dare use him during the tight finish of the final Test.

Australian Cricket Memorabilia   Stephen W. Gibbs, *Wisden Australia* 2001-02

An item with a connection with a current player, Shane Warne, being a set of Victorian car registration plates – WARNEY – had no offers at an estimate of $1,500-1800. What consequences did the potential buyers see in the display of these plates on their car?

2001

News Register   *WCM*, July 2001

Shane Warne's seven-year association with Nike has ended. He will wear Mitre boots until he finds a new sponsor.

THE ASHES, 2001

How to Beat the Aussies   Lawrence Booth and Christian Ryan, *WCM*, July 2001

Hit Warne out
To conquer Shane Warne a three-point plan is in order for England's batsmen. Move your feet, hit hard and memorise that old L. P. Hartley chestnut: "The past is a foreign country." For all his talk of new tricks, and a return to his golden days, Warne

post-shoulder-and-finger operation is a shadow (and a considerably wider one) of Warne circa '93. Where once he spun the ball two feet, he now spins it closer to two inches. Where once he flung the ball down with a vigorous flick of his arm, he now rolls it out more gingerly. Where once his flipper made Saqlain's doosra look tame, it now sits up obediently and is simpler to pick.

From day one at Edgbaston Warne must be denied the chance to settle and dictate terms. The man for the job is Graham Thorpe, who is not only left-handed but is batting with more verve than any English player since Graham Gooch. Thorpe must not be content with simply hitting Warne out of the attack – he must hit him out of the series. Australia missed a trick by letting Stuart MacGill rust away back in Sydney; when Colin Miller is your No. 1 spinning option things suddenly seem a little blue.

England v Australia, Birmingham   Gideon Haigh, *Wisden Australia* 2001-02
(First Test, July 5-8)

In fact, after the loss of Marcus Trescothick to Jason Gillespie's first delivery, Michael Atherton and [Mark] Butcher added an affirmative 104 for the second wicket from 138 deliveries, setting the tone for a day of batting so positive that it almost bordered on the riotous. Australia regained the ascendancy through Warne who, having described himself wryly before the match as no more than a "back-up bowler", commenced a teasing spell by inducing a bat-pad catch from Butcher with his second delivery in the last over before lunch. When Atherton's first Ashes fifty in 17 innings was ended by a clinking delivery from Gillespie, and Hussain misjudged Glenn McGrath's line in playing no shot, Warne clinically disposed of Afzaal, White, Giles and Darren Gough in the space of 19 deliveries, securing five wickets in a Test innings for the 17th time.

England v Australia, Nottingham   Gideon Haigh, *Wisden Australia* 2001-02
(Third Test, August 2-4)

Trescothick again showed his class but was unlucky to be caught off Warne by Gilchrist, the ball having rebounded from a full-blooded sweep that connected with Hayden's ankle at short leg. Television replays also demonstrated that he was twice cursed: Warne's front foot was clearly over the crease. Under darkened skies, and rain from which the umpires gave the batsmen periodic respite, a patient partnership of 56 between Atherton and Mark Ramprakash from 117 balls kept them in the match until Warne interposed again. Atherton was given out caught at the wicket pushing forward – another dubious decision – beginning a spell of four for 11 from 36 balls. Alec Stewart dragged on rather casually, Ramprakash charged down the wicket crazily, and Craig White popped the last ball of the day to silly point.

...

Warne's six for 33 was his 17th bag of five in a Test, his sixth against England, and his best figures since November 1995, before the finger and shoulder operations that had threatened his career.

...

The Australians performed a lap of Trent Bridge, during which Warne was the subject of fulsome tributes, and also the odd boo from a small contingent of Barmy Army irregulars, which was a form of tribute in itself.

England v Australia, The Oval   Gideon Haigh, *Wisden Australia* 2001-02

(Fifth Test, August 23-27)

In the end England negotiated the day's remaining 20 overs positively. They lost Atherton to a magical Warne delivery that jagged from outside leg stump to strike the top of off stump, but were sustained by a bold half-century from Marcus Trescothick in 49 balls. Trescothick succumbed to Warne's skidder from the fifth ball next morning and Mark Butcher followed swiftly, but Nasser Hussain played with impressive poise and Afzaal with something approaching audacity in their half-centuries. Warne might have had Afzaal as his 400th Test wicket, but third umpire Mervyn Kitchen rejected a stumping appeal to which either verdict seemed possible depending on the camera angle. The leg-spinner finally became the sixth bowler to overtake the landmark when, given the sixth over with the second new ball, he had Alec Stewart caught at the wicket, then trapped Caddick next ball.

. . .

As the fifth morning commenced, England had nine second-innings wickets available and needed 169 to make Australia bat again; they did not even go close. Four wickets fell in the first hour: Warne confounded Butcher and Hussain, while McGrath produced a ball of steepling bounce to unseat Trescothick and angled another across Afzaal. Steve Waugh attacked relentlessly, with five and six men around the bat for Warne, and six in the cordon for McGrath. Ramprakash again suggested composure before Hayden took a smart slip catch, and Stewart lingered, then played no stroke at a baffling leg-break that ripped out of the rough to strike leg stump.

The Australians in England 2001   Gideon Haigh, *Wisden Australia* 2001-02

Australia's victory was built around the accomplishments of Glenn McGrath and Shane Warne, who not only took 11 more wickets between them than all of England's bowlers put together, but were the only bowlers on either side to concede under three runs an over. For McGrath, this was merely more of the same; for Warne, a remarkable redemption after the travail of the Indian tour. It is amazing to recall that he was viewed at the outset as lucky to have retained his place at Stuart MacGill's expense. Both bowlers achieved significant landmarks. By dismissing Mark Ramprakash at The Oval, Warne passed Curtly Ambrose's wicket total, moving to fifth on the Test list. By dismissing Uzman Afzaal in the same game, McGrath left Dennis Lillee behind, moving to second on the Australian list. It is strange that we think of bowling partnerships only in terms of new-ball attacks: Hall and Griffith, Lindwall and Miller *et al.* In fact, with both Warne and McGrath in his charge, Steve Waugh has had perhaps the ideal coupling, covering all possible conditions and contingencies. They even worked in complementary fashion: 25 of McGrath's 32 victims were in England's top seven, 13 of Warne's 31 in England's last four.

Book Review   Gideon Haigh, *WCM*, September 2001

My Autobiography – by Shane Warne with Richard Hobson (Hodder & Stoughton, 2001)

Shane Warne's autobiography is probably the most widely anticipated cricket book of the year. This is easy to understand on one hand, hard on the other. Warne is a genuine giant of the game. Yet how many giants of the game have written interesting books, as distinct from books of interest because of who they're by?

It's an old problem. A century or so ago, when W. G. Grace was commissioned for his *Reminiscences*, the religious affairs journalist Arthur Porritt was recruited as court scribe. Prising anything from Grace proved desperately difficult.

"Often I left his house in absolute despair," Porritt recalled. "Once, at least, I asked to abandon the enterprise."

Porritt would ask Grace how he felt during a particular innings. The Doctor would be puzzled. Felt? He hadn't felt anything. "I had too much to do to watch the bowling and see how the fieldsmen were moved about to think about anything." Grace even chided Porritt for using the word "inimical", remonstrating that team-mates would ask: "Look here, W. G., where did you get that word from?"

Warne is something similar. He's a doer, not a talker. Early on, he candidly concedes: "I can honestly say I have never read a complete book in my life." He is also, as part of Steve Waugh's tight circle, restricted in what he can say.

And there's another problem for Warne's co-author, Richard Hobson of *The Times*, one Arthur Porritt never had with Dr Grace. For the last decade Warne has been probably the most newsworthy cricket figure on the planet. If you have followed his career with any interest much of this book will be, if not predictable, then at least rather familiar. It's only four years, in fact, since Warne last put pen to paper, or name to cover, in his first autobiography *My Own Story*.

So is there a point to this book? There is probably a solid commercial one. Warne's story has already been related in sundry "quickie" biographies without his cooperation. Coming into the market re-establishes Warne's ownership of the franchise he has become. The title is significant, the tautology for emphasis. This is the official product. Beware of imitations.

Yet it would be wrong to write off *My Autobiography* as a purely financial exercise. For all his braggadocio on the field, Warne is a rather more sensitive character off it than he appears to be. "I am a cricketer," he comments wearily at one point, "and a human being."

He hankers to express his side of the dramas in his career. He is even capable of repentance. His to-do with Andrew Hudson at Johannesburg in 1994, for example, causes him excruciating embarrassment. "Every time I see the clip now I cringe." Warne is especially forthright on last year's bizarre Scott Muller saga and the tawdry folly of his "dirty talking" dalliance with an English nurse. The latter story, a weekend wonder in the UK, developed a strange momentum in Australia – strange because Australians are so fond of regarding themselves as the uninhibited ones and the Poms as the stuffed shirts. Warne was subsequently stripped of the Australian vice-captaincy and still smarts at the slight.

"I wonder what might happen if the backgrounds of the 14 [Australian Cricket Board] directors themselves were investigated," he says. "If the same rules apply, as they should, then they, too, must have led unblemished lives or they are not fit to do their jobs."

His general views on the game come as little surprise. He is the latest Australian player to use his book as an apologia for sledging, which is designed not merely to intimidate but "to switch myself on for the contest". He is, moreover, unapologetic: "There are no mates out on a cricket field." Elsewhere, however, he gives perhaps unintended glimpses of a more generous nature. Despite his punishment at Sachin Tendulkar's hands in India three years ago, he comments that "it was a pleasure to bowl to him".

Warne is also candid about the travails of Mark Taylor on the last Ashes tour. The captain might have needed "a few more arms around the shoulder", thinks Warne. "I would say 'keep going Tubs' now and then, but never really sought him out for a longer chat.

"He was always there for us, and maybe we could have given a little more back. It is always hard to know what to do but I think we all let him down a bit." As Ian Healy has already revealed in his *Hands And Heals* that Taylor's form was a more contentious issue within the team than was admitted at the time, perhaps the Australians were more vulnerable on their last visit than they appeared.

The best chapter by far, however, is Warne on leg-spin. It is captivating, full of insights, bursting with joy. He pays warm forthright tribute to his teachers: Terry Jenner, Ian Chappell, Bob Simpson et al. He recalls swapping tips with Mushtaq Ahmed – his flipper for Mushie's wrong'un – which made more than one Australian batsman question "what I had done".

There is also a wonderfully sage comment during Warne's description of the various deliveries in his repertoire: "The other delivery is natural variation off the wicket!" Wilfred Rhodes – "if the batsman thinks ahm's spinnin' 'em, ah'm spinnin' 'em" – would nod his head at that.

Don't get your hopes too high with this book. It is generally pretty circumspect in its judgements by a cricketer who, against his instincts, has found this the most prudent course. In places, though, it diverts and delights. And as for Warne, savour him while you can.

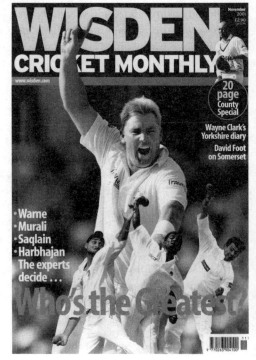

Wisden Cricket Monthly, November 2001

2001-02

Still No. 1		*WCM*, November 2001

Mike Atherton

When I began my career there were very few spinners to worry about. Greg Matthews and John Bracewell were decent enough offies but rarely won matches for their teams, while England had Phil Tufnell and Eddie Hemmings. Occasionally a spinner would burst briefly on to the scene, as Narendra Hirwani did with his 16 wickets against West Indies, but in general it was a time of pace.

Shane Warne changed all that, and then Saqlain Mushtaq and Muttiah Muralitharan did for off-spin what Warne did for leg-spin. In technical terms Warne is entirely orthodox; Murali is entirely unorthodox. Warne bowls all the varieties leg-spinner, top-spinner, googly, flipper and the back-spinner out of the front of the hand. He has the ability to vary the amount of side and over-spin at will, and often during an over you will see him going "around the loop".

Murali spins the ball even further than Warne – or anyone else in the game. At Galle last winter he virtually had to pitch the ball on the edge of the cut strip to hit the stumps. His off-spin comes from the wrist and it is the unbelievably flexible, almost rubbery, nature of his wrist that allows the rotation which, in turn, imparts spin on the ball.

Because of his incredible spin, and the fact that batsmen began to use their pad as a second line of defence, Murali realised the need to beat the outside as well as the inside edge of the bat. So he developed his own type of top-spinner which, when he gets his wrist far enough around, actually turns to the off. At Lancashire this summer he was developing a flipper. Murali's weakness is that he is less capable than Warne of varying the amount of spin. It is often all or nothing.

One of Warne's great strengths is that he spins the ball huge distances while remaining phenomenally accurate. He is a captain's dream – a bowler who is at once both attacking and defensive and when conditions are in his favour he has the ability to dry up the runs and to wreak havoc. The amount of spin he imparts on the ball also gives him more drift than other spinners. I have always felt it is Warne's drift which makes it so hard to come down the wicket to play him.

Where he departs from the orthodox is his line. To right-handers he nearly always attacks at middle and leg stump and, if the pitch is really turning, he will often look to pitch outside leg. Past leg-spinners, such as Richie Benaud, occasionally exploited the rough outside leg but none did so with the frequency or success of Warne.

Murali runs into problems because, in order to bowl off spin from the wrist, he has a chest-on action. This means that he rarely drifts the ball and is less effective round the wicket. Consequently he really dislikes bowling against left-handers and often struggles to dislodge even the most moderate of them. By the end of our Sri Lankan tour last winter he was bowling without hope against Graham Thorpe.

Saqlain is the other offie who has revitalised his art, although I rate him behind Murali. He has the distinct advantage of bowling in tandem with Mushtaq Ahmed and coming on after Wasim Akram and Waqar Younis. Unlike Murali he is a finger spinner and bowls his off-spinners in orthodox fashion. As a result he gets less spin and bounce than either Warne or Murali.

Where he is unorthodox is in his ability to bowl a ball – the doosra – that spins the other way off his first and second fingers. It is a wonderful delivery that is more difficult to pick than any variation I have played against. I struggled to pick it from the hand and looked instead for a slight change in flight – it always came with a slightly higher trajectory because of the top-spin. But that variation is Saqlain's main danger ball and, if you can come to grips with it, you are well on the way to succeeding against him.

It is unlikely that England's batsmen this winter will of face any spinners of the calibre of these three. Anil Kumble is recovering from shoulder problems and it remains to be seen if he can recapture former glories. Harbhajan Singh may be the main threat: against Australia he seemed to spin the ball, bowl a "slider" and get bounce from his height. However, he lacked the mystery which sets Murali and Saqlain apart.

Ultimately it comes down to mental strength. Murali relies on his natural ability and phenomenal spin but is no match for Warne when it comes to thinking a batsman out. Murali rarely alters his lines or his tactics, though he is not helped by the fact that Sri Lanka are so reliant on him that he virtually bowls non-stop at one end, allowing a batsman to get in against him and get used to his variations.

Warne never shies away when a batsman looks to be aggressive. Instead he thrives on the challenge. Using his wicketkeeper and first slip as allies, he is quick to sniff out a batsman's weakness and has an unerring ability to exploit it. He is undoubtedly the smartest bowler of my generation. It is his ability to out-think a batsman that sets him apart and makes him the best bowler I played against.

Atherton verdict: 1. Warne, 2. Muralitharan, 3. Saqlain

Mike Atherton played in 22 Test matches against Shane Warne.

Derek Pringle

Warne's supreme skill is to spin the ball big but land it small, usually in an area no bigger than a hula-hoop around the right-hander's leg stump. His consistency is a captain's dream and only Indian batsmen, in India, have dominated him to the extent where he has been removed from the attack.

His accuracy comes from minimising the amount of moving parts in his action. A short walking approach allows him to unwind himself with perfect timing. A strong right shoulder and chunky spinning wrist allow him to get both action and momentum on the ball.

Over 10 years that explosive movement has taken its toll on said shoulder and spinning finger, and variations such as googles and the flipper – Warne's previous favourite – are rarely used. Instead he relies on leg-breaks of differing magnitude, top-spinners and knowing looks – the last, as Mark Ramprakash and Nasser Hussain could tell you, are intent on provoking batsmen toward indiscretion.

Kidology is a huge part of a spinner's repertoire and Warne's talk of zooters and sliders is all part of his con. The real test comes from reading his subtle and deliberate variations, clearly highlighted for TV viewers by super slo-mo cameras but largely unseen by the batsman facing him.

Warne's closest rival is Murali, an off-spinner who uses more wrist than finger and gets as many rotations on the ball as a wrist-spinner, thus ensuring big turn and occasional steep bounce. Yet such lavish movement makes bowling at left-handers who sweep and cut well a problem, as Murali's ideal line of attack – well outside their leg stump – makes lbws impossible. Graham Thorpe played him this way and averaged 67 in Sri Lanka last winter.

Good batsmen can allow and adjust for spin, however big. So Murali, like Warne and Harbhajan, also looks for dip and drift, caused by over-spin and side-spin respectively. Misreading the length, rather than the amount of turn, is what usually undoes the best batsmen.

Saqlain lags behind the others in this respect, which is why he developed his mystery ball – the one that looks like an off-break yet leaves the right-hander off the pitch. He delivers this ball with a higher arm action than his off-spinner, but clever use of the crease to alter the angle means that many are lured into playing an inappropriate stroke before the deception becomes apparent.

Harbhajan is taller than the others. With his high loose-swinging arms his action appears to have been modelled on the former West Indies fast bowler Colin Croft rather than a spinner. Unlike Kumble, whose wickets come from accuracy and dip rather than turn, Harbhajan gives the ball a big rip but complements this with a quicker, well-disguised arm ball. He gets high bounce too, which makes it difficult to control shots against him.

To have Warne, Murali, Saqlain and Harbhajan dominating the scene at once is truly remarkable. With only a penchant for eschewing the coaching manual in common, their unique skills and individuality would make it possible for all four to operate in the same team and still offer something different.

Pringle verdict: 1. Warne, 2. Muralitharan, 3. Saqlain

Derek Pringle played in 30 Test matches for England and was the cricket correspondent of The Daily Telegraph.

Abdul Qadir

The thing about Murali is he is always making the batsman play. He is accurate, too, so he causes problems all the time.

Murali wins my vote because of the problems Warne encounters against batsmen from India, Pakistan and Sri Lanka. He is clearly a great bowler and I like him very much as a man. It was obvious that he would be successful in England earlier this year because English batsmen are weak against leg-spin, always looking to defend.

But Asian batsmen are determined to attack him, punish his good balls as well as his bad balls. When happens to a bowler he begins thinking only of how to save runs – not how to get a batsman out – and Warne has failed against Asian batsmen, particularly in India. Mind you, he's not alone: when I played for Pakistan it was always my dream to perform extraordinarily against India. I ended with 27 wickets at 51 in 16 Tests against them.

There is no comparison between Murali and Saqlain whom I would actually rate behind his team-mate Mushtaq Ahmed. Saqlain is not a big spinner of the ball and relies on his delivery that goes the other way. Murali has that ball too but he is more dangerous because he bowls from wider than Saqlain and spins the ball sharply from the off into the batsman. He also flights the ball better than Saqlain, whose faster pace plays into the batsman's hands.

But this is an easy time to be a spinner because the golden era of batting, when there were players like Viv Richards, Greg Chappell and Sunil Gavaskar, has passed. Back then the fast bowlers ruled and, as a result, the current generation do not play spin well. Average spinners can take a lot of wickets.

The unluckiest spinner around is Stuart MacGill, who has lived in Warne's shadow. He is not as big-hearted as Warne but he has all the ability and superb variety. If I was an Australian selector I would have played them together. I enjoy watching MacGill bowl because he has the art that is missing these days.

Qadir verdict: 1. Muralitharan, 2. Warne, 3. Mushtaq

Abdul Qadir played in 67 Test matches for Pakistan, taking 236 wickets.

Harsha Bhogle
Shane Warne is still unquestionably the best spinner in the game today, even if this seems a strange opinion coming from India where he has had so little success. In terms of sheer numbers he suffers a bit in comparison with Murali, but their strike-rates are virtually identical – which tells me that Murali bowls a lot more balls per Test than Warne.

If Warne has had the advantage of Glenn McGrath and others softening up the opposition for him, he has also suffered from not being his team's single attacking bowler. This gives Murali a huge bonus because the ball keeps getting tossed to him. Both have achieved great success overseas, primarily because the big turner is their stock ball, so there is little to choose between them on that count.

My primary reason for voting Warne is that he is a more classical and, dare I say it, a cleaner spinner. Murali became a greater bowler after he developed the away-going ball, but he is a long way from convincing people that this specific ball abides by the current law governing fair deliveries.

I'll go for Kumble ahead of Saqlain because a spinner from the subcontinent must consistently win matches for his side in home conditions. Kumble's record in India – 175 wickets at 21.38 in 31 Tests – is brilliant and, although he lacks the stock big-spinner of a Warne or a Murali, he has done as much as Sachin Tendulkar in giving India its outstanding record at home. Pakistan, by contrast, have lost a lot of home matches during Saqlain' reign.

My only reason for not picking MacGill ahead of any of the others is that he has played only 16 Tests – and that is possibly too small a sample from which to judge him.

Bhogle verdict: 1. Warne, 2. Muralitharan, 3. Kumble

Harsha Bogle is a leading Indian commentator and journalist.

Terry Jenner

There is no doubt that in Warne, Murali and Saqlain three of the greatest spinners in Test history are gracing the world's ovals. Common denominators among all three include above-average spin and a willingness to risk being hit in pursuit of a wicket. Each has contributed something unique to his chosen art. Each has been pivotal to his team's success.

I like Saqlain a lot. His unique approach, containing dozens of short steps, belies his beautiful action during release. He moves into a lovely side-on position, uses his front arm powerfully and completes his action with a consistent follow-through. In fact Saqlain, stuttering steps aside, is a perfect role model for any aspiring off-spinner.

The same cannot be said of Murali, whose extraordinary spin comes from his unusual arm and wrist action. He bowls from a chest-on position with his front foot opening out, and his method of release is freakish – kids will not be coached to bowl that way. We will never see its like again.

I am also impressed by Harbhajan, after his sensational series against Australia, and South Africa's Paul Adams, who is the most successful left-arm wrist spinner in history but, like MacGill, cannot find a spot in his national team.

Warne is something else. His ability to spin his leg-break exceptional distances while landing the ball consistently in the batsman's danger area has changed the whole perception and expectation of wrist-spinners. Warne also gets my nod for his courage and longevity, combined with his willingness to work hard in the nets. Two operations on his spinning finger, a major one on his bowling shoulder and surgery on his left knee are testimony to his bravery. That he is able to compete at all is amazing; the fact that he is still taking quality wickets is even more incredible.

Warne's impact on our great game should never be understated. On the day he bowled Mike Gatting with his first ball in England, Test cricket became exciting again. We had endured too many years of the four-pronged pace attack and people seriously believed Test cricket was close to death. Warne changed all that. Not only does he sit on top of all other spin bowlers but he revolutionised leg-spin and rejuvenated the game. Each of his 407 Test wickets are etched indelibly in the minds of wrist-spin devotees.

We are privileged that he came along in our lifetime.

Jenner verdict: 1. Warne, 2. Saqlain, 3. Muralitharan

Terry Jenner was a leg-spinner who played in nine Tests for Australia. He was Shane Warne's career mentor.

How to Beat Australia   Bob Woolmer, *WCM*, January 2002

Whack Warne

The most important factor is how South Africa's batsmen play Shane Warne. They have to have a game plan that is a cross between having a go at him and taking him for singles. It is nothing new or revolutionary but it is easier said than done. Warne took a lot of wickets last summer but that was largely to do with England's batsmen committing hara-kiri, rather than him bowling well. If he bowls the way he did during the Ashes series then there will be too many full tosses and long hops – and the South Africans won't have much to worry about.

Australia v New Zealand, Perth   Gideon Haigh, *WCM*, January 2002
(Third Test, November 30-December 4)

But the New Zealanders squandered the rare chance to force Australia to follow-on, Astle and Cairns both missing chances from Warne. Thus spared, the wannabe all-rounder proceeded to a robust Test best before joining his skipper, Kim Hughes and Geoff Boycott among those who have been marooned a run shy of a hundred at the WACA. A pity that Mark Richardson, who accepted his miscue at deep midwicket, had to demonstrate his glee with a boorish bow to the crowd: imagine the furore if Warne had been perpetrator rather than disappointed onlooker in the burlesque.

Australia v South Africa, Adelaide   Gideon Haigh, *Wisden* 2003
(First Test, December 14-18)

Warne returned to something like his best, recovering his menacing drift into the right-hander, and bowling over and round the wicket with all his old facility. His plot to uproot Gibbs was one for the scrapbook: a beguiling leg-break into the footmarks spun round the advancing batsman for Gilchrist to execute the stumping. After bagging five in an innings for the 20th time in Tests, Warne volunteered that a target of 250 in the fourth innings would be demanding: "The pitch is going to get worse, and it will keep lower for the fast bowlers." His prognosis showed why John the Bookie had once valued his opinions.
    ...
    ... the old stager Warne won the match award with eight. His first-innings five for 113 was the best by a leg-spinner at Adelaide since Richie Benaud's five for 96 against West Indies in 1960-61. It took Warne past 50 Test wickets in the calendar year and lifted him to fourth in the all-time Test bowlers' table, passing Wasim Akram's 414.

Australia v New Zealand, Melbourne   Ken Piesse, *Wisden Australia* 2002-03
(VB Series, January 29)

Shane Warne's first over cost 19 runs, and at one point the inventive Craig McMillan faced up to him with an impudent, ever-so-open stance and glanced the delivery for three.

VB Series   Richard Boock and Paul Coupar, *Wisden* 2003

Shane Warne disappointed: the loss of 17lbs on a diet of cereal, baked beans and water seemed to shear his powers, and he took only six at 54.

Surviving Warne
Barry Richards, WAC, March 2002

Shane Warne returns to South Africa with his reputation still intact, but the feeling among the inner circle of international players is that he is not the bowler he was a few years ago. Underestimating Warne is hazardous, but South Africa need to take a cue from New Zealand who attacked Warne on his home soil. They almost pulled off what would have been their finest-ever series victory, and much of that was due to the way they played Warne and their attitude to him.

In the coming series in South Africa, however, the pitches are expected to have a lot more grass than what we saw in Australia. If that's the case, the key to the points could well rest in a battle between Glenn McGrath and Shaun Pollock. McGrath came out on top in Australia but don't count Pollock out – he's regained a lot of his confidence with that win in the VB Series. Still, the Warne threat looms large. South Africa must come to grips with their old nemesis.

Attack, for heaven's sake
At the death of the Sydney Test, when it was all but over, Pollock took to Warne. I hope it is still fresh in Pollock's mind – and in the mind of every South African player. There's no doubt that Warne is a better bowler when players are edgy about playing shots and worried about using their feet. South Africa's middle order must make some mental strides to combat Warne for he, at the moment, has the psychological edge, even though it is diminishing.

In this regard, Sachin Tendulkar has shown the way, and as a consequence, Warne fears Sachin rather than the other way round. Warne's formidable variety has depleted since the shoulder operation: his control over the flipper and googly is not as good. This means there are more stock balls, i.e. leg-spinners, which provides the batsman with an opportunity to plan an assault.

The grounds in South Africa are smaller which means that you don't have to hit the ball absolutely in the middle of the bat to clear the fence, as you do in Australia. It is a plus that South Africa must exploit, and early.

Step up, Jacques Kallis
Pollock has got to have the courage to instruct his better players – Jacques Kallis and Herschelle Gibbs – that they not only have the licence, but the responsibility, to take the attack to Warne. Sachin does it naturally but others, though not quite as talented but good enough still, must have the courage to do it – with the captain's (and selectors') blessings. Each South Africa player is different in style and temperament, so deciding who must attack is important.

To my mind, Kallis is the man for the job. He has the class and skill to get onto the offensive against Warne, but it must not be a half-hearted effort. Through the Australian season, he seemed content to "sit" on Warne and just pinch the odd single. It's hard to be critical because for most of the series South Africa were down and out by the second day, so it was always a fight for survival. This time around Kallis must back himself more, but the team management needs to understand that this might result in the odd failure too.

The MacGill factor

The unknown in all of this is the dual leg-spin attack of Stuart MacGill and Warne – not bosom buddies, and both very competitive. My perception is that when they operate in tandem, it is MacGill who thrives. Warne, for all his greatness and proven ability, does not relish bowling in tandem with another leggie. This perhaps is when he is under most pressure: something the South Africans will do well to keep in mind.

CLASSIC TEST 5

South Africa v Australia, Cape Town   Neil Manthorp, *Wisden* 2003
(Second Test)
March 8, 9, 10, 11, 12 – Australia won by four wickets. Toss: South Africa.
Debuts: A. J. Hall, D. Pretorius, G. C. Smith

Shane Warne flew 16 friends and relatives to Cape Town for his 100th Test, and they saw him bowl 98 overs, take eight wickets, score a half-century, win the match award – and propel his team to yet another series triumph, which cemented their place at the head of the Test Championship. In the end, it was a memorable five-day battle. But that hardly looked likely when South Africa crashed to 92 for six on the opening day in the face of some tremendous fast bowling inspired by McGrath. They clawed their way back to 239, thanks to the street-fighting qualities of Andrew Hall, who scored 70 on debut, while Adams marked his first Test in nearly 11 months with an unorthodox but hugely welcome 35.

As Australia cruised to 130 for one, the script seemed depressingly familiar. But when Hayden top-edged a hook at Kallis to fine leg, the innings took a dramatic turn. Australia lost four more wickets in the next 20 overs, slithering to 185 for six – still 54 behind. The fact that those wickets were shared by a Cape-coloured spinner, Adams, and a Xhosa pace bowler, Ntini, stoked a frenetic atmosphere in the country's best-supported stadium. The controversy over quotas made a packed house cheer all the more loudly.

Then came Gilchrist. Again. It was impossible to imagine he could equal his feats at Johannesburg, but he did. Within five minutes, he was charging down the track at Adams, and after his first 26 balls he was on 42, with nine blazing fours. As a statement, it was devastating, and his form actually improved. A modicum of caution as Australia reached parity meant his first fifty took 53 deliveries, but then came feverish butchery

South Africa v Australia, Cape Town, 2002

SOUTH AFRICA	First innings		Second innings	
H. H. Gibbs c M. E. Waugh b Gillespie	12	–	c Ponting b Warne	39
G. Kirsten c M. E. Waugh b Lee	7	–	lbw b Lee	87
G. C. Smith c Ponting b McGrath	3	–	c Gilchrist b Warne	68
J. H. Kallis c Gilchrist b McGrath	23	–	lbw b Warne	73
N. D. McKenzie b Warne	20	–	run out (Martyn)	99
A. G. Prince c Gilchrist b McGrath	10	–	c Ponting b Warne	20
*†M. V. Boucher c Gilchrist b Lee	26	–	lbw b Gillespie	37
A. J. Hall c Gilchrist b Gillespie	70	–	run out (Lee/Gillespie)	0
P. R. Adams c Warne b Gillespie	35	–	not out	23
M. Ntini c M. E. Waugh b Warne	14	–	c Langer b Warne	11
D. Pretorius not out	5	–	c M. E. Waugh b Warne	0
B 4, lb 5, nb 5	14		B 8, lb 3, w 2, nb 3	16

1/15 (1) 2/18 (3) 3/25 (2)   239
4/70 (5) 5/73 (4) 6/92 (6)
7/147 (7) 8/216 (9) 9/229 (8) 10/239 (10)

1/84 (1) 2/183 (2)   473
3/254 (3) 4/284 (4)
5/350 (6) 6/431 (7) 7/433 (8)
8/440 (5) 9/464 (10) 10/473 (11)

First innings—McGrath 20–4–42–3; Gillespie 15–4–52–3; Lee 16–1–65–2; Warne 28–10–70–2; M. E. Waugh 1–0–1–0.

Second innings—McGrath 25–7–56–0; Gillespie 29–10–81–1; Warne 70–15–161–6; Lee 22–3–99–1; M. E. Waugh 9–3–34–0; Martyn 4–0–15–0; S. R. Waugh 3–0–16–0.

AUSTRALIA	First innings		Second innings	
J. L. Langer b Ntini	37	–	b Pretorius	58
M. L. Hayden c Hall b Kallis	63	–	c Boucher b Kallis	96
R. T. Ponting c Boucher b Adams	47	–	not out	100
M. E. Waugh c Gibbs b Ntini	25	–	c Boucher b Ntini	16
*S. R. Waugh b Adams	0	–	b Adams	14
D. R. Martyn c Boucher b Ntini	2	–	lbw b Adams	0
†A. C. Gilchrist not out	138	–	c McKenzie b Kallis	24
S. K. Warne c Kallis b Adams	63	–	not out	15
B. Lee c Prince b Kallis	0			
J. N. Gillespie c Kallis b Adams	0			
G. D. McGrath lbw b Ntini	2			
B 2, lb 1, w 2	5		Lb 6, nb 5	11

1/67 (1) 2/130 (2) 3/162 (3)   382
4/168 (5) 5/176 (4) 6/185 (6)
7/317 (8) 8/338 (9) 9/343 (10) 10/382 (11)

1/44 (2) 2/45 (3)   (6 wkts) 334
3/50 (4) 4/55 (1)
5/84 (5) 6/158 (7) 7/170 (8)
8/177 (6) 9/188 (9) 10/200 (10)

First innings—Ntini 22.5–5–93–4; Pretorius 11–1–72–0; Kallis 16–1–65–2; Hall 11–1–47–0; Adams 20–1–102–4.
Second innings—Ntini 24–4–90–1; Pretorius 14–5–60–1; Adams 21.1–0–104–2; Hall 3–0–6–0; Kallis 17–2–68–2.

Umpires: S. A. Bucknor and R. E. Koertzen.   Third umpire: D. L. Orchard.
Referee: C. W. Smith

as Gilchrist made fun of the bowlers. His second fifty needed 38 balls, and his final 38 runs just 17. He hit Adams's last two overs for 36. Like a dog that has been kicked too often, the South African attack were reduced to hiding, relieved by every delivery that wasn't drilled to the fence. Most memorable was Gilchrist's ability to hit good-length deliveries square of the wicket, cutting or pulling, while he drove yorker-length balls off the back foot like half-volleys. Australia had trailed by 63 when he came to the crease. When he ran out of partners 36 overs later, they led by 143 – thanks also to a mightily enjoyable 66-ball 63 by Warne, who gleaned plenty of wheat from the chaff of Gilchrist's harvest.

For once, South Africa's top five were undaunted second time around. They accumulated 366 runs between them – no centuries, but McKenzie fell only one short when Martyn ran him out with a direct hit from cover. Warne was made to work harder than ever before: it took 70 overs from him to dismiss South Africa, finally, for 473. Warne, slimmed down but not wholly reformed, compared his marathon to "a big night out when you think you're gone several times, but you get a couple of second winds".

Australia required 331, the tenth-highest fourth-innings total to win in Test history. But as they were responsible for five of the top nine, history was no barrier. Langer and Hayden launched the assault in fearless style, sharing their sixth century stand in 14 starts. When Dewald Pretorius, who was mostly outclassed, bowled Langer off an inside edge, Ponting helped take the score to 201 before Hayden edged Kallis to the keeper. He failed by four runs to become the second player to score centuries in five consecutive Tests, after Bradman (1936-37 to 1938), who went on to six. Some welcome tension entered the chase when Ntini removed Mark Waugh just before lunch. Then Adams's googlies bowled Steve Waugh and cornered Martyn lbw in successive overs, leaving Australia 268 for five; but Gilchrist effectively finished the job with a carefree, run-a-ball 24. Ponting had the last word in the drama: six short of a meticulous century, but needing only three for victory, he achieved both with a single blow against Adams. The script decreed that Warne should be there at the other end. Not for the first time, he had grabbed the headlines, and he could be proud of every word in them.

Man of the Match: S. K. Warne. **Attendance:** 52,105.

The Australians in South Africa 2001-02   Neil Manthorp, *Wisden* 2003

In reality, for the umpteenth time, Warne and Glenn McGrath were instrumental in Australia's triumph. McGrath took 12 wickets at 19, while Warne took 20 and moved into second place in the all-time Test wicket-takers' list. In his 100th Test, at Newlands, he put in a heroic effort, bowling 70 overs in a single innings, and claimed the match award.

2002

News Register   *WCM*, April 2002

Five people were arrested after a man attempted to blackmail the ACB, claiming Shane Warne and Brett Lee had acted improperly during a January encounter with two teenage girls. "It's all rubbish," said Warne. "It's disappointing and sad that people have tried to take advantage of my high profile."

2002 — Chronicle   *Wisden* 2003

Shane Warne was fined and banned from driving on British roads for three months for reaching 120mph on the M1 in Derbyshire. The case had been adjourned nine times because of problems serving papers on Warne, who admitted the offence in a letter to Ilkeston magistrates. "Thanks for your patience," he wrote. "I'm sorry, I was going too fast in your country. I love playing cricket in England." (*Daily Telegraph*, May 9).

Hollywood and The Tiger   Frank Tyson, *WAC*, May 2002

The cowboy film *Shane* made Alan Ladd a hero to every American youngster. The modern Shane – Warne – is a cult figure for every young Australian aspiring to bowl the slow stuff. He is hero-worshipped by the masses and idolised by the Australian media for whom he is a second Bill "Tiger" O'Reilly – albeit with more blond hair.

The comparison between O'Reilly and Warne is fascinating, for they are those rare birds: leg-spinners who succeeded in English conditions. Australian leg-spinners have a rich legacy of match-winning performances: Clarrie Grimmett snared 33 South African batsmen in 1931-32, and 44 more in 1935-36. O'Reilly took 27 wickets against England in the Bodyline series in 1932-33, another 27 against South Africa in 1935-36, and 25 against England in 1936-37. Later, Richie Benaud took 30 wickets against South Africa in 1957-58, 31 against England in 1958-59 and 29 against India in 1959-60. Outstanding performances these, but without exception, they were achieved on the harder, bouncier or more spin-friendly Australian, South African or Indian pitches. I did not expect Warne to be the decisive force he proved to be in 1993 in England.

Only the performances of Grimmett and O'Reilly in the English summer of 1934 bear any comparison to Warne's 34-wicket triumph of 1993. The victory of Bill Woodfull's Aussies over Bob Wyatt's England that year owed as much to the irresistible batting of Don Bradman (758 runs) and the post Bodyline turbulence in the corridors of Lord's as to the bowling successes of Grimmett and O'Reilly, who between them captured 53 Test wickets – O'Reilly being the more successful with 28 victims to Grimmett's 25.

These were outstanding bowling figures, considering that English playing conditions are notoriously unsympathetic to the wrist-spinner's art. While the leg-spinner turns the ball more than the finger-spinner, he is much slower through the air and off the pitch, giving the batsman more time organise his response. The sluggish

English wickets retard the leggie's turn even more, allowing the batsman to adjust his stroke according to the degree of deviation. Importantly, softer pitches negate top-spin, depriving the wrist-spinner of the bounce of the drier, harder surfaces, and reducing the chances of lofted strokes and the resulting catches.

Looking at the equation in reverse, wrist-spinners who master English conditions must possess certain attributes to compensate for the lack of nip and bounce, which are their stock-in-trade on harder pitches. There were striking similarities between the Warne of '93 and the O'Reilly of '34. Warne captured six wickets more, O'Reilly had to share his booty with Grimmett. But the averages were remarkably alike – Warne's was 25.79 to O'Reilly's 24.92 – and so were the strike rates: Warne struck every 12.8 overs and O'Reilly every 11.8 overs. But it was the manner in which O'Reilly and Warne claimed their wickets which provides the most illuminating commentary on their similarities.

Grimmett's flighted offerings outside the off stump yielded him six stumping victims and even Tim May, Warne's off-spin partner in '93, used to draw batsmen forward to their doom. In contrast, not a single English batsman was discovered out of his ground by O'Reilly in '34 and Warne only lured one batsman out of his crease in '93. The effectiveness of Warne and O'Reilly was founded on frontal attack. O'Reilly bowled eight of his opponents (29.6%) and Warne ten (29.5%), O'Reilly won four lbw victims (14.8%) and Warne seven (20.5%). Both depended on catches for most of their wickets. But most of those catches were taken as result of attacking bowling, in positions close to the batsman's stumps. Warne had the assistance of Ian Healy behind the stumps on five occasions, and of Mark Taylor at slip who took seven of the 14 catches off Warne's bowling. Three of O'Reilly's victims were caught behind by Bertie Oldfield, and a fair proportion of the remaining 12 went to close fieldsmen.

O'Reilly's bowling style was different from Warne's. He was near medium pace and turned the ball much less than Warne, but he commanded every possible delivery known to a leg-spinner and used his height – 6ft 1in – to extract disconcerting bounce from the most lifeless tracks. Warne is slower in the air and relies more on his ability to extract prodigious turn. But aggression was, and is, an important part of both their armouries.

Through his English campaigns, the full gamut of Warne's clever weaponry homed in on the batsman's stumps. His approach was multi-faceted, disconcerting the batsman with flippers from over the wicket or leg-spinners from around the wicket; pitching in the bowler's rough outside the batsman's pads; and turning the ball across the face of the stumps. But the objective was always the same: to make his opponent play at every delivery and to hit the wicket. Rarely did he permit the slip and gully fieldsmen to retreat into a defensive ring. O'Reilly was of the same ilk, always pressuring and probing and pushing the ball through on to the batsman, on or about the middle and off stumps. Tiger's colleague of the pre-war days, Australian opening bat Bill Brown, once described batting against O'Reilly's bowling in Shield games thus: "The ball just kept coming at you and climbing all the time. You simply could not get your bat out of the way."

To me, one of the most interesting insights into the comparative virtues of the front and oblique attacks – for which read the differing methods of O'Reilly and

Grimmett respectively – was provided during Australia's tour of South Africa in 1935-36. In the five Tests during that Cape Summer, Grimmett took 44 wickets and O'Reilly 27. Grimmett's flightier methods were obviously more suited to teasing out the batsmen in South African conditions. The message which rings out loud and clear from Grimmett's superiority in South Africa, and of the greater effectiveness of Warne and O'Reilly in England, is the lesson of evolution: to survive and succeed one must adapt to one's environment.

But the over-the-top, lap-dog adulation heaped on Warne would almost have one believe that he invented leg-spin, and that bowlers like Bernard Bosanquet, Warwick Armstrong, Herbert Hordern, Arthur Mailey, Grimmett, Chuck Fleetwood Smith and O'Reilly himself, never existed. Warne is undoubtedly a fine leggie: a prodigious spinner of the ball with a varied repertoire and a canny cricket brain. But does he fully deserve the extravagant praise heaped on him? The truth is that, while Warne's record is formidable, he does bowl the occasional bad ball, and many of his victims have been culled from the ranks of Test sides which, had they been on the scene in the old days, would have vastly inflated the wicket tallies of O'Reilly and Grimmett.

No less a batsman than Don Bradman felt that O'Reilly was the greatest bowler – not just spinner – he ever saw. There was a certain ferocity and spitefulness to his bowling. Warne may turn the ball more than O'Reilly, but I doubt if he bowls with the same venom as O'Reilly. O'Reilly was impossible to attack – even Bradman had limited success against him in Sheffield Shield games – and had a better disguised googly. He also bowled to many more classy batsmen than Warne has – Jack Hobbs, Herbert Sutcliffe, Wally Hammond, Len Hutton, Denis Compton, Dudley Nourse – and was rarely subjugated. Warne has had the opportunities to pick up many cheap wickets, but his unimpressive record in the subcontinent, where he has been mastered by many batsmen, goes against him. O'Reilly, I feel, would have done well in the subcontinent, like Chandrasekhar, for the simple reason that he came through the air a lot quicker, spun the ball hard and would have got a lot of bounce, since he was much taller than Warne.

In my book, O'Reilly gets 9 on 10 to Warne's 7.

Frank Tyson played in 17 Test matches for England, taking 76 wickets.

News Register   WCM, June 2002

Shane Warne threatened legal action against Melbourne newspaper *The Herald-Sun* over an article that linked his name to match-fixing. Warne settled out of court and the paper issued a full apology.

News Register   WCM, June 2002

Shane Warne, Glenn McGrath and Mark Waugh said they would not tour Pakistan in August due to safety fears.

| Hampshire | Rob Steen, *WCM*, August 2002 |

To the burning question: whither Shane Warne? Well, he popped into West End in early July and [Tim] Tremlett is, shall we say, cautiously optimistic. "It's up to him. We'd like him for a couple of years, which may work out for him. I reckon he needs another ten Tests to get 500 Test wickets and that will probably take him into 2003-04 and then there's the 2005 Ashes series to aim for. Watch this space."

| News Register | *WCM*, October 2002 |

Shane Warne was reappointed Victoria captain despite international commitments that mean he is unlikely to play many, or any, state matches. Matthew Elliott will captain in Warne's absence. Warne also suggested he may retire from one-day internationals after the 2003 World Cup in order to prolong his Test career.

2002-03

| Pakistan v Australia, P. Saravanamuttu Stadium, Colombo | Martin Blake, *Wisden* 2004 |
| (First Test, October 3-7) | |

In reply, the inexperienced openers did not contribute a single run and, with Warne showing the benefits of his new fitness regime, Pakistan only just avoided the follow-on. Faisal Iqbal danced down the wicket to carve Warne through the off side on his way to a run-a-ball 83, which went some way to vindicating Pakistan's youth policy. Rashid Latif backed him up with 66, but Warne, indefatigable, wheeled away in the heat to take seven for 94.

| Pakistan v Australia, Sharjah | Martin Blake, *Wisden* 2004 |
| (Second Test, October 11-12) | |

After Waqar Younis was granted his wish to bat first on one of world cricket's most benign strips, the Pakistanis were rolled over for their lowest-ever score, a pathetic 59, three below their previous worst at Perth in 1981-82. They had lasted less than 32 overs. The openers Imran Nazir and Taufeeq Umar repeated the pair of ducks they managed in the first innings in Colombo, and only Abdul Razzaq, who endured almost two hours for 21, reached double figures. Warne caused the damage again, taking four for 11 and bewitching the batsmen with his new "slider". Pushing forward, they found themselves trapped lbw by deliveries that were doing precisely nothing.

Pakistan v Australia, Sharjah	Martin Blake, *Wisden* 2004
(Third Test, October 19-22)	

Pakistan soon fell under Warne's spell again. He mesmerised batsmen and took five wickets with his combination of sharp spin and disguised straighter balls.

The Australians in Sri Lanka and Sharjah 2002-03	John Stern, *WCM*, December 2002

By the third match it was the Shane Warne show. McGrath became the eighth bowler to take 400 Test wickets but his milestone was overshadowed by another work of art from Warne. He finished the series with 27 wickets at 12.66. It was the highest total by an Australian in a three-match series, beating the 23 of Dennis Lillee and Richie Benaud. Of his 27 wickets 13 were leg-before – testament to the success of his new "slider" delivery. The slider is similar to the flipper but, according to Warne himself, is bowled more slowly, at the pace of his leg-break. Like the flipper, it has a hint of back-spin and goes straight on. The Pakistan batsmen continually played Warne with their pad heading down the line of the ball expecting it to turn. When it did not, they were stuck.

Is it the Slider or the Shiraz?	John Stern, *WCM*, January 2003

One minute he's banging on about the slider and the flipper, the next minute he's talking about "cab-sav-merlot" blends. Please welcome the new Shane Warne: wine drinker. The Shane Warne Collection, launched in Melbourne at the end of October, sounds as preposterous an idea as Darren Gough endorsing Harrod's hampers.

It just does not seem right. Warne, to his credit, concedes the incongruity of him having his own wine label – not that it bothers him. His opportunism, on and off the field, knows no bounds and the chance to cash in on his reinvented self-image was too good to miss. The wine will be marketed in England next summer when Warne returns to county cricket to captain Hampshire. "I've always been more of a beer man but I've been off the beer over the last 12 months while I went on a fitness campaign," Warne says, though the change in chosen tipple seems not to have dimmed a predilection for intoxication. "Over the last year, I've got stuck into a few too many bottles of white … a few too many bottles of red and started to develop a taste for it."

Warne reckons he has lost the best part of two stone over the past year after surveying the size of the international schedule for the next 12 months. Giving up the beer was one of the prerequisites but going teetotal was clearly never an option.

The cheekiness of Warne's venture into viticulture is not lost on team-mates. The genuine wine drinkers in the team, such as Adam Gilchrist, struggle to take it seriously. Quite what Stuart MacGill, rival leg-spinner and pukka wine expert, makes of it is anyone's guess.

Warne was more than happy to talk about his wines though the depth of knowledge will not be giving Oz Clarke sleepless nights. "The white is a chardonnay," said Warne (pronounced with emphasis on the -ay) with certainty. But he was less sure about the red. "It's a mixture between 'cab-sav' and, er, merlot, I think, and, er, maybe a shiraz." Two out of three ain't bad. The Zilzie Wines website reveals that the red is a cabernet-merlot-petit-verdot blend that has "a velvety palate".

English cricket writers got the chance to taste the collection during the Adelaide Test and the fact that few took up the offer says as much about their sobriety as the wine. Like most Australian wine, it is drunk very young. The red and the white are the 2002 vintage, which is good but not yet. Derek Pringle, who knows a thing or two about wine, remarked that the chardonnay was "not very structured and a bit flabby". Christopher Martin-Jenkins detected a faint metallic aftertaste; Mike Atherton said it went right through him, perhaps like the slider. In the interests of investigative journalism, WCM editor Stephen Fay drank the red blend of cabernet-merlot-petit-verdot. It was also young and unstructured and not as fruity as the advertising suggests. As for "the long, soft finish", Shane had left it in the nets.

Australia v England, Brisbane   David Frith, *Wisden Australia* 2003-04
(First Test, November 7-10)

True to their promise the openers attacked whenever possible. Marcus Trescothick, a left-hander as burly as Hayden, if without quite the shoulder power, chipped Warne into the crowd then cut him for four. The lean Vaughan drove classically and hustled Australia in the field. Mark Butcher too found no danger in Warne's bowling, and the pleasure and relief of it all beamed from English faces either side of the fence. It was like being told that your favourite uncle wasn't dead after all.

Australia v England, Adelaide   Warwick Franks, *Wisden Australia* 2003-04
(Second Test, November 21-24)

Warne again underlined his mastery of the craft of leg-spin bowling in a spell of 25 successive overs during which his relentless probing of his opponents reminded onlookers of the sheer aesthetic delight in watching one of the great slow bowlers of the game's history at work.

Australia v England, Melbourne   Nick Hoult, *Wisden* 2004
(VB Series, December 15)

The image of a distraught Shane Warne leaving on a stretcher overshadowed another imperious Australian performance. Diving to try and save a single off his own bowling, he had dislocated his right shoulder. Within an hour, Warne was being checked by the surgeon who had operated on the same joint in 1998; scans confirmed ligament damage, which put his World Cup place in jeopardy, but Warne would be back before this tournament was over.

Australia v England, Sydney
(VB Series, January 23)

Ken Piesse, *Wisden Australia* 2003-04

Paul Collingwood top-scored again before falling victim to Shane Warne, back for the first time since his shoulder dislocation just five weeks earlier. Warne had announced on the eve of the game that he would retire from limited-overs games after the World Cup, and while well short of his big-spinning best, he bowled economically.

Australia v England, Melbourne
(VB Series, January 25)

Nick Hoult, *Wisden* 2004

In the end, Lee emerged triumphant – though it was Warne, in what he said would be his last one-day international at his MCG home, who was chaired from the field.

Warne for the Road
Gideon Haigh, *WCM*, March 2003

The 2002-03 summer in Australia, overshadowed by "will-he-won't-he do-they-dare?" conjecture about the future of the country's Test captain, took an unexpected turn on January 23 when another player went without anyone asking, or even looking like they might. It was Shane Warne who got a taste of the tributes that Test cricket might have in store for him when he announced that he would renounce the one-day game after the World Cup.

Warne left no one in doubt, however, that the decision was about prolongation as much as termination. Speaking at the usual packed press conference – Warne has to hold one if he takes out the rubbish nowadays – he said: "It's not a decision that has come lightly. I love playing cricket for Australia but the No. 1 priority for me is to play Test cricket for as long as I can."

Warne had experienced intimations of mortality on December 15 when he had been stretchered off the MCG with a shoulder dislocated by an awkward dive; the injury cost him most of the VB Series and at one stage seemed to threaten his World Cup ambitions. "I think the rigours of one-day international cricket – throwing yourself around, fielding on the fence and all those sorts of things – take their toll," he said. "The amount of stress on your body is considerable and I didn't really come to my conclusion until I was carried off on a stretcher at Melbourne with the dislocated shoulder. If I stay in the same fitness condition as I have this last year, I hope I can play for a long time. This could prolong my Test career by five or six years. Who knows?"

Who does know where Warne is concerned? He is 34 in September but has never looked fitter: draped in the singlet of which he has grown rather fond, he bears a growing resemblance to the big-chested, big-chinned antipodean advertising icon Chesty Bond. He is also moving into a statistical terra incognita, with 491 Test wickets at an average that has actually been shrinking for the last year. Quite how the two seasons as captain of Hampshire to which he agreed last September fit into this regime is a bit of a mystery – though Warne is, of course, not averse to a touch of mystery now and again.

Another factor at which Warne hinted was to do with his sense of himself. Australia's soft-talking and big-stick-carrying chairman of selectors Trevor Hohns unsettled his men, as he upset many fans, with his unsentimental dismissals of the Waugh twins from limited-overs cricket a year ago. Warne has not been a player notable for his dignity down the years, but choosing his exit now pre-empts any ugly scenes that might portend. "A year or so down the track I don't particularly want to get the tap on the shoulder," he said.

Warne knows he is on firmer ground where Test cricket is concerned; in fact, it's granite-hard. Remember when Warne's mere presence was going to presage a wrist-spin revolution in Australia? It didn't happen. Stuart MacGill remain an attendant lord, but as he showed in the Fourth and Fifth Tests lacks both Warne's variety and accuracy. Victorian Cameron White, 19, has pluck with the bat but needs luck with the ball.

Warne, it is steadily being recognised, was a one-in-a-lifetime talent that could not be replicated, for all the promotional programmes, youth teams and academies one could wish for.

Warne's popularity in Australia, too, has probably never been greater, a generation of cricket fans having grown up with him. He is favourite singer or soap star whom they have been able to watch mature; even better, one whose best work isn't ten or 20 years behind him. For he still does it, time and again. When Australia was under pressure during his last one-day game on Australian soil, the second one-day final at the MCG, it was Warne who winkled out England's top scorers Michael Vaughan and Alec Stewart before being chaired off on his team mates' shoulders. One wondered about a future in which he was not around to carry them on his.

"Pretty Suss"   Christian Ryan, *WCM*, April 2003

He's out. So screeched the front page of Sydney's *Sun-Herald* on February 23. And as was the case 73 light years ago, when Don Bradman stirred the same headline after a rare dismissal against England, nobody needed to ask who or why or what.

Shane Warne's one-year ban for swallowing two prohibited diuretics was trumpeted by Australia's national broadcaster as the "biggest story in the nation's sporting history". But this went way beyond sport. Financial pundits tut-tutted over Warne's forfeited income (£770,000-£1.15 million). Fashion columnists fussed about what his family wore to the tribunal hearing. The *Age*, Warne's hometown broadsheet, interviewed a concreter called Lou who was working on a nearby apartment block. The concreter's conclusion? "It looked pretty suss."

"Pretty suss" pretty neatly summed up the nation's mood – and this, for once, was an issue on which almost everyone had a view. The prime minister John Howard, pilloried for not 'fessing up to whether Australian troops were committed to war in Iraq, showed no such reticence when buttonholed about Mothergate. "It would be a great shame," mourned the PM, "If we were to lose his [Warne's] services."

Opinions split more widely once news broke of the 12-month suspension. "Muddled logic," cried Geoff Lawson. "Very harsh," agreed Warne's Victorian coach David Hookes. Those with only a passing interest in cricket, meanwhile, tended to feel he had escaped lightly. "They've copped out," spluttered Brad McGee, a cyclist. "Warne dodged a bullet," said the World Anti-Doping Agency chairman Dick Pound, who was promptly mocked for being a Canadian. A *Canadian!* What could *he* possibly know about cricket?

The deepest intrigue surrounding Warne's ban was not its rights or wrongs but, more specifically, its length. If found guilty of using a prohibited method, which he was, the rules demanded a mandatory two years. If there were "exceptional circumstances" – that is, if Warne was more dopey than devious – then three months seemed appropriate. Twelve months sounded like a bet each way.

Perhaps the three-member tribunal was swayed by Warne's $20,000-a-day legal team and $350-an-hour spin doctor, hired to shore up his reputation. Oddities abounded. The tribunal insisted the absence of steroids in Warne's blood system counted in his favour. Yet all that proved, surely, was that if he had taken steroids the diuretics – prohibited for the very reason that they mask them – worked like a dream. The tribunal accepted medical assurances that a few pills could neither hasten Warne's recovery from injury nor help him spin the ball further. But could they not improve his stamina, his endurance?

All the while a nation was examining its feelings for a treasured son. Talkback radio callers were gobsmacked by Warne's lack of contrition and eagerness to blame Mum. Then there was his evasiveness. He said nothing for days before splashing out with an "exclusive column" in the Murdoch tabloids, where his grizzliness about the media invading his family's privacy was undermined by a front-page portrait, freshly commissioned, of Mr & Mrs Warne with their three children. Two weeks after the initial revelations Warne finally granted his first public interview – to the TV journalist Ray Martin, friendly as a labrador, on Kerry Packer's Nine Network, where Warne is on the payroll. It was there that Warne dropped his bombshell: he took not one but two of Mum's Moduretics.

It was not the deception – or Warne's "extreme vagueness", as the tribunal put it – that shocked people. His 1994 dalliance with John the bookmaker had already highlighted his talent for omitting incriminating information. His grubby behaviour when caught smoking had exposed his larrikin side; his pestering of an English nurse proved he could be a twerp.

Now a new Warne was emerging. Not a larrikin or twerp, but someone vain and narcissistic, someone altogether less likeable. Stories seeped out of Warne cavorting naked round the Victorian dressing room, nonchalantly parading his incredible physique. Team-mates mocked him for wearing sleeveless shirts in public. This was a man who swallowed one tablet to lose "a double chin" and another to "look nice" for a press conference. This was not a man

Australian dads wanted their sons to aspire to. Better, almost, if he had been a drug cheat. "I used to be sad that Bill O'Reilly wasn't around to enjoy Shane Warne," wrote Neville Ward of Arkstone to the *Sydney Morning Herald*. "Now I'm glad."

Warne, the bowler, plans to bounce back next year. Warne, the man, might find his skinny reputation takes longer to heal.

The World Cup Malcolm Conn, *Wisden Australia* 2003-04

The loss of an unrepentant Shane Warne for the illegal use of a masking agent on the eve of the opening match against Pakistan invigorated the Australians. Remarkably, he was not missed. After being a surprise choice to replace an injured Warne earlier in the summer, Brad Hogg stepped up as an admirable replacement spinner...

Cricket and The Media Alex Buzo, *Wisden Australia* 2003-04

The biological clock said it was time for a Shane Warne scandal and, sure enough, we had one just before the cup was about to start. Many hectares of print were taken up by the diuretic saga but the only succinct commentary was provided by cartoonist Jenny Coopes – who depicted a pedestrian walking past the following newsagents' placards: "War War War Warne War – and by one of Warnie's biographers, Louis Nowra, who wrote in the *Sydney Morning Herald*: "Reading through newspaper pieces on him is to trawl through some of the most pompous, sanctimonious articles and Tall Poppy bashing I have ever read."

Shane Warne: Celebrity in the Firing Line Mark Ray, *Wisden Australia* 2003-04

Is there any event that so excites Australian public interest as the fall of a celebrity? Shane Warne once said his life resembled a soap opera, and his latest misadventures – his one-year suspension for using a prohibited substance and the revelations about his habit of sending messages on his mobile phone to various women – confirm the other talent in his life beside cricket, his propensity for getting into strife.

Apart from the occasional allegation of sledging against him, Warne has never been accused of unfair play. His contributions to the game have been unmatched, albeit under-appreciated in some quarters. Not since Dennis Lillee has there been a cricketer capable of sending such a buzz of anticipation around cricket grounds when thrown the ball for his first over. But the drugs episode is different, as it casts doubt on his integrity. Even if, as he maintains, he took those diuretic tablets without realising they were banned (because of their capacity to mask performance-enhancing drugs), Warne's integrity as a fair-playing cricketer will henceforth be subject to doubt. His status as the first international cricketer to be banned for use of a prohibited substance is a dark blot on his brilliant career. That his evidence before the tribunal that banned him was deemed "not entirely truthful" is another black mark.

Yet the question remains: is Warne more sinned against than sinning? Your answer to that question depends on how you react to his fame and fortune. Do you, above all else, admire his talent and tolerate his human failings? Or do you demand that he uphold the highest standards of public behaviour in all areas of his life? Warne's many detractors follow the latter path and seem to apply higher ethical expectations on the leg-spinner than on politicians, church and business leaders, let alone athletes in other sports.

Perspective is all and in Warne's case it is often blurred. Certainly leading athletes are role models but the expectations on them often appear out of proportion to their influence on society. Corporate crooks, an area of high expertise in Australian life, cost the nation and its hard-working families millions of dollars. Predatory priests and the superiors who protect them ruin innocent lives. These sins cause profound suffering. What has Warne's latest sin cost us? Probably nothing more than a tiny amount of the remaining vestige of faith we have in sports stars. In late July, a Newspoll revealed that two out of three Australians believed the federal government misled them about the reasons for going to war with Iraq. The same poll revealed that none of those questioned would change the way they vote. So, Australians are prepared to be deceived by their political leaders in a matter as serious as war but not by a cricketer in matters as essentially trivial as sport or as private as his personal relationships. Where is the perspective in that?

Social commentator Hugh Mackay, writing in the *Sydney Morning Herald* on July 26, in the middle of a number of sporting contests against New Zealand, discussed this Newspoll and his long-held views about the "disengagement" from public life of contemporary Australian society. "Some things matter and some don't," Mackay wrote. "It doesn't matter how long or short your teenage son wants to wear his hair. It doesn't matter which brand of joggers your children wear. It doesn't matter whether your nail polish absolutely matches your lipstick. It doesn't matter whether New Zealand beats us at netball or football. But surely it does matter if our government has lied to us, again." In discussing this "disengagement" Mackay suggested that being "relaxed and comfortable", Prime Minister John Howard's mantra-like goal, had become a national ambition. If we can vent a little frustration on some sporting miscreant, all the better. It is a convenient distraction from the main game.

Why does Warne attract so much animosity? He is brilliant at what he does but for many his flaws are unforgivable. Actors and pop stars can divorce every two years, spend obscenely, abuse alcohol and narcotics, and trash hotel rooms, but they are treated with fawning affection. Perhaps most Australians are distanced from such superstars because most of us cannot act or sing and have never had pretensions to either. But most male Australians have tried to bowl a leg-break at some stage in their starry-eyed youth. Seeing Warne perform such a difficult feat so easily and so successfully seems to get under the skin of some people, especially the more cynical sports journalists. Many of these people appear to be motivated by little more than envy. In many press boxes you are more likely to hear derisory comments about players' mistakes during a match than praise for their skilful efforts, despite the fact that the journalists are often watching the best in the world. When such journalists get their chance they appease their envy by turning on sports stars with relish. In Warne's case this attitude has led some journalists to argue that Stuart MacGill is a better leg-spinner than Warne. Those who know anything about the game scoff at this suggestion, including MacGill, who acknowledges Warne as the greatest wrist-spinner in history.

Australians have a confused relationship to fame. The traditional Australian attitude of distrusting prominent people is still there somewhere in the national psyche but it is being overpowered by the cult of celebrity. We like to think we distrust fame, yet more often than not we grovel before it. Sections of the media that should have a sceptical attitude to the rich and famous often lead the fawning. The purportedly more serious sections of the media love to attack pretension and mistakes by the rich and famous, yet they still follow the dictates of fame, reporting its most trivial activities and promoting the fashions it creates.

Warne was widely pilloried for claiming he took the diuretic for reasons of vanity. One newspaper described him at a media conference as having "his spiked hair gelled to perfection". This was a cheap shot at his vanity. Yet every newspaper office has people with similarly gelled or fashionable hair. Had Warne turned up looking dishevelled, he would have been accused of disrespect or of not coping with the stress of the drugs affair. In Warne's case every trick is used to sustain the attack.

In one way or another, our consumerist, fame-obsessed swimming in vanity. The public and its media have it both ways. They are obsessed by the doings of the famous – reading and publishing their inanities in interviews, dissecting their so-called private lives and paying to see their mass-produced films or listen to their inane music. It is no coincidence that many film and pop stars want to be sports stars, often cricketers in nations of British background. And no coincidence that many cricketers want to be film or pop stars. These days there is little difference in the worlds they inhabit. It was no coincidence that Warne was a noted guest at actor Russell Crowe's wedding during his enforced absence from the game.

During these controversies, the media took delight in cataloguing Warne's crimes and misdemeanours. Yes, Warne was guilty of making suggestive phone calls to a British nurse. Yes, he smoked before he had fulfilled his contractual obligation to quit. But no, he did not criticise Test team-mate Scott Muller with the infamous words "can't throw, can't bowl". Although voice analysis exonerated him and television footage showed his lips were not moving when those words were spoken, Warne is still accused by many in the media of saying them and considered guilty of doing so by many people.

Warne often does not help himself in this regard. In the midst of his terrible off-season, he accompanied ten ill children to the USA for a Melbourne charity. That organisation and the parents of the children were keen to speak on his behalf, but Warne would not let them. He does a lot of charity work but, unlike Steve Waugh's very public support for needy Indian children, Warne keeps his charity work private.

Warne's admission that he never listened to lectures by sports administrators about banned drugs was seen as further evidence of his stupidity. It confirmed the public's view. Steve Waugh's admission a few days later that he too never listened was largely ignored as it did not fit the public's perception of the intelligent, worldly leader, the man described by John Howard as holding the second-most important job in the country.

That absurd notion brings us to another factor which skews perspective in these matters. Cricket has long assumed the role of sport's moral leader. This stance has been based on a fictional moral history invented by the British Empire. Was it not Neville Cardus who wrote that no one who was not a native speaker of English could ever play cricket properly? Simon Rae's recent book *It's Not Cricket: A History of Skulduggery,*

A fresh-faced Shane Warne at an Australia net session early in 1993. It was in the 1992-93 Test series against West Indies that he burst into the limelight with seven for 52 in the Second Test at Melbourne.

The moment that changed Warne's life: he has just bowled England's Mike Gatting with his first delivery in an Ashes Test. Within days the *Sunday Times* journalist Robin Marlar dubbed it "the ball of the century" and the label stuck.

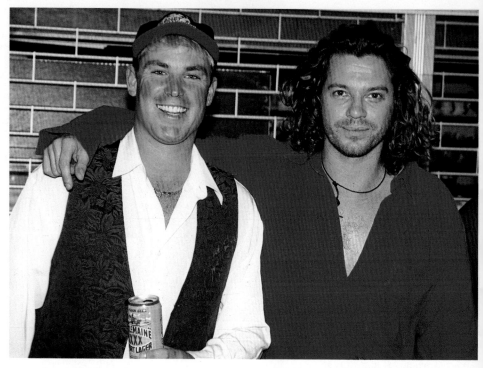

From the start, Warne was comfortable with the celebrity lifestyle. During his first Ashes tour in 1993, he shares a drink with Michael Hutchence, lead singer of the Australian band INXS. © Getty Images

By having Devon Malcolm brilliantly caught by David Boon at short leg, Warne completed a hat-trick in the victory over England at Melbourne during the 1994-95 Ashes series.
© Patrick Eagar/Getty Images

Pakistan batsman Salim Malik hits
Warne through the off side for four
during his 75 on the opening day of
the Third Test in Lahore in November
1994. Later, Warne alleged that Malik
had offered him and teammate Tim
May a bribe to lose this match, and
the first match of the series in Karachi.

© David Munden/Getty Images

Warne's celebrations after Australia had
won at Trent Bridge to complete their fifth
successive Ashes victory in 1997 were
attacked as graceless and over the top.
But he later explained he was reacting to
the way he had been treated by English
crowds. © Clive Mason/Getty Images

Warne and Mark Waugh prepare to face the press at the Adelaide Oval in December 1998 after it was revealed that several years earlier they had accepted money from an Indian bookmaker.
© Laurence Griffiths/Getty Images

During Warne's nine-month absence after surgery on his shoulder, Australia unearthed a new match-winning leg-spinner in Stuart MacGill. As Warne prepared for his comeback against England at Sydney in January 1999, the world pondered what damage they might wreak as a partnership. © Clive Mason/Getty Images

"Come on!" Warne exhorts his teammates after bowling Gary Kirsten to bring Australia back into an epic World Cup semi-final against South Africa at Edgbaston in 1999. He won the match award in this game and the final. © Patrick Eagar/Getty Images

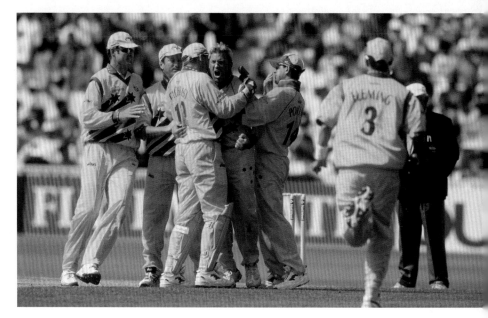

Warne achieved his ambition of captaining Australia in a one-day triangular series against England and Sri Lanka in early 1999. He proved an outstanding leader. Here, he celebrates with Ricky Ponting after victory over England had clinched the tournament title. © William West/Getty Images

Warne has just dismissed New Zealand's Paul Wiseman to complete victory in the First Test of the 1999-2000 series at Eden Park, Auckland. Wiseman was his 356th Test victim – one more than Dennis Lillee's record – making him Australia's leading wicket-taker. © Jack Atley/Getty Images

The most glamorous cricketer in the world gets used to the privations of the tiny dressing-room at Hampshire's Northlands Road ground after beginning his first season in county cricket in 2000. Robin Smith, right, shows the new boy around. © Adrian Dennis/Getty Images

On the eve of the 2003 World Cup in South Africa, Warne failed a drugs test and was banned from the tournament, and subsequently for a year. He makes his way to face the music at a packed press conference.

© Hamish Blair/Getty Images

Warne celebrates after capturing the wicket of Sri Lanka's Sanath Jayasuriya at Galle on his return to Test cricket in March 2004 after being banned for taking an illegal substance. He took ten wickets in the match.

© Hamish Blair/Getty Images

In February 2005, Warne returned to the Galle ground in Sri Lanka and joined forces with his great spin-bowling rival, Muttiah Muralitharan, right, in an effort to boost relief efforts after the Boxing Day tsunami devastated the country. © Getty Images

Warne holds up the ball to an appreciative Old Trafford crowd during the 2005 Ashes, after dismissing England's Marcus Trescothick to become the first man to take 600 Test wickets.
© Alessandro Abbonizio/Getty Images

Warne bids farewell to Test cricket at the Sydney Cricket Ground in January 2007 at the end of a 5-0 whitewash of England. © Mark Nolan/Getty Images

In the inaugural Indian Premier League tournament in 2008, Warne proved an inspirational captain of Rajasthan Royals, steering them to the title. Here, he sets his field during a match against Kolkata Knight Riders. © WENN/Alamy

After retiring as a player, Warne turned his hand to TV commentary. He quickly became outstanding in his new role, an enthusiastic and perceptive observer of the game. His former Australia captain Ricky Ponting was also part of the team for the 2019 Ashes. © Visionhaus/Getty Images

Sharp Practice and Downright Cheating in the Noble Game catalogues cricket's long list of sins, as C. L. R. James's classic *Beyond a Boundary* exposes the game's moral myth-making. This fiction has led to a situation where cricketers are judged by far higher standards than other sports people, standards that have never applied in practice.

A week after the furore about Australia's sledging in the Test match in Antigua in 2002-03, it became known that New South Wales rugby union player Matt Dunning had broken the nose of a team-mate in a drunken fight in public during "traditional" end-of-season celebrations. This attracted a few ripples of comment but hardly the widespread condemnation the cricketers received. In May, St George Illawarra rugby league coach Nathan Brown was fined $10,000 for using the f-word repeatedly during a media conference. Again, the public's response seemed to be: "Oh well, that's football." A cricketer steps out of line a little, say by swearing at an opponent out in the middle of the field, and he is seen as the lowest of the low.

The most damaging drug Warne has taken is the drug of fame. His attitude to fame is not as complex as that of the wider society. He was seduced by it long ago. The result has been that he seems to have to come to believe that he manipulate it and the public's view of him as easily as he can a cricket ball. But the world beyond the boundary is more complex than that. Warne's fumbled attempts to spin himself out of the drugs scandal confirmed this. By using a firm of spin doctors and his contacts in the media – largely the unquestioning Ray Martin on the Nine Network's *A Current Affair* – Warne tried to slip through a vital piece of evidence which had not yet come to light: that he had taken an earlier diuretic which, he thought, had not been detected by an earlier drug test. In fact, it had left detectable traces, but not enough warrant a "charge". This information was known only to one or two people at the Australian Sports Drug Agency. Warne knew nothing of the system, therefore did not realise that there was a chance the Agency already had evidence that he had taken a diuretic before the second testing in December 2002 that led to a positive finding and his suspension. Warne's naive belief in his fame seemed to encourage him and his advisers to think that every Australian believes Ray Martin and would be satisfied by Warne's plea for understanding on *A Current Affair*. But the world is not that simple, neither are some of its lawyers, drug testers and sports administrators.

When society has made you rich and famous for being a great leg-spinner – a talent that requires no moral or social understanding, a talent that is in the end profoundly useless and that came to you largely as a result of natural, unexplained physical talent – It is tempting to think the rest of life might come just as easily. Warne's simple view of life in the fishbowl encourages him to believe that people will fall for equally simplistic explanations. This tendency for famous people to see themselves as somehow beyond normal standards of behaviour is called "pedestal complex" by psychologists. Warne has never realised that smart and cynical people in the world are watching and analysing his every move. Such tactics as his appearance on *A Current Affair* might seem smart to him but to others they are merely more evidence of his disingenuousness.

Ignorance of the law is no excuse. Every professional cricketer should know that he must check the status of every pill he puts in his mouth. On a kind interpretation Warne was extremely foolish to take those pills and, if only to serve as an example to others, deserved his one-year suspension. That the tribunal was not satisfied by his evidence is another concern. That he threatened to sue one newspaper if it ran the story saying he had taken more than one pill, a story that later evidence confirmed was true, suggests either poor management by those around him or a dangerous naivety on Warne's part – or both.

However, it is worth reiterating that Warne has not declared war on anyone, not molested a minor, not swindled gullible people out of their life savings, not assaulted someone in a public brawl. As Hugh Mackay noted in the *Sydney Morning Herald* on July 21, professional athletes are now commodities, often the product of hothouse coaching from their teenage years, who often lack a "realistic appreciation of the place of sport in a balanced life". He continued: "In sport as in merchant banking, politics, medicine or bus driving, some people are pleasant, and some are unpleasant, some have integrity and some don't... So perhaps we shouldn't be too harsh on our sporting stars. If you can bowl a ball – or hit one – with enough skill you too can be a celebrity, right up there with pop stars and an assortment of showbiz wannabes. You will earn a fortune for your efforts, and the rest of us should just clap and cheer, I guess. If you've entertained us, why should we expect you to be nice as well?"

The "text message" scandal reconfirmed Warne's recklessness. English nurse Donna Smith was the first Warne text message recipient to go public and was paid by a tabloid newspaper for her story. Following her example other female gold-diggers were bound to emerge. South African woman Helen Cohen Alon's accusations of phone message harassment were the second instance of this syndrome, and at the time of writing South African police were considering whether to charge her with extortion. As well there was the case of the teenage girl on the Gold Coast who made allegations against Warne and whose uncle was charged with trying to blackmail the then Australian Cricket Board. Then came talk of celebrity manager Harry M. Miller hawking the story of a Melbourne exotic dancer who wanted to tell her affair with the spinner. Not surprisingly James Sutherland, CEO of Cricket Australia, conceded that such accusations were damaging the game. Australia's media, finally following the example of the British tabloids, were more prepared to give space to people claiming to have dirt on a celebrity sportsman's private life. Warne had become a laughing stock in the eyes of the public, and his reputation was damaged badly, perhaps beyond redemption. As Glenn McGrath noted in mid-August, Australian players were not given lessons in handling fame.

Where does all this leave Warne the cricketer? In the lead-up to season 2003-04 there were rumblings that Warne's team-mates might prefer to carry on without him. Warne's career, one that had reached the highest peaks while dabbling in farce, was threatening to end as a sporting tragedy.

WORDS ON WARNE

"Any association Warne has with the Australian team at present is something I'm not comfortable with."

James Sutherland, Cricket Australia Chief Executive – WAC, September 2003

2003

News Register	WCM, April 2003

Hampshire were considering signing Wasim Akram as a replacement for Shane Warne. Warne was due to be their overseas star this season before his drugs ban.

News Register	WCM, May 2003

Despite his ban, Shane Warne received £3,315 from Australia's World Cup prize money on the basis of the number of days each player spent in South Africa. Warne, who returned to South Africa during the World Cup for a series of speaking engagements because they had been pre-arranged, spent ten days with the team before he was sent home. The ACB asked Warne not to play for Kent club Lashings as they do not deem it "appropriate activity".

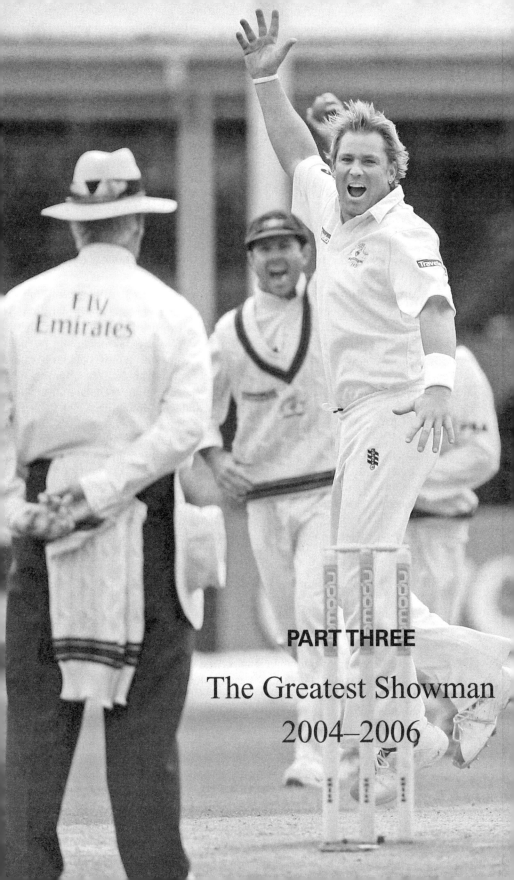

PART THREE

The Greatest Showman

2004–2006

The Greatest Showman:
2004–2006

"The first thing that comes to mind with Warne is his resilience, his adaptability in all facets, in any hemisphere. Then there is his uncomplicated run-up and delivery stride, and his ability to be a shock or stock bowler, which is a testimony to his stamina. And he has that coil-like wrist; he was born for greatness with that first ball he bowled in the UK to Mike Gatting."

Rex Sellers, former Australia leg-spinner, *Wisden Australia* 2004-05

Whatever the depth and breadth of their career portfolio, most sporting greats come to be inextricably associated with one contest, tournament, series or season. For Muhammad Ali, it's his 1974 Rumble in the Jungle victory over George Foreman, for Pelé, the 1970 World Cup, for Michael Jordan, the Chicago Bulls' second hat-trick of NBA titles between 1996 and 1998, and for Olga Korbut, the beguiling performances that brought her three gold medals at the 1972 Olympics.

With Shane Warne, many would opt for the Ashes series in England in 2005, a pulsating five-match contest of sustained drama and brilliance during which two well-matched teams scrapped like bare-knuckle fighters from the first day to the last. Yet, unlike Ali in Zaire, Pelé in Mexico City, Jordan in the United Center or Korbut in the gymnastics hall in Munich, Warne did not emerge as a winner from this epic struggle. It is perhaps the greatest paradox of his career.

When Australia finally surrendered the tiny terracotta urn after 16 years of virtually unchallenged domination on the final day of the Fifth Test at The Oval, Warne was, for the only time in his career, on the wrong side of an Ashes series outcome. Moreover, on that stomach-clenching final day, he had dropped a catch that might have turned the result in Australia's favour. None of this mattered. Over five Tests, Warne's performances were so superhumanly heroic that he earned the admiration and respect of the home crowds. He was serenaded on the Oval outfield with choruses of "We wish you were English."

To take 40 wickets at a fraction under 20 in a losing cause was astonishing (Brett Lee was the next-best Australian with 20), especially when he consistently added useful runs. Only four times has a bowler taken more wickets in an Ashes series. Warne accepted the defeat chivalrously but it hurt. "The image of Warnie sitting shattered in a corner stays with me," wrote Australia captain Ricky Ponting in his autobiography *At The Close of Play*. "He was the one guy in our line-up who'd been at his best."

What made Warne's performances still more remarkable was that his private life was once again in turmoil. He had arrived early in England for a pre-Ashes stint with Hampshire, and was joined by his wife Simone and their three children just before the First Test at Lord's. But within days of their arrival they were heading back to Australia after Warne featured in another rash of kiss-and-tell front-pages. It put him under extreme stress – "I would just go back to my hotel room and drink," he admitted in the

2022 Netflix documentary *Shane* – but did not seem to impact on his cricket. Australia coach John Buchanan, with whom Warne had an uneasy relationship, asked him how he did it. "He told me no matter what else was happening in his life, he could close the door on it and arrive at a cricket ground 'fresh and relaxed' and ready to play," Buchanan said.

Defeat in England banished any thoughts Warne might be harbouring about retirement. He could not leave the stage with the Ashes in English custody. When the rivalry resumed at Brisbane in November 2006, Australia were tuned to concert pitch. They won the First Test comfortably but England seemed to have regrouped in the second at the Adelaide Oval. On the fourth evening, Warne ordered room-service pizza and watched the film *American Pie* with teammate Michael Clarke. England were 59 for one, 97 ahead and apparently safe on a pitch on which both first innings had topped 500. But Warne glimpsed the possibility of victory where none seemed to exist. He convinced Ponting that if Australia took early wickets, England would not know whether to defend or attack, and may not be able to establish a lead that was beyond Australia's reach.

It worked out exactly as he had envisaged. In two hours, the force of Warne's personality as much as his bowling mesmerised England. At lunch they were 89 for five and teetering on the edge of the abyss. By tea they were 129 all out, leaving Australia ruthlessly to chase down in 32.5 overs to complete one of the most extraordinary come-from-behind victories in Ashes history. Hollywood would have been proud to have scripted such a heist. "Warne is the great eater of minds," wrote Simon Barnes in *The Times*. "His spinning of cricket balls is a secondary talent; his biggest talent is centrifuging the souls of his opponents. What we saw on that long, sad Tuesday was a succession of cricketers who unmistakably lost their minds in their attempt to play Warne."

Naturally, Warne took the wicket that ensured the Ashes were regained in the next Test at Perth, which left him free to contemplate the future. "What I would like is to finish on my own terms," he had told Gideon Haigh in an interview in *The Wisden Cricketer* in March 2004. Now he could. In the build-up to the Boxing Day Test at the MCG, his home ground, Warne announced he would retire from international cricket at the end of the series. "Australian cricket will miss him terribly and so will we all," said Derek Pringle in *The Daily Telegraph*.

He was not quite done. During the afternoon session of the opening day of the Fourth Test, he bowled Andrew Strauss for his 700th Test wicket, prompting a volcanic eruption of noise from the majority of the 89,155 present. "Warne's introduction had the effect of a detonator," wrote Greg Baum in his *Almanack* match report. In his swansong at Sydney, he took his career tally to 708 wickets while a *Wisden* table revealed that a staggering 63% of his 145 Test appearances had ended in victories. As he strolled around the outfield with his children and fellow retirees Glenn McGrath and Justin Langer, it was clear that a golden era had ended.

It was all a far cry from the beginning of 2004 when there was speculation about whether Warne would have the hunger to return after the furore over his year-long drugs ban. In his comeback Test against Sri Lanka at Galle, he took ten wickets and helped inspire Australia to a stirring victory. The doubters should have known better.

RW

2003-04

News Register   *WCM*, June 2003

Shane Warne was on the ACB's 25-man list of contracted players for the 2003-04 season, although he was to be paid on a pro-rata basis. Michael Clarke, on tour in the West Indies, was included for the first time.

The XI Best Shane Warne Deliveries   Greg Baum, *TWC*, December 2003

1. Mike Gatting – bowled, Old Trafford 1993

This is where Warne started. He had been a Test player for less than 18 months. It was his first ball in England, his first in Ashes cricket, and the captain of all deliveries. The look on Gatting's face, as if he had just seen a flying saucer, told us that all the old verities were defunct – something new and impossible was among us. Some batsmen are defined by a single innings; Warne is defined by this one ball.

2. Graham Gooch – bowled, Edgbaston 1993

Warne bowled Gooch around his legs with a ball that pitched so wide and spun so far that not even that imposing batsman's left leg, fully outstretched, could keep it out. Now all England knew that not even textbook defensive technique would be enough.

3. Richie Richardson – bowled, Melbourne 1992-93

Warne announced himself by bowling Australia to a rare victory over West Indies with seven wickets. The keepsake wicket was captain Richardson, a peculiar ball that scuttled like a crab under his hesitant defence. It is odd to think we were still learning the name of this new ball, the flipper. Before Warne a flipper was for swimming.

4. Shivnarine Chanderpaul – bowled, Sydney 1996-97

Chanderpaul hit Warne out of the attack in a furious counter-charge on the last morning. Warne, recalled for the over before lunch, gave one ball such a rip it seemed his surgically tightened shoulder tendons would loosen again. It looked to be going to Taylor at slip but rounded on Chanderpaul (who was shaping to cut) like a slobbering bloodhound and spun so far it would have missed leg stump had it not cannoned off the batsman's back leg.

5. Herschelle Gibbs – bowled, Edgbaston 1989

Australia's World Cup campaign looked destined to end until Warne produced a fiendish leg-spinner that turned Gibbs inside out and bowled him. It was the one-day equivalent of the Gatting ball. Both teams later said it had changed the course of the match.

6. Daryll Cullinan – bowled, Sydney 1993-94

Cullinan's cocksure attitude irritated Warne when South Africa returned to the Test fold – a bad mistake. Warne shot a flipper like a pip beneath the uncomprehending Cullinan's bat. Strictly, no Cullinan wicket should belong in this collection because they were fish in a barrel to Warne, but the macabre theatre they provided was always irresistible.

7. Basit Ali – bowled, Sydney 1995-96

With one ball remaining in the day's play, Warne and Ian Healy made an elaborate show of consulting mid-pitch whereupon Warne bowled Basit Ali with a ball that fizzed through his legs. Keeper and bowler claimed it was as they had planned it.

8. Alec Stewart – bowled, Brisbane 1994-95

Warne's three-card trick. Stewart cut a fast, flat ball for four. Warne muttered and cursed and scratched his head as if he didn't know what had gone wrong. The next ball looked the same but by the time it dawned on Stewart that it was the deadly flipper, he was bowled. Mike Atherton had fallen similarly, and soon both Englishmen were on the roof of the old commentary box at the Gabba, binoculars in hand, trying to fathom the secrets.

9. Jacques Kallis – bowled, Sydney 1997-98

The apocalypse looked to be upon us. As lightning crackled and thunder rumbled, a Warne top-spinner burrowed through where there had been no gap in Kallis's sandbagged defence. It was his 300th wicket. Warne shot out South Africa and within an hour another Test was over.

10. Brian Lara – caught behind, Adelaide 1996-97

Lara was bravely propping up a lost cause until he misunderstood an apparent leg-break that instead slid on with the arm, nicked the outside edge and nestled in Healy's gloves. Not a spectacular wicket in its mechanics but important because it showed that Warne had tricks even for left-handers.

11. Inzamam ul-Haq – last ball, Karachi 1994-95

So good it was too good. Pakistan were nine down and trailing by two as Inzamam shuffled down to drive to midwicket, where Warne had left a tempting gap. It was the springing of a trap. At the key moment the ball dipped and spun past Inzamam's bat, flicked his pad, missed off stump by a whisker and flew past the aghast Healy, who thought it must hit the stumps. Four leg-byes and match over. There have been many like it but none with such profound consequences.

Letters

TWC, January 2004

Regarding the Warne ball which dismissed Richie Richardson (The XI best Shane Warne deliveries, *TWC*, Dec), surely the flipper has a long history. There's a story about "Tich" Freeman showing his repertoire to an umpire: one ball was a flipper and the story ends with the umpire joining in the appeal!
Richard Fleet, Berkhamsted, Herts

I enjoyed reading The XI best Shane Warne deliveries but I was surprised to read that "before Warne a flipper was for swimming". The flipper was an important and successful part of Richie Benaud's armoury throughout his career and was one of the skills that helped him to 248 Test wickets.
Les Horner, Keighley, Yorks

© Nick Newman

News Register

WAC, December 2003

Shane Warne may end up as a film star in Hollywood at the conclusion of his cricket career, according to his manager Michael Cohen. "I definitely think that Hollywood would be an option for Shane," Cohen was quoted as saying. "He's good looking, he has a tremendous brain and he's a natural in front of the cameras."

News: Bets Are Off

TWC, January 2004

Shane Warne's brother and manager Jason has denied claims that Shane was given free betting money to spend in casinos. The claim was made in a book by Graham Halbish, a former ACB chief executive. Jason Warne dismissed the claims saying: "It's not 100% factual so we have nothing to say on it."

The Indians in Australia 2003-04

Sambit Bal, *Wisden* 2005

If there was less discussion about Australia missing Shane Warne, who was serving a 12-month drugs ban, it was because he had been collared by the Indians before. Warne remained a presence in the Channel Nine commentary box, occasionally straying into the press box to pick a bone with a journalist or two.

Shane Warne hinted that he wants to return to one-day internationals once his 12-month suspension for taking a banned substance is lifted on February 10. Warne announced his retirement from one-day cricket shortly before the 2003 World Cup to concentrate on prolonging his Test career. After a year-long break, Warne now feels that he can play in both forms of the game.

A Hero at Home?   Soumya Bhattacharya, *WAC*, June 2004

I still have the email. An Australian friend at the *Sydney Morning Herald* had sent it after Sachin Tendulkar had scored 241 not out at the SCG this year. "What an innings! It is such a pleasure to watch a player who is a delight on the field and a role model off it. The longer a disgrace like Shane Warne stays out of the Australian team the better."

Warne, the man who turned the waddle into a statement, who dusted off the art of leg-spin from cricket's history books and transformed it into one of the most compelling aspects of the contemporary game, a disgrace? Sorry, mate, I don't get this, I would have said, had I not been in Australia for more than a month by then.

When I got the message, though, I had got the message. I had heard the same thing over and over again ever since I had arrived in Sydney. I had the attitude sussed; but it seemed no less intriguing in spite of its familiarity.

But get this: Shane Warne is not half the hero we think he is in Australia. Correction: Shane Warne is not half the hero in Australia that he is in other parts of the cricket-playing world.

It's to do with a sense of typically Australian anxiety (which dominates the country's collective consciousness) about how they want to be seen by the rest of the world; about the gap between who they really are and who we think they really are.

For a nation so anxious about its identity, it's unsurprising that Australians fret about stereotypes. The construct of the sport-crazy Australian fan goes something like this: he – and it is almost always a he – is never seen without a pint of beer in his hand; his swagger matches his team's abilities; he adores players who play hard and party harder. The iconic hero for this fan is a cricketer who is charismatic, a swashbuckler, a wizard on the pitch, a hell-raiser off it. In short, someone who is rather like Shane Warne.

Nothing could be further from the truth.

Aussies have a word for Warne; they call him a "yobbo". They do not for a moment doubt that he is the most potent match-winning bowler Australia has produced in the last decade. But role model he is not. Not many Australian parents want their sons to grow up and become like Warne. Well, they'd love to see them play like Warne; but they'd want them to behave like Steve Waugh or Sachin Tendulkar. Warne perfectly fits the template of the stereotype of the cricketer who should be the idol of the typical Australian fan we have from popular imagination. Trouble is, the template is flawed.

Ricky Ponting must have realised this to some extent. His image makeover – from pub brawler to crown prince of Australian cricket to its undisputed king and genial ambassador – has seen the numbers of his fans rise meteorically in the recent past. Waugh has the following he has in the country because of his roots (working-class boy from Bankstown in Sydney), what he has made of them (one of the richest players in Australia) and how he has not let that change his life (he is a proud husband, a doting father and well documented do-gooder). Tendulkar's following in Australia has as much to do with his status as the best batsman in the world as with the dignity with which he conducts his private life.

The Wisden Cricketer, March 2004

Tendulkar, of course, is rooted in the middle-class values that Indian tradition celebrates; at the same time he is a poster boy for the kind of post-modern, 21st century (shining, if you will) India that we love to believe we belong to. It is difficult to place – or match – those parameters in an Australian context. But solid middle-class values seem to be qualities that Australians prize. A recent poll to determine what defines the Australian male revealed that being attached to the family is at the top of the agenda, a quality at odds with the beer-swilling Australian of popular perception.

The image that we have of the Australian cricket fan is a myth. Thing is, you won't be able to tell unless you've had a few glasses of wine (yes, another survey shows Aussies prefer wine to beer) with him.

Interview   Gideon Haigh, *TWC*, March 2004

"It is sometimes not a bad thing for a professional sportsman to sit in the crowd and watch from the other side. It is a reminder of how much you miss it when it's not there."

When Shane Warne confided this reflection in *My Autobiography* in 2001, it was with regard to past incidences of involuntary spectating rather than an expectation of a future exile. But at the end of perhaps the most frustrating year of his career, during which he has seldom been fitter and never less occupied, it is too tempting not to ask him how the thesis stands up.

Pretty well, he reckons: "I did write that. And it is true. When you're watching, in fact, you tend to pick up other things. Sledging. Style of play. Appealing. Body language. Which, when you're involved in the game, you're less aware of, because you're focused on the match and your opposition; because you're emotional. Some of the things I've seen I've learned from. I might even have been guilty of them a few times in my career."

Not, Warne admits, despite a season behind the microphone in the Channel 9 commentary box while suspended for the heedless popping of a banned diuretic, that he is one of nature's watchers. "I've enjoyed the commentating," he says. "They've all looked after me in the box, and I think I'm quite good at it. I mean, I do love cricket, and I've watched more of it than I ever have this summer. But I'm not someone who has to watch it all the time. If someone's been bowling a good spell, one of the quicks, or MacGill, or Katich, or one of the batsmen have gotten on top, I've watched it pretty closely. But I prefer doing it. There've been times when Zimbabwe and Bangladesh have played this summer when I've had a bit of a snooze."

Watching the World Cup, which should have been the crowning glory of Warne's limited-overs career, was particularly difficult; sitting up late at night to follow his mates in the West Indies a little less so, though still frustrating. But Warne operates in a negativity no-fly zone. "I'm looking at the positive side," is a phrase he scatters freely in conversation, and he manages to make it sound like a creed rather than merely a cliché.

The loss of a year? Think again. Warne regards it as the gaining of two – at least – on the end of what might by now have been a completed career. Positive person? Warne agrees he is: "Maybe that's why I play cricket the way I do." Perhaps it's intrinsic to leg-spin. Remember how Richie Benaud was nicknamed Diamonds, because "Dusty" Rhodes thought that if he put his head in a bucket of shit, he'd come up with a mouthful of gems. Warne would find at least a pile of casino chips.

Even the indiscretion that cost him the year has been rationalised away. Warne dismisses it as "not checking a book" – the book that would have told him that the fluid tablets he took had the "potential" to act as masking agents for steroids – with the implication that checking a book is something it's a bit hard to expect of people.

The only question that gives him pause, even momentarily, is what might have happened had he received the two-year ban many thought *de rigueur*. "Not sure. Don't know. What I would say is that, if I'd been guilty of trying to hide something, if I'd taken the diuretic to cover up a performance-enhancing drug, I should have been rubbed out for life. But I didn't."

So is there anything he has missed? The answer is interesting. "I've had a fair bit of contact with the guys over the last year. Darren Lehmann, Punter, Damien Martyn, Binger, Haydos. In fact I'm catching up with Punter tonight. But it's different to when we're playing. You know the thing I really enjoy about walking onto a field for a game – any game, whether it's a Test, or a one-dayer, or a club game? It's that you don't know what's going to happen. You don't know whether you're going to knock 'em over, or you're going to get slogged, whether you'll have a bad day, or take a couple of screamers." The baggy green? "Yeah, don't get me wrong. That means a lot to me. But what I miss when I'm not playing is that unpredictability."

What he would not miss is the unpredictability of his personal life, which reached something of a zenith last August when he was accused of harassment by a South African model and of infidelity by a Melbourne stripper. "He told me he had an open marriage," said the latter on television. "I asked him about his wife and he led me to believe they weren't together." And for a time, they almost weren't. Simone, whom Warne married in September 1995, took their daughters Brooke and Summer and went to live with her parents; Warne was left with his son Jackson in the palatial residence that he has spent almost three years turning into a cricketer's Xanadu: complete with cinema and popcorn machine.

Warne is less positive and forthcoming where marriage is concerned. "Marriage is a tough job at the best of times," he says. "Simone and I have been through a lot together, most of which, unfortunately, has been my fault. But that's in the past now, and we're looking forward to getting on with our lives." If he doesn't invite you further, that's because the media has tended to make itself welcome into Warne's personal life regardless; the extent of intrusion last year startled even a hardened campaigner like Warne. On one occasion, Warne and his wife agreed to meet for a conciliatory talk in his car in Port Melbourne; within 10 minutes, two Channel 7 vehicles containing film crews had pulled up on either side, boxing them in. "I still don't know how it happened," says Warne, "If you hear anything, let me know."

Publicly, mind you, Warne handled this affair perhaps better than any other in his career, maintaining his silence and his dignity while all about him were losing theirs, and at the height of hysteria rather shrewdly disappearing to Spain and the UK. Whose idea was that? "Mine. Well, both of ours. I said: 'Where would you like to go Simone?' She said: 'Spain.' I said: 'Let's go.'"

It proved a tonic. It turned out that, in this affair, being suspended had advantages, there being no need to create a pretence of normality and continue playing cricket. Observers were also relieved of the unedifying spectacle of Cricket Australia acting as a moral arbiter. Where Warne's indiscretions with a nurse three and a half years ago cost him the Australian vice-captaincy, Cricket Australia CEO James Sutherland this time offered support: "There are obligations and standards incumbent on players, but there is also a boundary between their public lives and their lives as private citizens."

Warne appreciated Sutherland's sensitivity; indeed, he thinks highly of the administrator, who is, of course, a former Victorian teammate. But the irony of the situation was not lost on Warne, who commented tartly in *My Autobiography* that Cricket Australia's directors paid too much attention to the media, and that the relationship between sins and first stones might profitably be explored: "I wonder what might happen if the backgrounds of the 14 directors themselves were investigated. If the same rules apply, as they should, then they, too, must have led unblemished lives or they are not fit to do their jobs."

"Well, maybe they read my book and took the advice," Warne jokes now. "But yes, one minute my personal life was their affair; next minute it was none of their business.

Then again, there wasn't really much they would do. I wasn't vice-captain any more. I was a contracted player but the contract was suspended and I was receiving no money. If that had been their attitude in 2000, then I might have stayed vice-captain and things might be different today. Who knows?"

Who does? If the rigour of his regimen is anything to go by, Warne certainly planning to be around for a while. In line with Terry Jenner's advice, he did not recommence bowling too early. But since he resumed training on December 27, his routine has involved three bowling sessions a week of 50 deliveries each, bike rides, swimming sessions, sprint work, weight programmes, skipping, boxing and karate. His cross-training has even involved kicks of the football with his friend Aaron Hamill of the St Kilda Australian rules club, where Warne played in the reserve grades 15 years ago and which over the years has been a favourite haunt. Nobody seriously doubts that Warne's old Test berth is his for the taking, and that he will form part of the team Ricky Ponting leads to Sri Lanka for the tour beginning on March 8. It might be a year since his last game, but it is only two years since perhaps his best: that 100th Test in Cape Town where he extracted eight wickets from 98 overs, scored 63 and 15 not out, and won it almost single-handedly.

The question is not so much about his place in the Australian team as it is about his role in Australian cricket. Times are changing. Warne may have extended his career, but under what circumstances will it be played? On more than one occasion, Warne has said he would have enjoyed playing for Australia during the 1970s. He has been thinking primarily of the scrutiny of players' lives, but there is also the issue of the way the game is played.

Warne's approach to cricket suggests a player not completely at ease with Buchananite precepts. In *My Autobiography*, he confessed a preference for using "the old brain" when he played; computers could only be a "back-up". He now goes a little further: too much analysis of cricket can be harmful. "When you come off the field, I think you have a bit of a chat, think about the things you got right, what you might do differently, then you move on, and you pick it up the next day. The danger is that if there's too much analysis, people get confused, or bored, or switch off."

His admiration for the encyclopaedic but intuitive Ian Chappell, with whom he is now close enough to have played a seven-hour game of backgammon in Darwin during the Test against Bangladesh, is unstinting. "We check up on him," says Warne. "We'll look up a game he's talking about, and once or twice what he remembers as a 50 turns out to be a 15, but we hardly ever catch him out. I've never met anyone with his memory for games."

Warne reckons his mindset is similar. "I'm pretty good. The one-dayers, they get a bit blurred. I've played several against South Africa in Johannesburg, for instance, and I have a bit of trouble telling them apart. But I do think I read the game well. I understand it. I've enjoyed my opportunities as a leader. I enjoy the role of a senior player, and hopefully my experience can make a contribution to the team in future." The opportunity to skipper Hampshire, too, was fundamental to his decision to take up the cudgels there again this season.

What about the end? When we digress, as two Melburnians are wont to do, into the *lingua franca* of Aussie rules footy, I remind him one of St Kilda's best games last season, the finale to the career of their indestructible Nathan Burke. The crowd's salute to Burke at the end of the game was definitely one of the more moving tributes to a player I can remember – the St Kilda fan next to me burst into tears, the Richmond fans who'd seen their team utterly thrashed solemnly shook hands with their counterparts, as though at a funeral.

Is this what Warne would like? Something simply spontaneous and demotic in front of a home crowd. Or would he prefer a Waugh-like pageant, in which each city has the opportunity to say farewell and vice versa? Excitement about his career's resumption, it turns out, hasn't curtailed consideration of its conclusion. "What I would like is to finish on my own terms," Warne says. "I think I deserve that." He doesn't believe that his lost year will tempt him to play more cricket than he should. "There's plenty of it, though, isn't there?" he says. "Too much, really." But, at the moment, better too much than not enough.

CLASSIC TEST 6

Sri Lanka v Australia, Galle   Paul Coupar, *Wisden* 2005
(First Test)
March 8, 9, 10, 11, 12 – Australia won by 197 runs. Toss: Australia. Debut: A. Symonds.

After the first innings of this fabulous Test, Sri Lanka's position looked as impregnable as the stone fort that dwarfs the Galle stadium. They had a lead of 161, the world's most complete spinner ready to bowl on an arid pitch, and history overwhelmingly in their favour – only nine Test sides since 1900 had overcome such a deficit and won. Ponting's honeymoon as Test captain looked likely to last around four days.

But Australia turned it round. The last Tests to see such a swing pivoted round a freakishly brilliant spell by Shoaib Akhtar for Pakistan against New Zealand at Wellington ten weeks earlier and a miraculous innings by V. V. S. Laxman for India against Australia at Kolkata in 2000-01. This time it was just hard cricket and self-belief that won it. In horrible heat, Hayden hit a century of little style but match-changing substance, and the middle order ground Sri Lanka into the dust. Warne and MacGill then bowled them out on the last afternoon. But it was Australia's batsmen who manufactured the win.

Australia made four changes to the side that had struggled against India's batsmen at Sydney two months before. Warne, available after a 12-month drugs ban, was predictably, and gladly, welcomed straight back. Kasprowicz was recalled in place of the injured Lee, and Lehmann stepped into Steve Waugh's huge shoes. English-born Andrew Symonds played as an off-spinning all-rounder; had he chosen England, his Test debut would probably have come much earlier. As it was, he had played a record 94 one-day internationals before he displaced poor Simon Katich who was dropped the Test after scoring a century.

Sri Lanka began with a clear plan: prepare a bone-dry pitch and pack the side with spinners, five in total. One visiting journalist, looking at the wicket set in a lush outfield, said it was the first time he'd seen a drought 22 yards long and three yards wide. It is not the normal response to a visit from Shane Warne, so it was risky but, for the first two days, it worked. The pitch did turn but only slowly, and too many Australian batsmen were over-keen to make an attacking statement. Lehmann reached the top score of 63 before being flummoxed by Muralitharan's doosra, one of his six victims for 59. Australia's 220 looked paltry.

In reply, Sri Lanka showed the patience Australia lacked. After a hot, tough second day they were 132 ahead, with four wickets standing and the match under control. Dilshan, who used his feet and a straight bat to make 104, continued his golden form from the England series. But in fading light he top-edged a pull against the second new ball. It was reward for the persevering attack and it kept the door an inch open for Australia.

On day three, the most gripping of a gripping series, they somehow prised it open. Sri Lanka's last wickets fell quickly, as Samaraweera, the final recognised batsman, made a poor 36 not out, neither shepherding the tail nor playing shots. Then, in blazing afternoon heat, and on a wearing pitch, Australia began the long trek towards safety. Hayden led the way. He put on 91 with Langer and 84 with Ponting, before running him out. It was as compelling as cricket gets: some of the world's best batsmen against Murali. Despite several scrapes, Hayden attacked sensibly and refused to let the bowler settle. By the close, he had 106 of Australia's 193 for two.

Hayden was finally caught at slip on the fourth morning. He had battled more than five hours for 130, using little more than the sweep shot, iron willpower and a multi-coloured umbrella, brought on to provide welcome shade during breaks in play. Martyn then stockpiled runs unobtrusively, making his first Test hundred in two years. And Lehmann, less studious, followed three balls later. They were so successful that, despite five expensive wickets for Murali (giving him match figures of 11 for 212), Australia could even declare, 351 ahead.

Sri Lanka's spirits had wilted, and they managed just 154. Their demoralised batsmen fell to a masterly display of controlled leg-spin from Warne, in his first post-ban Test. As he approached 500 wickets, the "Warnie Wicket Count", painted on a bedsheet by the travelling Australian fans, ticked on, while the huge sign counting Murali's wickets was stuck on 496. They started the last day level. Atapattu fended a quicker ball – 497. Dilshan played inside the straight one – 498. Jayawardene edged to slip – 499. And finally, at 1.38 p.m., with the Dutch fort and most of Australia behind him, Warne found Tillekeratne's top edge and became only the second man in history, after Courtney Walsh, to 500. The last three wickets were a formality, though Dharmasena provided not only Warne's tenth victim of the match – one behind Murali – but Hayden's seventh catch, equalling the Test record. Australia won by 197 runs: comebacks don't come much more comprehensive.

Man of the Match: M. L. Hayden

Sri Lanka v Australia, Galle, 2004

AUSTRALIA	_First innings_			_Second innings_	
J. L. Langer c Sangakkara b Dharmasena	12	–	lbw b Jayasuriya		32
M. L. Hayden c Chandana b Muralitharan	41	–	c Jayawardene b Muralitharan		130
*R. T. Ponting st Sangakkara b Chandana	21	–	run out (Chandana/Sangakkara)		28
D. R. Martyn c Jayawardene b Dharmasena	42	–	c sub (K. S. Lokuarachchi) b Muralitharan		110
D. S. Lehmann b Muralitharan	63	–	c and b Muralitharan		129
A. Symonds c Jayawardene b Muralitharan	0	–	st Sangakkara b Muralitharan		24
†A. C. Gilchrist c Dharmasena b Muralitharan	4	–	lbw b Chandana		0
S. K. Warne c Sangakkara b Vaas	23	–	st Sangakkara b Muralitharan		0
J. N. Gillespie not out	4	–	not out		11
M. S. Kasprowicz b Muralitharan	1	–	not out		3
S. C. G. MacGill lbw b Muralitharan	0				
B 3, lb 6	9		B 15, lb 28, nb 2		45

1/31 (1) 2/62 (2) 3/76 (3) **220** 1/91 (1) (8 wkts dec.) **512**
4/148 (4) 5/153 (6) 2/175 (3) 3/245 (2)
6/163 (7) 7/215 (5) 8/219 (8) 4/451 (4) 5/480 (5)
9/220 (10) 10/220 (11) 6/498 (6) 7/498 (7) 8/498 (8)

First innings—Vaas 12–2–39–1; Dharmasena 20–4–52–2; Muralitharan 21.3–5–59–6; Chandana 14–1–59–1; Jayasuriya 1–0–2–0.

Second innings—Vaas 27–3–67–0; Dharmasena 24–1–100–0; Muralitharan 56–9–153–5; Dilshan 6–3–9–0; Jayasuriya 14.3–2–38–1; Chandana 24.3–2–102–1.

SRI LANKA	_First innings_			_Second innings_	
M. S. Atapattu b Gillespie	47	–	c Hayden b Warne		16
S. T. Jayasuriya lbw b Warne	35	–	(5) c Hayden b MacGill		5
†K. C. Sangakkara c and b Kasprowicz	22	–	(2) lbw b Kasprowicz		7
D. P. M. D. Jayawardene c Hayden b Symonds	68	–	(3) c Hayden b Warne		21
T. M. Dilshan c Langer b Kasprowicz	104	–	(4) lbw b Warne		6
*H. P. Tillekeratne lbw b Warne	33	–	c Symonds b Warne		25
T. T. Samaraweera not out	36	–	b MacGill		15
U. D. U. Chandana c Gilchrist b Warne	27	–	c Langer b MacGill		43
W. P. U. J. C. Vaas c Hayden b MacGill	0	–	not out		10
H. D. P. K. Dharmasena c Hayden b Warne	6	–	c Hayden b Warne		0
M. Muralitharan c and b Warne	0	–	st Gilchrist b MacGill		0
B 2, nb 1	3		B 4, w 1, nb 1		6

1/53 (2) 2/92 (3) 3/123 (1) **381** 1/14 (2) 2/41 (1) **154**
4/198 (4) 5/298 (6) 6/323 (5) 3/49 (4) 4/56 (3)
7/369 (8) 8/372 (9) 9/381 (10) 10/381 (11) 5/56 (5) 6/89 (7) 7/119 (6)
8/153 (8) 9/153 (10) 10/154 (11)

First innings—Gillespie 28–9–61–1; Kasprowicz 23–3–56–2; Warne 42.4–9–116–5; Symonds 19–3–68–1; MacGill 22–4–69–1; Lehmann 2–0–9–0.

Second innings—Warne 15–5–43–5; Gillespie 9–2–20–0; Kasprowicz 5–1–13–1; MacGill 16.2–2–74–4.

Umpires: R. E. Koertzen and. D. R. Shepherd.   Third umpire: M. G. Silva.
Referee: B. C. Broad

WORDS ON WARNE

"Abdul Qadir was the best spinner I have ever seen for his unbelievable variety if not anything else. He made leg-spin acceptable, Warne made it fashionable."

Iqbal Qasim, former Pakistan left-arm spinner – *WAC*, February 2004

Sri Lanka v Australia, Kandy Paul Coupar, *Wisden* 2005
(Second Test, March 16-20)

Sri Lankan smiles were doubly broad because, when Kasprowicz was bowled, local hero Muralitharan had his 500th wicket. Congratulatory banners unfurled in the ground, and firecrackers echoed off the green hillsides as news spread. But it proved a bittersweet game for Murali, partly because Warne had beaten him to 500 in the previous Test and claimed another ten here, and partly because fleet-footed Australian batting in the second innings forced him to retreat into a containing round-the-wicket line. The key battle of the series had been won.

The Australians in Sri Lanka 2003-04 Paul Coupar, *Wisden* 2005

Both Murali and Warne began the series approaching 500 Test wickets, and the Great Race became an extraordinary sideshow, heavily pushed by the cash-strapped home board who hoped, mistakenly, it might boost abysmal Test attendances. The race was won by Warne. After his year-long ban for taking a prohibited drug, he returned better than before, ripping his leg-break a touch harder. Helped by receptive pitches, tight support bowling and a lean physique, he took 26 wickets at 20.03, and his control proved crucial on last-day pitches. Without him, Galle and Colombo might have been draws.

Warne's Moments of Magic Peter Roebuck, *WAC*, April 2004

1. 7 for 32 v West Indies, Melbourne, 1992-93

Everyone remembers the breakthrough. Everyone remembers the day, hour and minute when a man sets himself apart. In Warne's case, it was a single delivery. Till this match, Warne was not so much a performer as an idea, scarcely midway between promise and achievement. Then came a teasing, probing spell on a wearing pitch. Then came a ball to Richie Richardson that was like a bolt from the blue.

Warne had been toiling away, bowling very accurately but without penetration. He was a novice and felt it in front of a huge crowd in a great stadium. With the match evenly poised, he decided to try his flipper, an unknown and unreliable ball in his armoury. It was a gamble that paid dividends. The ball was perfectly pitched and heavily disguised.

Richardson did not pick it. Imagining it dropping short, he shaped to pull. At the last minute he realised his mistake, understood that the delivery was a temptation from Eve, but it was too late. After pitching, the ball skidded like a puck along ice, whereupon Warne raised his arms in triumph. He did not look back. Richardson's successors were mesmerised. Warne had won a match for his country. He was on his way.

2. 78 runs and 6 for 161 v South Africa, Cape Town, 2001-02

Warne's hundredth Test match was a memorable occasion. Doubtless the young surfer and footy player from Melbourne was as much amazed as delighted that spinning a cricket ball could take a man so far. To mark the occasion he flew his family across the world to watch. He has always had a strong sense of cricket history and his place in it.

Warne rewarded his followers with a characteristically wholehearted performance that helped his team to victory in a crucial and keenly contested match. He bowled tirelessly almost throughout South Africa's long second innings, holding his side together as the hosts threatened to take charge. Combining commitment, accuracy and imagination, Warne's effort said as much about the man as the bowler. He bowled 70 overs in the innings, scored 78 runs for once out, and was the decisive influence in a match played between proud teams seeking to establish their supremacy.

3. 5 for 43 v Sri Lanka, Galle, 2003-04

Warne had been in trouble again. Banned for a year after substances were found in his bloodstream, he had been busying himself with commentary and other trifles. A light had been turned off in his life. He could not perform, could not compete, could not squeeze the last drop from his gift. Naturally he yearned to return to the cricket field where he belonged, yearned for the satisfaction of wickets and the glories of victory.

By the time the team was chosen for the tour to Sri Lanka, Warne had been away for a long time. Inside he worried that he would perhaps not be able to recapture his former abilities. Accordingly the first match of the series in Sri Lanka was crucial to his state of mind. Australia conceded a substantial lead but fought back so effectively that their opponents faced the task of batting through the last day to save the match.

Warne went to work. From the depths of his memory and the forefront of his ambitions he summoned a dazzling display of flight and guile that destroyed the Sri Lankan batting order. Batsmen lunged forwards and were taken at slip. They lunged at the pitch of the ball and were deceived. Every delivery was part of the plot, a dipping, curling, wicked invitation to self-destruction. Warne took his 500th wicket in Test cricket. He bowled Australia to a famous victory. He was back.

4. 7 for 23 v Pakistan, Brisbane, 1995-96

Sometimes figures tell the story. With this performance Shane Warne proved how much he had changed the game. Few men had the ability required to challenge orthodox thinking. Cricket had convinced itself that spin no longer mattered. Slow bowlers were dismissed as "step and fetch it" merchants. Warne changed all of that with a superb performance on a pitch that traditionally favours faster bowlers. He marched into the front room of his rival and produced a performance that brooked no argument.

By taking 7 for 23 Warne confirmed that the Pakistanis were not as comfortable against the turning ball as had been supposed. He demonstrated that a leg-spinner could demolish a Test side on a dry pitch for a handful of runs. In many ways this performance was Warne's statement of greatness. He created havoc in the opposition ranks, dominated with his brain as much as his prodigious skills.

With this withering spell Warne scattered to the winds all remaining doubts about the value of spin, especially wrist-spin, in top class cricket. Suddenly the period of West Indian domination seemed long ago and far away. Cricket had recovered its sense of adventure. Warne had reminded the world about his game's possibilities. In a time of the machine, he had reasserted the value of the individual.

5. 6 for 64 & 3 for 16 v England, Melbourne, 1994-95

Warne's first ball in Ashes cricket pitched outside leg stump and turned a yard to remove the off bail. Ever since, English batsmen had treated every delivery from him as if it might contain gunpowder. By the time the teams reached Melbourne for the fourth Test of the 1994-95 series, Warne was regarded as a veritable demon. Australia had begun a period of domination over their oldest rivals and the precious urn had already been retained. Nevertheless Mark Taylor's side was determined to rub salt into the wound. Warne was determined to show his wares in a Boxing Day Test played at his beloved MCG.

In the event, he bowled admirably throughout but saved his best for last. Australia needed three wickets to win as Warne bowled to Phillip DeFreitas. Three balls later the match was over as England's tail was routed. Devon Malcolm was the last victim as David Boon dived from his perch at short leg to accept a sharp chance. Warne had taken a hat-trick. Australians roared and Englishmen trudged from the field. A man does not have many such moments.

Cricket Memorabilia   Stephen W. Gibbs, *Wisden Australia* 2004-05

It has been a buoyant 12 months for the cricket memorabilia market in Australia, with various intriguing items coming into the public domain. Most intriguing of all was the ball with which Shane Warne dismissed Sri Lanka's Upal Chandana in Cairns to capture his record-equalling 527th Test wicket. Warne, in a generous gesture, allowed the ball to be sold through eBay in July 2004, with the proceeds going to his children's charity, the Shane Warne Foundation. The winning bid was $42,700.

2004

Hampshire v Durham, Southampton   Pat Symes, *Wisden* 2005
(County Championship Division Two, April 16-19)

Shane Warne's first match as Hampshire captain ended in victory – as pre-season hype demanded – though not before a youthful and understrength Durham had competed to the last. Hampshire needed just 109, yet Warne had to pad up and watch anxiously as Davies and Plunkett, after a day and a half had been lost to rain, exploited the damp conditions and reduced them to 52 for seven.

Hampshire v Leicestershire, Southampton   Pat Symes, *Wisden* 2005
(County Championship Division Two, April 28-May 1)

Hampshire were already dominant by the end of the first day after Leicestershire failed to cope with a sporting pitch. Even so, there seemed little prospect of a result when play resumed under a watery sun on the last day. Yet Warne sensed a chance and instructed his batsmen to hurry towards a declaration ... Warne's declaration, 129 ahead, left Leicestershire 53 overs to save themselves, but Mascarenhas wobbled through the top order for Warne and Udal to polish off what remained.

Hampshire v Derbyshire, Southampton   Pat Symes, *Wisden* 2005
(County Championship Division Two, May 7-10)

Derbyshire's last pair, Mohammad Ali and Nick Walker, survived 14 balls to achieve a draw and deny Hampshire a third Championship win in three starts. Warne accused Derbyshire of "negative tactics" and admitted his irritation had led him to delay his declaration until they could not win.

Gloucestershire v Hampshire, Bristol   Graham Russell, *Wisden* 2005
(totesport League Division One, May 23)

Warne flew in from Zimbabwe after Australia's Tests were cancelled – and promptly starred with ball and bat. The Gloucestershire openers had put on 88 when he had Spearman stumped in his first over and – unlike the other Hampshire bowlers – he continued to cause trouble. Warne grabbed four for 27 from his nine overs; the only other wicket to fall was a run-out. In the Hampshire reply, he smashed a run-a-ball 48 and shared a partnership of 68 with the Tasmanian Michael Dighton, who was standing in for Michael Clarke.

Australia v Sri Lanka, Cairns   Robert Craddock, *Wisden* 2005
(Second Test, July 9-13)

There are rare and captivating moments in cricket history when the pursuit of an individual milestone completely overshadows the match going on around it. There are even more special ones when the milestone and the maelstrom go hand in hand. This was such an occasion. Warne needed seven wickets to equal Muralitharan's Test record and eight to beat it. He got seven, after bowling unchanged through the last two sessions, but Sri Lanka held on for a draw.

The record bobbled along in the background for the first four days before surging into focus on that final afternoon – for everyone except Murali. When told, back in Colombo, that Warne had pulled level, he replied "Oh, he's got it, has he? Well done. I've been out practising."

| The Sri Lankans in Australia 2004 | Robert Craddock, *Wisden* 2005 |

Officials from the cricketing outposts of Darwin and Cairns thought it would be Christmas in July. Shane Warne and Muttiah Muralitharan were expected in the Australian tropics to duel for one of cricket's most coveted records – most Test wickets. It would have been like Tiger Woods and Ernie Els turning up at the municipal pitch-and-putt to shoot for golf's No. 1 ranking. Sadly, only half of the fairytale came true. Warne, whose place was threatened when he damaged a finger playing for Hampshire, made the trip, but Muralitharan withdrew for "personal reasons" four days before his side left home. He claimed he needed a break, but there was no doubt sorrowful memories of Australia helped make up his mind. Not only had he been no-balled by three Australian umpires on Australian soil for throwing; on his most recent visit, in 2002-03, he was viciously taunted by Australian crowds, the low point being a humid night in Brisbane when he was catcalled after breaking down with a hamstring injury. And the English referee, Chris Broad, who had reported his action after the home series with Australia in March, was to preside again.

Australian prime minister John Howard may have sealed the boycott in May when he branded Murali a chucker at a political lunch. Muralitharan was then touring Zimbabwe, where he claimed top spot by overtaking Courtney Walsh's record of 519 wickets, and told Howard to mind his own business. The Northern Territory government, anxious to entice Murali to Darwin, sent an official to Colombo to beg him to come; he wrote a touching letter saying he appreciated the gesture but needed time away from the game.

The rivalry between Warne and Muralitharan, the most dominant slow bowlers in cricket history, developed an icy edge through long-distance media taunts, as both were inevitably pressed to assess the other. Warne, who needed 11 wickets in two Tests to gain outright ownership of the record, branded Muralitharan "thin-skinned" for pulling out. After taking ten, to finish the series tied on 527, he said he felt they were not on a level playing field – unlike Warne, Muralitharan had home wickets prepared to favour him, and was guaranteed to bowl more overs, given Sri Lanka's weaker attack. Even the sight of Warne equalling the record gave Cairns's unpretentious Bundaberg Rum Stadium a highlight worthy of Lord's on a balmy July evening or the MCG on Boxing Day. Still, Warne could not claim it outright, or complete the victory that would have given Australia their second whitewash of Sri Lanka in five months. They had crushed the tourists on a seamers' pitch in Darwin, but a friendlier strip at Cairns saw Matthew Hayden score twin hundreds and Sri Lanka hang on for the draw.

WORDS ON WARNE

"They'll all great bowlers but Warne's probably the best spinner I have seen. It's amazing what he can do with a cricket ball and I've always enjoyed watching him bowl. When we do get to meet, we share a few thoughts about each other's bowling."

Anil Kumble, India leg-spinner – *WAC*, March 2002

Glamorgan v Hampshire, Cardiff   Edward Bevan, *Wisden* 2005
(County Championship Division Two, July 29-31)

Clarke led the recovery with his third successive Championship century – a feat last achieved for Hampshire by Gordon Greenidge in 1986 – and Warne kept up the momentum with the ball. His second-innings six for 65 were his best figures of the summer, and he made everyone struggle except Elliott, his Victorian team-mate, who carried his bat…

Hampshire v Essex, Southampton   Pat Symes, *Wisden* 2005
(County Championship Division Two, August 3-5)

This was Essex's biggest first-class win in terms of runs and Hampshire's heaviest defeat, eclipsing their previous worst of 380, against Surrey at Northlands Road in 1896. The thrashing was especially painful for their captain Warne, who chose to field first and watched Essex compile 416 on what turned out to be one of the Rose Bowl's more reliable pitches … As Essex were extending their lead in the second innings, Warne exchanged unpleasantries with the batsman Irani and both were called to a meeting next morning, with their coaches, to be warned by the umpires. Irani issued a statement denying reports that Warne had called him "the son of a whore".

Somerset v Hampshire, Taunton   David Foot, *Wisden* 2005
(County Championship Division Two, August 18-21)

In a game truncated by rain, the two captains managed, through predetermined declarations, to introduce purpose and competition to the final day. Somerset were set 351 in 85 overs and gave every indication of scoring the runs. They were strongly placed on 300 for three, only to crumble miserably against Warne. He took four wickets, which gave him six for the innings, and played a cool hand in two of Somerset's three panicky run-outs.

Hampshire in 2004   Pat Symes, *Wisden* 2005

In the spring of 2004, as jubilant players sang their newly created club victory song "Glory, Glory, we are Hampshire" down a mobile phone to the chairman on his yacht in the Caribbean, it became clear that the face of county cricket in Hampshire had changed. It was not a club Philip Mead or Lionel Tennyson would have recognised, though the hedonistic Tennyson might have enjoyed the yacht. However, they would surely have approved of both the Rose Bowl, the club's imposing headquarters, and the impressive tally of wins in 2004.

This was Hampshire's best year in terms of results since they left Mead and Tennyson's county ground in 2000. The song (lyrics: Kendall and Prittipaul) was part of a forging of a new Hampshire ethos, which helped induce a togetherness and spirit missing since the break-up of Mark Nicholas's team in the 1980s. Players travelled to away matches by coach and "gaffe of the day", chosen by the team, earned the culprit a fetching pink T-shirt for the evening.

While one man does not make a team, Shane Warne came close. Yacht-owing Rod Bransgrove fought with determination to persuade Warne to return as captain, talisman and master tactician, and Warne lit up Hampshire cricket as no man since Malcolm Marshall in his prime. After his year's suspension, the great leg-spinner approached the task of raising the club's playing profile with a gusto and depth of involvement which inspired consistent underperformers by exuberant example. Warne's pre-match team talks were more like battle cries, and his reward came with much-improved results in all competitions. While his 51 wickets in 12 Championship matches may not have been exceptional, his fierce desire to win every game and his sharp tactical acumen were major factors in Hampshire's success. His mere presence was often enough.

The new victory song was rendered most often, and with greatest relish, during a Championship campaign which led to promotion as runners-up. The total of nine wins, up by seven from 2003, was a fair reflection of Warne's influence.

WORDS ON WARNE

"Warney has been such an influence. He has been positive and that has had a great effect on the club. He has shown us how to enjoy our cricket. After all Warney has been through, his love for the game is amazing. That rubbed off on everyone else and there were very few if any sessions when we were not totally up for it."

Paul Terry, Hampshire first-team manager – *The Wisden Cricketer*, November 2004

Rose Tinted Spectacle?
Will Kendall, *TWC*, January 2005

When Shane Warne walked through the gates of Hampshire's old ground at Northlands Road during the first April of the new millennium, it was like trying to fit a size 11 foot into a size 7 shoe. Everyone tried to make it work but, particularly on the pitch, we were overwhelmed.

From the first moment he cruised into a post-practice lunch and presented us each with a firm handshake, engaging eye contact and an unnecessary "Hi, I'm Shane Warne", we were transfixed. The greatest spinner, perhaps the finest bowler of them all, and certainly one of the game's largest personalities was in our dressing room. We were a young side in transition and simply unable to deal with it. He did not let anyone down – he took 70 first-class wickets and 99 in all cricket (perhaps the only thing missing was the odd fourth day match-winning spell) – but the team failed to respond and we bombed in a grim summer.

Warne returned in 2004. Where four years earlier his friendship with the then captain Robin Smith and a sizeable purse attracted him to Hampshire, this time the motivation was different. "The Judge" had retired and Warne took a pay cut. He puts a high price on loyalty but he clearly saw unfinished business. Warne does not do losing – not for long. A born winner, driven by immense pride and an insatiable desire to achieve, he took the reins and inspired Hampshire to comfortably their best season for more than a decade.

Though Warne's influence was immense, there are other major factors that have paved the way for this overdue success. Importantly the club now has that size 11 ambition and capability to accommodate Warne's formidable presence. As an entity, from the dressing room to the kitchens, Hampshire is better equipped to cope than in 2000, though it has been a long and difficult path.

In 2001, Hampshire swapped the cosy city centre venue of Northlands Road for the grand and expansive Rose Bowl site on the edge of Southampton. The move was not only about a venue; it meant an upscaling of the entire business. It was a courageous change, one intended to launch the county into the new millennium and to put down a stake for cricket in the south of England. The plans were ambitious, incorporating two cricket grounds, an indoor school, health club and a nine-hole golf course, and a desire to host national cricket in the future.

But such projects are rarely without their problems and these arrived by the bucket-load. Despite support from Sport England and the sale of the old ground for housing, funding was tight. After many nervy moments, the chairman Rod Bransgrove stepped in to back the site and the financial future of the club. Bransgrove has a passion for Hampshire cricket but the money he put into the county, a small fortune, was not a donation but an investment that needed a business structure to safeguard it. Rose Bowl plc emerged, an umbrella body that enveloped Hampshire Cricket, attracting other shareholders, and the business is now run with them in mind. This meant an end to the traditional committees, resolving a sensitive transition period; there was no option.

Of course, these changes in themselves do not make for a successful club but they created a focus. Hampshire is now driven by a responsibility to its shareholders, not simply a need to cover the costs of the operation. Naturally there were complications and drawbacks – cricket was no longer everything and had to sit as part of a business rather than the business itself – but the adjustment was made.

Certain areas are flourishing – on-site conference and banqueting is booming and Wise Catering, part of Rose Bowl plc, is taking contracts at venues from Twickenham rugby internationals to the Paris Air Show – but development plans for a golf driving range, an indoor sports centre and a media stand will go ahead only as and when the finance is available.

Cricket, though, remains and will remain a fundamental part of the business. A Golden Share scheme ensures that, whoever owns the club, the Rose Bowl will always stage cricket, which hopes to offer a regular diet of international fixtures in the future. The ground co-hosted the recent ICC Champions Trophy, and Test cricket is a realistic dream.

But, although the venue has now seen several one-day internationals and will host the inaugural Twenty20 international between England and Australia next summer, there are clearly areas to improve. Road access, the park-and-ride scheme that failed spectacularly during the Champions Trophy and the unpredictable pitch are all areas for address. Teething problems are inevitable but Bransgrove's drive for perfection will not miss a detail. Despite these hiccups, Hampshire is now a long way from Northlands Road.

Though county cricket might not be the only part of the business, it is inextricably linked to its overall success. In past years the team has often let down the club when good results would have made marketing, sponsorship and investment opportunities so much easier. At last the team might be starting to repay a debt. The ambition of the chairman and board has taken a while to seep into the dressing room but the players are now well aware of the need to deliver. Combined with a distinct and increasing Australian influence among the players and support staff, the upshot is an infinitely more accommodating environment for Shane Warne's style and personality. In essence the conditions for a successful relationship this time round were in place.

The final cog was Warne himself and, crucially, his positioning in the piece. Whereas the Warne of 2000 came along to help, the Warne of 2004 came along to lead.

Overseas players almost invariably do well in county cricket but the most successful are those whose influence goes beyond the weight of their performance. Warne has a natural ability to bowl magical leg-spin but he also has a born gift for directing, inspiring and motivating the people around him. As a captain he sweeps players up and they follow his lead. Combine this with his instinctive and insatiable appetite for success and you have a winning formula.

His influence is tangible. Of course, his wicket-taking ability is a key factor but his reputation means that cricketers want to play with him. Kevin Pietersen signed from Nottinghamshire in October, clearly prepared to take a chance on pressing for an England batting spot on the most bowler-friendly pitch in the country so he could play alongside Warne.

His overall impact is immeasurable as it goes beyond statistics. He is both the captain and the star turn. He galvanises the troops but also provides the cutting edge on the field. His presence intimidates many opposing players, making them wary and hesitant. He has the mouth on the pitch and the trousers to go with it. He makes his team push their shoulders back and believe that they are greater than the sum of their parts. It is impossible to quantify his worth in runs, wickets or match-winning performances. You cannot put a price on it. No team, not even Australia, would be the same without him.

But, if this upturn in fortunes is purely down to the influence of Warne, then it can all unravel as quickly as it has come together. The 2004 squad had not changed significantly from the one that flopped a year earlier and perhaps his presence only papered over the cracks. Recent signings will undoubtedly provide extra strength and depth but Warne will always remain the key man. If Cricket Australia do not grant him leave before next summer's Ashes, can the team reproduce the goods without him?

If he is not around, a residue of this influence will surely remain. At Hampshire we saw it last summer: without him, we reached the quarter-final of Twenty20 Cup and won three Championship matches out of three. The side had the habit – nine Championship victories in a season is more than double the county's return from 2002 and 2003 combined – and confidence from this is bound to carry over. But ultimately someone else will have to stand up to the plate and provide the inspiration, the cutting edge and the drive.

And there are encouraging signs here for Hampshire. In terms of statistics Warne is not irreplaceable. Though he may be the bowler the opposition fear most, three others – Dimitri Mascarenhas, Chris Tremlett and Shaun Udal – were above him in the 2004 averages, though each would admit to profiting from bowling with him. Leadership and tactical nous are apparent in the experience of Udal, John Crawley and Nic Pothas and instinct and flair lie in the capable hands of Mascarenhas and Pietersen. There is also plenty of young talent in the squad, the product of a regularly successful 2nd XI and youth system, who are champing at the bit for opportunities. There is no reason to feel that success in Division One is beyond them – the standard is not so different – but can it be done without Warne at the helm?

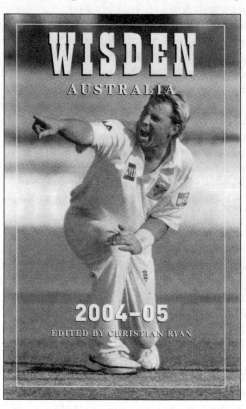

It will be hard because fundamentally the great leg-spinner is the ace in Hampshire's pack, the card that enticed Pietersen, the magnetism that gels the players and the irresistible force behind the county's revival. As long as Warne remains, the county is heading for good times.

There is a feeling about the Rose Bowl that 2004 has been a watershed year, that the club is finally making the strides on the pitch to catch up with advancement it has made off it.

Wisden Australia 2004-05

Will Kendall played for Hampshire from 1996 to 2004.

2004-05

Notes by the Editor   Christian Ryan, *Wisden Australia* 2004-05

A star is Warne

You often hear it said that Warne ain't the bowler he used to be. It is as if he hit his peak with the humungous leg-break that gazoodled Mike Gatting at Old Trafford in 1993 and has been in steady decline ever since. When did you last see him land a flipper?

Does he even have a wrong'un? To suggest there is a lick of difference between his zooter, slider, toppie or back-spinner is considered rank gullibility; swallow that and you'll probably believe those two diet pills really were his mum's fault.

There is an element of truth in all that. Yet from this vantage point Warne, never easy to turn away from, was at his most unturnawayable in 2004. Like the great classical painters he stumbled upon the art of simplicity. More than ever he relied on his two oldest friends, his accuracy and his leg-break. Except that instead of one leg-break he had at least six. There was one that spun an inch, one that spun a foot and one that kept going and going and going. Then there was one drifting in, another sloping out and yet another that sailed gun-barrel straight until it cuffed the pitch. The genius lay in the way he seemed able to vary at will the precise degree of turn, taking chance out of cricket's chanciest occupation: that of the leg-spin bowler. His bowling has never been simpler, nor more effective, nor lovelier to look at.

It was tempting to suppose that his various nadirs were actually integral episodes of some masterplan. His shoulder and finger injuries made him focus on his leg-break. His 12-month ban for ingesting diuretics concentrated his mind and desire. In his first three Tests back, on hostile terrain, a laughing stock among many of his countrymen, he swept aside 26 Sri Lankan batsmen and made Muttiah Muralitharan look a novice by comparison. As comebacks go, this was without parallel.

Few Australians in any walk of life can have polarised opinion the way Warne does. Either he was "born for greatness" with "that coil-like wrist", as the 1950s leg-spinner Rex Sellers contends in the following article, or he is "a giant sleazy hamster with terrible hair", as a female colleague of mine suggested by email earlier this year. Indeed your gender tends to have a lot to do with what you think of him. So does your acquaintance with history. To condemn Warne for shooting off salacious text messages is to forget that cricketers have been known to flirt with pretty admirers and shag themselves silly on tour for decades. His cheap dig at Murali – that he specialises in bowling out bunnies on bunsens – was as graceless as his walk-up trot is graceful. But like all Warne's worst sins, it happened off the field. On it he brings sweet joy.

So long as he keeps spinning the cover off the ball, we'll keep putting him on our cover. He is not only the inaugural cover star of *Wisden Australia*; he is the cover star of our generation. May he bowl on till he's 50.

That Coil-Like Wrist *Wisden Australia 2004-05*

We approached six Australian Test leg-spinners – one from every decade since World War II – and invited them to compare themselves to Warne. What does he do that they couldn't? How does he do it? And can there ever be another like him?

Rex Sellers, 1950s

I was a novice compared with Warne. I only played one Test and my style of getting wickets was completely different. I used to throw the ball up, land it just inside off stump and the batsmen came down the wicket to me. I hardly ever bowled with a square leg; I had one man behind square, a midwicket and a deep mid-on with everyone else on the off side. It would have been a bad ball for me to be bowling on leg stump because I was far too slow through the air. I think Warne is the forerunner, the benchmark, of pushing the ball through. When I went to England in 1964 I found it difficult. The wickets are slow and you don't get the same bounce, so you have push the ball through and move your line closer to the leg stump. You become a different bowler – and I found it hard to do that.

That's why the first thing that comes to mind with Warne is his resilience, his adaptability in all facets, in any hemisphere. Then there is his uncomplicated run-up and delivery stride, and his ability to be a shock or stock bowler, which is a testimony to his stamina. And he has that coil-like wrist; he was born for greatness with that first ball he bowled in the UK to Mike Gatting. The biggest spinner I've ever seen, including Warne, was the left-armer David Sincock. His bosie or wrong'un was as big as his stock ball – can you imagine what would Warne be like if he spun it back the other way with the same amount of lateral spin? But David was very inaccurate, the ball used to fly around everywhere. Warne has huge turn and accuracy, which is hard to do. His accuracy, the coil-like spin of his leg-break, his speed through the air and his ability to bowl for so long are what sets him apart.

And he has so many variations. Longevity gives him that. I used to try to learn one new ball a year, so that people hadn't worked me out the next year. I think Warnie has done that too, and he's been playing nearly 15 years, so he's developed lots of balls and variations. I daresay he's got two or three wrong'uns, even though he doesn't have a great one. Then there's his flippers and straight balls and zooters and top-spinners. He definitely has variations of what looks like the same ball.

I couldn't bowl the flipper. My hands were too small to be able to hold over the top of the ball, which is what you have to do. I played around the same time as Richie Benaud and I think Warne is more potent than Richie was. Richie only had a small wrong'un – Bobby Simpson probably bowled a better wrong'un than Richie – but he did have a leg-spinner and a flipper. Warne has got more wickets with his flipper but, gee, Richie's was very good. I think their flippers were on a par; Warnie just uses his more often. Richie was a past master at giving the sucker short leg-spinner – pull! Then another short leg-spinner – pull! And then he'd bowl the flipper which would shoot straight through and get you lbw.

When Warne came back from injury he was really only able to bowl leggies for about 18 months. Batsmen started taking risks against him and getting away with it. But gradually he's lost weight and his strength and his flipper have come back. He's lethal again. He has taken the ability to bowl leg-spin to a new level, I think. He is in the super club. He is unquestionably the best spin bowler ever.

Rex Sellers played one Test match for Australia, and took 121 first-class wickets.

John Gleeson, 1960s

The main thing is his control. Fellows who have been big spinners of the ball – Johnny Martin and David Sincock and Stuart MacGill – their control is not within a bull's roar of this bloke's. The ball can do only three things: it either goes straight or spins from the leg or goes from the off. It can't do anything else. It doesn't disappear or explode. So I think the main thing that sticks to Warne is his control and knowledge of the game. He showed that when he had the captaincy a couple of times.

I didn't see Bill O'Reilly, and apparently he was pretty handy, but this fella has got to be the best leggie since the war, at least. Normally people with Warne's control have to give something up, usually the amount or the variety of spin. But this bloke's got everything – variety and control – although I think a bit of baloney goes on about the eight different balls he says he can bowl. As I said, basically you do three things, so there's a certain amount of bluff there.

But as a spinner you've got to use a bit of guile. It's not as if you can bounce somebody; you've got to be aggressive in different ways, with field placings and thinking about the game. I used to always make people look for something that wasn't there. I reckon I knew two or three fellas who could pick what I was doing most of the time, but that never worried me. I never thought I couldn't get them out. I had one advantage in that I had eight balls an over – Warne's only got six – and that gives you more time to work on a fellow. He's got an edge with all the protection they've got. Guys can field a lot closer and feel confident they won't get hurt, and they intimidate the batsmen. It allows you to get that extra over-spin and make the ball bounce higher, looking for catches.

My biggest problem was we lacked quick bowling, so I did the donkey-work. I wasn't used the way Warne is. Economically we'd probably work out about the same, however he's a far bigger spinner. Also he bowled a flipper – I bowled a sort of a one, but you wouldn't really call it a flipper – so he's got that ammunition I didn't have. For me, the newer the ball and greener the wicket the better. I tried to get the ball off the track as quick as possible, to commit a batsmen to a stroke and give him no time to get out of it. The lbw rule was different too. You had to pitch between wicket and wicket, and hit wicket, so lbw was virtually out of the game. The Poms used to kick it through cover quicker than I could hit it. If you struck a bloke on the full or close to the full you had no chance in the world. You wouldn't even have the hide to appeal, let alone bellow, which they do nowadays. I'd like to be playing now. The men with the finger, they throw them up quick smart – more than they should I believe.

I heard it mentioned that Warne said he might ring me during his year off to work out a new mystery ball, but he never did. I was at Alan Davidson's farewell lunch a while ago and John Buchanan, the Australian coach, suggested that with the technology they should put a bit of my action on film and keep archives, in case somebody might use it down the line. One day that might occur. But they'd want to start soon – I'm getting too old to start bowling again.

If I could change one thing about Warne, I'd make him run through the crease more. Sometimes he just takes one step and stops dead – boom, boom – and then he's an ordinary bowler, you've him by short and curlies. I always reckon when you finish four or five steps down the wicket it gives the ball extra vim and vigour. He had great flipper and good wrong'un early on, and both seem have disappeared. But he's got away with it. The rest of his game has developed to the extent that he's still as good as he was when he had more variety. Very talented character. I don't we'll ever see another one like him. We'll see someone different, who might even be as productive, but there'll another Warne. Never. Like there'll never be another Gleeson.

John Gleeson played in 29 Test matches for Australia, taking 93 wickets.

Jim Higgs, 1970s

I first came in contact with him when he was St Kilda and Jack Edwards, the club president, asked me to have a few sessions him. He wasn't bowling the flipper at that stage, he was more fiddling around with it than anything. All I did was show him what I used to do. He got a bit of help from Terry Jenner but everyone works things out for themselves. What is certain is that Shane has always been his own bowler.

It was obvious that he was going to have a huge impact on the game, although not everyone could see it. He was struggling to get a start with Victoria in the early 1990s. I was one of the national selection committee at the time and had to wonder why. He could do most things with the ball. He developed few things later on, like the flipper and using the subtleties of back-spin and square-spin to create different flight paths. But the thing that stood out was that he was so strong. Without that, a spinner will struggle. Shane had that – and obviously a bit more.

From a technical point of view, there have been a lot of slow bowlers over the years – some finger-spinners, some leggies – who can bowl accurately and consistently for a long period of time. Then there are those who can spin the bejesus out of it. As far as I've seen, he's the first that's really been able to do both. You look at Anil Kumble. He's consistent but he's nowhere near as potent as Warnie in terms of getting blokes out – and in conditions that are made for batting. That's the key rider.

I used to try to spin the crap out of it and hope it landed in the right place. I'd try to confuse the bloke at the other end. That was a product of the times; we played on hard and fast wickets that offered very little turn, so you had to rip it hard if you were to have any chance of taking wickets. I played at a time when finger-spin wasn't popular and just about every Sheffield Shield team had a leggie. That's gone out because of the need for consistency. Leg-spin has disappeared to the point where only the ones who can bowl accurately survive. Shane is one of those bowlers.

The most intriguing thing about him is the way he has been able to re-invent himself when he's had to. Having had one myself, a shoulder reconstruction is very debilitating. You lose a lot of strength. So he had to change. His brute power was gone. He couldn't just blast them out the way he used to. Now he uses a refined approach whereby he unnerves batsmen until they get themselves out.

He has been a great advertisement for wrist-spin bowling. In the 1970s, the only people who could see what you were doing with the flight of the ball were the ones sitting in the front row of the member's stand. Television has demystified things for the average punter. They can see through slow-motion the curve and flight path of the ball. I think that's been his biggest legacy. He has added a dimension that never used to be there.

Jim Higgs played in 22 Test matches for Australia, taking 66 wickets.

Bob Holland, 1980s

I've watched his career with huge interest. What impresses me most is his ability to read a batsman. When he screws his face up after a delivery, as if to say "that nearly got through", I can see what he's thinking. He sums up a batsman in about three balls. He realises that this guy isn't so good off the back foot or doesn't like to use his feet. Then he hones in. The difference between him and others is that he bowls exactly the right delivery in exactly the right spot at exactly the right time.

I tried to spin the ball as much as possible so I had my fair share of bad deliveries. If you put a lot of revs on it, you have to control it. Shane has exceptional control all of the time. And a lot of variation. He has a great wrong'un but he doesn't bowl it very much because he usually has the flipper going. There are two deliveries that stand out for me. There's his leg-spinner that drifts from middle to leg and then spins a lot, that's an incredible delivery; and the other one is the flipper that's quick and straight and usually around the mark. They are both lethal.

There was never too much bluff about the way I bowled. It wasn't something I went home to work on. Shane has always conjured up the idea of mystery balls. He's always mentioned new deliveries, like the zooter. I used to bowl a variety of it but at the time it was called a flipper. In essence, they're the same: both spin backwards and go straight, except that one comes out one side of the hand and one comes out the other. He's a strong fella and that allows him to vary his pace. He normally bowls at 82kph but he can bowl the flipper at 90 to 100kph. You can basically only bowl leg-breaks, wrong'uns or one that goes straight. It's the degree to which you bowl them that's the key. And that's where a lot of Shane's mystery comes from.

It's been a good time to bowl, of course. He's been in a successful team. He's had runs to bowl to and there are fewer slow bowlers these days, so batsmen aren't getting much practice against leggies. He's also had someone keeping it tight at the other end. When a promising partnership is developing, and Shane is having to work hard, Glenn McGrath is at the other end either keeping them quiet or getting them out. Australia have rarely known success like it. Is it because Shane's there? Or is it just his good luck to have been around at the right time? I'd say it's a bit of both.

It's very unlikely that we'll see a leggie like him again – although it is possible. I went to England in 1985 and someone asked me if I would be the last Australian leg-spinner to tour. I said I hoped not. Almost 20 years later we have a bowler who has revolutionised leg-spin bowling. Now every leggie has a little bit of Warne in them. But I'd like to think he's got a bit of every leggie that came before in him as well.

Bob Holland played in 11 Test matches for Australia, taking 34 wickets.

Peter McIntyre, 1990s

I guess if I had my time again I'd love to be born in a different era. We were together at the Academy in Adelaide for a while – I was part-time, he was full-time – and Terry Jenner, myself and Warnie were standing around spinning balls to ourselves, as you do. The revolutions on his ball were almost twice as much as ours. I remember TJ giving me a nudge and saying: "Have a look at Warnie when he spins the ball up." It just kept going and going, it had a lot more noise on it. He wasn't overly fit in those early days – he was a fat boy, and he'll admit that – but he had this enormous strength.

It was a real adventure. We both started out in club cricket, him at St Kilda and me at Essendon, and then we went to Zimbabwe on a Young Australia tour in 1991. Ever since Abdul Qadir, there hadn't been any focus leg-spin. We were discovering these balls that had been dormant since Clarrie Grimmett, and batsmen just didn't know what they were. There was this real hype. We were talking about flippers and zooters and back-spinners. We named our flipper "the Butchie ball" because Ian Butchart, who used to play for Zimbabwe, got cleaned with it every time – by both of us.

We were both par. Then Warnie took a seven-for on that tour and you could almost predict, even then, that he was going to be a freak. But we always had a nice rapport going; it was never a competition. It wasn't about who was better; it was just the whole adventure of leg-spin coming back into vogue.

I had a better wrong'un. He had a pretty unique grip where held the ball with his forefinger and middle finger together, and it's always difficult to bowl the wrong'un like that. He did have one but he didn't rip it enough to be any sort of weapon. But he definitely had a better flipper and back-spinner than me. The other factor was his drift – that's his biggest weapon. When he really drifts it and then puts the big spin on it too, it's very hard work out where the ball going. He's like a swing bowler. Drift is not something you can work on – it's a natural thing – and the fact that he had so many more revolutions on the ball other leg-spinners is what made it drift more. The ball was grabbing the air as it went down. And his accuracy is probably the best of any bowler ever.

When we played our one Test together in Adelaide there was a lot of conjecture about whether two leg-spinners would work. But we were different kinds of bowlers. He was this big drifting, leg-spinning thing and I was just using a bit of subtle variation, some wrong'uns and back-spin. Before he did his finger, his flipper was a huge weapon. It was well-disguised, he used to drift it and it was bang on target every time. He could bowl it a lot easier because of those two fingers together, he used them as the axis.

I think he had the perfect action too. He still has. If you look at his wrist it's almost square to the batsman every time he bowls, so he gets maximum side-spin. Apparently George Tribe, a left-arm wrist-spinner of the 1940s and 50s, was a similar sort of bowler in that he got lots of rip and drift and bounce. Qadir had all those tricks too, especially his wrong'un, but he wasn't as accurate. Warnie is just a unique bowler – we may not see another like him for a very long time. Who'd ever have thought leg-spinners would be used in one-day cricket? He changed that whole thought process. He's set the standard for how leggies will bowl in the future. It was great to go along for the ride.

Peter McIntyre played in two Test matches for Australia, taking five wickets.

Cameron White, 2000s

I didn't grow up as a kid thinking I wanted to bowl like Shane Warne, although I'm sure there are thousands out there who do. I was more of a batsman who tried to bowl medium-pace occasionally. I didn't start to play around with leg-spin until I was 13, and by then Warnie had really made a name for himself. So I guess my take on him is a bit different to leg-spinners of the past. I've had an opportunity, as a young fan, to grow up watching him on TV – and now, in the last few seasons, to bowl alongside him as a player. I've been able to watch him and get a real insight into how he's done it, and how he's still doing it.

A lot of people have different opinions about why he has had such a big effect on the game. He is obviously a great bowler because of the things he can do with the ball, his different deliveries and his variations on those deliveries. He has every part of the game covered. But for me, what stands out most is his ability to do exactly what he's thinking and the way he prepares to get batsmen out. It's something the average person might not appreciate. When Shane pitches one on middle and it spins sharply and the batsman nicks to slip, it's easy to think it's simply a great delivery. But being out there in the middle with him, you get to learn how it unfolds. Every game, he's always telling his team-mates that he's going to bowl one here, then another there, then one around there. And then he does exactly that four or five balls later. Sometimes it might be five overs later. He sets a batsman up perfectly. Now he's teaching me to think more about that type of execution.

Usually, spinners either have a lot of accuracy or they can put a lot of spin on the ball – and if they do turn it dramatically they have to put up with bowling plenty of bad ones. But Shane can do both, and he has been doing both for a long time. There were a lot of comparisons between us when I was first coming on, probably because we're both Victorians and we're both leg-spinners. But we are totally different. For me, accuracy is the main thing because I can't spin it as much as him. I have to rely on bounce and drift and my changes of pace.

I really only have three deliveries: the wrong'un, a leg-break and a top-spinner. It would be good to have a bit more mystery to what I'm doing, like Shane's always had. He has been working with me on that. I guess I'm blessed in a way – he's not a bad teacher to have. I don't think I could have hoped for anyone better.

Cameron White played in four Test matches for Australia, taking five wickets.

My Other Life – Golf   Shane Warne, *TWC*, November 2004

Did your handicap go down during your year out of the game?
During the year I had out of the game – the enforced lay-off – I played three or four days a week. I was practising and having lessons: the lowest my handicap got to was 8.6. Now I'm playing off 9.6. Every time I play, I mark a card and send it back to keep my handicap up to date.

How competitive are you?
I'm competitive at everything I do and golf is no exception. I don't like to lose, but, playing golf, I probably lose more than I win. The big games, though, I've actually won – like the ones with Ian Botham. I've taken his money more times than he's taken mine. That's been very enjoyable. He had to pay for a helicopter for myself and [Aussie golfer] Peter O'Malley last year when we played the Dunhill Links Championship in Scotland. It was me, Ian Woosnam, Peter O'Malley and Beefy. Whoever lost between Beefy and me had to pay for a helicopter to get us to Carnoustie, rather than sit in a bus for an hour. He lost convincingly.

When did you start playing?
When I was 15 or 16. My brother and I played a bit, were no good and hacked about. I never had much time to play as I was growing up with cricket. Any break I had I'd go and play – but I never improved. In the last five or six years I have played a lot more. I've had a few lessons in Australia, but they actually stuffed me up: they made me too conscious of what I was doing wrong, or how things could go wrong.

Who's the best golfer in the Australian team?

Ricky Ponting's the best: he plays off three. He gives it an absolute smash – he gets up on his toes and whacks it over 300 yards. I can hit it 260 yards or if I really jump on one maybe 280. My longest was 309 metres – 340 yards – on the Capital Golf Course in Melbourne, 9th hole, 409 metres. I didn't make the birdie: I took three putts: I'm a terrible putter.

Do you ever play golf with the opposition?

All the time. A lot of cricketers love their golf – me, Beefy, Mark Nicholas, Ian Smith, we play all the time. I've played with Brian Lara a few times, too: he's a good golfer.

Do your cricketing skills help with your golf?

As a ball sportsman, the hand-eye co-ordination helps each sport. But the way a cricketer naturally wants to hit a golf ball makes it carve out to the right. Sometimes cricket can affect your golf, sometimes the other way round. But most cricketers have natural timing and it's a matter of playing enough to find out what you are doing and actually get better. It is a pretty frustrating game for the best players in the world, let alone us hacks.

What do you like best about the sport?

If you get a good four-ball with three good buddies and go and play, there are not too many better things. I get to play on wonderful courses. I'm lucky because, with what I have achieved on the cricket field, I can get on to most courses without being a member. Some won't let you on, but most will.

How far do you think you can go with your golf?

I'd like to play on the Seniors Tour one day. I mean, I've got a way to go, but I reckon I could do it: I do have 16 years to practise!

Interview by Edward Craig

India v Australia, Bengaluru　　　　　　　Dilip Premachandran, *TWC*, December 2004
(First Test, October 6-10)

Warne came out in red-tipped boots on the final morning, having reached 531 wickets – one behind Murali – the night before, but perhaps enraged by his lack of sartorial taste Pathan took him on with panache, smacking two deliveries into the stand en route to a first Test 50.

India v Australia, Chennai　　　　　　　　　　　Paul Weaver, *Wisden* 2005
(Second Test, October 14-18)

Warne bowled almost as well as Kumble. His record in India had been a poor one, with just 24 wickets at 51 before this match, and a lack of form and fitness had blighted his previous tours. Now, though, he took six for 125. His second wicket came in his fifth over of the second day when he had Pathan caught by Hayden at slip. It was his 533rd Test wicket and for the first time in his wonderful career he was the outright leading wicket-taker in the game, one ahead of his great rival Muttiah Muralitharan. "I would have been happy to take one Test wicket when I started my career," he said afterwards.

The Australians in India 2004-05
Paul Weaver, Wisden 2005

McGrath and Shane Warne, who had missed the previous, drawn series between the sides in Australia through injury and suspension respectively, were back. Warne, who had never been at his best in India, was something like his old self and at Chennai became the leading wicket-taker in Test history, passing Muttiah Muralitharan's record of 532.

Letters
TWC, November 2004

It is a great pity that the inaugural ICC awards ended up becoming a farce. How could a panel of judges overlook world record bowler Muttiah Muralitharan? Muralitharan took the most Test wickets this year with 68. Shane Warne, however, appears to have gained his place by virtue of reputation. The fact he was serving a drugs ban during the voting period should have been taken into consideration by the panel of judges but Warne is one of those characters whose flaws and misdemeanours are constantly brushed aside or ignored. Muralitharan, whose only flaw is mesmerising the opposition, endlessly pays the price for his bowling action. Where is the justification?
Hareen Marcelline, Aberdeen

Australia v New Zealand, Brisbane
Adrian McGregor, Wisden Australia 2005-06

(First Test, November 18-21)

Next day Oram nursed his score to 98, and the team to nine for 325, whereupon we were treated to the ludicrous scene of Shane Warne bowling wide of the leg stump to a field ringing the boundary, all to deny Oram his 100. Umpire Aleem Dar called two balls wide, disputed by Warne, who was then firmly chipped by Dar.

New Zealand in Australia 2004-05
Max Bonnell, Wisden Australia 2005-06

The series proved little about the Australian side that was not already known – Langer's reliabilty, Gilchrist's strike power – although the team would have been encouraged by Clarke's sparkling century in Brisbane, which came at the only point in the series at which Australia were subjected to real pressure. That innings made Clarke only the third Australian to post a century in his first game both abroad and at home, and confirmed his standing as the most marketable Australian player of his generation. The presence of another blond, gelled-up hairstyle in the Australian team seemed to have a direct influence on Shane Warne, who played the series with an alarmingly vertical hairdo, a cross-breed of mullet and mohawk.

Australia v Pakistan, Melbourne   Ron Reed, *Wisden Australia* 2005-06
(Second Test, December 26-29)

Younis went hard, too, hitting 11 fours in 87 off 157 balls, but Youhana's classy 111 – his twelfth century – best exemplified the Pakistanis' determination to take the fight to the Australians. He imparted a rare thrashing to Shane Warne in front of the leg-spinner's home crowd, three times driving him for six. But Warne laughed last, as he so often does. Before the match he had astutely observed that his remarkable strike rate against Pakistan was because "they either block you or hit you for six... there's no in-between."

New Zealand v Australia, Christchurch   Andrew Ramsey, *Wisden* 2006
(First Test, March 10-13)

New Zealand had first-innings lead, but only by one run. They looked demoralised, and duly capitulated. Their batsmen seemed neither able nor willing to find a way of combating Warne, who bowled round the wicket into the deep footmarks created by the fast bowlers at the Hadlee Stand End. The dismissal of Marshall was doubly significant: first, it exemplified the depth of New Zealand's problems because the ball cannoned out of a pothole and shot behind the batsman's legs as he played no stroke; second, it was Warne's 1,000th in first-class cricket. Among current players, only Phil DeFreitas, Mushtaq Ahmed, Martin Bicknell and Muttiah Muralitharan had more. McMillan was equally at sea, padding up to balls he should have hit, and then playing at a wide leg-break and pushing a catch to short leg.

Warne finished with the 29th five-wicket haul of his Test career as New Zealand were rolled over for 131, with seven lbws – equalling the Test record set in Zimbabwe's first innings at Chester-le-Street in 2003.

WORDS ON WARNE

"Ravi Shastri played him exceptionally well; he had an inglorious start to his Test career and had a long way to come back. He learned from that, learned how to bowl to players who were adept at playing spin. He had a lot of confidence in his ability and fitted in well. I fielded at bat-pad and you could hear his fingers snap and the ball coming down."

David Boon, former Australia batsman – *TWC*, July 2005

Chronicle	Wisden 2006

Shane Warne, still chasing his maiden century four years later, was told he was wrongfully denied the chance of scoring one in a Test in 2001, when he was caught in the outfielder for 99 against New Zealand at Perth. Channel 9 had unearthed previously unseen footage showing that the crucial ball, bowled by Daniel Vettori, should have been called a no-ball. The tape was played at the Allan Border Medal dinner last night. Asked how he felt, Warne said: "We're on TV so I can't swear." (*Herald Sun, Melbourne*, February 1)

Still the Man	WAC, January 2005

Have you still got it?
I suppose. Since I've been back, I've bowled as good as I ever have. In the last 20-25 Tests, I've got something like 130 wickets. I'm fitter than I have ever been, so I feel good. I'm not sure if I ever had it, but I feel pretty confident with my bowling.

But can you rip through a side like you used to?
Sometimes I can change a match by just taking one wicket and then the bowler at the other end might get three or four. There are different ways to influence a game. It's not just running through a side and getting seven or eight wickets. It depends on who you are playing. Some sides play spin better than others.

Colin Miller has said that you are just a leg-spinner now and Ian Healy says that it looks like it's taking more effort than ever for you to bowl that delivery.
I have not heard that from those guys and don't take much notice of what other people say. My numbers are holding up to any stage of my career. Those guys see it their way and it doesn't mean they are right. It's funny, after I play a game people say I'm back to my best or past it. In my years of playing Test cricket I've had ups and downs, but I am happy with how I am going and the results.

Have you still got a flipper and a wrong'un?
Yeah, I've still got all my deliveries, but I don't use the flipper as much as I'd like. It's not coming out as I'd like. I don't land it as consistently as I want. I'm still trying to work on that. I still have the wrong'un.

What's wrong with the flipper?
Confidence. Since my finger operations, it doesn't come out like it used to. The ball gets caught up in my finger because I have a bent finger now. It has a completely different feel. That has taken me time to get used to. It's slowly getting better and I'm working on it, so by the time the summer is in full swing I hope I am bowling it more.

Are you the bowler you were after your year off?
I think I am. It sort of gets annoying, after every game I get that same question. All I can do is play. I'm bowling as well as ever, bar the flipper. My numbers back it up.

Is that what annoys you most about the media?

I'd just like them to get their facts right. I understand how they want to sensationalise things. I just don't like rumours or "sources" saying things. If someone says or writes something and I respect them, I'll give them a call to talk about what they wrote. If I don't respect them, I won't bother because they are just trying to make their name at my expense.

What about the rumours that you and Adam Gilchrist don't get along?

Gilly and I get along fine. We have had a few disagreements over a few things. But that doesn't mean we don't get along or that we are not friends. That's press talk. There were rumours during the [1999] World Cup that myself and Steve Waugh were at loggerheads as vice-captain and captain, and I don't know where that came from. We are fine too. To say Gilly and I are not friends is wrong.

What's the biggest disappointment of your career to date? Was it losing the vice-captaincy?

It was losing a Test match to the West Indies by one run in Adelaide, and the 1996 World Cup. The vice-captaincy is five or six years ago. You've got to let it go and move on. That was a long time ago. There are no such things as mistakes, only lessons to be learnt. At the time it was disappointing, but I'm over that. Way over that.

You must wonder what it would have been like to be a long-term Test captain?

I'd be lying if I said that I wouldn't have wanted to be captain. I had my chances, but unfortunately it was not to be. I would have liked to have done it and I think I would have done a pretty good job. When I captained in the one-dayers, we seemed to play well – my record was good. It's not like I lie awake at night harping on it. But I think that Ricky Ponting has done a great job. He has my 100 per cent support and you can ask him that if you don't think I am telling the truth.

How has David Hookes's death affected you?

David Hookes and I got off to a rocky start when I first met him 15 years ago. We had massive arguments. Then just before he came to Victoria, we talked through things. We ended up being very, very close. He stuck up for me and supported me and he was fantastic. I miss him. He was a really good friend. Shit I miss him mate.

You're looking fit; there's no more need for any of those slimming tablets.

I've trained hard for the last three years. Sometimes you need time off, but I'm not eating as much of that junk food.

What's the best sledge you've copped?

Ricky Ponting told me not to rush off the field at lunch one day so that there would be something left for the rest of the players.

Most annoying batsman?

Arjuna Ranatunga. He was a shocker. He bent the rules. He played the game in the wrong spirit and I never liked him and I still don't. There is no love lost between us. He says stupid things all the time.

Player you respect most?

Sachin Tendulkar. He is so good and so humble.

Who's the second-best spinner in Australian cricket?

I think Stuey MacGill. His numbers are great. We have a couple of good young spinners in Cameron White and Nathan Hauritz, but they are pretty inexperienced. It would have been nice to have Stuey in India, but you can understand why the selectors did what they did.

What keeps you going?

I think it is all about enjoyment. If I wasn't enjoying it, I would be doing something else. I've been very lucky to be part of a successful era in Australian cricket. I'm fitter than ever and I will continue to keep going while I'm enjoying it. I won't hang around if I'm not having fun.

How close have you come to retirement?

I have thought about it. That's why I retired from one-day cricket. I wanted to keep my Test career going, and think you will see that more and more with international players. It was a big decision for me to quit the one-day stuff because it is such good fun. If I want to play until I am 37 or 38, I had to do that.

How will you feel the day you quit cricket?

Don't know. Ask me then. It has been a major part of my life for 15 seasons, I've had to grow up and learn about life whilst playing. Speaking to those blokes who have retired, I think I will miss the camaraderie.

Interview by Danny Weidler

WORDS ON WARNE

"The problem with people like Warne is that everything is fine as long as you shut your mouth and listen to all the crap they dish out. For a while our policy was to concentrate on our game and not to respond. But it was getting out of hand, so we decided to fight fire with fire and soon realised they couldn't take it."

Arjuna Ranatunga, former Sri Lanka captain – *TWC*, December 2008

News Register	WAC, March 2005

Shane Warne has pledged a sum of $1 million to help rebuild Galle Stadium which was severely damaged by the South East Asian tsunami last December, and where Warne took his 500th Test wicket. Jayananda Warnaweera, the curator of the ground, said that Warne had promised an initial payment from the Shane Warne Foundation to help rebuild the stadium.

News Register	WAC, April 2005

Shane Warne's successful return from a one-year drugs ban and England's unbeaten streak in 2004 have been nominated for the 2005 Laureus World Comeback of the Year award.

2005

Leading Cricketer in the World 2004	Greg Baum, *Wisden* 2005

In Shane Warne's prodigious career of spin, twist and revolution, no turn has been more startling than his comeback after a year's suspension to his former mastery at the venerable age of 34. In the soap opera of his life, the star was written out and wrote himself back in again, larger than before. But Warne's whole career has been about the inspiration he finds in the smell of the greasepaint and the roar of the crowd, and above all in the scale of the challenge.

He was thoughtless for a moment and idle for a year, and it was trying. The World Anti-Doping Authority, the Australian government and the cricket board were three of many forces who stayed on his back, and there were the several rods he made for himself, too, for he was never discreet. He remained in the limelight, but as a shadow. Some doubted that he could come back. Steve Waugh thought he would need time, but Terry Jenner, his mentor, felt he would return renewed.

His first step back was in a Victorian Second XI game at Melbourne's Junction Oval, a humble fixture suddenly made incongruously glamorous. He got hit for six an over in the second innings. But these were the wings, where he has never thrived; the selectors scarcely hesitated before putting him on the plane to Sri Lanka shortly afterwards. Immediately, it was as if he had never been away, as he took ten wickets in each of his first two Tests. This was the big stage, and he was the big player. The Sri Lankans, who had played him deftly in the past, succumbed at home (26 wickets in three matches), and again in an off-season series in Australia (ten in two). India, previously fallow ground, also yielded wickets (14 in three) as Indian batsmen who had previously treated him with contempt now faltered.

More wickets ensued in home series against New Zealand (11 in two) and Pakistan (nine in two, plus five more in the first week of 2005), two countries who have never relished him. He ended with 70 wickets in 12 Tests in 2004, comparable to 1993 (72 in 16) and 1994 (70 in ten) when he was the new sensation. Warne missed matches against

India in Sydney (still suspended) and Mumbai (injured) that on historical indications would have brought him many more wickets – without him, on a maverick pitch in Mumbai, Australia suffered their only defeat of the year.

He and Muttiah Muralitharan raced for the world record, and for a time shared it, until Muralitharan's personal boycott of Australia and another injury left Warne supremely alone. Meantime, he summered in England, leading Hampshire to their most successful season for more than a decade. Though he was on less money and attracted less fanfare than in a previous stint, his sheer zest for the game stood out amid the prevailing dullness. Warne was not a better bowler than before; that would have been impossible.

But he was at least as good, and that was itself a redoubtable achievement. Like Dennis Lillee before him, he reinvented the wheel. He bowled almost no flippers, nor many wrong'uns, but depended on craft, wile and guile. He took wickets by skill, by force of personality, by subterfuge. Sometimes umpires were as transfixed as batsmen.

He was as indefatigable as ever, and as willing, maintaining his career average of around 46 overs a Test, and his economy rate of around 2.5 an over. Others – MacGill, Hogg, sometimes Katich – had served Australia well enough during Warne's absence, but Australia looked a complete side again with him back in it.

Everything was restored, even the melodrama that has characterised his career as surely as his wickets. He broke his thumb. He made tactless remarks about the advantages Muralitharan had enjoyed. After his successful return in Sri Lanka, he commented on how satisfying it was to play under a captain who had faith in spin in a crisis, an apparent jibe at the retired Waugh. He lived in the headlines, his old habitat.

After he appeared in the tsunami relief match at the MCG in January 2005, Australian captain Ricky Ponting hinted that Warne would come out of retirement in time for the 2007 World Cup if other spinners did not mature sufficiently. Warne, significantly, did not discount it. He has never tired of the thrill of the contest, nor the view from the top. He had missed a year and played a year, and there could be no doubt which year was preferable. So the natural order of the last decade was restored, but at the end of 2004 all were reminded to presume nothing. Warne was assuredly back, but the ground at Galle on which he had made his return nine months earlier was in ruins.

My Favourite Cricketer   Tanya Aldred, *WAC*, April 2005

Reasons to hate Shane Warne: 1. His links with bookmakers, 2. His flirtation with diet pills, 3. His laissez-faire attitude to marriage, 4. The availability of his mobile phone number to sexy nurses, 5. His bad language, 6. His vulgar post-match celebrations, 7. His nationality, 8. His Success, 9. Stuart MacGill.

Reasons to love Shane Warne: Because. He is who he is – a rogue and a knave but the best thing to have happened to cricket since decimalisation – a superstar with magic in his wrists.

Do you remember cricket before he came along? In England at least, some of us grew up thinking that spinners were men of premature middle age who went by the names of John and Phil. Their job, we had learnt, was to hold up one end while the fast bowlers (or nearest imitators, in England's case) took wickets at the other. A spinner was by necessity, possibly by birth, boring. And what was a leg-spinner anyway?

Now, the wrist-spinner is the master of the known universe. The two current players to have taken 500 wickets are Warne and Muttiah Muralitharan. The one bowler to be voted into the top five cricketers of the twentieth century? Warne. With due respect to Abdul Qadir, Warne single-handedly popularised a dying art.

And all this from a bad boy who hails from the seaside suburb of St Kilda. A beach bum with a fondness for the bleach bottle, chunky jewellery, and the odd diamond earring. A young man who got into scrapes, who wasn't very keen on regimented practice, and was kicked out of the Australian academy.

In the early days he looked like an old-fashioned garage mechanic with a preference for a liquid lunch. His tummy swayed as he walked in to bowl, just covered by the slightly creased shirt that was never tucked into his trousers. It didn't matter though. With boulders for hands and hams for arms, he had all the right equipment for 36 inch-perfect leg-breaks, a quick scratch and a slice or 12 of pizza afterwards.

Now, post-ban, he has gone all streamlined. A friend of mine swore she saw a six-pack nestling within his shirt. But the ghost of laid-back guzzler remains; even with a dinner suit he is given to wearing vest and flops. Mark Ray took a great black and white picture of Warne making a snack. Barefoot and with a cheese sandwich he looked completely at home – how could you not warm to a man like that? But the charm and insouciance would all be for nothing if he was no good.

Take one Warne. Give him the ball and put him on the field with 12 other men. Then try to flick through your paper or to concentrate on someone else. He makes it impossible. Warne with the ball is horrible addiction. With each gesture: flick, ball toss, lip suck, trigger of the finger to the temple, he intimidates the batsman. His slightly lop-sided skip is full of menace, and that's before even bowls: old fashioned leg-break, zooter, flipper, slider, back-spinner.

Of course he left his calling card early: in his 12th Test in Manchester on 4 June 1993. His timing, as always, was perfect – it was his first delivery in an Ashes contest and eagerly awaited on both sides. The ball sprung from his hand, drifted to leg, fizzed like a top, and shot back two feet to knock out Mike Gatting's off stump. The ball of the century they say – not a bad achievement in itself – which also succeeded in scarring a generation of English batsmen.

My favourite memory of him is during a Championship game for Hampshire against Kent in 2000. The sun had been blazing since dawn and salt prickled your face like a shaggy dog. Rahul Dravid was playing for Kent and the day became an epic battle between the two. Dravid came off the victor, making a beautiful century, but Warne tried every trick in the book in two sensational spells from the pavilion end – a twirling dervish from the antipodes with a white stripe of sun cream on his nose, bewitching the crowd.

For someone of such talent, he has managed a surprising number of comebacks. There was the 1999 World Cup campaign which started disastrously and ended with Australia victorious and Warne being named man of the match in the final. Then there was the dodgy diuretic (for which he blamed his mum and her diet pills, which wasn't his finest hour) discovered on the eve of Australia's first game of the 2003 World Cup in South Africa. He was sent home and banned for a year. Few believed that he could successfully come back but he returned fitter than ever, went to Sri Lanka and became the first spinner to take 500 Test wickets.

It is the little things that make Warne who he is. His promotion with Nicorette which ended in fabulous style when he was caught on camera having a fag. His charitable work. His almost lone willingness among Australians to stand up for his big rival Muralitharan's action.

Warne gets it wrong, often spectacularly. He isn't a cardboard cut-out. He is a real-life star who has cocked up but has made cricket, and life, immeasurably more fun. This summer's Ashes will be the last chance to see him at his favourite sport – eating Englishmen for lunch.

Though genius does not beget genius – and the other Test teams are hardly awash in leg-spinners – this very minute a boy is whipping his wrist because of Warne. His legacy will come good someday soon.

Sussex v Hampshire, Hove   Andy Arlidge, *Wisden* 2006
(County Championship Division One, April 20-23)

A row between the captains overshadowed a thrilling draw. Adams accused Warne of trying to humiliate Prior with sledging; Warne said he wanted to get under Prior's skin after a confrontation with Katich. Umpire Gould referred to the game's "Test match intensity" but there was no reprimand.

Kent v Hampshire, Canterbury   Mark Pennell, *Wisden* 2006
(County Championship Division One, May 11-14)

Warne fielded in a beanie hat for much of a bitterly cold game, but one event gave him a warm feeling. When he joined Hampshire in 2000, he said he craved a first-class hundred. In his 321st first-class innings, he got there, and in a hurry. It took just 72 balls, as he oversaw a first-day recovery from 130 for seven. England selector Geoff Miller, a famous late centurion himself, was there to see it.

Hampshire v Surrey, Southampton   Pat Symes, *Wisden* 2006
(County Championship Division One, June 15-17)

Again, Warne's combative captaincy caused irritation along the way: the game was just four overs old when he was involved in a finger-pointing row with umpire Whitehead after an appeal for a catch at the wicket off Taylor had been rejected. The escapee was Newman, on 14, who went on to score the match's only century and set up a total Hampshire could not match in two attempts.

Middlesex v Hampshire, Southgate   Norman De Mesquita, *Wisden* 2006
(County Championship Division One, July 8-11)

Hampshire's first innings owed much to Warne, in his last game before joining the Australian tourists, who – after waiting 14 years for a century – clouted his second in two months. This came from just 79 balls, as he put on 100 for the eighth wicket with Mascarenhas.

County Round-Up – Hampshire   Paul Coupar, *TWC*, August 2005

In the 1990s when the side was led by Mark Nicholas – famous for schmooze and champers – they were known affectionately as "Happy Hampshire". But throughout this successful season there have been murmurings on the county circuit that the club are becoming unpopular.

Some experienced local journalists and club members cannot stomach Hampshire's new spikier approach under Shane Warne. They do not like the captain's swearing, sledging and bust-ups with umpires, the latest of which was a prolonged finger-wagging argument (supporters of Warne that his chat is simply an attempting to "educate" English umpires about his bowling variations). There was also mutterings that Kevin Pietersen's directness has bruised the feelings of some junior club officials.

Glamorgan v Hampshire, Cardiff   Edward Bevan, *Wisden* 2006
(County Championship Division One, September 15-18)

Glamorgan's wretched season ended with their 14th defeat. For the first time in their history, they lost every match at Cardiff. But Warne and Katich had returned to Hampshire, still hoping to win the Championship despite losing the Ashes and, after a first-day washout, they made up for lost time by racing to four batting points plus a wicket on the second day. Warne himself hit Cosker for three sixes and a four in successive balls. He went on to take four wickets as Glamorgan conceded a 101-run deficit then juggled his batting order in the quest for quick runs, even though news of Nottinghamshire's victory at Canterbury meant Hampshire were now chasing second place.

Hampshire v Nottinghamshire, Southampton   Pat Symes, *Wisden* 2006
(County Championship Division One, September 21-23)

Second against first should have been the perfect climax to the Championship season, but Nottinghamshire's controversial victory over Kent had already made them champions. Even so, this was a memorable match because Warne was still livid at Kent's tactics and in no mood to ease off.

THE ASHES, 2005

Playing Shane Warne   *TWC*, August 2005

Nasser Hussain

I reckon Warne was at his best about 10 years ago. Now his bowling doesn't have the same fizz, and he hasn't got the flipper after his shoulder operations. But he's still a pretty good bowler because he has more guile and can out-think people. He has developed this straight-on delivery that comes out the front of the hand and drifts in, to get batsmen lbw as they play what they think is a perfect forward-defensive.

We must be wary that we don't end up playing Shane the myth rather than Shane Warne the leg-spinner. This happened to me at Edgbaston in 1997, when I was on about 80 and hadn't faced much of Warne. I kept wondering to myself how long it would be before they brought on Warne and I kept remembering the "Gatting ball" four years earlier. I had to convince myself just to have a look at each ball.

Not many English batsmen have gone after Shane and some others like Laxman and Tendulkar have been successful doing that. If Flintoff does have a battle with him the public should encourage it. If he gets Flintoff or Pietersen it doesn't matter as long as they know what they are doing, sticking to their worked-out game plan.

Rahul Dravid

They have to be positive against Warne, which does not mean taking him on blindly. You must look to create scoring opportunities. If he gains the mental ascendancy over England early in the series it will be difficult. But England have a good batting line-up, they will score runs but the key is to do it at the critical times, sometimes in difficult conditions.

The Big Personalities – Shane Warne   Will Kendall, *TWC*, August 2005

The public image of Shane Warne takes many forms, from spinning genius to bookies' accomplice, from all-Australian hero and chief Pom destroyer to drug offender and philanderer. To the Hampshire dressing room the man beneath the headlines has remained an amiable constant, largely unaffected by fame and fortune and – just like many Aussies – ultra-competitive, generous, good-natured and good fun. As a person, not just a cricketer, he is held in high esteem and warm affection, appreciated not only for his on-field knowledge and skill and the success he has brought but because he is polite, funny and considerate.

Though he has the nickname of Hollywood, there are no airs about him and no special demands. The only time he might seem different is when it comes to meals. He eschews the standard pasta for something far more straightforward: cheese or, to be precise, mild cheddar cheese. This is the common denominator of most meals. The only thing that changes is what accompanies it – white bread, a white baguette, a white roll, nachos or chips. To him, exotic is a margherita pizza.

Within the dressing room, he is just like anyone else. He likes cars, clothes, gadgets and golf and happily talks about nothing in particular until the cows come home. During breaks in play he will share out some of his excess kit, play cards and lose his cash, sign autographs and talk about St Kilda footie team to anyone who will listen.

His corner of the dressing room at the Rose Bowl is a bomb site – heaps of stuff sprawling over his two lockers. International cricketers are swamped with free gear. Aside from the equipment, shoes and a sackload of cricket whites are a couple of packets of fags, chewing gum, empty wrappers, a pile of autographs waiting to be done, a pile of envelopes waiting to be sent, a few marker pens, several dozen golf balls and some grated cheese trodden into the floor. Pride of place goes to a gleaming new set of golf irons.

Talking cricket, he is candid and opinionated and his insights and experience ensure enthralling listening. He is always conjuring plans and mooting ideas, some preposterous, others merely outrageous. What makes him different is that he believes in these ideas and that belief is inspiringly infectious. Hampshire have won games in the past 12 months that were to all intents and purposes lost. While most players would be thinking about packing the kit bag and the journey home, he dared to think they could be won. Warne pushed and prodded at the opposition both with his bowling and with his captaincy, before finally finding the weakness and pouring through the gap in the defences, taking the rest of the team with him.

Players love a winner but they respond because of his personal qualities. He does not shy away from the truth but he supports and appreciates those he plays with, often going out of his way to praise those who have done well and equally to encourage those who have not, not out of duty as captain but as a normal human being. People like to spend time with him, not because of who he is but because he is good company. He is just a regular guy living an irregular life.

When there is no cricket, life is no less hectic. Though many Australian labels prefer the clean-cut Adam Gilchrist and Brett Lee, Warne has big demands on his time, from sponsors' obligations to TV interviews, writing newspaper columns to unveiling portraits, all of which has to be juggled around family life (though he separated his wife Simone at the end of June) and the lure of the golf course.

So, why does a regular guy like this come out with an often different public perception? Part of the problem is that the attributes that are his biggest strengths with ball in hand on the field are often the ones that let him down off it. He is impulsive, with a desire to push boundaries and the self-belief to say that anything is possible. His optimism knows no bounds and he does not admit failings or weaknesses to team-mates let alone opponents – except at football, where he has two left feet and the touch of a pinball machine. These mental factors are the essence of the Warne armoury, the source of the imagination, persistence and sheer will that have taken him to the top of the tree.

While they are clearly assets seen through one lens, they can be liabilities seen through another. Take his batting. Warne is a talented and clean striker of the ball but his record could and should be far better. His problem is that he bats at one progressive tempo, starting fast and getting faster. He will keep swinging, believing he can hit the ball

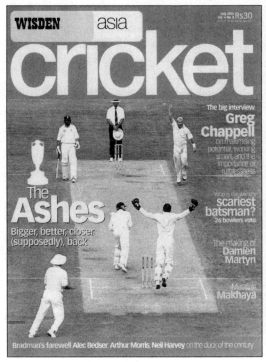

Wisden Asia Cricket, July 2005

further and further until it goes wrong and the whole lot comes crashing down. If his batting is taken as a metaphor for life, one can see how the result could be construed as careless and crass.

He knows his limitations now. There will be no more ripping leggies and pinpoint flippers but the oohs and aahs, the hustle and bluster, will be as big a factor as ever in the coming weeks.

England v Australia, Lord's   Gideon Haigh, *Wisden Australia* 2005-06
(First Test, July 21-24)

England needed 420 to win, or cleansing and prolonged rain to draw. They set off as if in pursuit of victory, Trescothick and Strauss calmly negotiating the opening burst of McGrath and Brett Lee. The breach was opened when Strauss aborted a pull and Lee intercepted the bunt by diving forward at short cover, whereupon Shane Warne induced catatonia among the batsmen. Trescothick was handily snared at slip, Bell baffled by a straight ball, Flintoff snaffled behind, and Lee finished off Vaughan's strokeless three quarters of an hour with a ball that held its line and flattened off stump.

CLASSIC TEST 7

England v Australia, Birmingham   Steven Lynch, *Wisden* 2006
(Second Test)
August 4, 5, 6, 7 – England won by 2 runs. Toss: Australia

If Australia had been rolled over in a couple of balls on the fourth morning, which was wholly possible, this would still be remembered as a great Test match: it produced exciting, fluctuating, often brilliant cricket from day one. But the crowd that turned up and filled Edgbaston on the Sunday seemed to sense they would be seeing something more worthwhile than three minutes' cricket and a victory singsong.

They still got the win they desperately wanted and expected, but in a manner that will never be forgotten. When the Old Trafford Test began four days later, *The Greatest Test* DVD was on sale. And no one was arguing with the description. On that sunlit fourth morning, England strode out on to the field with Australia 175 for eight, chasing 282. The main batsmen were all gone, and so was the swaggering confidence that had characterised Australia's Test performances for almost the whole of the previous 16 years.

But sometimes there is nothing quite as invigorating as a hopeless situation. Warne started brightly, Lee jumped solidly behind the ball, collecting bruises as well as runs, and the target ticked down. Warne trod on his stumps with 62 wanted, but still it wasn't over. The bowlers dug the ball in too short and too straight, aiming for catches off the splice rather than in the well-stocked slip cordon. England's confidence turned to concern to alarm to panic. And the last pair, Lee and Kasprowicz – with plenty of help from Extras – whittled the target down towards single figures.

With 15 required, Kasprowicz flicked Flintoff uppishly to third man, where Simon Jones failed to hold on to a difficult catch as he dived forward. England's last chance appeared to have gone. But finally, with just three wanted, Harmison banged one into the left glove of Kasprowicz, who hunched down horrified as the ball looped down the leg side and Geraint Jones plunged for the winning catch, the signal for tumultuous celebrations. A mournful Kasprowicz said afterwards. "It just got big quick, and I didn't see too much of it." Nor did umpire Bowden.

After umpteen TV replays, it was possible to conclude that Kasprowicz's left hand was off the bat at the moment of impact and, technically, he was not out. Bowden, however, would have needed superhuman vision to see this, and an armed escort involving several regiments to escape the crowd had he actually refused to give it out. It was also the right decision for cricket: 2-0 to Australia would have been the signal for the football season to begin; 1-1 lit the blue touchpaper. The Greatest Test became the Greatest Series, and the pyrotechnics illuminated the summer. The final margin was the closest in England-Australia Tests, edging the three-run thrillers at Old Trafford 1902 and Melbourne 1982-83 – and neither of those could match this one in its relentless unmissability.

The drama began before the toss, when McGrath trod on a ball during practice and tore his ankle ligaments. Despite losing his leading fast bowler, Ponting decided to field on a cloudy morning, influenced by some gloomy predictions about the pitch, which had been under water less than a week beforehand after Birmingham was struck by a mini-tornado. But, in keeping with Australia's flawed backroom work throughout the tour, Ponting's decision ignored well-informed local opinion on both the weather and the tendency of Edgbaston wickets to deteriorate.

Vaughan could hardly believe his luck, and Ponting rapidly got the sinking feeling of a captain who has made a very, very big mistake. Against a McGrathless attack, England shed their inhibitions and their vulnerability, and hurtled to 407 inside 80 overs – not the full 90 – the most conceded by Australia on the first day of any Test since 1938. Trescothick led the way with a blazing 90, as the bowlers obligingly served the ball into the perfect groove for his crunching cover and off-drives. He hit 15 fours and two sixes, but was out shortly after lunch, in sight of his first Ashes century. Bell followed third ball, and Vaughan hooked straight to long leg, but that set up a crucial stand of 103 between the big-hitting pair of Pietersen and Flintoff.

Unsure at first against Warne, who wheeled away through 25.2 overs, Flintoff hit his way out of trouble, carting Warne into the stands and once swatting a Lee bouncer over the rope despite taking his eye off the ball and trying to withdraw the bat. Few innings of such power and importance have conveyed so little authority: Flintoff was feeling his way uncertainly into the series but, once he got there, he commandeered it. After 45 overs, the official halfway mark, England were already 236 for four, a day's ration in the dour 1950s and '60s.

Flintoff had carved five sixes and six fours when he became Gillespie's 250th Test victim, just after tea. But then Pietersen, who had intelligently held back while Flintoff flailed, took over to score his third half-century in his first three Test innings, this time wafting a forthright 71 with a six and ten fours, several from a whipped forehand drive to midwicket reminiscent of the tennis court, more Borg than Border. The tail joined in too: Simon Jones was the fifth man to hit a six on a day which featured ten of them, as well as 54 fours, and the eventual scoring rate was a breathless 5.13 an over. Australia did manage to bowl England out on the first day – but for 407.

Rain prevented Australia from batting on the first evening, and they started badly next day when Hayden drove his first ball straight to cover, his first Test duck for 40 months and 68 innings. Langer dug in after being hit on the head in Harmison's first over – he said his old coach always liked to see him get hit early on, as it sharpened him up. And he resisted for four and a half hours, lasting long after Ponting had gone for a pleasant 61. But the middle order misfired, and Gilchrist was stranded on 49 when Flintoff struck twice in two balls, leaving England with a handy lead of 99. That increased by another 25 on the second evening, for the loss of Strauss, who was fooled by Warne's second ball, a huge turner which fizzed across his body and crashed into the stumps. It made Warne the first overseas bowler to take 100 Test wickets in England, and brought – for England – unnerving comparisons with the Gatting ball of 1993.

Indeed, after an initial burst from Lee reduced England to 31 for four – Vaughan's off stump was sent flying by a 91mph nip-backer – Warne dominated the third day. He bowled unchanged from the City End, usually round the wicket into the rough, often turning the ball unfeasible distances. Bell and Pietersen might have been unlucky to be given out caught behind, but Pietersen, whose 20 included two huge sixes over midwicket off Warne, had survived a confident caught-behind appeal from Lee first ball.

Warne's fifth wicket reduced England to 131 for nine, 230 ahead, but Flintoff then cut loose, slamming four more sixes to take his match total to nine, an Ashes record, outbeefing Ian Botham's six at Manchester in 1981. Now, this was Flintoff in full command of both his shots and the situation. One Kasprowicz over went for 20, despite a ring of fielders on the boundary, then Lee disappeared for 18, with one of two sixes being fished out of the TV cables on the pavilion roof by Graham Gooch. Flintoff was finally bowled for 73 – Warne's tenth wicket of the match and 599th in Tests – but the last-gasp stand of 51 with Simon Jones had swelled the lead and given England's dressing-room the scent of victory.

The frenetic pace continued in a three-and-a-half-hour session on the third evening. Australia galloped to 47 in 12 overs before Flintoff, almost inevitably, shook things up. Langer dragged his second delivery into his stumps, and Ponting nicked the seventh (after a no-ball), a leg-cutter, having kept out some searing inswingers. Hayden grafted to 31 before being well caught by the tumbling Trescothick at slip – Simon Jones's over-the-top send-off cost him 20% of his match fee – and three more went down before Flintoff, in his second spell, thudded a straight one into Gillespie's pads.

With the score at 140 for seven, England claimed the extra half-hour in a bid to polish the match off in three days. But Warne went on the offensive, lofting Giles for two sixes, and the only casualty of the extra period was Clarke, bamboozled by Harmison's rare slower ball after another easy-on-the-eye innings. That turned out to be the final ball of the day. At the time, it seemed slightly unfortunate that there would probably be so little left for a full house on the fourth day. But for the crowd the simple prospect of beating Australia was unmissable. Soon, their enthusiasm was to ripple out across the whole country.

Man of the Match: A. Flintoff. **Attendance:** 81,870.

England v Australia, Birmingham, 2005

ENGLAND	First innings		Second innings	
M. E. Trescothick c Gilchrist b Kasprowicz	90	–	c Gilchrist b Lee	21
A. J. Strauss b Warne	48	–	b Warne	6
*M. P. Vaughan c Lee b Gillespie	24	–	(4) b Lee	1
I. R. Bell c Gilchrist b Kasprowicz	6	–	(5) c Gilchrist b Warne	21
K. P. Pietersen c Katich b Lee	71	–	(6) c Gilchrist b Warne	20
A. Flintoff c Gilchrist b Gillespie	68	–	(7) b Warne	73
†G. O. Jones c Gilchrist b Kasprowicz	1	–	(8) c Ponting b Lee	9
A. F. Giles lbw b Warne	23	–	(9) c Hayden b Warne	8
M. J. Hoggard lbw b Warne	16	–	(3) c Hayden b Lee	1
S. J. Harmison b Warne	17	–	c Ponting b Warne	0
S. P. Jones not out	19	–	c Gilchrist b Lee	21
Lb 9, w 1, nb 14	24		Lb 1, nb 9	10

1/112 (2) 2/164 (1) 3/170 (4)   407
4/187 (3) 5/290 (6) 6/293 (7)
7/342 (8) 8/348 (5) 9/375 (10) 10/407 (9)

1/25 (2) 2/27 (1)   182
3/29 (4) 4/31 (3)
5/72 (6) 6/75 (5) 7/101 (8)
8/131 (9) 9/131 (10) 10/182 (7)

First innings—Lee 17–1–111–1; Gillespie 22–3–91–2; Kasprowicz 15–3–80–3; Warne 25.2–4–116–4.
Second innings—Lee 18–1–82–4; Gillespie 8–0–24–0; Kasprowicz 3–0–29–0; Warne 23.1–7–46–6.

AUSTRALIA	First innings		Second innings	
J. L. Langer lbw b S. P. Jones	82	–	b Flintoff	28
M. L. Hayden c Strauss b Hoggard	0	–	c Trescothick b S. P. Jones	31
*R. T. Ponting c Vaughan b Giles	61	–	c G. O. Jones b Flintoff	0
D. R. Martyn run out (Vaughan)	20	–	c Bell b Hoggard	28
M. J. Clarke c G. O. Jones b Giles	40	–	b Harmison	30
S. M. Katich c G. O. Jones b Flintoff	4	–	c Trescothick b Giles	16
†A. C. Gilchrist not out	49	–	c Flintoff b Giles	1
S. K. Warne b Giles	8	–	(9) hit wkt b Flintoff	42
B. Lee c Flintoff b S. P. Jones	6	–	(10) not out	43
J. N. Gillespie lbw b Flintoff	7	–	(8) lbw b Flintoff	0
M. S. Kasprowicz lbw b Flintoff	0	–	c G. O. Jones b Harmison	20
B 13, lb 7, w 1, nb 10	31		B 13, lb 8, w 1, nb 18	40

1/0 (2) 2/88 (3) 3/118 (4)   308
4/194 (5) 5/208 (6) 6/262 (1)
7/273 (8) 8/282 (9) 9/308 (10) 10/308 (11)

1/47 (1) 2/48 (3)   279
3/82 (2) 4/107 (4)
5/134 (6) 6/136 (7) 7/137 (8)
8/175 (5) 9/220 (9) 10/279 (11)

First innings—Harmison 11–1–48–0; Hoggard 8–0–41–1; S. P. Jones 16–2–69–2; Flintoff 15–1–52–3; Giles 26–2–78–3.
Second innings—Harmison 17.3–3–62–2; Hoggard 5–0–26–1; Giles 15–3–68–2; Flintoff 22–3–79–4; S. P. Jones 5–1–23–1.

Umpires: B. F. Bowden and R. E. Koertzen.   Third umpire: J. W. Lloyds.
Referee: R. S. Madugalle.

England v Australia, Manchester   Chloe Saltau, *Wisden* 2006

(Third Test, August 11-15)

Vaughan shared the first-day headlines with Shane Warne, who became the first bowler to take 600 Test wickets when Trescothick tried to sweep him and was caught by Gilchrist. Warne kissed a white wristband given to him by his daughter Brooke, who had urged him to "be strong", and continued to bowl tirelessly.

...

... the highest scorer in the first innings was the incomparable Warne. He blunted the reverse swing where his more highly regarded colleagues could not, saved the follow-on during the 14 overs that survived the rain on Saturday, and came within ten of a much-coveted maiden Test century.

England v Australia, Nottingham   Lawrence Booth, *Wisden* 2006

At 32 without loss after five overs, they were coasting. But cricket has never had a scene-stealer – not even Ian Botham – who could match Warne. He removed Trescothick and Vaughan with the opening deliveries of his first two overs, then snared Strauss at leg slip in his fifth to make it 57 for three.

The Spin Genius Etched in Time   Michael Henderson, *TWC*, October 2005

Whatever happens at The Oval (this column is being composed two days before the final Test), this late flowering of the summer owes much of its glory to Shane Warne. The incomparable wrist-spinner has given so much to the game that it seemed impossible that he could add to his reputation. Surely we know everything about him we needed to know. But, with his bowling, his batting, and his astonishing tour de force on the last day of the Trent Bridge Test when he led the Australian challenge, indeed appeared to be in charge of the side, he has taken his leave of us (in Tests that is: he will carry on playing for Hampshire) in the most remarkable manner.

That Warne is a true great is not in doubt. The figures prove, though, that it is wrong to rely too much on figures where greatness is concerned. Ted Dexter's Test average (47.89) would suggest that he was very good, rather than great, but the bowlers who ran in at him tell a different tale. Ian Botham, of course, was great – greater than his figures, good as they are, might suggest. There are plenty of others, too, in all sports, who achieved greatness by imposing their personality on games and opponents.

At a time when Australia are in decline, when the English batsmen have blasted Jason Gillespie out of Test cricket and refused to bend their knee to the other bowlers, Warne has shown his real mettle. He has also taken his punishment, particularly when Andrew Flintoff got after him at Edgbaston, but he has shown the character of a true champion in his response, not least in his batting, which has improved so much that he may call himself an all-rounder.

We can all admire greatness, whether it is Warne taking wickets with sheer force of personality, or Roger Federer feathering the ball beyond the range of harder hitters.

Even the partisan crowds that have congregated this summer – and, by word, they have been partisan! – have warmed to Warne's compelling skills. We have seen it so often now it fails to surprise us, and yet it is still something to observe: his cunning, his persistence, the showmanship of the born troubadour.

Admire him while you can, because when he departs the international stage we shall not see his like again. That is often said of great players, but it is still true. Warne is the greatest slow bowler in the history of a game that has produced many notable ones, and cricket-lovers will be talking of him 100 years from now, just as people talk today of Victor Trumper and Ranji. Of course, it is possible that they will also talk of Muttiah Muralitharan, but not necessarily for the same reasons.

Great players deserve to be celebrated with fine writing, and Warne has found a worthy scribe this summer in the person of Gideon Haigh, the Anglo-Australian who has spent the series in the bosom of *The Guardian* family. The coverage of this mighty Ashes contest has produced some excellent writing (James Lawton and Peter Roebuck in *The Independent*, the Stephens Brenkley and Fay in the *Indy on Sunday*, Atherton in the *Sunday Telegraph*) but *The Guardian's* coverage, like the series itself, has established fresh standards. Mike Selvey (who looks more and more like Brando in *Apocalypse Now*!) has led the way and Haigh, after getting his eye in, has creamed the ball round the meadow like Hammond at Bristol.

One cavil, though. All this talk of cricket becoming "the new football" is the most dreadful mush. Who actually came up with a phrase like that? Whoever it is, he should be marched to the stocks at once. Either that, or the cat. Football, whether we like it or not, will always remain the most popular game in the world, and for that reason it is often followed by people with whom we might not care to share a noggin. Cricket does not need to be promoted as a form of showbiz. That way madness lies. It is the game of games, and this summer the players of both sides have given us so many reasons to celebrate its greatness that we should simply say: thank you, gentlemen.

England v Australia, The Oval   Hugh Chevallier, *Wisden* 2006
(Fifth Test, September 8-12)

Far from a commanding lead, Australia trailed by six, failing to make 400 in a series of four or more Tests for the first time since 1978-79. Ponting's only option was to blast England out double quick, but the light remained sepulchral. McGrath idiotically bowled a bouncer, and they were off – though not before Warne found extravagant, anxiety-inducing spin to remove Strauss. On their return, in marginally brighter conditions, all the Australian players sported sunglasses. The pantomime caught on: with Warne a constant threat, some spectators theatrically unfurled umbrellas against non-existent rain. Nearby Aussies promptly stripped off their shirts and basked in illusory sunshine. The umbrellas won. To applause that might have been thunder, everyone trooped off. It meant no more cricket; the paying public, for once, didn't care.

The final day dawned, brightly, with every result possible and tension upgraded from danger level to crisis point. England were 34 for one, but they had to get through a notional 98 overs without giving Australia a look-in. With the score on 67, McGrath struck twice with two exquisite deliveries. The hat-trick ball looped into the slips, sparking huge appeals and much queasiness. Somehow, umpire Bowden got it right. Not out: it had hit Pietersen's shoulder. Next over, he was dropped off Warne; had it stuck, England would have been 68 for four. They were nurturing the shoots of a recovery when Lee found Pietersen's edge. The ball flashed at head height to Warne, safest of first slips. He parried it. As his despairing lunge failed to grab the rebound, the stands erupted.

The release of tension was shortlived. Warne snaffled Trescothick and Flintoff to give Australia the edge: at lunch, they were 133 behind, just five wickets to filch and more than 70 overs left. Some found it all too much. David Graveney, the chairman of selectors, headed for the car park to calm himself down, missing an epic shoot-out between Pietersen, oozing conviction, confidence and courage, and Lee, touching 95mph.

Australia in England, 2005   Gideon Haigh, *Wisden Australia* 2005-06

In any other summer, Shane Warne's 40 wickets at 19 and 249 runs at 27 would have guaranteed some individual awards. It carried, indeed, its own badge of distinction. Warne, for long a great player in a grand side, was here seen in a new guise: Australia's best, last and sometimes only hope. Time and again he redeemed Australia's cause on his own, apparently by sheer force of will. In the only Test in which he did not clean up with the ball, at Old Trafford, he hefted 90 and 32. Warne's build-up to the series had been what might euphemistically called less than ideal; in particular, publicity about a new round of sexual peccadilloes finally drove off his long-suffering wife. Yet once on the field, he sunk himself entirely in his task. The crowd at The Oval paid him warm tribute with a chant of "we wish you were English" – taking the words, as it were, from the tabloid newspapermen's mouth.

Notes by the Editor   Matthew Engel, *Wisden* 2006

The guiding myth of cricket is that it's a team game. The ethos is always that the individual must subordinate himself to the collective: celebrate a victory even if he has contributed nothing and faces the chop, or pretend that his own century is meaningless if it failed to secure the team's objective. This applies on the village green just as it does in a Test match.

But this misrepresents cricket's appeal, both to the player and the spectator. It's a game of character and personality – individuals operating within the team's framework, like wheels within wheels. The Ashes provided the classic example of this. It would have been half the contest but for two amazing men: Andrew Flintoff and Shane Warne.

These two extraordinary physical specimens brought to the summer all the qualities associated with the medieval joust: heroic endeavour laced with good humour and magnanimity. Many of the most interesting figures in cricket history have been built on this scale (Grace, Barnes, Compton, Miller, Botham, Lara...). They are freaks of nature who play the game without fear; their careers are never smooth progressions from one success to the next – their failures are spectacular and disproportionately criticised; they irritate authority; in some cases, their personal lives are equally tempestuous. Yet they bring more to the game than a dozen well-disciplined mortals.

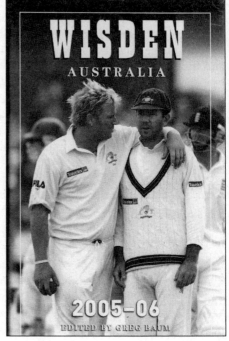

Wisden Cricketers' Almanack 2006   Wisden Australia 2005-06

Warne's Amazing Summer   Alex Brown, *Wisden* 2006

During the final session of the Oval Test, the trash-talking bully boy of Australian cricket stood on the boundary as the Ashes slid away from his team. Was he mocked? No, thousands of English fans offered an extended, emotional chant of "There's only one Shane Warne."

Everyone knew that. But, though his career has been defined by success, it took defeat for Warne to be truly embraced in England. And his journey in 2005 was an extraordinary one: from mirth to myth.

Before a ball had been bowled in the Ashes, Warne's public (and often pathetically embarrassing) sexual dalliances prompted his wife Simone to announce she was ending the marriage. For a man whose career has included a drugs ban and betting allegations, personal turmoil was hardly a novelty, but now his reputation seemed in tatters along with his domestic life.

Redemption came, not through the victory at Lord's, but through the trials that followed. At Edgbaston, with the Australian attack suddenly toothless, Warne unleashed an outrageous leg-break that pitched in the footmarks, bit like a rabid dog and bowled a startled Andrew Strauss around his legs. That was just one of ten wickets. And then there were his deeds with the bat, that dragged Australia to the chance of victory.

When Australia lost, one might have expected the delirious Edgbaston crowd to jeer him. After all, they had taunted him with "Where's your missus gone?" earlier in the match. Instead, they stood and applauded a worthy opponent.

The theme continued in Manchester, where Warne fought valiantly for the draw and became the first man to take 600 Test wickets, whereupon he kissed a white bracelet. A marketing stunt? A sponsor's ploy? No, he explained. His daughter Brooke had given it to him just before the family's return to Australia.

On to Trent Bridge, and the aura became yet brighter. So often defensive and surly in his dealings with the media, Warne grew ever more engaging, witty and incisive. Sometimes you felt he didn't want the press conferences to end. He was certainly loving the duel on the field. While others wavered, Warne took eight wickets and scored what were almost match-winning runs.

His sweat-drenched efforts at The Oval also failed to produce victory. But they did not go unrewarded. As he stood at fine leg, the English applause came like thunder. And after the match, while his opponents headed for their victory ride and a long rest, he rushed off to try – in vain again – to lead Hampshire to the County Championship. What a summer! What a cricketer!

The Wisden Forty   Lawrence Booth and Rob Smyth, *Wisden* 2006

Just when we thought we had seen it all from Warne, he showed us more. He obliterated Dennis Lillee's record for Test wickets in a calendar year, ending with 96, became the first person to pass 600 wickets in Tests, and thwanged his maiden first-class century for good measure. And his Ashes performances were the stuff of legend: a glorious fusion of brain, brawn and box-office against the backdrop of the crumbling Australian hegemony, and of his marriage. Rarely had anyone emerged from such disaster so triumphantly. Where the intensity of England's challenge cowed others, it fascinated and inspired Warne to produce the best series of his career: 40 wickets and 249 streetwise runs, an absolute champion at the peak of his powers and a never-ending well of mental strength to which his team-mates turned every single time they were in trouble. One by one, the Australians had their will broken but with every baggy-green bottle that went down Warne just stood taller, prouder, stronger. The compelling manner in which he held court confirmed his place as cricket's great lost captain and, when his every delivery was anticipated like a sudden-death penalty shoot-out, it felt like it was Warne against All-England. His brilliance made it even more brutal that he should drop Pietersen so crucially at the final day at The Oval, but he took that and defeat on the most famous double chin in sport. Business continued as usual in the Australian summer, as it had in New Zealand before the Ashes, and he ended the year with 700 wickets on the horizon, along with the small matter of Ashes revenge. With Warne, there was always something new to look forward to.

2005-06

Australia v West Indies, Adelaide　　　　　　　Peter English, *Wisden* 2006

(Third Test, November 25-29)

Warne bowled unchanged throughout the first two sessions – 29 overs – to take six for 80, and moved within one of Dennis Lillee's 1981 record of 85 Test victims in a calendar year. Bravo proved harder to dislodge, and he capped a strong all-round match by hitting 64. This made sure of a reasonable target before the innings was finished off by Lee and Warne, who was later cleared by Mike Procter, the referee, of a dissent charge following a rejected bat-pad appeal off Powell in the final over of the third day.

Australia v South Africa, Perth　　　　　　　Neil Manthorp, *Wisden* 2006

(First Test, December 16-20)

South Africa's batting also promised more than it delivered. There was an opening stand of 83 between Smith and de Villiers, who hooked the first ball of the innings for four and put a poor trot behind him with a spirited 68. But Smith drove at a wide one and edged to second slip, Lee chipped in with two quick wickets and, when Warne trapped Prince in front – his 86th wicket of 2005, breaking Dennis Lillee's calendar year record from 1981 – the innings threatened to implode at 187 for six, still 71 adrift.

WORDS ON WARNE

"Your hope is the record goes to someone you rate very highly, and I rate him as the best I have ever seen so it's perfect."

Dennis Lillee, former Australia bowler – *TWC*, February 2006

Australia v South Africa 2005-06　　　　　　　Neil Manthorp, *Wisden* 2006

Buoyed by a compelling contest at the WACA after years of one-sided home Tests, the Australian public's interest was drawn further to the series when Warne previewed the Boxing Day Test by describing Smith as "unimaginative and uninspiring" and a "typical" South African captain. Far from bowing down and biting his lip, which would have been a typical South African response, Smith gave journalists and headline writers the perfect Christmas present when he described Warne as a frustrated captain who tried to "take control of the team when the pressure is on", and who "put Ricky under a lot of pressure".

Warne was livid, while most South Africans could hardly believe that their young captain had allowed himself to be dragged into such a public no-win situation. Smith said after the series that it had been a calculated tactic to get under Warne's skin and deflect media attention away from the younger, more vulnerable members of his own squad. Both goals were achieved but, while neither man enjoyed his best series, the cost to South Africa may have been far greater: Warne's 14 wickets at 33 were more valuable than Smith's 155 runs at 25.83.

...

When it was all over, the final sight of Warne and Smith was of them sitting next to each other in the South African dressing-room at the SCG, sharing a bottle of wine and showing that all was fair in sport, if not life, after all.

South Africa v Australia, Cape Town   Neil Manthorp, *Wisden* 2007

(First Test, March 16-18)

Players play and groundsmen prepare pitches. Or that's the theory. But when the South African team arrived in Cape Town before the First Test, they decided to get involved with pitch preparation. Senior players persuaded team management to encourage Christo Erasmus, the head groundsman, to give the pitch an unscheduled watering two days before the match started – despite his insistence that it was a good batting surface that would not especially take spin.

The South Africans had just one man in mind, and to their eyes the bare patches looked terrifying and the small cracks cavernous. After dominating South Africa's batsmen for more than a decade, Shane Warne (and his reputation) had once again influenced the outcome of the match – before he had even had a net.

South Africa v Australia 2005-06   Neil Manthorp, *Wisden* 2007

Warne, naturally, rose to the on-field challenges, though compared to previous tours he seemed content to step back and let the seamers enjoy the greener pitches prepared in the hope of nullifying his threat. But as always he couldn't keep his mouth shut, and continually goaded Smith for his "unimaginative" leadership. It was too much for Smith, who was left gasping at a press conference: "Do you guys really take him seriously? I can't believe you take him seriously..."

2006

News   *TWC*, March 2006

Shane Warne, who has quashed rumours of an ODI return, is set to make his acting debut in a cameo appearance in the soap *Neighbours*. His character apparently has plenty of skeletons in the cupboard: he is playing himself.

Appealing   Gideon Haigh, *TWC*, April 2006

Growing up in Melbourne, Shane Warne's first cricket aspiration was famously to emulate his hero Dennis Lillee. And if it turned out he lacked the speed, part of Lillee's game he certainly mastered: the appeal.

The action photograph that Warne chose for his autobiography is not of himself flicking out a flipper or speculating about a slider. He is instead red-faced and roaring, bent backwards by the effort of demanding justice from an unseen and unfortunate umpire. It reveals a few too many chins to be a flattering portrait but it is a faithful rendering nevertheless. Like his bowling, Warne's appealing has multiple dimensions, being inquiry, assertion, celebration, exhibition, denunciation and defiance all at once and sometimes, also, annoyance.

The appeal is the elephant in the dressing room – a feature that is a huge part of the game's ritual yet is routinely overlooked. Just occasionally, though, someone gets a glimpse of a trunk or an ear. So it has been this summer in Australia. After defeat at Melbourne, South Africa's coach Mickey Arthur described Ricky Ponting's Australians as "masters" of putting pressure on umpires with their "histrionics" and singled out Warne as first among equals. The ICC match referee Chris Broad agreed that the Australians were pushing the boundaries of fair play and spoke to both Warne and their coach John Buchanan during the game.

Not surprisingly Ponting was having none of that: "It's another little niggly thing they are trying to have a go at us with. We are out there appealing every time we think something is out. We don't think there's anything wrong and we don't think there's been any over-appealing in this game." Justin Langer even channelled the Lillee spirit himself: "It's indicative of his [Warne's] passion for the game. I remember as a kid watching Dennis Lillee appeal. It was one of the great sights of cricket. I used to run around as a 10-year-old, bowl and then appeal like Lillee. He [Warne] thinks it's out and he gives it a big appeal. To me that's just part of the game, part of the great theatre of the great Shane Warne."

World News   *TWC*, April 2006

Shane Warne has dropped a hint that he will still be around for the 2009 Ashes by signing a four-year footwear deal with Mitre. Warne has been reluctant to announce his retirement plans, going as far as to say only that he intends to have a decent stint in county cricket with Hampshire.

Warwickshire v Hampshire, Birmingham   Paul Bolton, *Wisden* 2007
(County Championship Division One, May 9-12)

Warwickshire looked all at sea against Warne, who found increasing turn, and wound up with the 60th five-for of his career.

World News   *TWC*, June 2006

Shane Warne is expected to regain his Channel 9 television contract after it was terminated last year due to his off-field behaviour. The deal, believed to be worth A$300,00 (around £125,000) a year, is expected to involve more than just commentary work.

Hampshire v Kent, Southampton   Pat Symes, *Wisden* 2007
(County Championship Division One, May 24-27)

Warne's lingering ill-feeling towards Kent – he believed Fulton, their former captain, denied Hampshire a fair crack at the 2005 Championship when he struck a deal with Nottinghamshire – spilled over at the end of a rain-affected game. This time, Warne accused them of negativity after he set a last-afternoon target of 225 from a minimum 48 overs. When bad light and drizzle ended play an hour early, Kent were well adrift.

    ...

    Kent showed a flicker of interest in victory until Key, Fulton's successor, had his middle stump uprooted by a Warne leg-break; thereafter survival became the one concern. Key countered Warne's accusations by claiming he had acted realistically.

Nottinghamshire v Hampshire, Nottingham   Simon Cleaves, *Wisden* 2007
(County Championship Division One, July 14-17)

A feud between Warne and [David] Hussey, apparently dating back to disputes in the Victoria dressing-room 18 months earlier, boiled over into angry words in the middle, resulting in Warne pointedly refusing to applaud any of Hussey's landmarks on the way to an undefeated 150.

Hampshire v Worcestershire, Southampton   Pat Symes, *Wisden* 2007
(NatWest Pro40 League Division Two, September 13)

Pride came before a fall for Shane Warne on his 37th birthday: after receiving an honorary doctorate from Southampton Solent University for services to cricket, he top-edged a ball through the grille of his helmet and was struck above an eyebrow. Stitched up, he returned at the end of Hampshire's innings.

Hampshire v Lancashire, Southampton   Pat Symes, *Wisden* 2007
(County Championship Division One, September 20-23)

With the top three places now set in stone, Warne, keen to make a game of things in the fourth-day sunshine, suggested a contrived run chase. But Chilton declined, needled by what he saw as premature declaration bowling – and maybe the sense that Warne was pressurising him. He later regretted the decision. Once it became clear Lancashire were batting on, the circus really began: Warne bowled bouncers off a 20-yard run-up one moment, lobs that threatened to go into orbit the next, while Benham revealed his ambidexterity by bowling right- and left-arm spin. It all ensured a largely meaningless return for Anderson, limited to 12 overs a day by the ECB during his recovery from injury. Warne even contemplated forfeiting the match if a late declaration – to give Anderson a few more overs – materialised. It didn't, but accusations from Warne that spectators and the spirit of the game were being ignored certainly did.

Liverpool Victoria County Championship

Wisden 2007

Hampshire, certainly the most interesting team in the Championship, had a useful spinner of their own in Shane Warne, although Warne's bowling was rarely overwhelming. His genius went more into the all-round gusto he put into the captaincy, ensuring that each game he played had some kind of entertainment, even if it was just a blazing row with the opposition.

Hampshire in 2006

Pat Symes, *Wisden* 2007

Warne's value cannot be overstated: leader; mentor of a predominantly young side; tireless world-beating bowler; belligerent late-order batsman. There were two Hampshires in 2006 – a combative, occasionally confrontational outfit (especially in some hostile battles with Sussex) led by Warne, and a meeker, less confident team when he wasn't there to hide behind.

Missing the Bus in Trafalgar Square

Craig Butcher, *TWC*, July 2006

A giant, polystyrene Shane Warne paraded along Tower Bridge, Piccadilly Circus and Trafalgar Square, and mingled with befuddled tourists and curious fans late in May. Nearly two weeks in the making, the 28 feet high model was all part of a TV advertisement filmed around London's West End and destined for Australian television in late June. And without a word being said or a ball bowled, big Warne's appearance created quite a stir.

"It was massive – pretty amazing," said Shabs Bazdar. "Everyone was looking at it." The oversized Warne appeared in trademark appeal stance, complete with zinc and earring. "He looked like he'd probably had a couple of cases before sitting for it – his eyes were red," said Jacques de Sousa, a security guard at Lillywhite's sports shop in Piccadilly Circus.

Not everyone was certain of the likeness. Passer-by Tony Bloomer said: "I've seen him a lot of times but from a distance I thought it was Ian Botham. The hair and, er, the chubbiness, to put it lightly."

The sculpture soon struggled in the damp, flaking around the hairline. Then his shirt-collar snapped in two and his drivers escorted him to a back street. Some thought that too good for him. "Hopefully he's going down the Thames and getting pushed in," said Kevin Hole, a comment swiftly dismissed by Mark Gibbons of Believe Media, the company behind the campaign: "We're worried we'd get arrested."

Warne did seem to lift spirits on a miserable squally day. "A little bit of a laugh will give people encouragement – why not?" said De Sousa. "If I was Australian, I'd be proud." Eugene Barber echoed this thought: "I think he's great for the sport and he should have pride of place in Trafalgar Square."

Chronicle *Wisden, 2007*

Shane Warne is the hero of Australia's young males, according to Paul Merrill, editor of the country's top-selling lads' mag, *Zoo*. "He's supposedly shagged 1,000 women, he's fat, he smokes and he drinks beer." (*The Times*, September 26).

***

Victoria Coverdale, 39, who runs a B&B west of Melbourne, has produced a book of 28 poems devoted to Shane Warne. She published them herself after being turned down by a vanity publisher, who told her: "I've never known anything so singularly obsessive." The poems include "A good introduction" devoted to *the* ball:

Mike Gatting's mouth became an O,
With a single delivery that changed the world,
Mike's, Shane's and mine, you know (*The Times*, December 1).

THE ASHES, 2006-07

Warne of Words with Buchanan Kevin Mitchell, *TWC*, November 2006

Ian Chappell once said coaches at international level were a waste of time. Clive Lloyd used to say captaining a great side, as he did, was one the easiest jobs in cricket. And Angelo Dundee helped Muhammad Ali only when he put his stool in the right place at the end of each round. Champions do not or want or need cosseting. They are not the best listeners. If they are going to triumph, they want it to be their terms, otherwise it dilutes the achievement.

The freewheeling Shane Warne, who has taken 685 wickets in 140 Tests and whose early-career mentor Terry Jenner is now a more avuncular and peripheral influence, would agree. John Buchanan, probably, would not.

Buchanan, the former teacher and university lecturer who played seven first-class games for Queensland in 1978-79, averaging 12.30 with the bat, has always seen another, more cerebral, dimension to the game. A great fan of Sun Tzu, he famously tried to share the Chinese warlord's wisdom with the Australian team on the 2001 Ashes tour. He had the backing of the then captain, Steve Waugh, but not all the players welcomed Buchanan's input. And he left the lightest footprint at Middlesex, whose players regarded his stint at Lord's as coach in 1998 as a dismal episode.

Warne and Buchanan have never gelled but their most recent falling-out goes beyond cricketing philosophy. It betrays a fundamental division in the Australian team. After Warne mused recently on the merits of Buchanan – "Does the coach make the team does the team make the coach?" – it came as no surprise that he quickly claimed he had been quoted "completely out of context". If you regularly open your mouth to change feet, this is an accepted sequence. Gaffe followed by limp excuse.

There is plenty of previous between Warne and Buchanan. In his latest book Warne damns him with faintest of praise, saying "Some people" go along with the coach's methods. Elsewhere he moaned about Buchanan's utterly ridiculous boot camp for the Australian squad. Then, after a benefit bash for Liam Botham, a *Daily Telegraph* diary writer claimed Warne told Buchanan at boot camp: "I hate your guts and I want to go home. You're a dickhead."

It is all good, robust stuff and very Australian, in the tradition of the former Labor Prime Ministers Bob Hawke and Paul Keating – and quite a few of their 20 million compatriots. It is fine having an opinion. But Ricky Ponting, Warne's captain (in name at least), would contend it is not so fine having an opinion that undermines the authority and credibility of your coach and sharing it with the enemy – which, in this case, is the media.

At least Warne is candid. I happen to agree with him that coaches are regarded with too much reverence – though I am not about to share a dressing room with Buchanan this winter. I did briefly share a dressing room with both of them in 2005 – and very interesting it was. I was ghosting a column Buchanan was contributing to *The Observer* and he was always accommodating and polite, even when the series came to an unsatisfactory end for the Australians at The Oval. On the Saturday of that Fifth Test, Buchanan could have been excused for sidestepping his obligation or for asking for more time to compose his thoughts after a frustrating day but we duly met at the appointed time.

As we spoke in the dressing room Buchanan reflected on the Test and the series, conceding that England had produced a couple of aces in Andrew Flintoff and Simon Jones, whose reverse swing took them by surprise. He said that maybe the Australians did not have enough practice time between Tests. Then, as he sought to balance self-justification with positives, he looked over my shoulder and paused. We should not forget, he went on, that Shane Warne had had a great series (he would end with 40 wickets). There had never been a bowler like him, and so on.

"Just as well you got that in," Warne said as he walked from behind me and out of the door. He had been listening for a couple of minutes. It was a light-hearted aside but a telling one. It is not that Buchanan was currying favour with The Blond. Who could argue that Warne did not have a wonderful series? But it was the nuance of the exchange, the senior player chipping the hired help. There was no question who had the upper hand in that dressing room.

Warne, rightly or wrongly, has long regarded himself as undroppable. He generally puts on a good public show of solidarity with whoever is lumbered with ruling his unruly life but sometimes he cannot help himself, either privately or in the media.

A couple of days after Warne's criticism of Buchanan, the good folk from Cricket Australia sought to paper over their embarrassment. Warne, they said, had subsequently spoken by phone with the coach and the captain. "It was an amicable call," they announced, "and the team now moves on."

So, where have we moved on to? On balance, Warne's spat with Buchanan will matter little. The coach is leaving after the World Cup and the player will still be there, bamboozling batsmen without any help from the boundary.

Warne has a more fascinating relationship with Ponting, just as he had with Waugh, who got the captaincy ahead of him when Warne's indiscretions had piled too high for the moralistic administrators of Cricket Australia.

Bowler and captain will close ranks for the Ashes and there may well be no further disturbances. But it is the unspoken truth in the Australian dressing room that Warne has a cricket brain twice the size of Ponting's and, "moving on" towards the end of his illustrious career, fewer inhibitions about saying exactly what he thinks.

Australia's Boot Camp   Shane Warne, *TWC*, November 2006

What did you think of the idea?

I couldn't see the point of it. Three months before the first Test of the Ashes you have a bonding camp, then you all disappear and do your own thing for three months. But having gone through the camp and given it a chance – we all had our concerns or a lot of players did but we all went in with an open mind to try to get something out of it – the whole 25 players became a lot closer together after what we went through, so you'd have to say it was a success in that regard.

What did you actually do?

Pushing cars up hills on gravel – that was great fun. Walking up hills carrying 25-kilo water cans, with a 25-kilo backpack. Sleeping out under the stars in a sleeping bag with no tent, that was just wonderful, getting bitten by mozzies. It sounded like a For-mula 1 Grand Prix as they were going round in your ear. I've got mozzie bites all over me. Getting woken up in the middle of the night and going orienteering when there's kangaroos out there jumping around… It was just a wonderful time to be honest, it's just been fantastic. I think, if it was *Survivor*, myself and Stuart MacGill would have been certainties to be voted first off, absolute certainties.

Did you eat witchetty grubs?

No we didn't go that far, two slices of bread and a bit of water – that was pretty good.

How would you assess John Buchanan's role as coach?

I disagree with certain tactics and some of his methods I thought just complicated issues. At stages, too, he lacked a little bit of common sense. You've got to say he's played in a successful era but it's the old question: does the coach make the team or does the team make the coach? I'm a big believer, as Ian Chappell is, that the coach is something you travel in to and from the ground.

Interview by Paul Coupar

WORDS ON WARNE

"A lot of people ask me about Shane Warne but let me tell you, I never competed with another player – it's not massively helpful. Having him in the side was a huge advantage, predominantly because he was such a superstar."

Stuart MacGill, Australia leg-spinner – *TWC*, January 2011

Nasser's 10-Point Plan
Nasser Hussain, TWC, December 2006

Warne and McGrath

For the first time in a long while Australia are not certain about the make-up of their bowling attack. They don't have the luxury of a settled and proven four-man attack that has served them so well for years.

The slight decline of Jason Gillespie has left them in a position where they will probably use a five-man attack with Shane Watson and possibly Mitchell Johnson backing up the established trio of Shane Warne, Glenn McGrath and Brett Lee.

The McGrath-Warne axis is the greatest bowling partnership of all time and, although still formidable, there are signs of decline there too. England will feel that if they can get through McGrath's new-ball spell and the occasional wonderful spell from Warne there will be runs to be had elsewhere. Stuart MacGill is likely to play at least a couple of Tests and, while he is an excellent leg-spinner, he does bowl the odd bad delivery. England definitely have the batsmen to score heavily on good pitches.

At Last – The Ashes
Lawrence Booth, TWC, January 2007

Shane Warne summed it up with pomposity-pricking finality. "I'm fed up of talking to you guys. I want it all to start." Tell us about it, Shane. So he did. Three days before the First Test at Brisbane, Warne explained why it was madness to drop Chris Read and why Ashley Giles was Fletcher's teacher's pet. Oh, and he had been working on the flipper. And the googly was coming out nicely. And England had better watch out. In the circumstances, it seemed futile to argue.

Australia v England, Brisbane   Stephen Fay, *TWC*, January 2007
(First Test, November 23-27)

Oddly enough, the most absorbing cricket was played by Kevin Pietersen and Paul Collingwood when they took on Shane Warne on the fourth day. KP was at his magical, unorthodox best, irritating Warne by using his feet to turn defence into offence. Warne did not like it and words beginning with 'F' were exchanged. When Pietersen was out on 92, it was not Warne who got him, though he did tempt Collingwood on 96 to charge down the wicket and get stumped instead of his hundred. Collingwood, an unlikely No. 4, drove Warne magnificently and matched the imperious KP's scoring rate, minute for minute and ball for ball.

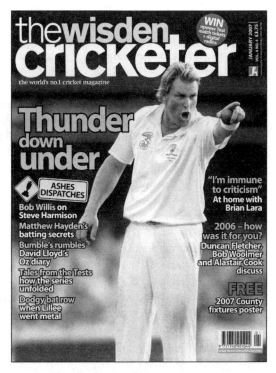

The Wisden Cricketer, January 2007

CLASSIC TEST 8

Australia v England, Adelaide   Matthew Engel, *Wisden* 2007
(Second Test)
December 1, 2, 3, 4, 5 – Australia won by six wickets. Toss: England

Great Man theory, originally associated with the philosopher Thomas Carlyle, holds that the whole of human history has been determined by a handful of people. In cricketing terms, it has always been hard to dispute, especially when you're sitting at Don Bradman's home ground.

For four days and 43 minutes of this Test match, there was plenty of time to think about such matters, and also whether it might be more amusing to spend the final afternoon hiring a pedalo on the River Torrens instead of watching this turgid contest dribble away to its inevitable draw. Then came the Great Man.

Shane Warne conjured up perhaps the most astounding victory of even his career. Here was a pitch that, all along, had offered the possibility to a batsman with sufficient stamina and perseverance of staying at the crease until the 2010-11 Ashes. Suddenly the placid earth began to crack and crumble and boil and bubble, as if the San Andreas Fault had opened directly underneath. But the fault was all England's. In the first innings, they had convinced themselves the Wizard of Oz was no great magician but just a cunning illusionist. Now they thought he could make the earth move. And so he did.

He was given a shove by the first bad umpiring decision of the match: Steve Bucknor gifted Warne the wicket of Strauss, caught off his pad. From that moment, every demon that has haunted English cricket started to play inside the batsmen's heads. And the greatest of those demons was bowling at them.

From 69 for one, England withered to 129 all out. Australia's task – 168 in 36 overs – was no certainty. But the force was with them, and they won with 19 balls to spare. You could replay the final day a hundred times, and the game might be drawn every time. But it won't be replayed. Such a day could never happen quite like this again. To understand the drama of the turnaround, it is necessary to loll awhile amid the languor that came before. There was a shock at the start: both teams were unchanged, which meant England were defying public and pundits alike by again omitting Panesar and keeping both Anderson and Giles. There was a second shock too, in the sense that English fatalists presumed such an important toss was bound to be won by Australia. In fact, Flintoff correctly called heads, and he did not attempt a third shock by fielding.

There have been better batting pitches – some England players said it was the slowest they had seen all year – but few more disheartening for bowlers. Warne did get some first-day turn, which was remarkable. But it was soon clear this was unlikely to be one of McGrath's Tests and, when the second new ball came, it was handed to the wholehearted Clark. The only good news for Australia was that the Adelaide weather was unusually cool and breezy.

It took a while for England to establish any kind of command. Though Bell and Collingwood dug in, Bell wrecked his good work by mishooking on 60. That brought in Pietersen, but even he could not assert himself. Collingwood reached his hundred off the eighth ball of the second day; Pietersen followed him before lunch. And though the stand easily surpassed the 153 they had put on in adversity at Brisbane, England still had trouble upping the rate. This was due partly to the pitch, partly to the batsmen's caution, and partly to Warne opting for negative round-the-wicket bowling, which Pietersen could only kick away. He later claimed this showed he had Warne beaten.

Relentlessly, though, both men kept climbing. Collingwood's determination had never been in doubt; but he also soared above his presumed limitations as a primarily leg-side player, cutting and cover-driving, and then dancing down the track to straight drive Warne to reach 150. Shortly before tea, he became the first England player to score a Test double-century in Australia since Wally Hammond 70 years earlier. Not Hutton, not May, not Boycott, not Gooch, not Atherton... Collingwood. Moments later, he wearily fell for 206, after 515 minutes, 392 balls and 16 fours. The stand was worth 310, England's fourth-wicket record against Australia. Pietersen, however, failed to reach the strange landmark he craved: 159. He was out for 158 for the third time in his 20 Tests. Since he was run out, going for a twitchy single trying to get off his own personal version of 99 or Nelson, we may assume this was no coincidence.

The runs kept coming afterwards, not as fast as England wanted, but quickly enough for Flintoff to declare once the total had hit the 550 mark. Some thought at the time he should have batted on longer; Australia lost here with 556 only three years earlier. As it was, England soon found out what Australia had learned the hard way: it was no fun bowling on this. But they did make inroads with the new ball, and worried an unusually scratchy Ponting, who flirted with the exit several times. The most notable was on 35: he hooked Hoggard to the deep square boundary where Giles, in from the rope, misjudged the trajectory, and (some said) dropped the Ashes.

Ponting left scratchiness far behind but settled for a mere 142, his tenth hundred in the last 13 Tests, and a stand with Hussey of 192. Hussey hustled most impressively but narrowly missed his hundred; Clarke, only playing because Shane Watson was injured, asserted squatter's rights and made his. Gilchrist returned to form, and there was 43 from Warne – important in lots of ways, not least in helping England coach Duncan Fletcher justify his insistence on retaining Giles as a decent No. 8.

Hoggard finished with his third seven-for in Test cricket, a remarkable performance, bearing in mind that Warne (the 13th wicket of the match on the stroke of fourth-day tea) was arguably the first batsman who had not been dismissed by either the new ball or his own impetuosity.

Australia were just 38 behind, and only the TV commentators – paid to make the cricket sound interesting – and the English gloompot Geoff Boycott even tried to pretend there was any prospect of anything happening on the final day. Still, 20,000 turned up, but the weather was warmer now, and the Adelaide Oval an agreeably summery place to sit. They got their money's worth.

From the start, England's cricket seemed suddenly tentative. After Bucknor gave out Strauss (even the appeal sounded only three-quarter-hearted), the doubts turned into blind panic. Warne was turning the ball, but mainly out of the footmarks. And Lee was getting reverse swing. A few good hits, though, would have made England safe. They hit three fours in four hours.

Bell dithered disastrously over a single; Pietersen swept Warne and was bowled round his legs (the ball hit the outside of off stump). Mastery, eh? Then Flintoff swished aimlessly. Collingwood stood firm but was completely constricted and, though the tail did better than the body, England were gone by 3.42.

The gates were thrown open, and spectators began to arrive as they used to do when they heard Bradman was batting. Instead, it was his successors, Ponting and Hussey. There was a wobble when Ponting and Martyn went in quick succession; and Flintoff, leading the charge on his damaged ankle, nearly bowled what would have been the first maiden of the innings. But a wild Pietersen throw turned a last-ball three into a seven, and then for England there was only deflation.

Afterwards, the ageing Australian players galloped and danced with delight round the field before retreating into the evening shadows. Summed up the series, really.

Man of the Match: R. T. Ponting. **Attendance:** 136,761.

Australia v England, Adelaide, 2006

ENGLAND	*First innings*				*Second innings*	
A. J. Strauss c Martyn b Clark		14	–	c Hussey b Warne		34
A. N. Cook c Gilchrist b Clark		27	–	c Gilchrist b Clark		9
I. R. Bell c and b Lee		60	–	run out (Clarke/Warne)		26
P. D. Collingwood c Gilchrist b Clark		206	–	not out		22
K. P. Pietersen run out (Ponting)		158	–	b Warne		2
*A. Flintoff not out		38	–	c Gilchrist b Lee		2
†G. O. Jones c Martyn b Warne		1	–	c Hayden b Lee		10
A. F. Giles not out		27	–	c Hayden b Warne		0
M. J. Hoggard (did not bat)			–	b Warne		4
S. J. Harmison (did not bat)			–	lbw b McGrath		8
J. M. Anderson (did not bat)			–	lbw b McGrath		1
Lb 10, w 2, nb 8		20		B 3, lb 5, w 1, nb 2		11

1/32 (1) 2/45 (2)	(6 wkts dec.)	551	1/31 (2) 2/69 (1)		129
3/158 (3) 4/468 (4)			3/70 (3) 4/73 (5)		
5/489 (5) 6/491 (7)			5/77 (6) 6/94 (7) 7/97 (8)		
			8/105 (9) 9/119 (10) 10/129 (11)		

First innings—Lee 34–1–139–1; McGrath 30–5–107–0; Clark 34–6–75–3; Warne 53–9–167–1; Clarke 17–2–53–0.

Second innings—Lee 18–3–35–2; McGrath 10–6–15–2; Warne 32–12–49–4; Clark 13–4–22–1.

AUSTRALIA	*First innings*				*Second innings*	
J. L. Langer c Pietersen b Flintoff		4	–	c Bell b Hoggard		7
M. L. Hayden c Jones b Hoggard		12	–	c Collingwood b Flintoff		18
*R. T. Ponting c Jones b Hoggard		142	–	c Strauss b Giles		49
D. R. Martyn c Bell b Hoggard		11	–	(5) c Strauss b Flintoff		5
M. E. K. Hussey b Hoggard		91	–	(4) not out		61
M. J. Clarke c Giles b Hoggard		124	–	not out		21
†A. C. Gilchrist c Bell b Giles		64				
S. K. Warne lbw b Hoggard		43				
B. Lee not out		7				
S. R. Clark b Hoggard		0				
G. D. McGrath c Jones b Anderson		1				
B 4, lb 2, w 1, nb 7		14		B 2, lb 2, w 1, nb 2		7

1/8 (1) 2/35 (2) 3/65 (4)	513	1/14 (1)	(4 wkts)	168
4/257 (3) 5/286 (5) 6/384 (7)		2/33 (2) 3/116 (3)		
7/502 (8) 8/505 (6) 9/507 (10) 10/513 (11)		4/121 (5)		

First innings—Hoggard 42–6–109–7; Flintoff 26–5–82–1; Harmison 25–5–96–0; Anderson 21.3–3–85–1; Giles 42–7–103–1; Pietersen 9–0–32–0.

Second innings—Hoggard 4–0–29–1; Flintoff 9–0–44–2; Giles 10–0–46–1; Harmison 4–0–15–0; Anderson 3.5–0–23–0; Pietersen 2–0–7–0.

Umpires: S. A. Bucknor and R. E. Koertzen.   Third umpire: S. J. Davis.
Referee: J. J. Crowe.

Black Tuesday	Patrick Collins, *Wisden* 2007

And then the sky fell in. It was Warne, of course, that brought it down, with his grotesque repertoire of grunts and grimaces. His supporting cast, hovering around the bat, played its pantomime part: "Bowled, Shayyne! Noyce stuff, Warney!" When Pietersen was bowled around his legs, his father left the ground, scratching his head. Warne cackled at the chaos. As *The Guardian's* Mike Selvey observed: "Cricket against Australia is never over till the fat boy spins."

Australia v England, Perth	John Stern, *TWC*, February 2007
(Third Test, December 14-18)	

When Michael Clarke staggered towards cover point during his second-innings hundred, having just been cracked nastily on the thumb, Andrew Flintoff wandered over to show concern. When Ian Bell caught one in the unmentionables from Glenn McGrath, Ricky Ponting and Shane Warne did not budge an inch from the slip cordon. Ponting's lips moved but only to chew gum.

Revenge was a dish Australia served piping hot in Perth, where the third-day temperature approached 50°C. The Australians have been consumed by the idea of Ashes vengeance for 15 months. They said "No More Mr Nice Guy" and boy did they mean it. Fred cannot be anything other than a nice guy, which is a problem in these circumstances.

Australia v England, Melbourne	Greg Baum, *Wisden* 2007
(Fourth Test, December 26-28)	

Shane Warne stole his own show. From the moment he announced his retirement a few days beforehand, this Test was always going to be about Melbourne's farewell to its favourite cricketing son. Glenn McGrath's decision to quit, too, sharpened the sense of a grand occasion. Already, record crowds had been forecast to flock to the spectacularly refurbished MCG, which billed this as its 100th Test, though most records disregard the abandoned game in 1970-71. Now the match would surely be five festive days of farewell.

Two forces of nature intervened. One was rain over Christmas – much needed in a parched state, but not here, not now. It was a cold rain too, and trimmed the crowd figure on Boxing Day to a mere 89,155 (an Ashes record, but 1,645 below the 46-year-old record for any properly audited day's Test cricket). It also meant the pitch spent a sweaty Christmas under covers, leaving it underprepared. Mike Gatting, one of the innumerable guest stars invited to speak at innumerable functions attending this series, described it at breakfast one morning as a "slow shitheap".

The other force was Warne himself. His five wickets on the opening day thrilled the crowd, but put an end to the match before it had properly begun. It took Australia just two more days to complete victory, forcing Cricket Victoria not only to refund $A2.3m (more than £900,000) worth of tickets for day four, but to wring its hands at the thought of the takings lost on day five. Melbourne might not have been gasping for more, but the administrators were.

...

Midway through the day, England were 101 for two and glimpsing light beyond the pylons.

Warne's introduction had the effect of a detonator. Extra security appeared inside the fence. Soon, Collingwood fell to Lee, then Strauss, so watchful for three and a half hours that he managed just one four, suddenly hit over and around a conventional Warne leg-break and was bowled. Warne had his milestone wicket, the crowd its keepsake moment. England's resistance thereafter was minimal. Pietersen, again left with the tail, hit out and got out, and they finished up with 159. Warne took five in an innings for the 37th time in Tests, again transfixing England in conditions that should have put him at their mercy.

...

Warne had most enjoyed his cricket when Australia were in crisis and it was all up to him: in this match, England gave him no such challenge. At nine down, police and security again encircled the arena. The end came in an almost indecent rush. The last wicket fell (to Lee) at 5.44 p.m., and the news was scheduled for six o'clock. Warne waved, bowed deeply and rode from the ground on the unsteady shoulders of Hayden and Symonds, returned to receive a rather dubious match award, then was gone. The occasion called at least for a lap of honour, and the crowd had expected one. But television schedules wait for no man.

Australia did not apologise for winning the match so quickly, nor at such an awkward time of day. Their idea of giving Warne and McGrath a decent send-off was not to have gestures and ceremonies, but simply to win the series 5-0. But it did make Warne's exit from his Melbourne stage a flatter moment than had been envisaged. To Warne, the consummate cricketer, this was unimportant. But as a way for the instinctive showman to go, it was incongruous: a fading into the night.

Australia v England, Sydney   Matthew Engel, *Wisden* 2007
(Fifth Test, January 2-5)

After all the presentations were finally over, the Australian players were led by their three retiring heroes – Shane Warne, Glenn McGrath and Justin Langer – in an approximation of the traditional lap of honour. However, the exercise bore little relation to the theatrical farewell Steve Waugh had organised on this very ground precisely three years earlier.

It was more of an amble of honour. The players promenaded around the boundary, several of them clutching a child with one hand and waving vaguely with the other. A stroll in the park, like the series itself.

...

Warne found another companion in Clark, and they put on a further 68 for the ninth wicket. The Warne magic is so pervasive that many spectators convinced themselves he would, at the very last attempt, reach the Test century that had so cruelly eluded him. It was a slash-and-burn innings that had pretty much everything, including some characteristically lippy exchanges with Collingwood. But there was no century: after Clark went, Warne had insufficient trust in McGrath, and was stumped on 71, made in 65 balls.

England, 102 behind, found trouble right away. Cook went quickly and, two balls later, Lee felled Strauss with a 93mph bouncer that hit him on the base of the helmet. He resumed groggily, but not for long enough. England were soon 98 for four. They inched into the lead shortly before the third-day close. Then, to a thunderous cheer, Warne returned to the attack.

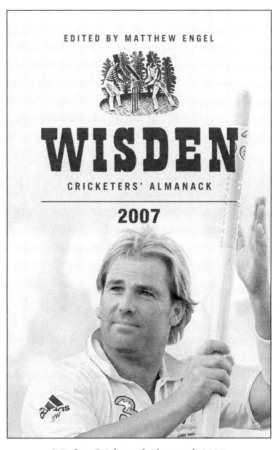

Wisden Cricketers' Almanack 2007

He had bowled an over before tea, possibly the worst of his life, including three full tosses which Bell smacked through the on side for four. The first over of his second spell was notably stiff. In the next, Flintoff reached right forward to stun a leg-break. He missed, wearily failed to get his back foot behind the line, and thus became Warne's 708th and last Test victim.

Sydney Notes *Wisden 2007*

Shane Warne took his three children – Brooke (9), Jackson (7) and Summer (5) – on to the outfield for a knockabout after the opening day to allay their fears that his retirement would put an end to their backyard games. "They said 'Can you still play cricket with us?' and I said I could." So he proved it.

Bowling's Bradman Malcolm Knox, *TWC*, February 2007

There are different kinds of intelligence and Warne is exceedingly "cricket-smart". Even among a generation of cricket-smart Australians – Mark Taylor, Steve Waugh, Ricky Ponting, Darren Lehmann – Warne stands out as having possessed an Einsteinian cricket brain.

What exactly is "cricket-smart"? In Warne's case it is not only knowing how to set his fields, how to plan an attack on a batsman, when to bowl the unexpected ball or even the expected one – though it includes all those things. Above all it is a certain gift of empathy, the ability to think the way a batsman is thinking. In his most candid moments, inside the dressing room, Warne is a gifted mimic, particularly of batsmen. He can "do" Ian Chappell, he can do Viv Richards, he can do everyone from Arjuna Ranatunga to Jacques Kallis. (In a spontaneous bow-and-kiss after the Melbourne Test he even did Andre Agassi). Terry Jenner, Warne's mentor, has always said the gift of mimicry stems from Warne having started his cricket career as a would-be batsman. He can place himself inside a batsman's skin and detect precisely where the batsman least wants him to bowl next.

He can get under a batsman's skin, too. Mark Taylor said Warne was continually "thinking up new ways to get under a batsman's skin". Or, he added as an afterthought, "just new ways to get them out".

How to get under the skin? To say that cricket is played 90% between the ears is a cliché but Warne practised psychology with a shamanistic mastery. Ian Botham, who never played Warne, said he had heard that Warne was "always thinking up new nicknames for opposing players... they'd go back to Google the name and find out what character Warne was naming them after". It was more than Warne standing at first slip and, as [Graeme] Smith said, "calling you a f-ing c- all day". It was Warne making them think about him even when he was not bowling: when he was fielding, talking non-stop; when they were in their hotel rooms. Like Oscar Wilde, Warne knew that much worse than people talking about you was people not talking about you. (It could even be said that his off-field peccadillos worked to his advantage; as long as he was in the headlines he was inside batsmen's heads.)

Thus, he would risk self-exposure by carrying out leg-spin masterclasses all around the world, showing off his full bag of tricks: exactly how he turned his wrist to deliver each variation. [Ian] Healy said that teammates would question the wisdom of this but Warne would shrug them off. "It's not how the ball comes out," he would say, "it's how it arrives." What he meant was: if a batsman can concentrate hard enough, he might pick how each ball will turn but Warne's trick, beyond all of what Bob Woolmer called "Mr Heinz's 38 varieties", was that he could cloud the batsman's concentration. Even when a batsman thought he could master Warne, he was still thinking about him. And the cards were, in the long run, stacked Warne's way. During the course of a contest the bowler could make several mistakes; the batsman could afford only one.

Never let it be said that Shane Warne came upon the cricket world by stealth. I was at the Sydney Cricket Ground when made his Test debut against India, in 1992.

When Allan Border threw the tubby long-haired blond the ball, the crowd broke into applause. Australia sensed that something special was happening.

Warne's legacy is not, as is often claimed, that he rejuvenated the art of leg-spin. The cliché is that Warne has prompted every blond-haired Australian boy to bowl over-the-wrist, yet there is little evidence of that. Warne is inimitable.

His legacy is that he rejuvenated the game itself. The fascination of his bowling, the aura of his personality and the overturning of an old expectation that teams could comfortably bat out draws on the last day... Warne reset the limits of the game. He laid the bedrock on which all the attractive, aggressive cricket of the Taylor, Waugh and Ponting eras was built.

With Warne gone, Australian self-confidence will become a touch brittle. While hard on the surface, it will crack more easily. And it will embolden opponents. Stephen Fleming spoke for every non-Australian Test cricketer when he said that Warne's late-December retirement was "a Christmas present for batsmen". No longer will they have to devote so much of their energy to thinking about him. Now that the owner of the centre wicket has gone, a few more of them might get beyond the sense of their own impermanence.

The Ashes 2006-07
Simon Briggs, Wisden 2007

The two old bowling soldiers, McGrath and Warne, were among Ponting's greatest assets. After an eight-month break, McGrath proved that age (he was 36) had not wearied him, wrecking England's first innings at Brisbane with six for 50. Then, on the final day at Adelaide, came Warne's devastating spell. He bowled 27 overs off the reel and, though he took only four wickets, his psychological hold was such that batsmen kept self-destructing at the other end.

Warne now had little left to achieve in cricket. A few days after the Ashes were secured at Perth, he announced he would be leaving the international game after the Sydney Test. "Getting the Ashes back was my mission, and I couldn't have worked the script better," he told a reverential press conference in Melbourne. Too true: five days later, he claimed his 700th Test wicket in front of an Ashes record crowd at the MCG, his home ground.

Ashes Afterthoughts (1)

John Woodcock, *Wisden* 2007

Of those Australians to have made this their swansong, the one whose like may never be seen again is, of course, Warne. Until he came along and, by hard work, native ability and force of character, took the fiendishly difficult art of accurate wrist-spin bowling to a new level, there was no argument as to the finest bowler there had ever been: it was Sydney (S. F.) Barnes, as gaunt a figure and austere a man as Warne is well-upholstered and outgoing. Although he was a more orthodox bowler than Warne, Barnes's long, strong fingers – I once shook his hand – enabled him to spin a leg-break out of the front of his hand at a brisk pace and with the same control, bristling aggression and high arm with which he bowled everything else.

Umpires, as well as batsmen, were in awe of Barnes, as they have been of Warne. Had they both bowled the same number of balls in Test cricket, at their respective strike-rates, Barnes would have finished with 977 wickets to Warne's 708. They are *primi inter pares*. Whether Barnes sledged or not I don't know. Warne does (and he has done much to popularise it) and it is beneath contempt, and no more than all his wonderful achievements should it go unrecorded.

Ashes Afterthoughts (2)

Ian Chappell, *Wisden* 2007

Judgment day is just around the corner for Australia; the moment when Shane Warne and Glenn McGrath are not in the Test side to stifle the opposition's scoring and secure their wickets.

It is this dual job that they did so effectively and makes them so hard to replace. Together they accounted for 9.63 wickets every time they partnered each other: that's half the 20 wickets required to win a Test taken care of before you pick any other bowlers. It's not surprising Australia won 68% of their matches with this pairing and lost only 15%.

Not only were they diametrically opposite in bowling styles, one slow, the other fast, they were outwardly vastly different in character. Warne was the showman, the bowler whose aura mesmerised the batsmen, before the fizzing leg-break finished the job. McGrath snuck up on his opponent. The ball came out of the hand with no apparent evil attached, except it always landed in an awkward spot, leaving so little margin for error that even the slightest movement off the seam was likely to be terminal. McGrath bored batsmen out and Warne bowled them over.

...

While Stuart MacGill is the logical and deserved replacement for Warne, he is purely an attacking bowler. MacGill won't contain and mesmerise batsmen the way Warne did; he will lure them to their downfall by encouraging strokeplay. Australia could not have won in Adelaide with MacGill playing in place of Warne. He was capable of taking the wickets, but he would also have conceded a lot more runs; England would have put the game beyond Australia's reach.

| Notes by the Editor | Matthew Engel, *Wisden* 2007 |

We can see it clearly now: Australia would have regained the Ashes even if England had played up to their 2005 standards. Anyone who has ever seen a western knows that when a group of old compadres get together for one last, vital mission, it cannot end in failure. And these compadres were way too good, way too committed. Even the most embittered England supporter should take pleasure in the fact that they have seen Ricky Ponting and Adam Gilchrist bat and, above all, seen Shane Warne bowl.

| The Mighty Craftsman | Mike Atherton, *Wisden* 2007 |

In the moments after the Ashes were won at Perth in December 2006, only one of the victors managed the moment with due dignity. As the Australians hugged each other and celebrated with the crowd, England's players, who had emerged to shake their conquerors' hands, were ignored. Only Shane Warne broke away from the pack to acknowledge the vanquished.

At the end of the next Test, at the MCG, I was waiting near the podium to interview Warne, chivvying him along because we were about to go off air. He started to walk over to me, then stopped. Andrew Flintoff was in the process of answering the usual post-match questions. Warne took off his cap, listened to Flintoff, applauded when Flintoff had finished, and then continued on his way towards me.

If anyone had an excuse to be self-obsessed at the MCG it was Warne, but his respect for the game, and for the people who play it, was an essential and often overlooked part of his greatness. Michael Vaughan touched on this point in his book *A Year in the Sun.* He said that Warne was "great to face because he gives you respect. If you do well against him he is not one to give you abuse. He will just say 'shot' and, after the game or your innings, he will come in and say 'well played.'"

It is true that such respect has not always been in evidence (contrast his behaviour at the end of the 2006-07 series with his loutish celebrations from the Trent Bridge balcony in 1997), but they are the reasons why Warne the showman and Warne the celebrity never quite consumed Warne the cricketer. He never forgot that he was but one link in an Australian leg-spinning chain that goes back generations. He never forgot that he was a craftsman as well as an entertainer.

The link with the great Australian leg-spinners of the past is enough to explain why nothing that Warne did was revolutionary. Despite his claims before each and every series, there were no new deliveries. The googly, of course, had been invented by the Englishman B. J. T. Bosanquet whilst experimenting with a tennis ball during a game called twisti-twosti; Clarrie Grimmett perfected the flipper and passed on the secret to Bruce Dooland and Cec Pepper; after the Lord's Test of 1953, Doug Ring picked up an apple on a train journey and showed a young Richie Benaud how he bowled the slider, pushed out of the front of the hand between the second and third fingers. And there, in essence, was Warne's armoury: the original leg-spinner and top-spinner, the googly, the flipper and the slider.

During his apprenticeship, and in an interesting echo of Bosanquet's experiments with his tennis ball, Warne used to entertain fellow inmates at the Australian Academy with his ability – from his strong forearm, wrist and fingers – to spin balls in all directions on a billiard table. At the Academy he learned how to perfect the variations on offer to a leggie, and at various stages throughout his career he revealed each delivery to perfection: the curving, dipping, viciously spinning leg-break that bowled Mike Gatting in 1993; the flipper that befuddled Alec Stewart at Brisbane in 1994; the top-spinner to bring him the only hat-trick of his career against a groping Devon Malcolm at Melbourne later that series; the googly that crept through Matthew Hoggard's defences towards the crushing denouement at Adelaide in 2006; and the sliders that put Ian Bell into a near-permanent state of confusion throughout 2005.

Within each variation, there were variations. Before the Ashes series of 1997, David Lloyd, aware that Warne's trade was a mystery to many of his players, invited the former New South Wales leggie, Peter Philpott, to talk to the England team. Philpott explained how leg-spinners would, to use his phrase, "go through the loop", varying the amounts of side-spin and over-spin. They could start with a leg-break that had just side-spin (the seam rotating at 90° towards extra cover, imparting maximum turn), gradually increasing the amount of over-spin (seam now rotating towards third man, with less turn but more dip and bounce) until reaching the top-spinner (seam rotating towards the batsman) and then the googly, which is simply an extension of that (seam now rotating towards fine leg). The flipper is the opposite of the top-spinner, being released from under the hand, imparting back-spin (seam now rotating back towards the bowler).

Later on that summer, during the one-day series that preceded the Ashes, I was watching from the commentary box, and saw Warne do exactly that – go through the loop – in the first over of a spell. He began with a side-spinning leg-spinner, then bowled a leggie with more over-spin, then a top-spinner, then a googly, then a slider and ended up with a flipper. Each delivery landed perfectly.

After his shoulder operation the following year, he gradually began to bowl fewer and fewer wrong'uns and flippers, relying instead on the leggie, in all its variations, and the slider. He even lost the ability to bowl a flipper for a while. His dismissal of Saj Mahmood in his last match at the MCG demonstrated both that he had rediscovered it, and that he had never stopped working at his craft.

Once he had perfected his stock ball and variations, he needed to learn where to bowl them. With help from Bobby Simpson and Allan Border, he devised tactics that would keep most right-handed batsmen in check for the next decade. Because he was such a big spinner of the ball, the traditional middle-and-off-stump line would be a waste, because most deliveries would not threaten the stumps. Instead, they devised a line – middle-and-leg if the pitch wasn't taking a great deal of spin, more leg-stump and outside if it was – that meant he would always be attacking.

Again this was not revolutionary. On an unresponsive pitch, Grimmett apparently bowled more round-arm at leg stump. Benaud, of course, out-thought England at Old Trafford in 1961 by bowling outside leg stump from round the wicket. For Warne, though, this was his default line, rather than a variation. And, as his mentor Terry

Jenner once explained, it was not so much where the ball ended up which caused such problems for a right-hander, but how it got there.

It got there, as The Ball (to Mike Gatting at Old Trafford in 1993) revealed, with a great deal of curve and drift. This presented serious problems for all but the very best players. Most right-handers moved forward down the initial line, only to find themselves in the wrong position by the time the ball arrived. As a result, most found themselves playing across their front pads and against the spin. This was exacerbated by the prevalent technique of the time – the forward press – whereby batsmen pushed their weight forward slightly before the ball had been bowled. Advancing down the pitch to Warne was difficult; the drift in the air often meant a batsman would end up too far to the off side of the ball, again resulting in him playing across the line.

So, as with all great bowlers, Warne demanded that batsmen think carefully about their technique and, in order to succeed, alter it. Salim Malik, for example, had the courage to bat outside leg, showing Warne all three stumps, so that he was still able to score through the off side. No right-hander, in my view, played him better than Kevin Pietersen, who had such exquisite balance that he was able to change direction – with the drift – while still advancing down the pitch. He battered Warne into submission at Adelaide in 2006, causing him to run up the white flag by bowling so wide of leg stump that a stalemate ensued. It was a rare admission of failure.

Has any slow bowler ever bowled his overs so slowly? Grimmett was once told by his captain to slow down so that the bowler at the other end could be given more of a breather. Warne didn't need to be told to slow down, because it was an essential part of his act. Occasionally during the last series, I timed his overs and, even when wickets were not falling, they could take up to four and a half minutes to complete. The long pause at the end of his run-up, the slow walk to the crease, the oohs and aahs after every delivery, the cold stare down the pitch at a batsman, a word or two in his ear, often a slight field change and a chat with the captain. All were designed not only to give him time to think, but to give the batsman time to think.

What did he bowl me there? More to the point, what's coming next? The thinking time he gave himself was put to good use. No bowler was more cunning. One example, from personal experience, will suffice. At Lord's in 2001, after miraculously surviving Glenn McGrath's opening spell, I was bowled round my legs by Warne. It wasn't a particularly great ball, nor a good shot but, since I'd felt a bit tangled up around leg stump, I decided to shift my guard towards leg stump during the next Test, at Trent Bridge, to open up the off side. In the second innings (I didn't face him in the first), he noticed the difference within three balls, and altered his line more towards off stump, so that I found myself defending with half a bat towards extra cover. I was soon caught behind.

In that same match, towards the end of the second day, Mark Ramprakash was a victim not so much of Warne's cricket craft but of his understanding of the game situation, and of his opponent's mind. Ramprakash had been batting well in a low-scoring affair and was torn between the desire to be positive against Warne and the need to bat out the day. Warne goaded him continually, urging him to come down the pitch: "Come on, Ramps, you know you want to." Ramps did want to, and eventually had a mad charge to be stumped by a distance. England ended the day six wickets down.

Umpires were there to be exploited and, in Warne's view, existed only to offer suitable judgment on appeal. No slow bowler ever worked an umpire so well. No slow bowler, in my time, ever got more lbws. Appeals were followed by the ritual "I-can't-believe-you-didn't-give-that-one-out" look, and maybe a little chat to let him know that was the straight-on-er: "What, you can't pick me either, Rudi?"

He might go too far with a batsman, but not with an umpire. When, in his last Test at Sydney, he told Aleem Dar not to worry about where his feet were landing, and "just take care of what's happening at the other end, mate", those were the words of a man who had already mentally retired. After all, Aleem Dar could be of no further use.

Days before the first Ashes Test of 1993, when Warne announced himself with the Gatting ball, Old Trafford was awash with rain. Warne had been belted around Worcester by Graeme Hick in the run-up to that Test and was by no means, in our estimation at least, a certain starter. The pitch was sticky – you could shove your thumb in it – and all the older players, those who had played on uncovered pitches, were certain that Australia should play their finger-spinner, Tim May. I can well recall David Lloyd saying that a leg-spinner would be of no use in the conditions.

Over the coming years, Warne would show everyone that leg-spin was not a luxury but an essential if a team were to have an attack for all conditions. In that sense, Warne has been the greatest advocate for his craft that there has ever been. Australia only ever left him out once when he was available: Antigua, 1998-99, and even then they still had a leg-spinner, Stuart MacGill.

He was at once aggressive and defensive, a wicket-taker and a sponge (to dry up runs), a captain's dream. Here was no revolutionary but an amalgam, the perfect amalgam, of all that had gone before: Arthur Mailey's carefree big-spinners, Grimmett's miserliness, O'Reilly's competitiveness and Benaud's cunning, all combined in a showman from the television age. In that sense, Warne might not have done his craft any favours at all.

Every leg-spinner will be compared to Warne; every leg-spinner will be expected to be at once accurate and incisive, and to have all the tools at their disposal, at a moment's notice, to be dropped on a length. We will never see anything closer to perfection.

The Wisden Forty   Lawrence Booth and Rob Smyth, *Wisden 2007*

It was no great surprise that Warne ended his Test career in magnificent fashion, with an Ashes whitewash and a 700th Test wicket in front of his home crowd at the MCG. With his powers waning ever so slightly, Warne had spent much of the year in the mode of rogue psychiatrist – inviting opponents on to his couch and persecuting them, encouraging them to torture themselves with imaginary demons. Even besieged umpires, who had to contend with incessant appeals of wildly varying credibility, could not escape his spell. Overall, his wickets cost more than 30 each for the first time since 2001 but, as always, Warne won the really big points: his legendary last-day performance at Adelaide, when his presence numbed England into a fatal strokelessness, turned a tight Ashes series into a walkover. His six for 86 on the final day at Durban, when he took Australia to a thrilling against-the-clock victory, was almost as good. The coup de grâce came on the first day of his beloved Boxing Day Test, when he ran through England with five for 39, including his 700th wicket (Strauss). A week later, he walked into retirement, putting a lump in the throats of even those Englishmen whose dreams he had wrecked for a decade and a half. Cricket would never see his like again.

PART FOUR

Still Crazy
2007–2021

Still Crazy:
2007–2021

"The Oval, Southampton, Canterbury, Edgbaston, Arundel, Chester-le-Street, Old Trafford, Worcester, Headingley. These are the grounds where (subject to fitness etc), Shane Warne is due to bowl for Hampshire in first-class cricket in 2007. If you have grandchildren, take them. If you don't, go anyway – so you can tell them."
Matthew Engel, *Wisden Cricketers' Almanack* 2007

There was no chance that Shane Warne would slip quietly into pipe-and-slippers retirement, reappearing only occasionally as a documentary talking head to discuss the Gatting ball or the 2005 Ashes. In fact, in some respects, he became even more famous after that final Test appearance at Sydney in the first few days of 2007. "I thought I would be sad to leave but people say you know when it is time to go and now I understand what they mean," he said at the press conference to announce his departure from the international game and domestic cricket in Australia. In his brilliant book *On Warne*, Gideon Haigh pointed out that his relationship with some of his long-serving teammates had become more distant; in England in 2005 he preferred the company of the comparative newcomer Michael Clarke after hours. But Haigh predicted that retirement would not frighten him. "He was only giving up cricket. He was not giving up being Shane Warne," he wrote.

He still had a two-year contract to play county cricket for Hampshire where his impact, especially since taking over the captaincy, had been enormous. But 2007 proved an unusually low-key summer for Warne and the county, and he opted not to fulfil the final year of his deal in 2008. Instead, he swapped the habitual chill and deserted grounds of early-season County Championship matches for the historic Indian city of Jaipur where he led Rajasthan Royals amid the frenzied hype of the newly launched Indian Premier League.

He had needed some persuading – the former England captain Tony Greig had made the first approach during the previous English summer. "It sounded interesting but I just couldn't convince myself I wanted to play cricket anywhere, least of all Twenty20 which I hadn't really played at all," he said. But the backers of the Rajasthan franchise offered him the chance to lead the team exactly as he chose, to shape it in his own image. Manoj Badale, the principal owner, told him: "It gives you the chance to show that you were the best captain Australia never had."

Although few anticipated the runaway success of this new tournament, once convinced Warne fell into its warm embrace. And it was a symbiotic relationship. Without the presence of imported marquee players such as Warne, the IPL would not have instantly acquired the mix of sport and showbiz glamour which quickly became its USP. There had been many occasions over the years when Warne seemed able to bend events to his will, even if "Who writes your scripts?" became something of a tired cliché.

But that gift was never better demonstrated than in the six weeks and 15 matches in which he appeared in the inaugural IPL.

After being thrashed by Delhi Daredevils in their opening match, the Royals embarked on a run of 11 wins out of 12 that took them to the semi-finals. There they gained revenge over Delhi to face Chennai Super Kings in the final. It went to the final ball, but Warne, having hit a boundary off Makhaya Ntini that brought the target within reach, was at the crease when Rajasthan completed a three-wicket victory amid ecstatic scenes. Throughout, his leadership and handling of a less than stellar line-up was exemplary. "Part Pied Piper, part Winston Churchill and part anti-John Buchanan," as Lawrence Booth wrote in *The Wisden Cricketer*.

"We had one of the great nights, a party to match any Ashes victory or anything else," Warne wrote in *No Spin*. "From the moment Manoj and Ravi [Krishnan] talked me into the IPL, to the party after the final that went deep into the next morning, this was one of the best experiences of my life." He returned for the next three editions of the competition – typically, he took a wicket in his farewell over – and also played for Melbourne Stars in two seasons of Australia's own T20 competition, the Big Bash League. His last appearance in professional cricket, aged 43, was in semi-final defeat by Perth Scorchers in January 2013.

By that time, he was almost a franchise in his own right. His three-year relationship with the English actor and celebrity Elizabeth Hurley may have lifted his profile even higher than it had been in his playing career. Although they broke off their engagement in 2013, he later described their time together as "the happiest of my life". He also played poker professionally, an activity which appealed to his competitive instincts and provided some of the shots of adrenaline he missed from big cricket. He was briefly a chat-show host in Australia and was the subject of a musical, several documentaries and a rash of books. In 2018, he published his second autobiography, *No Spin*, written with the broadcaster Mark Nicholas.

But it was for his work as a TV commentator that he became most respected in this phase of his life. On Channel 9 in Australia and Sky in the UK, Warne emerged as of the most astute and insightful members of the commentary teams. As Ian Healy writes in the foreword to this book: "Commentating alongside Warney was also full-on. It highlighted his cricket brain, he strategised as if he was out there, he argued if you disagreed and it continued over dinner. These were the same instincts he displayed as a player." Ian Smith, the former New Zealand wicketkeeper, agreed: "That's what he was like – he was combative on the field of play, so to commentate with him was like playing against him."

RW

2007

Terry Jenner Interview *TWC*, May 2007

Were you surprised when Shane Warne retired?

I was disappointed, not surprised. I remember meeting him for the first time. We shook hands, handshake like a rock, and we forged a friendship and a bond that day. First ball I saw, he bowled me a leg-break the like of which I'd never seen. Into a strong breeze it curved feet and spun sideways. He had all the ingredients to be the best – it was only fine-tuning and getting him hungry enough that he wanted to be the best there was. The ingredients alone aren't enough unless you formulate a willingness to improve and sacrifice. That didn't happen overnight, it took a few years and that's where our bond got stronger.

How did Shane cope with his injuries?

The amazing thing is the way he recovered from the injuries to his fingers, which affected the nerve endings, after ligaments were replaced. The "feel" that he had all the way through his developing years disappeared – bowling a leg-break felt different and he didn't like it. Even when he started to bowl well again he'd say, "If that ball was so good why didn't it feel any good?" That's what he worked through – twice. Does that make him a genius? I think it does. One thing with Warne, through all the changing body shapes you can never see the size of his heart. If you are going to be as good as Warne, you have to have courage – he's been hit for more sixes than any other bowler.

What about the future in Australia? Has Stuart MacGill been harshly treated?

I think if Shane Warne had not been around you could argue that Stuart MacGill would not have played much cricket at all. Warne set it up, meaning leg-spinners had respect. Stuey was the old fashioned type of leg-spinner, full-bungers, long hops and wicket-taking balls – whether Australia would have been able to put up with that as the lone spinner is problematical. Warne became the captain's go-to man. I don't know that Stuey would have become a go-to man. He would always have been an above-average leg-spin bowler but I can argue he may not have played as much Test cricket as he has already played without Warne.

Is MacGill a difficult character?

Being a non-abrasive person wouldn't help a leg-spin bowler. You've got to have some mettle and Stuey has plenty of that. He probably feels he needs to be aggressive to bring out the best in himself. He's still bowling well and would be in my Australian team. It's important that he gives two years for the young bowlers to develop. It is crucial that they are following Stuart MacGill rather than Shane Warne. The comparisons for a 21-year-old following Warne would be too great.

Should Warne be used to coach leg-spin worldwide?
He should be but it will be interesting to see where they get the funding from. Two facets of world cricket that are not budgeted for as they should be are wicketkeeping and wrist-spin.

Interview by Sam Collins

Notes by the Editor Matthew Engel, *Wisden* 2007

The Oval, Southampton, Canterbury, Edgbaston, Arundel, Chester-le-Street, Old Trafford, Worcester, Headingley. These are the grounds where (subject to fitness etc), Shane Warne is due to bowl for Hampshire in first-class cricket in 2007. If you have grandchildren, take them. If you don't, go anyway – so you can tell them.

Kent v Hampshire, Canterbury Mark Pennell, *Wisden* 2008
(County Championship Division One, May 23-26)

Warne, frustrated by the slow, grassy surface, showed his indignation at Kent batting on with an over lasting seven minutes, which only served to stall Key's declaration for another 12 overs. Warne had also protested when given lbw, which earned him six penalty points for dissent.

Chronicle *Wisden* 2008

Britain's advertisement regulators said an advert featuring Shane Warne should be banned. The Advertising Standards Authority said newspaper ads in which Warne implied the Advanced Hair Studio cured baldness were misleading (Reuters, May 30).

Sussex v Hampshire, Arundel   Andy Arlidge, *Wisden* 2008

(County Championship Division One, June 6-9)

This was an intriguing battle of the master leg-spinners: Warne took five wickets in the first innings as Sussex reached 341 thanks to Mushtaq Ahmed's 54 from 43 balls; then Mushtaq trumped him again with seven wickets as Hampshire subsided for 202. Mushtaq's wickets included his 400th for Sussex (Lumb), and the satisfying scalp of Warne, bowled between his legs – the first time Mushtaq could remember taking a wicket in such a way. Warne proved impotent in the second innings, going wicketless as Goodwin and Adams pushed the target beyond likely bounds.

...

There was a mini-battle between the two captains, conducted in their respective newspaper columns. Warne claimed in *The Times* that in 2006 the No. 1 on the back of Adams's shirt was bigger than his team-mates' numbers. Adams retorted in *The Independent* that at least his shirt size had stayed the same.

Hampshire v Durham, Southampton   Pat Symes, *Wisden* 2008

(County Championship Division One, June 15-18)

With an audacious declaration, two outstanding slip catches, and match figures of 11 for 133, Warne swung this match Hampshire's way. It was his 12th match ten-for, though only his second outside Tests and his first in 58 matches for Hampshire.

...

Rain wiped out the last morning, prompting Warne to declare on their overnight score, leaving Durham 66 overs to make 254. Di Venuto and Smith struck 83 for the first wicket and, at 173 for four, the outcome lay in the balance. Then Warne – who claimed seven lbws – and Tremlett helped polish off the last six wickets for 30.

Around the World   *TWC*, August 2007

After impressive receptions at workshops in Adelaide, *Shane Warne: The Musical* is set to make its full debut in Australia. Written and directed by Aussie comedian, Eddie Perfect, the musical includes the songs "S-M-Mess" and his mother singing "Take the F***ing Pill".

***

Eddie Perfect isn't the only person using Shane Warne's name for personal gain. After months of negotiation, Warne has been signed up by 6-Up, a new text betting company. Warne, who has been given a share in the company, says he has turned down a lot of offers since his retirement, including commentary. "If I wanted to be in Brisbane for the First Test, then Adelaide and Perth and Melbourne etc, I may as well have kept playing."

2007-08

Sri Lanka v England, Kandy Andrew Miller, *TWC*, February 2008
(First Test, December 1-5)

The congratulatory posters all around town implied that Murali's record was a done deal – even though his required tally was one more than he had managed in two Tests against Australia. But England's lack of enterprise was reminiscent of their efforts against Shane Warne at Adelaide a year earlier. Murali wheeled through 23 overs in the day at a cost of 30 runs, gleaning four wickets, and when he dismissed Ravi Bopara to draw level no mortal had a hope of halting his momentum. Instead the gods acted, dampening the ardour in the stands with a downpour that wrote off the rest of the day.

It was surely only a temporary hiatus. And yet, in Paul Collingwood and Ryan Sidebottom, England found an obdurate and essential seventh-wicket alliance. They repelled Murali for over an hour on the third morning, and it was not until the new ball arrived that Sidebottom was extracted for a Test-best 31. But Murali had been beaten back only temporarily and in the 89th over – his 33rd – he skidded the harder shiny ball through Collingwood's half-formed defences. "It was meant to be an off-break but it didn't turn," Murali later admitted, but no matter. Pandemonium ensued in the stands, as the hills came alive with the sound and smoke of 709 firecrackers.

From the Editor John Stern, *TWC*, January 2008

The Warne v Murali debate will rage as long as cricket is discussed, which is why it is such a delicious rivalry that boils down to cultural prejudice, gut instinct and personal taste.

If it comes down to a straight choice between the two, I go for Warne because of his overall package of competitiveness and tactical nous gives him an edge, not to mention his handy batting and slip fielding.

But Murali deserves the respect and admiration of every cricket lover for his resilience, his remarkably consistent good humour and for reinventing finger-spin. It is one thing to dispute the legitimacy of his action but quite another to label him a cheat, as people do. He is not diving in the penalty area, trying to con the referee.

Who is your genius of choice?	Lawrence Booth, *TWC*, January 2008

The cricket community has never much cared whether comparisons are odious: its sense of order and love of statistics are too ingrained for that. So no sooner had Muttiah Muralitharan bowled Paul Collingwood at Kandy to pass Shane Warne's Test tally of 708 wickets than the opinions began fizzing like a doosra. Or was it a zooter? Typically of the Murali v Warne debate, it was hard to decide.

First the similarities: both are geniuses. Both can do freakish things with their right wrist. And both have an even more famous body-part that has transcended the sports pages: in the blue corner, an elbow with a congenital kink of 11 degrees; in the red, a thumb adept at churning out ill-advised text messages. But the chucker/sleazebag debate is not our concern here. What matters is who has achieved what.

That Murali has taken 163 of his wickets against Bangladesh and Zimbabwe to Warne's 17 is usually held against him, as if it is his fault that Sri Lanka were not granted a proper Test series in, for example, England until 2002. Equally Warne's record in India (34 wickets at over 43 each) is considered as proof of his mortality while Murali's (31 at almost 40 apiece) tends to be overlooked.

Perhaps their respective records in Sri Lanka and Australia give us a clue. After taking six for 55 in the first innings against England at Kandy, Murali had 438 wickets at just under 19 in Sri Lanka (where Warne managed 48 wickets at 20.45 each), and 12 at 75.41 in Australia (where Warne took his 319 scalps at 26.39 apiece). Advantage Warne. But then can you imagine operating at 100% in a country where your professional essence has been so publicly undermined as Murali's has in Australia?

In his favour is a better average against all the other eight Test nations bar Pakistan, and that he needed only 116 Tests to surpass what Warne managed in 145. True, he has faced less competition than Warne for his wickets. But he has not always bowled to the same attacking fields allowed by Australia's batsmen.

Murali's one-day international record is also superior in terms of both average (22.68 to 25.7) and runs conceded per over (3.84 to 4.25). That seems to tie in with a recent comment made by the former South Africa opener Gary Kirsten, who reckoned there were "fewer moments against Murali, with the ball in the air, when I thought, 'Phew, at least this one won't get me out'". And yet... statistics can be manipulated this way and that, particularly when the margins between the two men are so slender; and Kirsten being a left-hander means he would instinctively have found Murali's off-breaks more dangerous than Warne's leggies.

What about presence, the indefinable quality of all sporting greats? Duncan Fletcher, in an understandably ignored section of his autobiography, says he would notice a slump in Murali's body language when he was swept; the Australians, who made Murali pay 100 runs for each of the four wickets he took against them in November, might argue the slump was more common than that. Irrepressible and impish when things are going his way, Murali can lose his sparkle when they not.

For Warne the *appearance* of sparkle was paramount, both to persuade the batsman that he was in control – just ask the England players who let him dictate terms on the last day at Adelaide a year ago – and to convince the umpire that the next front-foot lbw decision was no more than a top-spinner away. Perhaps Warne was consumed by wicket-taking, defined by it, with an intensity that not even Murali – for all his goggle-eyed energy – has been able to match.

Whether this makes Warne the greater bowler is another matter. After all the only cloud over his career was a self-induced drugs ban while Murali has spent more than a decade having his action scrutinised and vilified. Without a sense of perspective he might have given up. Instead he could reach 1,000, which suggests a thicker skin than those who accused him of sulkily refusing to tour Australia in 2004 would have one believe.

In the end it is a bit like music aficionados comparing Beethoven with Mozart. Stats be damned. This one is a matter of taste. And I reserve judgment.

Letters _TWC_, January 2008

Murali is the better bowler, just look at the statistics. Warne never come in bowled against the best batting side in the world – Australia – so the two bowlers can be compared only in terms of their performances against the second-ranked Test sides. These have, in recent years, been England and South Africa, followed by India and Pakistan. If you look at average and wickets per match, Murali's performances against England, South Africa and India are significantly better than Warne's. Warne edges it against Pakistan.
Bruce G. Charlton, Newcastle-upon-Tyne

While Murali has overtaken Warne's record the differences between the two world-class spinners lies in statistics. Murali, before the England series, has taken almost 23% – or 163 wickets – against Bangladesh and Zimbabwe while Warne has claimed 17 wickets – or 2.5% – against these two weaker cricket nations. I agree that Murali is a world-class spinner but is the record really comparing apples with apples here?
Graham Marshall, Devonport, Tasmania

WORDS ON WARNE

"In the Indian dressing room we didn't discuss any spinner as much as Murali. Shane Warne is a great bowler but Murali troubled us more than anyone else."

Rahul Dravid, India batsman – _TWC_, September 2010

2008

| Book Review | Patrick Collins, *Wisden* 2008 |

Shane Warne: Portrait of a Flawed Genius by Simon Wilde (John Murray, 2007)

In January 1992, an old leg-spinner named Kerry O'Keeffe watched a young leg-spinner play in his first Test match for Australia. He was not impressed. "Overweight, slightly round-arm, no variation, can't bowl," was his verdict. O'Keeffe may have been uncharitable but he was not alone. A few weeks earlier, Matthew Hayden had spotted the youngster acting as Victoria's twelfth man in a match against Queensland. He was sitting in front of the changing-rooms and, Hayden recalled: "He had a pie in one hand with a cigarette wedged between his fingers, and a can of coke in the other hand." Hayden said to a colleague: "Have a go at this bloke. He's absolutely no hope."

When they get round to making the movie of Shane Warne's life and times, those opinions will surely find their place; for the fact is that, with Warne, chronic self-indulgence has always loitered only a step or two behind glorious talent. But it is that talent, which may fairly be called genius, that will speak most loudly.

In the first chapter of his outstanding biography, *Shane Warne: Portrait of a Flawed Genius*, Simon Wilde imagines himself as a young English batsman, belatedly called upon to play in the New Year Test in Sydney and opening with Andrew Strauss. The pacemen are seen off after 15 overs, then it is time for spin. First, deceptively, an over from the gifted Stuart MacGill. And then Warne.

His method is dissected, his motives examined, his strategies analysed, his technique stripped down to its sadistic essentials in a protracted description of an imaginary patch of play. It is a daring conceit, and in less skilful hands it could have proved embarrassing. But Wilde brings it off quite superbly, so much so that by the close of the chapter this reader at least had learned a good deal about Warne and a great deal more about the art of spin bowling.

From there on, the story unfolds, occasionally familiar, yet always enthralling. Improved by the breadth and wisdom of those he has consulted – from Benaud R. to Waugh S. – and unconstrained by being an "official" biography, it is a sensitively written and intelligently researched account of an overweight, pie-scoffing, coke-swilling no hoper finished up with 708 Test wickets.

| Hampshire in 2008 | Pat Symes, *Wisden* 2009 |

Hampshire's dreadful early-season form was rooted in late resignations. In February, the improved pace bowler James Bruce preferred a career in the City and, at the end of March, Shane Warne decided not to return for the final year of his contract. To lose Warne was a huge setback, since he had been no ordinary overseas player for five of the past eight seasons; and no ordinary captain for the past four. His aggressive, idiosyncratic on-field approach defined an extraordinary era for the club, even if

Warne never achieved the Championship title he wanted. With the season almost upon them, Hampshire suddenly had to find an overseas player and a captain.

Clearing up after Shane
Pat Symes, *Wisden* 2009

Shane Warne welcomed Hampshire's second-half revival when he joined their end-of-season dinner as a guest. But he might not have been aware of the chaos his resignation had caused the club and individuals.

Several had their lives significantly altered by his sudden departure, not least Dimitri Mascarenhas, the Sri Lankan-born, Australian-raised all-rounder who replaced him as captain. Paul Terry, the manager, found the task of public leadership onerous, and, had Warne's retirement plans been known, Shaun Udal could have extended his Hampshire career for a 20th summer.

WORDS ON WARNE

"Someone with such a personality, intensity and confidence can lead to extra pressure being placed on other players. That is good pressure in a lot of ways. He brings the best out of you – if you can't take it, get out. So many times it brought good things, occasionally it would be too much."

Michael Brown, Hampshire batsman – *TWC*, July 2008

The Indian Premier League
Lawrence Booth, *Wisden* 2009

Most fortunate for the tournament organisers was the identity of the eventual winners. Warne's Rajasthan Royals charmed through their sheer improbability. None of the other seven franchises had spent as little at the first auction, in Mumbai, and none had been so written off in advance. But Warne's ability to get the best out of a motley crew of Indian youngsters and overseas imports was the story of the tournament. And by embodying one of sport's most enduring themes – the triumph of the underdog – it reminded observers that the IPL really could be about more than just money.

What Warne Did Next
Lawrence Booth, *TWC*, July 2008

It seems an odd thing to say about someone with 708 Test wickets but to watch Shane Warne inspire Rajasthan Royals to unexpected heights in the Indian Premier League was to witness a man who may just have answered his true calling. Graeme Smith, an improbable team-mate in India once derided Warne as a "frustrated captain" but, if a first-game mauling by Delhi Daredevils felt ominous, the Royals then won 13 of the next 15, including a last-ball victory in the final.

Warne's style of leadership was part Pied Piper (his young team worshipped him), part Winston Churchill (plenty of charisma and tub-thumping) and part anti-John Buchanan (count the gags about computers). He spurned a coach in the traditional sense, preferring as ever to ride in one to the ground and share organisational and motivational duties with Darren Berry and Jeremy Snape. And he refused to allow local politics to intrude on the actual cricket, a simple enough policy which escaped some of the richer franchises.

Tactically he was brilliant. He cherished surprises, successfully instructing his off-spinner Yusuf Pathan to deal with Adam Gilchrist in the second over of the game at Hyderabad, then plucking the diminutive opener Swapnil Asnodkar from nowhere to thrash 60 against a bewildered Kolkata. And he led from the front, notably carting Andrew Symonds for 16 in three balls to beat Deccan Chargers. There was even a rumour he was sampling the Indian cuisine. He was the story of the tournament.

Letters   *TWC*, July 2008

As an initial sceptic of the IPL I actually followed most of the competition and enjoyed this entertaining spectacle. It was pleasing to see the unfancied Rajasthan Royals win as they consistently played the best cricket. What can you say about their captain, Shane Warne? His impact on world cricket is still irresistible. His skills, both technical and tactical, transcend all formats of the game. Quite simply, he is a legend.
Timothy Bremner, Barking, Essex

Notes by the Editor   Scyld Berry, *Wisden* 2009

It was during the third IPL match, in Delhi, that the principal defect of 20-over cricket became apparent. Shane Warne led the Rajasthan Royals against the Delhi Daredevils – and was anonymous. It was not simply that his bowling was ineffective on a flat pitch, or his innings brief, or his captaincy unable to avert a large defeat. The defect was that he had no time to manifest his personality.

Warne's strength of character soon made itself felt, as he turned what had seemed in Delhi to be a bunch of Indian club cricketers into the first IPL champions. But on the field, such is the bustling pace of the 20-over game, Warne had no time to transmit his personality to spectators or television viewers; and the interplay of personalities is the essence of drama. A 50-over game can sometimes allow the necessary scope: remember how Warne, gradually but inexorably, bent the 1999 World Cup semi-final at Edgbaston to his will. But although a Twenty20 game offers plenty of action over three hours, and an exciting finish almost as often as not, it lacks the drama that a full day of intense cricket provides. As the novelty of 20-over cricket wears off, it will be seen that cricket's characters can only be formed in longer versions of the game.

2008-09

Chronicle

Wisden 2009

The real Shane Warne put aside his original annoyance and went to a preview of *Shane Warne: The Musical* before the official opening night in Melbourne. He described the experience as "weird", but admitted "I can't help but chuckle at parts" and congratulated the writer and star, Eddie Perfect. After the show opened (to warm reviews), Warne appeared on stage and took a curtain call *(Herald/Sun, Melbourne,* December 10).

Review

Geoff Piggott, *TWC*, February 2009

Shane Warne, throughout his career, was often heard to wonder who wrote his scripts. From that ball to Mike Gatting at Old Trafford, through the 1999 World Cup comeback and on to the vindication of nailing the Poms 5–0 in 2006-07, Warne was an irresistible phenomenon. Opposition batsmen, especially those from England, seemed destined to act as unwitting antagonists and supporting characters to Warne's hero.

Take his 700th wicket, for example. Somehow fate conspired to have him needing a single scalp in front of his home crowd in Melbourne, on Boxing Day, against England. Unsurprisingly, Andrew Strauss played the part by missing a regulation leg-break.

It is this Warne – an everyday man guided by destiny to perform acts of genius on the field and of stupidity off it – that the Melbourne comedian and writer Eddie Perfect presents in *Shane Warne the Musical*. It is a largely sympathetic portrait. The underlying point, beyond the text messaging and inflatable penis jokes, is that, as one song intones, "Everyone's a little bit like Shane".

Perfect (his real name) says he was attracted to Warne's character because "he was one of those people, in an Ancient Greek mythological way, that the gods said: 'Right, that guy is going to be a spin bowler for Australia.' He can smoke, he can drink, he can sleep around but it is going to happen."

The audience see a hero for whom life is something thrust upon him. He is chased by the cricket academy, harried by his mother to get off the couch and stop eating pizza and championed and cajoled by his redemption-seeking mentor Terry Jenner.

Warne's failures, too, occur largely despite his will. He naively gives into the temptation of wily, mystical, Bollywood villain John the Bookmaker; he is shamed into taking a diuretic pill by a mother concerned about his appearance; and how could he resist those girls throwing themselves and their mobile phone numbers at him?

While it might not be possible for Warne to emerge from the musical a rounder character, he certainly has greater depth than the larrikin ladies' man seen in women's glossies and tabloid front pages. Australian sporting culture, however, is not treated so kindly.

Perfect, who grew up in the same suburb as Warne, was always fascinated by the contrast between cricket's gentlemanly image and the hard-edged deeds of players like David Boon and Allan Border. His musical questions the win-at-all-costs attitude prevalent in Australia. One scene shows a coach from the cricket academy deriving just a little too much homoerotic enjoyment from pushing and pumping his charges through their fitness regime, while the players' hypocrisy is highlighted a song about sledging with the lyrics "Calling someone's mum a slut is fine, but we never cross the line".

Perfect also sees Warne as a typically Australian hero. His failures are significant and his redemption can come only through defying authority and "sticking it up the Poms". "That's why cricket is so important, because it's England's game and Australia likes nothing more than beating England at it," says Perfect.

Warne's failures are in his personal life and it is in his relationship with his wife Simone that the musical achieves poignancy. Following Simone's discovery of his infidelity via – what else – a series of text messages and an "erection in the frozen food section" of the supermarket, the tone turns genuinely sad. She laments his deceit and, in a swipe at the unwritten rule of "what goes on tour, stays on tour", asks her husband to imagine how he would feel if those he thought were friends were lying to him all along.

MY WIFE THINKS I'M SEEING THE SHANE WARNE MUSICAL!

© Nick Newman

Perfect's aim was to "shine a gentle light and offer a new perspective" on Warne. By showing the damage Warne's frailties have done to the man himself, the audience are reminded that, while there is much to laugh at and enjoy in the story of the bottle-blond from Black Rock, this is real life for a man not so different from themselves.

2009

Interview   *TWC, Heroes of Cricket*, February 2009

My favourite moment in my career was walking out on the SCG and looking up to the scoreboard and seeing it read: "Congratulations Shane Warne, you're the 350th Test cricketer to play for Australia." That made me realise that there weren't an awful lot of people who have actually represented Australia in over 100 years.

The best advice I got was from Ian Chappell: "Know yourself." This had so many different connotations – knowing how you react in certain situations, knowing about your preparation, knowing how you conduct yourself when you're bowling. As a 22-year-old you don't know this. That's why I was successful, because I was prepared to learn, I was a good listener and I learned quickly.

I never saw cricket as a job, I saw cricket as a passion, a hobby and as a sport. So I always went out with the attitude to do the best I could, to enjoy it and to have fun. My job now is to be the best father I can to my children – that's my job.

I've lived in England for four years. But now I see myself living back in Australia with my kids – with their mum for nine days and with me for five days.

I don't have any regrets. If I had regrets I'd be in a strait-jacket in a cell. The thing with the past is you can't change it. No matter what it is – how bad it is, how good it is, you can't change it, so there's no point harping on it. You just focus on today and tomorrow. I don't think about the past. It's gone.

You've got to read the newspapers. If you don't read it you will get it reported back to you. That's always worse.

The media have generally been good to me. It's only certain sections that continually make stuff up, or try and nail me at any chance for nothing. There are specific people that for some reason have it in for me – they will find the negative in anything. Some of the stuff I bring upon myself but that's passed.

I only ever take issue with a journalist if it's someone I respect. I'll ring them up and say "look mate, why have you written that piece", or "what was your angle, where are your facts behind that?" I'll have a chat about it. Then we agree to disagree, or they may apologise, or I may see their point.

My debut didn't go well. But after my first Test I had a taste of international cricket and I wanted to become the best that I could. If I wasn't good enough, then I wasn't good enough, but I had a direction.

I'm not going to tell you the biggest mistake I've made. I've made a few. I'm going to leave that to myself, thank you.

I am more respected in England than in Australia. In England there's more of a respect for the way I played. Respect for never giving up, no matter what has happened. In England, the off-field stuff is more commonplace, every day there's something in the tabloids about somebody. In Australia, that doesn't happen. The English think "move on", because they've had tabloid stories in their face for years now and they know that a lot of it is nonsense. Whereas in Australia they haven't had it, so it's like: "Wow, that's bad. Bad you."

I've had a lot more respect in Australia since I retired. Mainly because of the way I retired, the way I went out of the game – it had a lot of class about it.

They shouldn't do a play about anyone's life without their permission. I'm on record as saying that I think there should be a law against that.

I don't speak to Kevin Pietersen much any more. Occasionally. There are lots of reasons why. We are not as close as we were. Michael Clarke is my best friend. We are very similar. He is a very respectful guy. We just clicked.

People who stop me in the street say: "Please come back, are you coming back?" And in England it's like: "You're not coming back are you? Please don't come back."

Cricket has taught me to never give up. No matter what the situation is never, ever give up.

Interview by Edward Craig

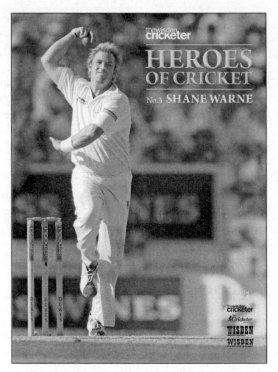

Heroes of Cricket (Wisden Cricketer supplement)

The Ashes Masters

David Frith, *Wisden* 2009

Warne was the swaying, enticing palm-tree, hula skirts all around and lethal coconuts dropping on to batsmen's heads. [Keith] Stackpole sees him as a "likeable rascal", and identifies the source of his success as not only power of wrist and fingers and boldness of character but his outstanding stamina too. "In some ways he was a bit of a con artist. He seemed to have certain umpires in his pocket. He played the mental game with batsmen even before he had bowled a ball." Warne spun, grunted, leered and teased his way to an astonishing Ashes-record 195 wickets, starting with that "ball of the century" to bowl Mike Gatting at Old Trafford in 1993 and finishing with the stumping of Andrew Flintoff at Sydney in 2006-07.

Dear Old Thing and a Brilliant New One

Kevin Mitchell, *TWC*, September 2009

The arrival of Shane Warne in the Sky commentary box this summer fizzed like a flipper through conventional cricket punditry. Alongside Blowers, there have been a few left-field characters allowed into print or near a microphone down the years – Dermot Reeve, Kerry O'Keeffe, Harsha Bhogle, David Lloyd and Phil Tufnell spring to mind – but, with all due respect, The Blond brings something unique to go with his persona, something that resembles a Third Eye.

Like John McEnroe at Wimbledon, Warne seems to see things before anyone else. He is not always right but he is not often wrong. Warne shares with McEnroe the gift of greatness as a player, of course, and that carries more clout than the ability to shape a smart line occasionally – not that he is a dummy in that department.

Warne does not spot buses but he sees momentum and tactical drift, mistakes and opportunities and has the sort of cricket brain you would like to hope is in the possession of any good Test captain.

Warne was denied that honour by his indiscretions and the rise of Steve Waugh but in a brief one-day stewardship, as well as when leading Hampshire and the Rajasthan Royals, he showed what he could do. He translates that ease of understanding to his TV work and has already put a bit of a fire under the Sky guys.

WORDS ON WARNE

"More than anything, Warne is fortunate that he has the confidence of the captain and the selectors. And he has delivered every time he has played. I am not taking anything away from Warne's ability as a great bowler. But I haven't seen a better bowler than Subhash Gupte. Sir Garfield Sobers rates him as the best leg-spinner he ever faced."

Bishan Bedi, former India left-arm spinner

2009-10

Chronicle

Wisden 2010

Andrew Flintoff and Shane Warne have become rivals as celebrity endorsers of socks, aimed at the Christmas present market. Flintoff has teamed up with artist Duncan Cargill to produce three "unique and exclusive" sock motifs. Two days later Warne's "Spinners" range is available in a "funky palette of colours and stripes in trendy fitted trunks and hipster briefs". Flintoff's profits were going to charity (*The Spin*, December 15).

***

A two-year-old pied cock pigeon called "Tubby" (named after Mark Taylor) beat 11 other contenders also called after cricket commentators in the inaugural Great Betfair Pink Pigeon Race over a 30km course from the Glenn McGrath Oval in Narromine to Trangic. The event was held to raise money for the McGrath Foundation, in honour of Glenn's late wife Jane. "Tubby" finished just ahead of "Scoop" (Simon O'Donnell) and "Warnie" (*Daily Liberal*, Dubbo, January 6).

David Shepherd Tribute   Shane Warne, *TWC*, January 2010

All umpires make mistakes but some behave like Eddie the Expert and can't bring themselves to admit it. With Shep you could have a rapport on the field. At the end of an over he'd be prepared to say, "Sorry boys, I got that one wrong." He was big enough to do that. We'd just say, "No worries, Shep, it doesn't matter," and move on.

Shep was probably the best umpire around during my time in world cricket. He was brilliant. One obvious reason is that he got a lot of decisions right but it went beyond that. What really impressed me – and all of us, I think – was the way he interacted with the players. That's what made him a class act.

I enjoyed winding him up when the score was 111 or anything Nelson related, maybe hopping back to my mark or all the way from slip at one end to the other at the end of an over. That worried him. He thought I was tempting fate. He was serious about his superstition; it wasn't just a gimmick to draw attention to himself.

One afternoon sticks in my mind, just the two of us quietly sat together in a bar in India during the 1996 World Cup, chatting about cricket and doing the old trick of upending our beer bottles into water to get the glycerine out. I played club cricket in Bristol in 1989 and made loads of friends there. Shep spent his career with Gloucestershire and had some great stories about the characters and the area in the 1970s.

He cared deeply about the game. Soon after he missed those no-balls in the England-Pakistan Test at Old Trafford in 2001 he came to do one of our tour matches. You could tell he was down, though I didn't realise he was thinking of packing it in. We tried to rally round, to give him a drink and say "Shep, you're with us now, you're fine."

You couldn't dislike him if you tried. He really was one of the good guys.

The Indian Premier League 2009-10   Nagraj Gollapudi, *Wisden* 2011

"I've played this game for 20-odd years. I've seen Sachin Tendulkar smash bowlers all around the park plenty of time, and I've seen some wonderful players, but this is probably the best innings I've ever seen." So said Shane Warne, the Rajasthan Royals captain, about Yusuf Pathan's 37-ball century against Mumbai Indians on the second day of the third IPL. He couldn't stop himself gushing, even though his side had lost by four runs.

It was a ridiculous statement; even Warne, the agent provocateur nonpareil, should have known he was not giving a pep talk in the dugout but making a declaration to the world. But hyperbole was one of the strongest bricks of the IPL's architect, Lalit Modi, used while constructing the league. Since day one, the likes of Warne have been strengthening that foundation.

2010

Loose Talk: Shane Warne   *TWC*, July 2010

Who were the toughest players mentally you played with or against?
Allan Border would be top, nobody comes close to him. It was just the way he carried himself. He was never on the treatment bench, never asked for any help. Everyone knows the way he played but that was only part of it. With opponents you can't really judge because you don't see them in the dressing room, around the hotel and so on. Kepler Wessels struck me as being tough – and Graham Gooch was probably the toughest I came across for England.

As a bowler you were famously quick to work out batsmen. What was your secret?
No secrets. I would like to think that most good bowlers can get a very good idea after an over or so. I look for things like stance, grip, whether the first movement is back and across or forward. Tossing one up early can give an insight into the batsman's mind-set. Will he play positively or cautiously? How does he use his feet? Variations can be good to see what he can pick and what he can't. Does he drive? Does he sweep? Over time you get a reputation. If I bowled a long-hop and it got clouted to a fielder for a catch, people thought it was all part of a great plan. That was fine by me.

Do you think people underestimate your intelligence because of some of the things that attracted bad publicity during your career?
Good question. I suppose my first reaction is "how would I know?" Perhaps some people's perception of me, because of some of the things that happened a long time ago, might affect their judgement. I think those I played with and against could see how I went about the game, they could see that I thought about it a lot. I think I learnt a fair bit during 20 years in the game. Whether people underestimate that, I don't know. I would hope not.

You are commentating for Sky Sports again this summer. Who are your favourite commentators?
I love working with David Lloyd – a funny, funny man. Everyone loves Richie Benaud. We have had some great chats, one leggie to another. He had so much respect all over the world. Ian Botham is a good mate and I like the way he tells things as he sees them. I would say that I learnt most from Ian Chappell. My favourite overall is probably Bill Lawry. His enthusiasm is amazing for a bloke in his 70s who has been doing the job for more than 30 years.

You have been critical of Monty Panesar in the past. How do you see his future?
My thing about Monty is that he has stayed the same bowler. I think he works hard but he didn't seem to learn as he went along. You need to sum up batsmen and conditions – and adapt. That is using your brain, being smart. I am not bagging him. As long as he improves, I think he could come back and play for England. He needs his mojo

back, his passion and hunger. He has to hold up his hand and say "you know what, I'm your man here". I hope he does come back because the crowds love him. He will bowl a lot of overs for Sussex this year and the pitches at Hove will help him. He should be looking to take 70 or 80 wickets and get on the Ashes tour.

Interview by Richard Hobson

2010-11

Sydney Test Notes and Quotes *Wisden* 2011

As England's New Year celebrations approached in Sydney, *Warnie* bit the dust. Channel 9 ditched Shane Warne's chat show early – its audience had fallen from 850,000 to 500,000. The broadcasters were quick to say that there was no slight on the host, but the resolution of the Ashes before the final Test meant there was no appropriate vehicle for the programme's scheduled concluding episode.

Warne still grabbed a share of centre-stage, though. Even as Alastair Cook was cementing England's position on the second day, the crowd was captivated by the sight of the world's greatest leg-spinner bowling, in front of the Bradman Stand, to *Baywatch* star – and Swann's diary contributor David Hasselhoff. "The Hoff" was in town to promote an ice-cream company, and did not look a natural with bat in hand.

Australian Cricket Peter English, *Wisden* 2011

The greatest waste occurred with the overlooking of the off-spinner Nathan Hauritz, who despite being the most potent of the 11 slow bowlers called on since Shane Warne retired in 2007, was not used at all in the Ashes series. Instead, two fringe slow left-armers – Xavier Doherty and Michael Beer – and the leg-spinning all-rounder Steve Smith were employed, and managed four wickets between them. The lack of options became so bad that after the Second Test there was a concerted public campaign – it was always going to fail – to bring back the 41-year-old Warne.

2011

The Indian Premier League Nagraj Gollapudi, *Wisden* 2012

Rajasthan Royals were in contention for a play-off spot at the halfway stage, but fell apart in the final stretch. However, they remained constantly in the news, mainly thanks to the various activities of Shane Warne, who signed off from the IPL with a wicket in his final over. He finished with 55 wickets over the league's four seasons. Heads **were** turned when Warne arrived for IPL4 slimmer and sleeker than ever, his new look leading to suggestions he had had a facelift or botox injections – suggestions he vigorously denied. He was usually accompanied by his girlfriend (later fiancée), the actor and model Elizabeth Hurley, keeping the photographers busy. But Warne became embroiled in an unnecessary dispute with Sanjay Dixit, the Rajasthan Cricket Association secretary, which started when Warne accused the local association of changing a pitch without notice. The IPL governing council slapped him with a $50,000 fine.

2011-12

Australian Cricket

Daniel Brettig, *Wisden* 2012

That series went head-to-head with the newly expanded domestic Twenty20 competition, which was marketed aggressively towards youth, and did away with traditional state colours and identities in favour of city-based teams in garish uniforms. While the Big Bash League had its detractors, not least because it deprived the domestic schedule of first-class fixtures for almost two months at a time while the Test team required reinforcement, its value as a television product was quickly asserted by rich viewing figures.

The tournament was helped by the return of a bevy of hired stars, including Shane Warne, Matthew Hayden, Stuart MacGill and Brad Hogg. None disgraced themselves: Warne thrilled watchers by foretelling his dismissal of Brendon McCullum via an on-field microphone...

Chronicle

Wisden 2012

The New Zealand prime minister John Key hit Shane Warne for four during a match in Wellington to raise money for victims of the Christchurch earthquake, thus earning £50,000 for the appeal (*NZPA*, March 13).

2012

Not Picking the Wrong'un

Jarrod Kimber, *Wisden* 2012

Shane Warne's first real victim wasn't a batsman, but a fellow leg-spinner – a fellow Victorian leg-spinner, in fact, with a wrong'un so brutal it would crash into the chest of those who lunged blindly forward; a leg-spinner who ran in like a graceful 1920s medium-pacer, but who then produced a dramatic twirl of his long arms and ripped the ball off the surface like few teenage leg-spinners before or since. This leg-spinner was so good that Warne said he had more talent than he did. His name was Craig Howard. And if you've never heard of him, it's probably not your fault: Howard doesn't even qualify for a single-line biography on ESPNcricinfo.

By December 3, 1995, Warne – who was by then closing in on 200 Test wickets – had already saved leg-spin. If the date sounds random, then for Howard it was not: it was his final day of first-class cricket. He was 21. Howard retired with 42 wickets in 16 first-class games at 40 apiece, which was no great shakes. But to understand how good he was, you had to be there – you had to see him hit a batsman with his wrong'un. Aged 19, he had returned second-innings figures of 24.5–9–42–5 at the MCG against the South Africans. *Wisden* noted: "Only Rhodes, with 59, made much of Howard's leg-spin second time around." Darren Berry, who kept to Howard at Victoria, said he would have named him in his all-time XI of those he had played with or against if it hadn't been for Warne. Yes, Craig Howard could definitely bowl.

Plenty of others have been bit parts in the story of Australia's post-Warne spin apocalypse, but no one has been a more intriguing bit part than Howard. He is the only Australian bowler to go through the Cricket Academy twice, once as the artistic leg-spinning prodigy from my teenage years, later – after one of his fingers packed in – as a 28-year-old, made-to-order journeyman off-spinner. And now Howard is back, plucked from his office job in telecommunications to coach Nathan Lyon, currently Australia's No. 1 tweaker.

Howard, as it happened, did play alongside Warne in four Sheffield Shield games in 1993-94. The comparison is unflattering: Warne took 27 wickets at 23, Howard – who bowled 100 overs to Warne's 247 – three at 108. But in between, with Warne away on international duty, Howard finally got a decent bowl: he took 5 for 112 against Tasmania, including the wicket of Ricky Ponting. More than 15 years later, when another leggie – Bryce McGain, who was almost 37 – was making his Test debut for Australia, the 34-year-old Howard was playing for Strathdale Maristians in Bendigo, up-country Victoria.

He is philosophical now. "Had I played Test cricket, my life would have turned out different," he says. "I probably would have ended up in some sex-text scandal and lost my wife and kids and ended up a lonely bum. Although, yes, playing Test cricket was the dream."

There are many reasons why Howard didn't make it: injuries, bad management, terrible advice, over-coaching, low self-confidence. But had he played in an era when Australia were desperate for a spinner, he might now be a household name – or at least someone with a decent blurb on the internet.

"At one stage, there were headlines saying I was going to play for Australia," he says. "I remember being about 20, and at the top of my mark at the MCG. Instead of thinking, 'How I am going to get out Jamie Siddons or Darren Lehmann?' I'm thinking about a small group of men in the ground who are judging me. It wasn't like that all the time, but when I was struggling this is how I felt. In the back of my mind I know the captain of my side doesn't like me, and has told me to f*** off to Tasmania. The coach believes that, because I can't bat or field, I am never going to be that useful. It was a dark time."

In the mid-1990s, no one needed to look for Warne's replacement, because he would play for ever and inspire so many kids to take up leg-spin that any who fell through the cracks wouldn't be missed. Junior sides each had four or five leggies – often with peroxide hair – and they all walked in slowly, ripped the ball hard, and barely bowled a wrong'un. But they weren't Warne. None had his physicality: Warne was built like a nightclub bouncer, not a spinner. Massive hands led into awe-inspiring wrists, the whole lot powered by an ox's shoulders. But kids who try the same quickly wear themselves out.

Howard knew how they felt: "My body never backed me up. I couldn't feel my pinky finger, had part of my right arm shortened, tendinitis in my shoulder was operated on, a wrist operation, stress fractures in my shins, tennis elbow in my knees from excessive squat thrusts, a spinning finger with bad ligaments, and barely the fitness to get through a two-day game, let alone four. There was no million-dollar microsurgery in the US for me. In the '90s, you still had to pay for a massage and work a day job.

"There were suddenly leg-spinning experts everywhere – not ex-spinners but just ex-cricketers, coaches and selectors who spent years ignoring leg-spin. No one ever came up to you and said: 'You should be more like Warne.' But every bit of advice seemed to be about making you more like him. It wasn't subtle. Everything just created doubt in your mind. And with leg-spin, if you have an ounce of doubt, you're cactus."

Warne's retirement sparked a desperate search for his replacement. One spinner simply begat the next: Stuart MacGill, Brad Hogg, Beau Casson, Cameron White, Jason Krejza, Nathan Hauritz, Marcus North, Bryce McGain, Hauritz again, Steve Smith, Xavier Doherty, Michael Beer, Nathan Lyon. Never mind Simon Katich, Michael Clarke or Andrew Symonds.

MacGill should have softened the blow of Warne's departure, but his knees gave way, his career as a lifestyle-show TV host took off, and it was clear he just didn't want to bowl any more. Even then, there was Hogg, the chinaman bowler with two World Cup wins to his name. But after one horrendous home summer against India, he retired as well – only to make a bizarre return to international cricket during the Twenty20 home series against the Indians once more, in February 2012, aged all but 41.

Along came Casson, another purveyor of chinamen, but a boyish one who seemed too pure for international cricket. His first (and only) Test was uneventful, and within 12 months he would be out of the Australian set-up altogether after an attack of the yips. A brief comeback was ended by Tetralogy of Fallot, a congenital heart defect.

White was captain of Victoria, where he virtually never bowled himself, but suddenly – a product of injuries to others and weird selection – he was Australia's frontline spinner. He was awful. Krejza eventually got a chance and, on Test debut in Nagpur, claimed 12 wickets. The problem was he also gave away 358 runs; he played only one more Test. Marcus North became a Test batsman because he could bowl handy off-spin, some said better than Hauritz. But despite a flattering six-wicket haul against Pakistan at Lord's, North's off-breaks were gentle; and they weren't much help when his batting faded.

McGain made his debut amid plenty of jokes about Bob Holland, who was 38 when he first played for Australia. McGain was an IT professional in a bank, who had never really been especially close to state selection. But he wouldn't go away. And while the search focused on big-turning kids, McGain sneaked into the Victoria side. In the 12 months before his Test debut, a shoulder injury had limited him to four first-class games. When the day finally came, at Newlands, McGain was roadkill: 18–2–149–0. That was it. McGain now plays part-time in the Big Bash League.

Hauritz was not deemed good enough even for New South Wales. He was a timid off-spinner from club cricket with a first-class bowling average of more than 50, but he fought hard and improved regularly. The trouble was Hauritz was neither an attacker nor a defender, and Chris Gayle said it was like facing himself. By the time Hauritz was dumped, he was in the best form of his career.

A young all-rounder named Steve Smith bowled leg-spin, and was brought in to play Pakistan in England. He made a dashing 77, was dropped and then later recalled in the Ashes as a batsman who bowled a bit – just not very well.

Xavier Doherty was given a go because Kevin Pietersen kept falling to left-arm spin. He got his man – but for 227. So in came Michael Beer, who admitted he probably wasn't ready for Test cricket, and then proved it.

The first anyone in Australian cricket heard of Nathan Lyon was when Kerry O'Keeffe mentioned him on radio. At that stage, Lyon was part of the Adelaide Oval groundstaff, and was travelling to Canberra to play for the second XI. After some good performances in the nets, Darren Berry – now Adelaide's Twenty20 coach – took a punt on him. Lyon suddenly looked like the best spin prospect in the country – which wasn't saying much.

Howard really had come along at the wrong time. But there were moments, before I finally spoke to him, when I wondered if he actually existed at all. Finding someone who remembered his name was hard enough; finding someone who'd seen him play next to impossible. I'd talk to a guy, who'd tell me to contact a guy, but that guy would also tell me to contact a guy. The leads never went anywhere. Craig Howard wasn't the missing link of Australian spin bowling: he was just missing.

Then I asked Gideon Haigh about Howard, and he gave a long stare, as if he was searching through his billion-terabyte memory. I had my breakthrough. Haigh talked about how Howard looked like an otherworldly artist – long shirt buttoned to the wrist, billowing madly in the wind; incredibly gawky, like a schoolkid. Howard didn't fit into Haigh's, or anyone else's, imaginings of an athlete. But it was the Howard of my youth. Someone else remembered my poet leggie.

After that I cornered O'Keeffe, leg-spin's court jester. He had coached Howard at the Academy, probably twice. O'Keeffe's eyes were full of regret: he said Howard had a biomechanically flawed action, and O'Keeffe hadn't tried to fix it. But that didn't stop him happily reminiscing about "a wrong'un batsmen had to play from their earhole".

I collared Damien Fleming, Howard's Victoria colleague. Fleming seemed surprised to hear the name again. He told stories about how he thought Victoria had a champion on their hands, but said his skin folds were thicker than those of Warne or Merv Hughes: "Basically bone and fat." He could have gone further with a more supportive coaching structure, said Fleming. He added, almost lustfully: "The best wrong'un I've seen." Then came the clincher. "If someone like him came on the scene now, he'd be given everything he needed to succeed. Like they treat Pat Cummins."

Haigh, O'Keeffe and Fleming all seemed to think Howard was a Test spinner we had missed out on. They could be right. But Howard was caught between two eras, relaxed and regimented. And Australia had Warne.

"My career is long over," says Howard. "It finished with me out of form and mostly injured. It wasn't one thing that ended my career, and I'm not coming up with excuses, but this is what happened to me. Due to my finger, I can't even bowl leg-spin any more – I have to bowl off-spin, but nothing can ever compare to being a leg-spinner. I'm younger than Hogg, McGain or MacGill and instead of preparing to play in my 100th Test and thinking about retirement, I am working in an office in Bendigo."

Craig Howard went from a freakishly talented wrist-spinner to a boring club offie. Australian spin did much the same.

Chronicle *Wisden* 2013

Liz Hurley and her partner Shane Warne are believed to have bought Donnington Hall, a £6m mansion near Ledbury, Herefordshire. "I think Shane would get a game for us," said Jim Sandford, chairman of nearby Eastnor CC (*Malvern Gazette*, August 27).

***

Australia's Transport Accident Commission defended their choice of Shane Warne to front a road-safety campaign less than a year after he was involved in a road-rage dispute with a cyclist (*Sydney Morning Herald*, December 19).

WORDS ON WARNE

"I would love to see Viv Richards play Shane Warne on a turning wicket. I'm sure in time he would have coped, but initially he might have got frustrated if he couldn't score quickly, and might have got himself out. I think he didn't have that much quality spin to face in that particular era. If ever I would like to see a contest between players from two eras pitted against each other, it would be Viv against Warne."

Barry Richards, former South Africa batsman – WAC, July 2003

2013

Book Review John Crace, *Wisden* 2013

On Warne by Gideon Haigh (Simon & Schuster, 2012)

I can't remember Gideon Haigh ever constructing a duff sentence, and *On Warne* more than maintains his reputation as the most literary of the current breed of Australian cricket writers. There have been countless biographies – not to mention autobiographies – of "the greatest spin bowler who ever lived™", and Haigh sensibly eschews this route, despite having spent more time with Warne over the years than many of his predecessors. Instead, as the title suggests, he has opted for something rather bolder: a philosophical treatise on the meaning of being Shane Warne; a deconstruction of genius.

If some of the material feels relatively familiar – the betting scandals, the weight-loss drugs, the infighting in the Australian dressing-room – Haigh's approach casts them in a new light. While never less than forensic in his analysis, he makes us reconsider the sheer physical exertion and contortion in imparting so many revolutions on a ball, hour after hour, year after year; the burden of being every captain's go-to bowler; the expectation of being asked consistently to win the unwinnable; and the sheer absurdity of finding a unique talent in someone who would be just as happy sitting on a beach, drinking beer with his mates.

My only small reservation is that Haigh perhaps loves his subject just a bit too much. Plenty have queued up to knock Warne for his off-field behaviour and, as an author, Haigh is within his rights not to join in. But, while never avoiding the difficult issues, he does tend to give Warne the benefit of the doubt. Take the incident in which Warne and Mark Waugh were found to have accepted money from an Indian bookmaker on the 1994-95 tour of Sri Lanka in exchange for information about pitch conditions and team selection. Haigh's view is that it was an act of naivety on a very demanding tour, no real harm was intended and, however badly Warne and Waugh might have acted, they looked like saints in comparison with the Australian board's handling of the situation.

All of which may, or may not, be true but it rather misses the central point that Warne and Waugh *did* take the money on offer and should have known better; deep down they probably did. But why did no one else in the Australian team do the same? Why did they not even think to ask their team-mates whether they thought it was a good idea? Haigh is equally lenient in regard to Warne's diet, drinking, gambling and womanising, his attitude being that countless other cricketers have done the same or worse; that Warne's behaviour away from cricket is a personal matter; and that he gets more flak simply because of his celebrity. These are valid points, but they close down the argument rather than open it up. The aim is not to pass moral judgment on Warne – as far as I'm concerned he can do pretty much what he likes – but to understand him. Why is he so self-destructive? Is there a relationship between his personality flaws and his bowling genius? I'm fairly sure there might be, if you looked carefully enough.

Old Trafford Test Notes and Quotes   *Wisden* 2014

Shane Warne used his post-match column in the *Daily Telegraph* to criticise the attitude of England's players. "A lot of us reporting and commentating on the game were really taken aback by the way the England players were interviewing," he wrote. "To me there were a few moments at Old Trafford when I thought 'Hang on, who do you think you are?' … it leads me to think perhaps it is a conscious effort or direction from Andy Flower to be arrogant and dismissive of the opposition."

Chester-le-Street Notes and Quotes

Wisden 2014

Alastair Cook was on the front foot in his pre-Test press conference, following Shane Warne's criticism of his team's attitude in Manchester. "I've got no qualms with the way we've gone about our business in this series," he said. "The way we've conducted ourselves has been very good."

Warne kept up his Twitter assault on Cook's captaincy throughout this Test, calling it "very defensive and negative" – at least until Australia's fatal collapse. He also questioned Cook's decision to bring on Tim Bresnan ahead of Stuart Broad after tea on the fourth day. Moments later, Bresnan removed David Warner, and the slide was on.

2014

Cricket and the Media

Marcus Berkmann, *Wisden* 2015

During the Test series against Sri Lanka, Shane Warne was gunning for Alastair Cook (in the *Telegraph*, inevitably). "His captaincy at Lord's was terrible, then on Monday at Headingley I witnessed the worst day of captaincy I have ever seen at international level in almost 25 years in the game... This column is not a personal attack and never has been, Alastair. Mate, you need to improve tactically or England need someone else in the job." One can only admire the brilliant tactical use of "mate", feigning friendly advice while firing both barrels into the twitching corpse.

2015

Chronicle

Wisden 2016

Bowling seam-up, Jackson Warne, 14, took four wickets in five balls, including a hat-trick, for the Year 10 team at Brighton Grammar School. His better-known father, Shane, was watching: "Jackson did it!!!!" he tweeted. Jackson had previously preferred football to cricket (*Sunday Herald Sun* Melbourne, February 8).

The Oval Notes and Quotes

Wisden 2016

Shane Warne, commentating on TV, attacked the Australian selectors for preferring Peter Siddle to Pat Cummins. Warne claimed Darren Lehmann and Michael Clarke – no longer a selector – were overruled by chairman of selectors Rod Marsh. "For me, they've got the selection wrong again, and Rod Marsh has to be accountable," said Warne. Lehmann responded: "Shane Warne doesn't know what goes on behind the scenes." Siddle took six wickets.

2016

Chronicle

Wisden 2017

Shane Warne agreed to close his charity, the Shane Warne Foundation, to avoid the possibility of it being deregistered after an 11-month investigation by Victoria state officials. Since 2011, the foundation had recorded that 11-32% of funds raised was being sent to sick and underprivileged children, contravening guidelines that suggest 35% as a minimum (*Sydney Morning Herald*, January 11).

***

Shane Warne told critics of his charity he had nothing to hide. "You can all get stuffed if you want to have a go at us for it, but we are very, very proud." he told an interviewer. "It's really disappointing that people want to come after some good people that have raised a lot of money and made serious difference to seriously underprivileged children" (BBC, March 11).

***

Shane Warne put forward the theory that humans are descended from extra-terrestrials. He was taking part in the Australian version of *I'm a Celebrity … Get Me Out of Here*, and musing with fellow contestant, dancer Bonnie Lythgoe, while in the Kruger National Park. Why, he wondered, had the monkey population not evolved into humans? "Because, I'm saying, aliens. We started from aliens" (*The Guardian*, February 15).

***

Three Channel 9 commentators – Shane Warne, Kevin Pietersen and Michael Slater – have each been fined $A300 by Tasmanian police for failing to wear seatbelts. The three were recording a close-of-play update from a car, and were issued with infringement notices after police saw a video on Facebook (ESPNcricinfo, November 22).

2017

A Mural in Time: Dreaming Up Shane Warne's Ultimate Party
Jonathan Liew, *TN*, June 2017

The film crew had been through almost every room of the house, and were just about to leave when the producer spotted the mural. At first, she thought nothing of it. Shane Warne's house in the Melbourne suburbs was like a shrine to bad art. The motivational posters featuring tropical sunsets and soaring eagles. The Matisse rip-offs that looked like a child's school macaroni project. The Barack Obama "Hope" poster, but with Merv Hughes in the main role. This, however, was on an entirely different scale.

The cameras started rolling. "I'll run you through a couple of the names," Warne said. "So there's Bruce Springsteen and myself just chilling in the corner, having a drink. Springsteen's got a cricket ball in his hand, he's just asking questions about cricket. The legend Mick Jagger, he's just sitting in the pool chilling. Then you've got Frank Sinatra and Muhammad Ali having a bit of a tune, just singing along. Then JFK's just mixing with Sharon Stone and Marilyn Monroe. Two of my closest friends, Chris Martin and Michael Clarke, just having a bit of a chat. I tell you what, the artist has looked after Pup with those guns!"

When the programme eventually aired on Sky Sports in 2015 under the title "Shane Warne: Living the Dream", Warne was widely ridiculed for his vanity. Warne feigned indifference, but deep down he allowed himself a wry chuckle. Sure, he could be a touch outspoken at times, perhaps even unsubtle. But vanity was the last thing you could accuse him of. Besides, he knew the truth. The mural was not some fanciful imagining of an idealised poolside reverie. It had been painted from life.

***

Darkness washed over The Oval like a cruel sea. The champagne corks on the outfield would not be seen again until morning. The confetti danced alone. Moths flapped at the pavilion window, the only square of light left in the ground. Inside the Australian dressing-room, however, illumination offered no solace.

For much of the evening, they had laughed and drunk away the pain. The English came in to visit, but had not stayed long, eager to clamber into their waiting taxis and begin the festivities in earnest. And so the Australians commiserated alone, flipping open the bottles of Victoria Bitter that had been purchased for victory but would do just as well in defeat.

A taut and awful silence gripped the room. Simon Katich stared at the backs of his hands. Shaun Tait blew a one-note tune across the neck of his bottle. The silence was momentarily broken by a cricket ball rolling off the bench and hitting the floor with a thud.

"Well, fellas," Adam Gilchrist began suddenly. "At least we can tell our grandkids we played in the greatest Test series of all time."

Ricky Ponting harrumphed. "How can it be the greatest of all time?" he retorted. "We lost."

The click of a cigarette lighter interjected before Gilchrist could respond. From behind a tall stack of pizza boxes, the slumped and cetacean figure of Warne slowly winched itself upright. Warne inhaled slowly and exhaled with violence, an angry cloud of smoke pouring from his mouth.

"Yeah, we lost," he spat. "But we're still Australia. They won, but they'll wake up tomorrow morning and they'll still be England. Ian Bell will still be Ian Bell. Ashley Giles will still be Ashley Giles. The ginger bloke who came in and made seven, he'll still be the ginger bloke. Who's going to remember these guys in 20 years' time?"

Warne paused for effect. "Nobody, that's who," he said. He had developed a habit of answering his own rhetorical questions, a trait that grated on colleagues to an unfathomable degree, and which they would occasionally remark upon when he was out of earshot. But before they could dwell on their irritation, Warne continued.

"Yeah, they're having a bit of a party tonight," he said. "But if Warney throws a party, it's going to be the greatest party the world has ever seen."

Already, Warne's mind was racing quicker than his tongue could follow. Warne was often this way when a grand idea seized him: catalysed, almost to the point of breathlessness. "In fact," he continued, "that's what I'm going to do. Soon as we get back home. Biggest party in the southern hemisphere. Who's coming?"

Again, there was a certain sceptical silence. Every single person in that room had first-hand experience of one of Warne's "mega-parties". Invariably, they failed to live up to their advance billing. Often, spectacularly so. One time, the promised "A-list celebrities from the world of acting" had turned out to be Alf and Ailsa from *Home and Away*. Then there was the time, a few years earlier, when most of the Australian team and their partners had turned up in anticipation of a "sumptuous moonlight dinner". When they arrived, they found that Warne's hot tub had been drained and filled with chips.

But it had been a long summer. Playing in the greatest series of all time takes a toll on the body, but it takes a toll on the mind as well. Nobody was in the mood to arrest Warne's flight of fancy. Many were already allowing their thoughts to wander homewards, to their own beds and home-cooked food and towels they had chosen themselves.

"You know those games where you have to pick your ideal party guests?" asked Warne, to nobody in particular. "Of course you do. Well, it'll be like that, except for real. Elvis Presley. James Dean. Frank Sinatra. Bruce Springsteen. Muhammad Ali. JFK. Marilyn Monroe. Princess Di."

It was at this point that John Buchanan, the coach, piped up: "Shane, you do realise half of these people are dead?"

Warne glowered at him. "Now that," he retorted, "is the sort of negative thinking that's been holding back Australian cricket for years. 'No nightwatchman.' 'No Hooters the night before a Test.' 'You can't invite this bloke to your party, mate, he's dead.' That's your problem: it's always 'can't' with you, John."

An unidentified yawn from the back of the dressing-room – it may have been Justin Langer, who had been up since 4am doing tai chi – seemed to spread like contagion. One by one, the Australians started stretching and rubbing their eyes and picking up their bags and drifting towards the door. "We'll have a barbecue," Warne announced as their descending footsteps cast echoes back up the stairs. "How's second week of October suit everyone?" But nobody was listening any more.

***

"Have you ever read *A Brief History of Time*?" Jason Gillespie asked. "Basically, it says that all time is a form of matter. It has a frequency and a position and a weight all of its own. If you could somehow create a gravitational field stronger than any field that currently exists in the universe, you could enter and exit the time curve at any point you choose. Are you going to have that side salad?"

Warne pushed the plate across the table, rapt in thought, or perhaps the lack of it. It was six months after the Ashes defeat and his party plans had yet to find any kind of definite shape. October had been a non-starter; most of the team had discovered immovable prior arrangements that prevented them from attending. So too November. December and January, at the height of the summer, were no good for anyone.

Meanwhile, a quick blast on Wikipedia had proven Buchanan right. Many of the prospective guests were now dead. But over a hastily arranged lunch in Fitzroy, Gillespie was enthusing about a potential solution.

"You know when you fizz one three feet outside leg stump?" Gillespie said. "And the ball kind of stops in the air? And it seems like time is standing still? That's not an effect. That's the gravitational field created by the revs on the ball. If you harness that, find a way to keep the ball spinning indefinitely, then essentially time is your servant. You can go wherever you want, in whatever direction you want, for as long as you want."

Warne looked unconvinced. It was not that the prospect of time travel was unappealing to him, or that the science underwhelmed him. It was more that he did not see the point. Why live 200 years in the future when you could live now, with the certainties of the present, when you knew where everything was in your fridge, and you had a pretty good idea what would be on TV that evening? Besides, people in the past would never have heard of him, and people in the future might already have forgotten him. He banished this last thought with a violent, involuntary shake of the head.

"What that means," Gillespie continued through a mouthful of rocket, "is that you can delve into history and grab anyone you want for this party of yours. JFK. Elvis. Leonardo da Vinci. Genghis Khan."

Warne nodded, a gesture that concealed a comprehension that was only partial. Over the months, the guest list had grown in his head. It now included Marlon Brando, Martin Luther King, Buddy Holly and Mother Teresa. But in his head it had remained, until Gillespie had called up out of the blue and asked to meet. Now he was talking about valvetrains and drive belts and hooking a spinning cricket ball up to his motorcycle engine.

"Remember the time I won a motorbike in that tour game in India?" Gillespie asked, spearing a radish with his fork. "It's still in the garage. So you attach the ball to the drive belt – that keeps it spinning – rig it up to a capacitor, beef up the hydraulics, spark it up, lift the throttle, and suddenly you're surfing the highways of time."

Warne pondered as he lit a cigarette. All sorts of thoughts were running through his head. What if Dizzy could actually pull this off? Even if he could go back in time and find JFK and Elvis Presley, how would he convince them to come to a party in Melbourne? And who was Genghis Khan? He could have sworn he had heard that name someplace. Indian? Off-spinner? 1950s? "Not famous enough," he thought to himself, and mentally scrawled his name off the guest list.

***

Once Gillespie got the bike running, things started to move pretty quickly. Warne sat pillion and operated the spinning motor: leggie to go back in time, slider to go forward. "It's so quiet," Gillespie remarked breathlessly as the years began to tick away, as the sharp edges and definite shapes of the garage around them began to blur and melt and warp and fade. The only sound was the ambient fizz of the Kookaburra ball behind them, wobbling furiously on its own axis, held in place only by its own eerie volition. "It's like a county game," Warne scoffed.

Some guests were easier to persuade than others. Mother Teresa refused on grounds of taste. Princess Diana offered her apologies, but she was due to be appearing in a haunting in Bristol later that afternoon and she had always prided herself on being a lady of her word. Buddy Holly had, for some reason, developed an aversion to long-distance travel. Monroe was sceptical, but agreed to come when she found out Kennedy would be there. Kennedy instantly agreed to come when he found out Monroe would be there. He told Jackie he was going to a Pacific trade summit.

But the big fish was Elvis Presley, who agreed to meet them at Graceland in 1972. Sprawled across his luxurious white-leather sofa, Presley refused point blank to accompany Warne and Gillespie to the future. The present was where his life was, and it contained all the food and prescription drugs and heartbreak he could ever want.

It took all Warne's powers of persuasion to lure Presley off his sofa and into the 21st century. "What are future generations going to say," he said in a vaguely scolding tone, "when they find out that the end of the world was coming, and you could have prevented it?" He paused for effect. "I think they'd find that pretty ordinary, if you ask me," he added.

***

And so, there it was. The weather was glorious, as glorious as it is in your dreams. Mick Jagger and Sharon Stone arrived first, having shared a cab together. "Incredible who you bump into in cosmetics," Stone remarked. Next came Jack Nicholson, bearing a giant slab of Victoria Bitter and with his 1998 Oscar for Best Actor in his pocket. He was followed in close order by Sean Connery. "Let me guess," Warne beamed. "Martini, shaken not stirred?"

"I'm driving," Connery grumbled. "Do us a Diet Coke for now."

Chris Martin was simply delighted to be there. Everyone he met was greeted with a fusillade of effusive compliments. "You're a fucking legend!" he shouted to Kennedy on meeting him. "I saw that Kevin Costner film about the Cuban Missile Crisis. I mean, what an amazing experience that must have been. Just, you know, knowing how close we were to nuclear war. It would have been major. So fucking... fair play, man. Fair play. Do you like cricket?"

"Not as such, no," Kennedy replied.

Dimitri Mascarenhas looked, if anything, a little lost. He tried to strike up a conversation with Presley, but seeing as Mascarenhas had never listened to Presley's music and Presley had never watched a Hampshire CB40 game, their chat quickly fizzled out, and Mascarenhas spent most of the afternoon picking at a bowl of Doritos and wondering what on earth he was doing there.

Sinatra requested some music: "Connie Francis, if you have it." Warne said he would search his iTunes library but might have to resort to one of his playlists. Sinatra, polite to a fault, had no objections. And so it is that in the painting, the tune that Sinatra and Ali are belting out is "Somebody Told Me" by The Killers.

Warne circled the party in quiet contemplation, quietly marvelling at the tableau he had brought together. It all felt too surreal for words. Was that really

Muhammad Ali reaching for the prawn skewers? Was that really Angelina Jolie lounged half-naked over a chair he had never seen before in his life? Was that really Anthony Hopkins in the character of Hannibal Lecter, flipping brains over on the barbecue?

In a funny way, he still had his doubts. Ever since he was young, he had always had a vivid imagination. It helped him as a bowler, too: not until late in his career did he realise that his ability to envisage what a batsman would do before he did it was not a skill all humans possessed, but a preternatural, almost supernatural, talent. There were times when he felt like an actor, in a film he had already seen many times before.

His reverie was broken by Martin, grabbing his shoulder and gushing about the ball that he had bowled to Andrew Strauss at Edgbaston. "It was fucking awesome," he said. "We were on tour all that summer and we've got the cricket on in the tour bus, and I'm sitting there thinking, 'fuck,' but it was an absolute genius ball. Seriously, what a genius. You, Freddie Flintoff and Curtly Ambrose are my absolute favourite cricketers of all time. And Botham, obviously. Martin Crowe. Lara. Shaun Pollock. Kumble. Sachin Tendulkar. What's he like to bowl at? I mean, Tendulkar, what a fucking genius..."

It had all gone more perfectly than Warne had dared to hope. Everybody was getting on famously. Sinatra and Michael Clarke exchanged telephone numbers and agreed to go for a drink the next time they were passing through the same spacetime. Bruce Springsteen learned how to bowl a googly and promised to teach the E Street Band when he got back home. Everybody was having so much fun, in fact, that nobody even noticed the two large trucks pulling up outside the back gate; one bearing a giant water pump, the other carrying 150 industrial-sized bags of chips.

Later, after the last of the guests had left and the sun was finally receding, Warne went back inside the house. He saw his phone on the dining table, and instantly a cold dread settled over him. Even before unlocking the home screen, he knew what he would find. There were 19 missed calls and eight unread texts from Gillespie. He had been at the front door all day, pleading for someone to let him in.

***

"OK, that'll be a wrap," the producer announced, checking her phone for the time of her next shoot, a bunch of AFL players visiting a petting zoo in Collingwood. "That was great, thanks. We'll just take some cutaways of the exterior, and then we'll be out of your hair."

"No worries," Warne said, but the film crew were already opening the door by that point. Warne fancied he saw a couple of them smirking conspiratorially to each other. They left promptly and without a second glance, and so they did not see the cricket ball above the garage door, hovering a few inches below the ceiling, still furiously spinning.

2018

Book Review   Tanya Aldred, *Wisden* 2019

No Spin: My autobiography by Shane Warne with Mark Nicholas (Ebury, 2018)

Shane Warne stares out from the cover of *No Spin*. His ghost is the aforementioned Mark Nicholas, who describes the book as a stream of consciousness. And that's exactly what you get, along with gallons of self-justification, a soupçon of self-knowledge, and fistfuls of exclamation marks. Whoa!

The usual suspects are nailed: John Buchanan and Steve Waugh get it in the neck – the famous loss in Kolkata in 2000-01 was Waugh's fault – as does both men's deification of the Baggy Green. Off-spin is decried as "limited and predictable", while Indians are "thoughtful and kind by nature". Warne's brush occasionally runs a little broad.

In many ways, he is old-fashioned, despite the friendship with the Packers, the private planes and the jet-skis. He adores his children, believes in the school of hard knocks, and thinks today's cricketers have it too easy. He also has a bee in his bonnet about good manners, which unfortunately did not translate on to the field. In fact it is striking that Warne, who had the world at his fingertips, felt so impelled to casual cruelty in the name of tactics. When he first bowls to Kevin Pietersen, he greets him with: "Everyone on this field hates you. Even the non-striker thinks you're a prick. I don't know what's wrong with you, but you must be a fuckwit." There is no shame, and there are many similar conversations.

That apart, Nicholas has things rattling along with his usual light touch. The book is fascinating on the intricacies of leg-spin, with its head-fizzing permutation, and on the thought and trickery behind it: the set-up, the angles, the revs, the patience. There are a few home truths for the English reader, too. While Warne loomed large in our psyches, few English players made an impression on him, and the Ashes grew insignificant as Australian victory followed victory followed victory.

Scandals are skimmed over: he was an ingénue to accept $5,000 from a man he met in a casino, naive not to have checked the contents of a diuretic that led to a drugs ban. His libido has a starring role (there must be something in the literary water), thanks to various blowzy trysts, and an unlikely relationship with Elizabeth Hurley. His attitude to booze, perhaps to life, is as enthusiastic: to borrow from Mike Brearley, shit or bust. "And by the way I'm no slouch. I can drink most people under the table." Bowled Shane.

Chronicle *Wisden* 2019

Playing on the Masters course at Augusta National, Shane Warne hit his first ever hole-in-one at the 16th: 155 yards and into the wind. "Can't believe it!!!!!!!!!!" he tweeted (Nine.com.au, March 19).

2019

Cricket and the Courts *Wisden* 2020

Shane Warne was banned from driving for 12 months by Wimbledon magistrates in September, after admitting his sixth speeding offence in two years. He was clocked doing 47mph in a hired Jaguar on a 40mph slip road on to the A40 in West London. Deputy District Judge Adrian Turner said that, while each incident on its own may not have been serious, "for points disqualification purposes, the triviality of the offences is not to be taken into account". Warne was also fined £1,845.

Chronicle *Wisden* 2020

A newly discovered range of about 100 underground volcanoes in the Australian outback have been named "The Warnie volcanic province", in Shane Warne's honour. The volcanoes are buried hundreds of metres beneath the rocks in the Cooper-Eromanga Basins, in the oil-and-gas-producing region shared by Queensland and South Australia. They are believed to be about 170m years old. Warne is about to turn 50 (Geologypage.com, August 14).

2020

Timeline of a Pandemic *Wisden* 2021

March 19: A gin distillery owned by Shane Warne turns production to hand sanitiser.

2021

London Spirit v Southern Brave, Lord's *Wisden* 2022
(The men's Hundred, August 1)

London Spirit, whose coach, Shane Warne, was in isolation after a positive Covid test, almost pulled off their first win.

The Final Curtain
2022

"He was a brilliant bowler – no one disputes that – but what made him so special was his showmanship, an ability to use the occasion in his favour. He seemed to understand what was going through your mind."
Sir Andrew Strauss, *Wisden Cricketers' Almanack* 2023

It was a little after midnight in Melbourne when the barely believable news began to circulate. The writer Gideon Haigh received a text from a friend relaying something he had heard in a bar: Shane Warne had died while on holiday in Thailand. Knowing *The Australian* newspaper and *The Times* in London would want articles, Haigh got out of bed and began to write. By 2am, the news now confirmed, he was appearing on TV in India via Skype, by 3am he was recording a podcast with his Australian colleague Peter Lalor, who was in Rawalpindi covering the national team's Test match against Pakistan.

The world of cricket operates in perpetually different time zones, and around its circumference there were similar stories of stunned reaction followed by a whirlwind of activity. In London, where it was a little after 2pm, Lawrence Booth, editor of *Wisden Cricketers' Almanack* and a *Daily Mail* cricket writer, missed a call from a friend in Thailand about half an hour before the news broke. It was followed by a bleak message "Warne's dead". He returned the call but details were still sketchy. Nevertheless, he contacted the *Mail* sports desk to tell them a major story might be about to break. While he was on the phone, Fox News in Australia confirmed the news on Twitter. Warne, 52, had suffered a heart attack at the villa he was sharing with friends on the Thai island of Koh Samui.

"I spent the next couple of hours writing a piece for the next day's paper, caught between a certain numbness and the demands of the job," Booth recalled. "It was not a piece I had expected to write for at least another couple of decades – if ever, since Warne was only five years older than me."

Mike Atherton, a former Ashes adversary of Warne's but now a colleague in the Sky Sports commentary box, was on a flight bound for Antigua to cover England's Test tour of the Caribbean for *The Times* and Sky. The photographer Philip Brown walked down the aisle, his eyes red with grief. "Warne's dead," he said. "I cannot think that I have ever been more shocked," Atherton wrote. Like Haigh, he began to write straight away and filed his tribute as soon as his plane touched down in Antigua.

"Having played against him for almost a decade, and having worked alongside him as a commentator for longer, I knew him very well," Atherton added. "But everyone knew him well because his character radiated from every minute of cricket he played."

The sense of shock was shared by current players. In Pakistan, the Australian players had boarded their bus and were waiting to drive back to their Rawalpindi hotel when David Warner broke the news. "The game was never the same after Warnie emerged... and the game will never be the same after his passing," said captain Pat Cummins.

That evening they gathered to share stories of their interactions with Warne, and there was a minute's silence before the start of the second day. In Antigua, the England players broke off from a warm-up game to hold their own silence. Captain Joe Root said: "My experiences of Shane were of someone who absolutely loved the game of cricket. He was always a joy to be around, he gave so much energy to the sport."

In the UK, Warne's death made the front page of all but one national newspaper, and there were pages of tributes. "You could try to measure his greatness in statistics, but they wouldn't ever really begin to capture it," wrote Andy Bull in *The Guardian*. The venerable former *Daily Telegraph* correspondent and *Wisden* editor Scyld Berry wrote: "He was the ultimate con man, deceiving batsmen either off the pitch or in the air or in their minds."

Australian cricket was already in mourning after the death of former wicketkeeper Rod Marsh, announced a few hours earlier. Warne had used social media to pay tribute to Marsh. "Sad to hear the news that Rod Marsh has passed," he posted on Twitter. "He was a legend of our great game and an inspiration to so many young boys and girls. Rod cared deeply about cricket and gave so much – especially to Australia and England players." Soon, came the news that Warne was dead too.

His trip to Thailand with friends had been the start of a global three-month jaunt, in part to celebrate the end of pandemic travel restrictions. After settling into the villa, he watched the cricket from Rawalpindi on TV and left briefly to order some new clothes from a local tailor he had used previously. He went to his room to rest, agreeing to meet his friends for drinks at 5pm. When he had not emerged by 5.15, they knocked on his door but there was no response. When they went in they found Warne unconscious. Frantic efforts to resuscitate him were unsuccessful. Paramedics were soon on the scene but their efforts were also to no avail. He was pronounced dead on arrival at Thai International Hospital after further resuscitation efforts failed.

Australia was plunged into mourning. "It's our Princess Diana moment," said the actor Rhys Muldoon. "Australians, comfortable with wealth but wary of the highfalutin, approved of his plain tastes and knockabout everydayness," reported London's *Sunday Times*. There was a stream of visitors to Warne's statue outside the Melbourne Cricket Ground. Some brought flowers but others left cans of beer, pizza boxes and pies. Warne would surely have chuckled. His funeral was private and for family only but there was a state memorial service at the MCG on March 30. It was an extraordinary event, attended by 50,000 people in the stadium and watched by an estimated global audience of a billion.

The tributes – some live, others by video link – were a testament to the extent of Warne's fame. Sir Elton John sang 'Don't Let the Sun Go Down on Me' and there were messages from Kylie Minogue, Ed Sheeran, Hugh Jackman and Chris Martin. Frank Sinatra's 'My Way' played over the speakers. There were emotional speeches from his father, Keith, and his children Brooke, Summer and Jackson. The MCG's vast Great Southern Stand was renamed the Shane Warne Stand during the course of the service.

It still seemed unreal. Only a few weeks earlier, in the Netflix documentary *Shane*, Warne had looked to the future with his customary zest for life. "I like loud music, I smoked, I drank, I bowled a bit of leg-spin, that's me," he said. "I don't have any regrets."

RW

2022

Shane Warne, 1969-2022 Phil Walker, *WCM*, April 2022

Shane Warne is gone and the game is broken. They say that cricketers die twice, once when they bowl their last, and then, well. Warne wasn't like that. Warne wasn't like anything else ever. There was no pause, no break in the flow. He rode on the tracks he built himself, never once got off and took everyone with him. He thrummed and danced and spoke his heart and did stupid things and took and gave it all. Always in the game, from the first slap of zinc to the last tip of the wink. He answered only to his vision for what cricket should be, only ever wanting to know if this casual muckabout, a thing he came to with a shrug, was up to it. He eyeballed the game, in its badges and stripes, and implored the thing to live a little, and he changed everything entirely by accident, which must be the purest, most sublime way of doing anything.

This is an Australian tragedy. But Warne more than any other cricketer across all our lifetimes belonged to the whole thing. English cricket adored him, took him in, a saviour and executioner all at once. And he gave back to it, even trod the boards at Southampton for a few years. Easy access routes to London, after all. He won the first IPL largely by dint of personality. He *was* the game.

You'll remember how he emerged in '91 as Benaud's boy, all jowls and spunk, ostensibly a social experiment, approved with caveats by Border, his visionary captain. Even then he had history on him. It seemed to fall to him to resurrect those great lost Aussie wristies, dragged from the past into the present and ragging into the future. With the juddering news of Rod Marsh's death, announced barely 24 hours earlier and eerily commemorated by Warne himself in his final tweet, three generations of Australian cricket are bound together in thick black tape. Somehow the current team, on tour in Pakistan, will have to keep going. Warne, at the start, would have drawn each and every one of them in. And Marsh, who caught everything and coached everyone, would have helped make them good.

First time I interviewed Warne was at Lord's, a couple of months before that valedictory whitewash in 2006-07, when he bent Boxing Day in his hometown to his will and took his 700th before walking off a week later, arm in arm with McGrath, at the SCG. That day at Lord's he was there to front up a new scheme to identify some young spinners from the gaggle of hopefuls in attendance. (Just think for a moment of the sheer number of days that Warne did this.) After the interview was done, off he went to get changed into his cricket gear and have a cigarette ("Smoko!" he announced at the interview's end, forever in search of a bike shed). He was about to give a masterclass in the indoor school, in front of the cameras and all that. Some of the journalists headed for the exit, and as we made our way through past the back door of the arena, Warne was there, in full whites, fag in hand, giving a solitary young lad, no more than nine, an impromptu tutorial in how to bowl the leg-break. He was bent over to the boy's height and was demonstrating the grip. The boy leaned on his bat and listened. There were no cameras to capture the moment, no PR person to usher him along. It was just a bloke and a kid, talking cricket. Everyone who's ever had a passing interest in cricket will have their own impressions, their own stories. The gap between him and his people was thinner than a silver Rizla.

At a swoop, the rest just falls away. None of it matters. All the other stuff, who cares now. The doomscroll of dodgy diuretics, iffy bookies, bad musicals, chat shows, filth scoops and captaincy craps, graceless Waugh games, pool parties, Twitter beefs – all of it just melts away, attached to the Warne story only like thin strands of molten cheese on a ham and pineapple special.

Sitting here at The Oval, where he doffed his filthy white floppy on that autumn evening two decades ago, with the day's highlights mutedly rolling on the TV in the corner, and this season's intake training out there on the outfield, every ball from every arm from London to Pindi to Mohali to Melbourne seems to belong to him and him alone. The language of sport is stuffed to excess, overstretched, routinely pulled out of shape. The torrents that now will flow for Shane Warne will all be true.

This piece was originally published on Wisden.com, a few hours after news broke of Warne's death.

'He crammed a number of lifetimes into those 52 years' Simon Katich, *WCM*, April 2022

I learned so much from Warnie and he had a huge impact on my career. Because I bowled part-time leggies, when we were in Sri Lanka for my first tour [with the Australian Test team in 1999] he took me aside to teach me about the art of leg-spin. A couple of those tips that he gave me about my action I kept with me throughout my career.

His love of sharing that knowledge was second to none. It's already been said so many times that he was a legendary player, but from our perspective as teammates and mates he was a legend of a bloke. You knew where you stood with Warnie. There was no grey, it was black and white, and I loved that about him. I loved how he cared about his teammates. He was always very, very good to me.

I saw first-hand at Hampshire how good he was with the young kids, taking time to have photos, sign autographs, all that sort of stuff. And I think that's what endeared him to people all around the world.

He was a magnificent captain. He didn't get the chance to do it as much for Australia as potentially he would have liked, but having seen him captain at Hampshire, he made the game fun. He was always making the game move forward, and he tried to bring in things that challenged us as teammates. We had a six-hitting competition at Hampshire, across all formats, because he wanted us to put pressure on the opposition. It probably wasn't my style as a player but I loved it because it took me out of my comfort zone and challenged me to be a little bit more aggressive, and in the end it had a really positive effect.

He thrived on being the man in the big contests and there's no bigger series for Australia than the Ashes in England. In 2005 we got off to a great start, won at Lord's, and then all of a sudden we found ourselves behind the eight-ball. He was the one that kept us in it, single-handedly at times.

Hearing that he had some issues off the field at the time, to be able to compartmentalise that and then still step out on the field was just a remarkable effort. It says a lot about him and his strength of character to be able to manage both scenarios and still be magnificent at his job, which was to play cricket for Australia. He did it so well.

There's no doubt that he kept the art of leg-spin bowling alive, and I think that it's going to keep going for generations and generations. I know when the news broke the other morning and I rang home, my 11-year-old son, who bowls leggies, started crying because he realised he was never going to meet Warnie. He desperately wanted to meet him and unfortunately I never got around to organising that for him. But I think it just highlights that it doesn't matter what generation it is; Warnie's legacy will remain for the history of the game, for centuries to come. He helped make Australia one of the greatest teams in the history of the game, and as teammates we were all very blessed to see that first-hand and be a part of it.

Yes, he's been taken far too soon, but we all know he lived life to the fullest, and he crammed a number of lifetimes into those 52 years. It was an absolute pleasure and privilege to call him a teammate and a mate. May he rest in peace, The King.

Simon Katich played in 17 Test matches with Shane Warne.

'I'd never seen a ball turn like that before'   Mark Butcher, *WCM*, April 2022

The first time I played against Shane Warne was in a tour match, Surrey versus Australia, all the way back in 1993. They tossed the ball to this slightly round, spiky-haired blond bloke with an earring, who was pretty much unknown. I remember him bowling this delivery, round the wicket to me as a left-hander, and it pitched just on the cut strip, outside my off stump. I thrust a pad out at it to try and cover the spin, and it turned and bounced and shot over my right shoulder. I'm just thinking, 'What the hell was that?' I'd never seen a ball turn like that before. I suppose it was a precursor to the ball of the century [which Warne produced at Old Trafford a week later].

During the 1994-95 Ashes series I was playing grade cricket and living in Melbourne and I just remember watching him have England on toast. The flipper was still working back then. He had the entire box of tricks in those early days, and he was just compelling to watch. I'm watching this thinking, 'Crikey, what happens if I get picked for England? How am I going to go about playing against this?'

I made my debut in the 1997 Ashes series. In the second Test at Lord's I made 80-odd in the second innings and he bowled me when I tried to hit him through extra-cover against the spin. I got a little bit cocky. Then in the third Test at Old Trafford a wet pitch dried out and really started to turn in the second innings, and that was when I started to see close-up just how good he was.

Later in my career I got the chance to play against Shane in county cricket, which was nice because there didn't seem to be quite so much pressure. It didn't mean that he bowled any differently or took it any easier, but you just had a little bit more mind space to try and figure out what you were going to do and what he was doing.

The smoke and mirrors about Shane Warne was that he was a leg-spinner with no googly, the flipper had stopped by then as well because of the shoulder injury, and so what you saw was varying degrees of leg-spin and a ball that went straight – and that was pretty much it. A lot of his mastery was based around the theatre of it all.

He'd come on to bowl and it would take him forever to set his field, it would take him forever to bowl the first ball, it was building up this anticipation. And then the field would move maybe a centimetre one way or six inches the other, and you're standing there going: 'Why's he doing that? Why's he making such a big deal of doing that?' Immediately the brain is starting to think, 'He's setting me up for something here', and he probably wasn't, but that was how he had command of the people he was playing against and the arena that he was playing in.

In 2005 he probably bowled as well as he ever did. He was just so completely in control of what he was doing. It wasn't as though he was struggling before, but by then his mastery of the entire art was supreme. It's just an absolute privilege to have played so many games of cricket against somebody that good, and to have had the odd day where it went my way, and tons more when it didn't!

When it comes to comparisons with Murali, there's not a great deal in it, you're splitting hairs between two greats. But in terms of nous and understanding of what batters were trying to do and getting inside their head, Warne had that advantage. And when the game appeared to be in your favour, when it seemed to be going your way, Shane was much better at wrestling that back. With Shane there was just that little bit extra, something unquantifiable.

There was this feeling that once he got his teeth into a situation – once he locked into the perfect pace for that particular day on that particular surface – it was unbelievably difficult to stop the momentum when it went his way. It was like a tiny little snowball rolling down the hill and, before you knew it, it was the size of a house, and just knocking everything over in its way. And the crowd got involved in that too.

Off the field, he was a lot of fun. The beer-drinking thing is perhaps another piece of smoke and mirrors really. He wasn't a massive drinker, at least not beers anyway, but he was very sociable and always wanting to talk cricket. He'd have a million and one stories about stuff going on outside cricket, but if you wanted to talk to him about something to do with the game, he came even more alive and was always willing to share his thoughts.

Murali is the same here – both of them were absolute badgers for the game of cricket. You'd imagine that being as great as they were they'd pack their boots away at the end of the day and want to do or talk about something else, but the pair of them – and Warnie to an extraordinary extent – absolutely loved the game, loved the strategy of it, loved the idea of trying to get one over on the opposition.

What he did for the rest of us, for all the mere mortals on the field, was to give cricket this glamour, this injection of being something that was worth watching even if you weren't a cricket fan. That excitement is rare from cricketers. Botham had a similar type of aura, Lara too at his very best, whereby everybody wanted to stop what they were doing and watch because this man was involved.

He was just an extraordinarily alive and vibrant human being. He had his faults, as we all do, but he had the ability to raise not only a room but 90,000 people at the MCG. He had everyone in the palm of his hand when he was the centre of attention. And he was nearly always the centre of attention.

Mark Butcher played 14 Test matches against Shane Warne and was dismissed by him seven times.

Moments of genius that made the man   *WCM,* April 2022

Daniel Norcross – 1993, 34 wickets in an Ashes series
My sister-in-law is American. Her punishment for marrying my brother was to spend much of the summer in the early part of her marriage holed up in England watching cricket on the TV, which she did with patience and grace but absolutely no enthusiasm. Her first exposure to a Test match was, unhelpfully, watching Australia amass 602 in 206.3 overs at Trent Bridge in 1989 including a 382-ball 138 for Geoff Marsh. Even for a devoted Anglophile like her, the game was nothing more than a perverse exercise in watching entropy played out in the most Byzantine method yet devised. For four summers she endured, unmoved by some of the greats of the game. Then in 1993, everything suddenly made sense. It wasn't so much *that ball*, though it did certainly help. It was that Shane Warne had turned a light on and illuminated the murky, inaccessible labyrinth of cricket.

In one fell swoop she finally understood what was possible; why bowlers were allowed to bowl the ball into the pitch. How they worked batters over. The deceit, the subtleties, the theatre. Now, instead of reading a book she would shout out to the kitchen to hurry up with the gin and tonic because "Warnie's bowling". She whooped with delight every time he took one of his 34 wickets that series, while the rest of us groaned and tried to explain that leg-spin was unsustainable at Test level. But she was having none of it. The slider was her favourite. The slow, straight one. She started to predict when it would come and was spookily, invariably right. My job today is to communicate the wonders of our great game. For four years I failed abjectly to make any headway with my sister-in-law until Warne. In an instant she was saved, and given the tools to educate me in the wonders of leg-spin. Neither of us have ever looked back. Thanks, Warnie.

Sam Perry – 12-128 v South Africa, Sydney, 1994
It's 1994, I'm nine years old, bushfires are pounding NSW, and for the third successive summer my dad takes me to the SCG Test match.

I am already spellbound by Shane Warne; everyone in Australia is. But my age is important. I'm new to cricket, yet like all kids I could intuit there was something special about Warne by the way even wizened adults were mesmerised by him.

Imprinting theory posits that people are innately attached to the first thing they see. I loved every iteration of Warne, but I think I loved his old stuff the most.

I went to every day of this Test match. It was 27 years ago, so I can't say I remember each wicket vividly. But I remember the feeling. This was early album Warne: he had every trick in the book, his body was strong and athletic, and he could spin the ball violently. Certain words accompanied descriptions of Warne's bowling through every stage of his career. At this point, it was "bamboozled". Here, on the old SCG track which actually spun, the South African batters had absolutely no idea.

It is the perfect collection of wickets. Seven in the first innings, five in the second. Five of them are with flippers. Flippers! At one point Gary Kirsten charges at one and gets stumped. He bowls the left-handed Kepler Wessels from around the wicket. He gets one with a wrong'un, which he rarely bowled. He bowls Pat Symcox around his legs. You've never heard Richie Benaud attempt to contain his enchantment so much. The supporting cast is involved. Healy, of course. But then there's Mark Taylor at first slip taking them one-handed, low to his left. Mark Waugh coolly intercepts one at silly point. Boon is under the lid. Every wicket is taken in-close. I was hooked for life.

Australia lost, by the way. But for me, it was secondary to Warne, as it usually was.

David Lloyd – 9-111 v England, Old Trafford, 1997

He was an absolute showman. Unshakeable belief and the skill to do it. He'd target us. He'd have them all ready and lined up. Atherton wouldn't take any truck, Stewie would shrug his shoulders, and Graham Thorpe didn't care who he was facing. But he basically had the wood over the lot. You'd tell them to play the ball not the man but he made sure you played the man.

It was all smoke and mirrors. He bowled a hard-spun leg-spinner, hardly ever showed you his googly, and the killer ball was the flipper. "Hey lads, I've got another mystery delivery!" The zooter, the suitor, the flooter, the shooter, as long as it rhymes! Everybody knew it was all bulls**t.

In 1997 we won the first Test and drew the second at Lord's. I was going round trying to speak to chief executives – I couldn't get to the groundsmen – to get them to keep their leg-spinner out of the game for as long as possible. And they couldn't give a toss. The third Test was at Old Trafford, where it would always spin, and he loved it there – it's where it all started. He took nine in that one, won the game for them, danced on the balcony, and then was basically unstoppable for the rest of the summer.

He was like a machine-gun with his ideas. One after the other. He was way ahead of the game. And forthright opinions. He'd dismiss any Test team that turned up without a spinner. He was a proper cricket bloke and a champion of the game. He had a life – my, what a life he had. But cricket was always front and centre of it.

He was such a good mate. Just the generosity of the bloke. It's well known he was a chain smoker, he'd go anywhere in the ground for a smoke and even give the steward a bob or two to look the other way! And they always did. Everyone was under his spell.

David Lloyd coached England in two Ashes series against Australia – 1997 and 1998-99.

Yas Rana – the Gibbs ball, v South Africa, World Cup semi-final, 1999

For me, it's the delivery that sums him up best in that it combines his supreme skill with his unabashed revelry for the big moment. South Africa are cruising. They're 166 runs away from a first World Cup final with all 10 wickets still in hand. If the Gatting ball was canonised partly for its surprise factor, the Gibbs ball is special precisely because you almost expected it. It drifts ominously and turns sharply from outside leg to dislodge the off bail, leaving Gibbs perplexed and Warne triumphant; he lets out a roar that signals a shift in the mood. His unbroken spell yields figures of 8-4-12-3; he returns later to remove Kallis at the death. Ironically, the only top-five batter Warne spared that day was Cullinan. Warne takes combined figures of 8-62 across the semi-final and final. Surely no man has had a greater impact on the business end of a World Cup and yet it probably doesn't even register as one of his headline achievements.

John Stern – 8-24 v Pakistan, Sharjah, 2002

Myth met reality in the desert. Home away from home for Pakistan who, in the ongoing aftermath of 9/11, could not host teams in their own country. This three-Test series began in Colombo where Pakistan had a shot, needing 86 to win with six wickets left. But Warne got Younis Khan leg before and they lost five for 26.

When the show moved to Sharjah, the heat was unbearable – 48 degrees at one point. Warne had shed two stone for the series, as he readied himself for another Ashes, and he'd have lost a few more pounds in those inhumane conditions. Seamer Andy Bichel, one of the fittest blokes in the game, bowled six overs and was on a drip in the dressing room.

This was the dawn of the slider: a new mystery ball or just a leggie that didn't turn much? But nothing Warne ever bowled was just anything. The Pakistanis played for sharp turn and half the time there was barely any. Pads were thrust, fingers went up – Warne took 27 wickets in the series, 13 of which were lbw.

The second Test was over in two days, Pakistan bowled out for 59 and 53, the fourth-lowest aggregate in Test history. Warne's figures in the first innings: 11-4-11-4. After an innings win in the third match, he duly picked up the player of the series and turned his thoughts to the following month's Ashes. He was bowling as well as ever, he said, and the flipper was back. England were bullish, he was told. "So Nasser's talking the talk but let's see how they play," he responded. No one ever talked the talk *and* walked the walk quite like Warney.

Alison Mitchell – 107 v Kent, Canterbury, 2005

Around the commentary boxes you would often hear him before you saw him; a hearty, mischievous laugh would ring down the corridor, and you knew that Shane Warne was in the house.

I knew him more professionally than personally, having first covered him as a radio reporter during his time at Hampshire, then shared a commentary box with him at the T20 World Cup in Bangladesh in 2014, and media centres during English and Australian summers ever since.

I'd like to offer something on his batting. I was a young reporter when he reached 99 not out for Hampshire against Kent in the lead-up to the 2005 Ashes series. At that point he'd never scored a first-class hundred, yet he was a batter of considerable ability. When he hammered Simon Cook off the back foot to reach three figures in just 72 balls he punched the air, jumped up and down, and spoke afterwards of how much it meant to him, admitting that he felt nervous as the milestone approached.

I've still got the commentary clip I recorded of that moment. It's not my finest piece of work – I'd barely commentated at all at that point and was only at the match as a reporter. I called 'the moment' into my mini-disc recorder for the BBC news desks and archives. It's a piece of audio I've never deleted.

Commentating with Warne at the T20 World Cup was a time I was determined to appreciate and remember. I was established as a cricket voice by that time, but I'd never sat next to Warnie in a commentary box before and I found myself really wanting to make a good impression. He could not have been more respectful and generous both on and off air, even deferring to me for knowledge at times. It was as if he knew I might have felt a bit overawed or intimidated, and without saying anything, wanted to make sure I didn't. His tactical brain was immense. Discussing the game with him was a thrill, and fun. I loved it.

He was my favourite cricketer, and I can't believe he's gone.

Jon Hotten – 4-31 v England, Trent Bridge, 2005

"And if Shane Warne is going to have to come on now," says Geoffrey Boycott on the Channel Four commentary, "then Ricky Ponting is obviously not happy with his seamers…"

Geoffrey is right. Ricky Ponting is not happy with his seamers. On that Nottingham afternoon, with England chasing 129, they have scored 32 from their first five overs. Michael Kasprowicz has figures of 2-0-19-0. England need less than a hundred with 10 wickets in hand and Tresco is biffing like it's a village-green Sunday, but we all know that the chase has not begun, not yet.

Shane Warne is in full Warnie mode, surfer hair spruiked and spiked, earring glinting, ridiculous flares making his feet look like hooves. It is, for the England fan, terrifying. He moves the field a bit, pretending that he doesn't know exactly what he is going to do, then comes round the wicket and has Trescothick caught first ball at silly mid-off. With the first ball of his next over, he catches Michael Vaughan's leading edge with a fizzer and it goes to Matthew Hayden at slip.

England were winning. Now they are not. From the penultimate ball of his fifth over, he gets Andrew Strauss caught at leg slip. Ian Bell goes in Brett Lee's next, and from 32-0, England are 57-4. Anything can happen now. That was Warne. That was Warnie.

Phil Walker – 12-246 v England, The Oval, 2005

At lunchtime we were a mess. No one could eat a thing. We just stood on the concourse and thought about the future.

Minutes earlier, Warne had obliged Flintoff to bunt a return catch. England were five down, 132 ahead. Pietersen was still there, just; luck ridden, chances spurned. After Warne dropped him at slip, Pietersen slapped two sixes off him in his next over. Pietersen made no sense. There were no frames of reference. England never took an Ashes into the final match anyway.

After lunch Pietersen went kamikaze against Brett Lee. From 13 bullets, one of which floated in at 96.7mph, Pietersen advanced his score by 35. There is no madder passage of play.

Warne wasn't done, though not every day belonged to him. When Pietersen finally went, clean-bowled by McGrath, he jogged over to him. You can lip-read it clear as day. "Well played, mate."

He would have to clean up the innings, bowling Giles round his legs and nicking off the last man for his 12th of the week and 40th of the summer. I can still see through the haze of those valedictions Warne standing on the boundary at the Vauxhall End, doffing his Stetson to the crowd.

Adam Collins – 7-85 v England, Melbourne, 2006

Before Shane Warne the colossus – with all his imposing might – there was Shane Warne the freak. At the core of this, in those early years before his body said otherwise, was the flipper. Sure, there was an abstract understanding of what he was doing with that click of the fingers but nobody could quite process how he could deliver it with such ferocity with the very same release that he did his stock ball. There are too many of them to recount – the Richardson, the Stewart, the Cullinan Cullinan Cullinan; all wondrous. As a boy in Melbourne through this stretch, I was obsessed with it. Everyone was. At the MCG we'd sit in the Great Southern Stand and roar his name and bow to him; he'd play along and life was perfect.

But then, he couldn't. After shoulder surgery, the flipper was, in effect, retired from his repertoire. That was until, nearly a decade on, he busted it out deep into his final Test innings at the 'G in a blatant piece of fan service. Sajid Mahmood was the recipient. Behind Warne's arm, the moment the ball pitched, my world stood still – this felt familiar. Before it arrived, I was out of my seat appealing in anticipation, up with Warne, then overcome when umpire Aleem Dar answered the call. Appropriately, Mark Taylor was on TV to explain to the untrained eye how rare and special it was. But for us, in the stand that will now carry his name, to see it one last time meant everything.

Melinda Farrell – 1-22 v Brisbane Heat, The Gabba, 2011

There was a sense of awe and mystery surrounding the magic balls bowled by Shane Warne throughout his career; how the actual hell did he do that? There were no player mics on hand to capture his plans to Mike Gatting or Andrew Strauss or Herschelle Gibbs.

But when it seemed his career was confined to the commentary box, Warne was tempted back onto the field to play for the Melbourne Stars in the inaugural Big Bash League.

There was much anxiety at Cricket Australia; they had largely bet the farm on the success of the T20 tournament. Warne's signing was a publicity boon, but he single-handedly made the BBL the talking point of world cricket when, mic'd up and bowling to the Brisbane Heat's Brendon McCullum, he gave viewers a real time insight to his cricketing genius.

"I think he'll probably try to shape a sweep after that first one, or maybe even go inside-out a bit harder," Warne told commentator Brendon Julian. "So I might try to slide one in there. Fast."

Warne trundled to the crease and bowled, McCullum attempted the sweep, and the ball slid through – fast – and shattered the stumps. "That worked pretty well," laughed Julian. "Yeah not bad, BJ," said Warne.

Not bad indeed, Shane.

Notes by the Editor Lawrence Booth, *Wisden* 2023

On a chilly night in Hobart in January 2022, Shane Warne was enjoying a cigarette outside his hotel. England had just lost the Ashes 4–0, and he was unimpressed by their lack of fight. For Warne, it made no sense. A few weeks later, he was dead, at the age of 52. That made no sense either.

Warne was a genius, but spoke like (and to) the man on the street. He was a playboy who raised money for Sri Lankan sea turtles. He spotted weakness from 22 yards, and bullshit a mile off. And could he bowl. When 100 experts chose *Wisden's* Five Cricketers of the Century, he alone was still playing, carved into Mount Rushmore, safe in the knowledge he would merit his place when he retired.

His contribution to leg-spin, cricket's toughest skill, hardly needs restating. Just as immense was the blow he struck for all bowlers. Three of the Cricketers of the Century – Don Bradman, Jack Hobbs, Viv Richards – were batters, and the all-rounder, Garry Sobers, averaged 57. But Warne drew the gaze to the other end of the pitch. He was a one-man theatre, a walking box office.

His ball to Mike Gatting in Manchester earned instant membership of a hall of fame, where stars are indistinguishable from their signature deed: Roger Bannister breaking the four-minute barrier, Geoff Hurst's hat-trick or Diego Maradona's Hand of God, Jonny Wilkinson and his drop goal. And, like many who transcend their sport, Warne held up a mirror to his society, exposing the puritanism just below Australia's sunny exterior. Even before he served a year's ban for taking a prohibited substance, he was the captain the Establishment could barely bring themselves to anoint. When he did get a brief go, in the late 1990s, he was innovative, provocative, daring. Without knowing it, he was one of Bazball's forebears. Warne is gone, but not his spirit.

Let's rip this Gideon Haigh, *Wisden* 2023

On the evening of June 4, 1993, the Carbine Club – bonded by "sport, fellowship and the community"– gathered at the Melbourne Cricket Ground for their annual dinner. Guest speaker was Terry Jenner, the cricketer-turned-coach who had recently been associated with Shane Warne, the rising leg-spinner. Before long, a television at the back of the room, tuned to Channel Nine, began screening the First Test of the Ashes from Old Trafford. As the night neared its end, a club member was standing beside Jenner as his protégé took the ball for the first time.

This part of the story we know: after veering to leg, Warne's leg-break reversed course and cuffed off stump, leaving Mike Gatting between wind and water, and the world agog. The reaction at the MCG? "You cunt!" said Jenner. "You fucking little cunt!" The club member couldn't believe what he was hearing. "But Terry," he pointed out. "That ball…" Jenner broke into a smile. He had, he explained, had a long conversation with Warne about how to approach his initial overs against England. Nothing special, they agreed. Feel your way into the contest. Be patient.

So much for that: Warne had decided he was the contest, and would not wait. He later transcribed his interior monologue: "You gotta go. Come on, go mate, pull the trigger, let's rip this."

Thirty years on, Warne is gone, but his signature feat and its impact abide. One of the most remarkable features of the Ball of the Century is that nobody had imagined such a notion until it happened. We were seven years from the new millennium before it was proposed that a single delivery could stand out from everything before it. Baseball had its Shot Heard Round the World, football its Hand of God. But cricket had never so isolated, analysed, celebrated or fetishised a single moment. Here was the mother of all highlights, ahead of a boom in the concept expedited by a format – T20 – geared to their mass manufacture.

Also leaning against the trend towards commodification was Warne, who never bowled a ball without expecting to appeal, was always shrugging off the ordinary in quest of the extraordinary, and forever reminded us that we love cricket because we don't know what will happen, rather than because we wish for an orderly procession of familiar events. Nobody saw Warne coming; nobody has replaced him. He benefited, to be sure, from the Australian initiative of a cricket academy in Adelaide, which is where he first encountered Jenner. Yet Warne was there only because his preferred career as an Australian Rules footballer in Melbourne had petered out. Even then, he was rejected at first for his youthful wildness. "Cricket found me," he was wont to say, which was not quite accurate, but as an idea uplifting.

The balance of his career, in some ways, had to contour itself to the template of that first ball. In the aftermath of his death, highlights reel after highlights reel was presented for our delectation, offering variations on the same theme. Warne's inimitable pause at the end of his run; Warne's seemingly artless approach; Warne's hugely powerful surge through the crease, for an instant almost airborne. Then came that little interlude of the ball's flight, beguiling but deceptive; and, at last, the springing of the trap, the baffling break, the bewildered response, the flying bails. He bowled only 16% of his 708 Test victims, but disintegrating stumps – the bowler's vindication and the batter's abjection – are an entire story, accessible to everyone.

Yet these reels hardly did his career justice. Warne bowled 51,346 balls in international cricket, which means 98% did not take wickets. What really counted was the anticipation experienced in watching him. You wouldn't be anywhere else, didn't dare look away. He stretched our imagination, and our credulity, even telling us so: "Part of the art of bowling spin is to make the batsman think something special is happening when it isn't." We were in the presence, then, of a master illusionist. To vary Arthur C. Clarke's line about technology, any sufficiently advanced leg-spin is indistinguishable from magic.

To reinforce this illusion, to practise what in magic is called misdirection, Warne summoned a deliciously expressive repertoire: gasps, grins, moues, imprecations, scowls and stares. He could not even stand at first slip inconspicuously, given his unmistakable crossing of the legs between deliveries, and his custom of favouring a broad-brimmed sunhat, lightly disturbing the Baggy Green consensus. But it was when he ceremoniously surrendered his hat to the umpire that you took your seat to enjoy the show, starting with the trademark rub of the disturbed dirt in the crease, and the saunter back.

The tennis writer Richard Evans once described the contrast between John McEnroe in repose and in action, how the spindly, puffy-haired, flat-footed figure at the baseline electrified when the ball was in flight. Warne accentuated this by first simply walking – walking! – to the crease. He might have been approaching the umpire to tap his shoulder. Then, to borrow a recent movie title, everything everywhere all at once, the seamless delivery stride and follow-through – the bowling action kept in trim by Jenner, but altered over the journey really only by age and attrition, and then but slightly.

Contrast, too, what was commonly believed about Warne's skill before June 1993, and how he compelled us to adjust our understanding. In the decades before him, only Bhagwat Chandrasekhar, *sui generis*, and Abdul Qadir, *rara avis*, had nourished belief in leg-spin's match-winning properties. It was, we were advised, an unpredictable faculty, an expensive luxury. It involved a great variety of deliveries. It lured batters to destruction by indiscretion. It needed congenial conditions, including dry, dusty or disintegrating pitches. It required constant innovation to stay ahead of the batter, which precluded attention to the game's other departments. Captains might deploy leg-spin to afford their fast bowlers respite. Otherwise it bordered on anachronism.

Apart from a fond regard he expressed for Qadir, Warne showed no sign of having watched any leg-spinner before him, or partaken of any of the skill's associated folk wisdom. By his own admission, his boyhood backyard heroes were Aussie pacemen, macho and theatrical, and batters, tough and leathery. That is understandable: when Warne came to England that first time, it had been fully 30 years since Australia tackled an Ashes with a world-class wrist-spinner. Coincidentally, that cricketer, Richie Benaud, was calling the Manchester Test when Warne bowled to Gatting, and was there to pronounce, now and ever more: "He's done it."

By the time Warne had departed the Test stage, he had repudiated all those prior beliefs. His cardinal virtue was as much his accuracy as his degree of spin. He bowled with prodigious precision and relatively few variations; he hemmed batters in from all angles, including round the wicket, and succeeded in all climes and countries, with the exception of India, previously held to be spin's great citadel, and to a lesser extent the West Indies. The discrepancy between his home and away bowling averages was less than two runs. Nor did Warne revert to the mean: after the Ball of the Century, his career average fluctuated little, while his most prolific years were separated by over a decade (72 wickets at 23 in 1993, and 96 at 22 in 2005).

Above all, Warne was never other than a frontline weapon. He saw bowling defensively as a contradiction in terms. He sought neither protection nor reinforcement. On the contrary, he rejoiced in being Australia's sole spinner, and was notably less effective in partnership with Stuart MacGill, another gifted leggie. When Colin Miller supplanted Warne for a Test in Antigua in April 1999, he never forgave his captain, Steve Waugh. His great confrère was instead Glenn McGrath, a pace bowler with similarly robust core skills, and the same mix of patience and aggression. Warne enjoyed batting, was handy enough at No. 8 to allow Australia to do without a bona fide all-rounder, and excelled in the field, taking 205 international catches. He was leaving accumulated knowledge and established ideas in the dust.

Warne was also busily transcending our conception of a cricketer. It need hardly be said that he rewrote the book on fame. In Australia before him, Don Bradman had set the standard for deportment in greatness – a monument as much as a man, an austere figure sealed off by his renown. Warne ascended no pedestal. By his colourful lifestyle he made privacy elusive, but by his personality he made public dealings easy. After his death, it seemed almost everyone had their own Warney story: he had a capacity for seeing others, for recognising them, for making them feel a little special. There had been other glamorous cricketers: Miller and Compton, Lillee and Imran. But nobody tackled fame so willingly, so hungrily, with an enthusiasm almost ingenuous.

Especially once introduced to social media, which allowed him to monitor and regulate his interaction with the outside world, he provided cheery relief from seriousness, and in a way that seemed breezily natural. "If you're happy all the time," he would say, "good things will happen to you." Never mind that the latter also helps the former: he matured into a splendid advertisement for being famous, apparently enjoying every minute.

But the celebrity perishes with him; it's as a cricketer Warne will endure. He unveiled his own statue at the MCG; now half the ground bears his name. When the Melbourne Cricket Club foreshadowed the Great Southern Stand in 1991 by explaining that the structure was "too significant in every sense to be named after any one individual cricketer, footballer, administrator or public figure", they expressed the conviction that "posterity will support the decision". When the Victorian government decided within hours of Warne's death that it would be rebaptised the Shane Warne Stand, it seemed the most natural thing in the world.

It's arguable that Warne has, inadvertently, proven a mixed blessing for those striving to follow his example. It was expected he would inspire a generation to take up slow bowling, and perhaps he did, but he also set a standard that made it difficult for them to persist. The Australian men's team restlessly turned over a dozen spinners in the five years after his retirement, before settling on the phlegmatic off-breaks of Nathan Lyon. Warne's most successful imitators, unexpectedly, have been female: Australia's Georgia Wareham, Amanda-Jade Wellington and Alana King.

The only bowler Warne did not overawe, perhaps, was himself. After the close that evening at Old Trafford, he and his colleagues sat around the dressing-room watching a BBC wrap of the day, and replay upon replay of that delivery. "Mate," said his wicketkeeper, Ian Healy, "that is as good a ball as you will ever bowl." A daunting idea, one might think, at 23. What to aim for now? What to do next? So it was that he started on the path to becoming as good a slow bowler as there will ever be.

Set phases to stun   Andy Zaltzman, *Wisden* 2023

Shane Warne's 15-year Test career can be statistically divided into four main phases: a brief apprenticeship, followed by two prolonged flowerings of unmatched mastery of cricket's most difficult art, either side of a three-year relative slump, aggravated by injuries – and Indians.

Phase 1 encompasses his first eight Tests, from January 1992 to January 1993, in which he managed 14 wickets at almost 50. Starting against India, he became part of a list – now numbering 14 – of bowlers who in their first two Tests took no more than one wicket for at least 200 runs. Ten of the other 13 finished their career with fewer than five wickets; apart from Warne, only Andrew Caddick went beyond 30.

Warne's early struggles were interrupted by a match-winning three-wicket burst against Sri Lanka in Colombo (until then, his Test figures were one for 335), and seven for 52 against West Indies at Melbourne. Even so, he had a poor start to his Test career. Of the 106 Australian men to have bowled at least 1,000 deliveries in their first eight Tests, only three had a higher average than his 49: Ian and Greg Chappell, both back-up bowlers, and leg-spinner Peter Sleep. And only five had a higher economy-rate than Warne's 3.25.

His greatness – **Phase 2** – emerged in New Zealand early in 1993, when he took 17 cheap wickets. Then came Old Trafford, where Warne erupted into Ashes immortality with his hypnotic, physics-querying ball to Mike Gatting, perhaps the most memorable delivery out of more than nine million in all international cricket.

England's collective batting psyche never recovered, although that summer they did not collapse to him. The Gatting ball was merely the first of Warne's 2,639 in the 1993 Ashes, still a record for any Test series, and he took just one five-for. But he conceded less than two an over, and bowled a staggering 178 maidens, almost 30 per game (only Alf Valentine, with 197 for West Indies in England in 1950, has bowled more six-ball maidens in a Test series). On batting-friendly pitches, then, England were rendered strokeless by a 23-year-old. No Australian spinner had bowled 40 overs in a Test innings in England since Ashley Mallett at The Oval in 1975. Warne did so seven times in 1993, including all six second innings. From then until the end of the 1997-98 Australian season, he was brilliant. This first period of supremacy brought him 289 wickets at 22, with an economy-rate of 2.23.

His one significant slump – **Phase 3** – began and ended with tours of India, early in 1998 and 2001, when he twice averaged over 50. He had undergone shoulder surgery in May 1998, and his 23 Tests in this period yielded 73 wickets at 38, including two for 268 in three Tests in the West Indies, where he was briefly dropped. Overall against India, Warne managed 43 wickets at 47 in 14 Tests, including 34 at 43 in nine in India, when the hosts' slow bowlers took 120 at 29. Elsewhere in Asia, he managed 93 at 20 in 16 games, while opposing slow bowlers averaged 38. But two of those 14 Tests against India came in his debut series, three not long before his surgery, and six in the three years after it. So Warne played just three Tests against India in his two peak periods combined – all away in 2004-05, when his 14 wickets at 30 helped Australia to a 2–0 lead, before a broken thumb forced him to miss the final Test on a Mumbai turner.

This was the only series in his two peak periods when Warne had a higher average than the opposition's spinners. He played in two or more Tests of a series 43 times, and had a better average than opposition spinners 36 times; four of the other seven were against India. In all, his average against them was almost 16 higher than the Indian spinners; against other Test opponents, Warne was better by at least 12. England's spinners, for instance, averaged 47 against Australia in Tests featuring Warne, who averaged 23. South Africa's spinners responded to his 130 wickets at 24 with 54 at 50.

His Test lull happened to encompass his greatest white-ball achievements: in the final three matches of the 1999 World Cup, he took ten for 95 in 29 overs. His ODI stats (293 wickets at 25) do not grab as much attention as his Himalayan Test numbers. And yet of the 62 spinners who bowled at least 150 ODI overs during Warne's career, from March 1993 to January 2005, only Saqlain Mushtaq and Muttiah Muralitharan had a better average. Warne's economy-rate (4.25) and strike-rate (36) were also excellent.

In three of his four World Cup semi-finals or finals, he took four wickets – the exception being the 1996 final, when he was hampered by a slippery ball under lights in Lahore, and went wicketless against superb Sri Lankan batting. Apart from Australia's Gary Gilmour in 1975, no other bowler has taken more than one four-for in World Cup semis or finals. In 68 ODIs after the 1999 final against Pakistan, until he was banned for taking an illegal substance just before the 2003 tournament, he managed just one more four-wicket haul, and averaged nearly 30 (he played only one more ODI after that, for the World XI against Asia at Melbourne early in 2005). Perhaps, big World Cup matches aside, one-day cricket did not fascinate him as much as the five-day game.

Warne found his Test form again in England in 2001 – the start of **Phase 4**. He took 31 wickets at 18 in five Tests, striking every 38 balls, twice as often as he had over the previous three years. (He also became the second bowler to take separate hauls of one, two, three, four, five, six and seven in a series, after India's Subhash Gupte, another leggie, against New Zealand in 1955-56.)

THE WARNE PHASEBOOK

	Dates	T	O	M	R	W	BB	5i	10m	Avge
Phase 1	Jan 1991–Jan 1993	8	214.3	40	699	14	7-52	1	0	49.92
Phase 2	Feb 1993–Jan 1998	56	2,917	955	6,517	289	8-71	13	4	22.55
Phase 3	Mar 1998–Mar 2001	23	937.4	231	2,794	73	5-52	2	0	38.27
Phase 4	Jul 2001–Jan 2007	58	2,715	535	7,985	332	7-94	21	6	24.05
		145	6,784	1,761	17,995	708	8-71	37	10	25.41

After an ineffective series against New Zealand later in 2001, Warne played 16 more Test series (plus the one-off match against an ICC World XI). Australia won 15. Even in the exception – the 2005 Ashes – Warne constructed his greatest all-round performance: 40 wickets at under 20, and 249 runs at 27. By now, his batting had evolved from handy to influential, while his slip catching was another asset. His last 70 Tests produced a batting average of 20 (it had previously been 14), with ten of his 12 half-centuries, and 72 catches.

It was appropriate that Warne's defining delivery and his greatest series both came in England. When he arrived in 1993, England had for decades been inimical to his art. Since the second of Bill O'Reilly's Ashes tours, in 1938, front-line wrist-spinners – including Gupte, Richie Benaud, Bhagwat Chandrasekhar and Abdul Qadir – had averaged over 40. The most wickets by a wrist-spinner in a series in England in the 50 years before Warne was Gupte's 17 in five Tests for the 1959 Indians.

By the end of his second Test in England, Warne had 16. By the end of the third, he had become the first touring wrist-spinner to take 20 in a series there since O'Reilly. By the end of the sixth, he had become the first to take 30, a total exceeded in 2001 and 2005. Not only did he stun, then surgically dismantle, England's batting, he became more dominant as his career progressed. On his four Ashes tours, England found more ways of scoring off him: 1.99 an over in 1993, 2.43 in 1997, 2.96 in 2001, 3.15 in 2005. But they also found more ways of getting out: his strike-rates were 77, 59, 37 and 37.

He maintained astonishing consistency. Between November 2001 and his penultimate Test, at the MCG in the 2006-07 Ashes, Warne took two wickets in one or both innings of 49 consecutive games – only Murali, with 52, has a longer sequence. This second period of greatness brought 332 wickets in 58 Tests at 24, with an economy-rate of 2.94.

Test batting had become more attacking during Warne's career, yet he still exerted mastery. That made this final phase arguably his greatest. While his average was a little higher (24 to 22), he took more wickets per match (5.72 to 5.16). He had become what had seemed impossible – an even better bowler.

After his international career finished, with a total of 1,001 wickets (999 for Australia, two for the World XI), Warne helped establish wrist-spin's pre-eminence in the early years of the T20 format, and was among the leading wicket-takers in the first four seasons of the IPL, with 57.

Alongside the second golden age of leg-spin, Muralitharan purveyed an unprecedented brand of off-spin. The only bowler with more Test wickets than Warne, Murali collected 800 at 22 each, to Warne's 25. Murali had a better economy-rate (2.47 to 2.64) and strike-rate (55 to 57); he took 67 five-fors to Warne's 37, and 22 match hauls of ten, a dozen more than Warne. And all from fewer Tests: 133 to Warne's 145.

But if you remove Tests against Zimbabwe and Bangladesh (of which Murali played 25, and Warne three), Murali took 624 wickets at 24, Warne 691 at 25. Away from home against top-eight sides, Warne took 372 wickets at 24, Murali 252 at 28. Murali shouldered the burden, and harvested the statistical rewards, of being his team's main bowler; for much of his career, he had only Chaminda Vaas as significant wicket-taking support. Warne played mostly in a potent attack, founded on the greatness of Glenn McGrath.

In a wider context, Warne's achievements are even more striking. Leg-spin, if not dying, was only occasionally emerging from its sickbed. Following its rapid evolution in the early 20th century, it was prominent between the two World Wars, when wrist-spinners collectively averaged 32, fractionally better than the combined figure for finger-spinners and seamers. From 1946 to 1976, wrist-spinners averaged 37, the rest 30; between 1977 and 1991, they averaged 36, the rest 30.

Warne's Test career began in January 1992, and lasted 15 years and four days. He finished with 708 Test wickets at 25. During his career, all other wrist-spinners – including some of its best exponents, such as Anil Kumble, Stuart MacGill and Mushtaq Ahmed – averaged 34, and non-wrist-spinners 32. After his retirement, it took 392 Tests, over more than ten years, for all wrist-spinners to match Warne's career aggregate; those 708 wickets cost 40 each.

TEST RECORD AGAINST EACH TEAM

	T	O	M	R	W	BB	5i	10m	Avge
Bangladesh	2	87.2	12	300	11	5-113	1	0	27.27
England	36	1,792.5	488	4,535	195	8-71	11	4	23.25
India	14	654.1	139	2,029	43	6-125	1	0	47.18
New Zealand	20	961.4	252	2,511	103	6-31	3	0	24.37
Pakistan	15	675	192	1,816	90	7-23	6	2	20.17
South Africa	24	1,321.2	367	3,142	130	7-56	7	2	24.16
Sri Lanka	13	527.5	132	1,507	59	5-43	5	2	25.54
West Indies	19	679.4	159	1,947	65	7-52	3	0	29.95
World XI	1	31	7	71	6	3-23	0	0	11.83
Zimbabwe	1	53.1	13	137	6	3-68	0	0	22.83
	145	6,784	1,761	17,995	708	8-71	37	10	25.41

Warne played 194 ODIs (including one for a World XI), taking 293 wickets at 25.73.

Cricket is one of the most measurable sports, though Warne, like all greats, cannot be measured in statistics alone, however staggering. It is impossible to quantify an aura, or the transmission of belief to team-mates, or doubts implanted in opposition minds. Numbers cannot capture the magnificence of his cricket, or the drama he created. He expanded the possibilities of his craft and his sport, enraptured the game for a decade and a half, and set standards of control, penetration and consistency which others could not hope to emulate. And yet statistics can illustrate the extent of his brilliance, give context to his achievements, and shine a light on the uniqueness of one of its defining giants.

Andy Zaltzman is the Test Match Special *statistician.*

Showman, mind reader, master *Wisden* 2023

Shane Warne took 708 Test wickets, behind only Muttiah Muralitharan's 800. His landmark victims – those he dismissed to notch up each century – reflect on what made him so hard to face.

100: Brian McMillan – lbw b Warne 4, v South Africa at Adelaide, 1993-94
Pat Symcox, Daryll Cullinan and I formed a think tank to decide the best way to play Shane Warne. We decided to treat every ball as if it was the flipper, seeing as we couldn't pick it. If it wasn't, then we would have time to adjust, and play it on merit. There would be no pulling – in case it was the flipper. So he would go round the wicket, we would pad away everything that pitched outside leg stump. Warney hated that, and he would invariably come back over the wicket, and we would revert to Plan A. His 100th wicket was… a flipper. Of course it was. The best-laid plans! I played back, and it hurried through.

Not long after, in South Africa, he spun one between my legs as I tried to kick it away, and bowled me. I looked a right prick, but then he made a few of us look pricks. He was incredibly competitive, but I loved playing against him. I am happy to say he was a genuine cricketing mate, and we enjoyed lots of banter and beers together. Sometimes brilliance isn't fully appreciated until it's gone, but we were all fully aware we were in the presence of greatness, even in those early years.

200: Chaminda Vaas – c Healy b Warne 4, v Sri Lanka at Perth, 1995-96
Most of the Sri Lankan side had not played a Test in Australia, so there was a lot of excitement. This was Perth, and all the talk was about how the pacies were going to dominate. But Warney was equally effective.

It was the first time I had played against him in any cricket, and he got me twice – both caught behind by Ian Healy. The second dismissal, the result of a big drive that went straight up in the air, was his 200th.

Looking back, I sense he had the wood over some of us. Rather than playing him on merit, we were obsessed with analysing him, and we paid the price. Aravinda de

Silva also got out to Warne twice in that game, for ten and 20. When he's making the team's best batsman look ordinary, there was little the rest of us could do. Warney was great, but not because of all his variations, his ability to turn the ball, or his accuracy; there were spinners more talented than him. Warney played with your mind – and cricket, after all, is a mind game.

300: Jacques Kallis – b Warne 45, v South Africa at Sydney, 1997-98
I loved playing against him, once I realised what he was all about, and I got over the fact that I was a youngster. No matter how intense the situation, it was fun. He was a showman and, as a batter, you were part of his show.

In the Boxing Day Test the week before the 300th, I helped save the game, and he was the first to come to our change-room with a couple of beers. He was generous enough to say was one of the best innings anyone had played against him, which pretty much summed him up. I still regard it as one of the best Test hundreds I scored, if not the best.

At Sydney he was all over us. He took five in the first innings, and he'd already taken five in the second by the time he got me. We were seven down for not many, but I'd been keeping him out. He came round the wicket, which we used to think was a good sign because he was getting frustrated. I was looking to use the pad as much as possible, but he was pitching everything in line with the stumps, so I had to play. He beat me in the flight with a googly – a googly from round the wicket! It just slipped under the bat, and hit two-thirds of the way up middle and off.

Strangely enough, I didn't find him too hard to read, but reading a ball and playing it are different skills. He was way too good for me that day.

400: Alec Stewart – c Gilchrist b Warne 29, v England at The Oval, 2001
I played a forward defence, and didn't quite cover the ball, which allowed it to pitch and turn. As I played it, I hit the bottom of my pad with my bat. I just felt I didn't hit the ball, and I got called into the match referee's room afterwards, as I'd been reported for dissent by umpire Peter Willey. It cost me £1,000.

I got out to Warne 14 times in Test cricket, more than anyone else, but if I had my time again, I would have attacked him more. We always found ourselves on the back foot against Australia, and trying to survive. We could have taken the game to them in a controlled way, yet we were too respectful, especially to Warne. I wish I'd not allowed him to dominate me and the team.

Of course, he was the master of setting you up, and I got done by his flipper in Brisbane the first time I faced him in Australia. I cut him for four, then he sent down what I thought was a long hop, went to pull it, and was bowled.

Leg-spin is the hardest art in the game, and Warne mastered it. He possessed an unbelievable cricket brain and, because of his control, he could put his plans in place seamlessly. We were never ahead in enough games against Australia to change his thinking.

500: Hashan Tillekeratne – c Symonds b Warne 25, v Sri Lanka at Galle, 2003-04
Shane was on his comeback after his 12-month ban [for taking a proscribed substance], and the race for 500 wickets was intense between him and Murali, who began the game on 485 to Warne's 491. I was Sri Lanka's captain, and we had done really well in the first three days, carving out a first-innings lead of 160 or so. But Australia made over 500 in their second, and Shane started turning things in their favour.

It was remarkable, as he had played just a couple of first-class games before this Test. By the time I was dismissed, they had the game in the bag. He came on for a fresh spell, and I scored a straight boundary from his first ball. Next ball, I went for a big sweep, but got a top edge and was easily caught close in by Andrew Symonds. We were kicking ourselves at losing that Test. That's what can happen when they have someone like Shane in the side.

I remember his parents were there to see him get to 500. He was player of the series, and unstoppable. We lost 3–0, and I never played Test cricket again. Murali took 11 wickets in that game to Warne's ten, but had to wait until the next Test to follow him to 500.

600: Marcus Trescothick – c Gilchrist b Warne 63, v England at Manchester, 2005
I knew what an important wicket it was – we were going well – but it was also really annoying, because I was so unlucky. The ball was outside off stump. I tried to sweep it, and it bounced round off my body, caught the back of my bat, deflected on to Adam Gilchrist's knee and popped up into his gloves. Lucky so and so! But the celebrations were quite special. Shane was the first to get 600 Test wickets, and on my wall at home I've got a picture of the ball in mid-flight, with Gilchrist about to complete the catch. Warne signed it at the end of the series.

It was the execution of his skills that made him so special. Other spinners tried different things, like coming round the wicket, or bowling into the rough with a different field, and you would always feel there was a period in which you could get a few away. I never felt like that with Warne.

As good as Muttiah Muralitharan and Anil Kumble were, you felt at some stage you had a chance to build momentum. Maybe playing against Murali in England was different from playing him in Sri Lanka, but wherever you played against Warne, it felt as if he pressured you the whole time. The only way I could counter him was to be really aggressive, and that meant taking chances. You never got to the stage of spreading the field and knocking him around.

700: Andrew Strauss – b Warne 50, v England at Melbourne, 2006-07
It was dank and overcast, and you didn't really expect Warne to be bowling. There wasn't a lot of turn, so it felt like an opportunity to score. He moved midwicket away, which was very clever. As a left-hander, you felt you were going to hit a lot of balls into that region off him – and he'd offered me a big gap. People who watch replays of the delivery ask why I played the shot, or how I could have missed it, as it didn't really do that much.

But it needs context. You have to take the field setting into consideration. He bowled the ball wider, and I tried to fetch it from outside off stump. Once again, Warne was one step ahead. He did me – not for the only time.

He was a brilliant bowler – no one disputes that – but what made him so special was his showmanship, an ability to use the occasion in his favour. He seemed to understand what was going through your mind. Then there was the task of simply facing him. He would play on this in any way he could, whether through smart field changes or making you feel as uncomfortable as possible. There wasn't a great deal of sledging. He would just project his presence on to you. It was intimidating.

In some ways, it can be more menacing facing a spinner than a seamer, because you have more decisions to make. Against a seamer, you just react to what comes down. Against a spinner, there are many more options to weigh up: run down the pitch, slog-sweep, or survive? Warne's skill was to know what you were going to do before you did it.

Interviews by Neil Manthorp, Rex Clementine and Richard Gibson.

Obituary *Wisden 2023*

WARNE, SHANE KEITH, AO, died of a heart attack on March 4, aged 52, while on holiday in Thailand – the news reported around the world. If his death came as a shock to millions, the wall-to-wall coverage did not. Warne had been nicknamed "Hollywood" in his teens, and felt like public property from the moment he bowled Mike Gatting with his first ball in Ashes cricket, a ferocious leg-break, at Manchester in 1993; he finished with 708 Test wickets, overtaken only by Muttiah Muralitharan. For a while, he was engaged to the British actor and model Liz Hurley, enthusiastically embracing the celebrity lifestyle. He also became a professional poker player. His memorial service at the MCG, his spiritual home, was attended by more than 50,000, including many big names from Australian public life. No compatriot since Don Bradman had transcended cricket like Warne. He was, simply, a superstar.

The legend was born with a single delivery. It was June 4, 1993, the second day of the First Ashes Test at Old Trafford, when Allan Border asked Warne – rosy-cheeked, nose smeared with cream, spiky hair bleached blond – to bowl. Warne later claimed he was "pumped up and rocking and rolling". Actually, he was nervous as a kitten: landing the ball somewhere close to the right spot would have been success enough. Instead, he created folklore. After a casual stroll to the crease and a whirring shoulder, he made the ball dip, swerve outside leg, spit across Gatting's half-forward defence at a set-square angle, and clip off stump. "First ball!" said BBC commentator Tony Lewis, who like many could not quite believe his eyes. "Now, what's happened? Mike Gatting's staying there. The bail is off. He's bowled him! Gatting can't believe it… First ball: lethal."

By the time Warne played the last of his 145 Tests, helping Australia to a 5-0 Ashes whitewash at Sydney in January 2007, only Muralitharan had more than his 1,001 international wickets. But a more important statistic remains unknown: the number of boys and girls drawn to cricket by Warne's energy and joy. He didn't just weaponise wrist-spin: he covered it with glitter and imbued it with glamour.

Accurately landing a leg-break is as hard as spinning it prodigiously. Warne could do both. While he had a flipper, top-spinner and a reasonable googly, it was his leggie that made him special. A serendipitous accident as a child – he broke both legs, and for a year wheeled himself around on a customised trolley – had built up his shoulders, which were so strong he barely needed a run-up. Thick sausage-fingers enveloped the ball, and his personality exerted a crushing grip too. According to Ramiz Raja, the former Pakistan batsman: "He created this slow death and slow drama." Some of the theatrics took place before the cricket began, and few Ashes build-ups were complete without Warne announcing his latest delivery – usually one of his normal balls rebranded as an innovation, such as the slider or the zooter.

Gatting considered him "without a doubt the No. 1 bowler ever"; Mike Atherton thought him the most intelligent he faced. Warne was a stock and strike bowler combined, in perhaps the greatest side of all time. Twice, between October 1999 and February 2001, then between December 2005 and January 2008, Australia won 16 Tests in a row, with Warne playing 11 times in the first sequence, and 12 in the second, before retirement. Glenn McGrath proved a wonderful foil, but they were chalk and cheese: Warne the look at-me star of mystery and style, McGrath straightforward and strictly top-of-off.

Warne relished the battle as much as the bouquets, and in this respect the cover images of the 2006 and 2007 *Wisdens* are revealing. Teeth shine and eyes gleam on the first, as Andrew Flintoff drapes an arm around him at the end of the epic 2005 Ashes. It is hard to conclude Warne had finished on the losing side. A year later, he is photographed leaving the field at the SCG, clapping a stump against his palm, mouth now shut, perhaps to hide the emotion. Australia have just hammered England, but there is a sadness: his international race is run.

Gatting besides, there were countless highlights along the way. In 2005 alone, he had astounded Andrew Strauss and Marcus Trescothick with deliveries that spun impossibly. Another left-hander, West Indies' Shivnarine Chanderpaul, had been done similarly a decade or so earlier, while the way Warne set up Pakistan's Basit Ali after a long conflab with wicketkeeper Ian Healy before the last ball of the day at Sydney in 1995-96 became another after-dinner story – appropriate, as they were chatting about where to eat that evening. Daryll Cullinan, meanwhile, was considered one of South Africa's best players of spin, until Warne got inside his head.

As late as 2011, miked up in the Big Bash League, Warne told commentator Brendon Julian he was about to slide one through a bit more quickly, because he fancied Brendon McCullum to sweep. On cue, the ball dipped under McCullum's horizontal bat and hit the stumps. "That worked pretty well," said Julian. "Yeah, not bad, BJ," said Warne with the familiarity that became well-known to viewers in the UK, where he was a regular and insightful member of Sky's commentary team. If he could be repetitive, he was easily forgiven, and usually fair.

And yet, until the 1993 Ashes, his career had been a slow-burner. Aussie Rules rather than cricket was his boyhood passion in the Melbourne suburbs; according to Warne, illness ruined a potential break in the sport, even if he owed the Hollywood nickname to Trevor Barker, his hero at the St Kilda football club. Warne made his first-class cricket debut relatively late, at 21, after summers with club sides in Bristol and Accrington remembered for hedonism as much as cricket. Whether, in 1990, he was told to leave the Australian Cricket Academy, or walked out of his own volition, depends on whom you ask.

But Australia had always backed leg-spin, and Warne was a talent. Within a year of playing for Victoria, he made his Test debut, against India at Sydney in 1991-92. It proved chastening: Ravi Shastri hit 206 before becoming his first Test wicket, and Sachin Tendulkar 148. Warne finished with one for 150, and never altered his opinion that Tendulkar was the best he bowled to. Three late wickets in a narrow win against Sri Lanka in Colombo seven months later were his first significant contribution, before he marked the 1992-93 Australian summer with seven for 52 against West Indies at Melbourne. Seventeen wickets at 15 in New Zealand cemented a trip to England.

They instantly became his favourite opponents, his tally of 195 Ashes wickets a record for any series. Gatting was the first of 34 English victims in 1993 – a performance that made him one of Wisden's Five – while his 27 in 1994-95 included a hat-trick at Melbourne. There were 24 more in England in 1997, then 31 four years later. Asked whether his players might cope better with Warne by fraternising with him, England captain Nasser Hussain, replied: "If you go out with Warne, you don't learn to pick his googly. You just learn he has bad taste in shirts." (His Baggy Green, meanwhile, would generally be discarded in favour of a floppy white sunhat.)

You also learned about his diet. When Graham Gooch joked that Gatting would not have let the ball through had it been a cheese roll, he missed the point: Warne would have eaten it himself. Thick butties lathered in spread and cheddar were among the few foods he ate, and Healy once observed that his "idea of a balanced diet is a cheeseburger in each hand". When Warne saw Ian Botham's foreword to his second autobiography, he was astonished his mate thought he loved ham and pineapple pizza. "He knows it's margheritas," Warne exclaimed, though he respected Botham too much to make the change. He was a heavy smoker, too, and courted trouble in 1999 when he was photographed in a Caribbean bar, cigarette in hand, having been sponsored by a chewing gum manufacturer to quit.

By then, long spells had taken a toll. In 1996, he needed surgery on his spinning finger; two years later, after more punishment from Tendulkar, he underwent a shoulder operation. Warne thought he was at his best between 1993 and 1998, and admitted he was overweight for the next three years. He remained formidable, except against India, who made him pay 47 for each of his 43 wickets. But he compensated for weaker muscles with his experience, growing more adroit at changing his position at the crease and accepting natural variation from wearing pitches. And he could still spin the occasional ball further than anyone. When *Wisden* chose its Five Cricketers of the Century in 2000, Warne was among them. He was the only one still playing – and without a knighthood.

He could be less savvy off the field, and remained vulnerable to a newspaper sting. Naivety also resulted in the two biggest controversies of his career. In 1994, after heavy losses on the roulette wheel in Colombo, he accepted $5,000 from a bookmaker posing as a supporter called "John", who then sought information on pitches and teams; Mark Waugh was also hoodwinked. Cricket Australia covered up the incident but, when the truth broke four years later, Warne appeared shady and duplicitous rather than misguided, having meanwhile reported an approach by Salim Malik to underperform in a Test against Pakistan.

Then, on the eve of the 2003 World Cup in South Africa, he was forced to fly home after a drug test revealed traces of a banned substance. Having dislocated his shoulder in a one-day game against England, he was suspected of taking the diuretic to mask detection of illegal steroids that would have hastened his recovery. (In *The Guardian*, David Hopps noted that even his urine now had highlights.) Warne's explanation, that his German-born mother, Brigitte, had given him the pill to lose weight, was ridiculed by Dick Pound, the head of the World Anti-Doping Agency, but plausible to those who knew his vanity. The one-year ban could have been career-ending; in the soap opera of Warne's life, it merely ended an episode. Returning with 26 wickets in three Tests against Sri Lanka, he convinced himself that his "enforced break" had been a blessing.

Back in 1993, Warne had taken his girlfriend, Simone Callahan, to the Lake District and proposed spontaneously in a rowing boat. Twelve years on, she finally tired of his infidelities, and dissolved the marriage. For Warne, more than most, sport was a sanctuary from the real world and, over eight memorable weeks in 2005, he fought the torment of lonely hotel nights to produce arguably Test cricket's greatest all-round performance in a losing cause: 40 wickets and 249 runs, even if he dropped Kevin Pietersen at slip on the last day at The Oval, 15 runs into his series-clinching 158. Warne's batting was a reminder that he was never far from all-rounder status: 3,154 Test runs at 17 included 12 half centuries and, to his ever-lasting irritation, a top score of 99 (replays showed the delivery he holed out to, from New Zealand's Daniel Vettori, was a no-ball). Had he not stepped on his stumps on the impossibly tense last day at Edgbaston, the 2005 summer might have taken a different course.

Spurred on by Australia's 2–1 defeat, Warne committed himself to one last Ashes, at home in 2006-07, and delivered in the Second Test at Adelaide, an illusionist persuading batsmen that a flat pitch was a bed of snakes. England lost nine for 60, and in these pages Matthew Engel evoked Thomas Carlyle's theory that the human story has been determined by only a few. Warne, he felt, now stood among those Great Men.

He was hardly less effective in one-day internationals. Wearing the No. 23 shirt, after his Aussie Rules hero Dermott Brereton, he took 293 wickets in 194 games, and shone when it mattered. Dropped during the preceding Test series in the West Indies – a slight for which he never forgave Australia's captain, Steve Waugh – he arrived in England for the 1999 World Cup with his shoulder and ego equally bruised, and Simone heavily pregnant back home with the second of their three children (Jackson, who was sandwiched by two girls, Brooke and Summer). As the tournament began, he was warned by the ICC over a newspaper column attacking Sri Lanka's Arjuna Ranatunga, and caused further opprobrium with a middle-finger gesture to a taunting spectator at Worcester.

Australia started the World Cup badly, but rallied as Warne rediscovered his mojo. In one of his most prescient observations, he told a team meeting that South Africa's Herschelle Gibbs sometimes threw the ball away in premature celebration when he took a catch. During a Super Six match at Headingley, Gibbs spilled Waugh in exactly that manner, leading to Waugh's apocryphal line about Gibbs dropping the World Cup. Warne was Man of the Match in the semi-final, also against South Africa, when his four wickets – including Gibbs, bowled by a replica of the Gatting delivery – set up a breathless tie. Australia progressed because of a better net run-rate earlier in the competition. And he claimed the award again in the final against Pakistan, thanks to another four-for. With the trophy secured, he suggested theatrically he might retire because his Test place was uncertain. It wasn't, and he didn't.

The Gibbs insight crystallised why Warne was considered the best Test captain his country never had, mainly because Cricket Australia would not tolerate such a larrikin. Hampshire had no such qualms, with club president Colin Ingleby-Mackenzie, a kindred spirit of yore, declaring at his appointment in 2004: "Lock up your daughters, because Warney's in town." Having coasted for years, Hampshire became ultra-competitive, narrowly missing a first Championship since 1973. Warne took ages to get over Kent captain David Fulton's decision to accept a chase of 420 in 70 overs rather than play for a draw against Nottinghamshire, Hampshire's main rivals, in the penultimate game of 2005. Nottinghamshire won, and pipped Hampshire by 2.5 points. No matter that Warne, who later had a stand at the Rose Bowl named after him, was a gambler himself, happily risking defeat for victory.

But he did triumph with the unfancied Rajasthan Royals in 2008, winning the inaugural Indian Premier League by force of his infectious self-belief on an awestruck group, and conferring on the tournament the stardust it craved in its first year; among the captains of the eight franchises, he was the only non-Indian. More easily forgotten were his 11 one-day internationals in charge of Australia, all but one in 1998-99, with Steve Waugh injured. He won ten, and *Wisden* said his "attacking field placings stopped singles and created pressure. He rallied his troops like a football coach, with plenty of backslaps and good communication."

Tributes to Warne spanned the social divide, from the political elite to the earthiest fan. Pies and fags were left by his statue outside the MCG, where the huge Southern Stand now bears his name. Any young spinner glancing in that direction should be in no doubt about the advice he would offer: whatever you do, give it a rip.

Part Openers

Part One (page 9)

A youthful Warne relishes some interaction with the crowd during the Second Test of the 1993 Ashes series at Lord's.

Credit: Philip Brown/Popperfoto via Getty Images

Part Two (page 61)

Warne bowls in Australia's World Cup victory over West Indies at Old Trafford in 1999. He took three for 11 in 10 overs.

Credit: Popperfoto via Getty Images/Getty Images

Part Three (page 133)

Warne and Ricky Ponting appeal for the catch, and Steve Harmison is out for a duck during England's second innings in the epic Edgbaston Test of 2005. The umpire is Rudi Koertzen.

Credit: Clive Mason/Getty Images

Part Four (page 211)

Another batsman lured to his doom... Warne celebrates with Rajasthan Royals wicketkeeper Dishant Yagnik after Parthiv Patel, of Kochi Tuskers Kerala, is stumped during an Indian Premier League match at Jaipur in April 2011.

Credit: Prakash Singh/AFP via Getty Images

Part Five (page 247)

To cricket-lovers from all over the world, and Australians in particular, Warne's death in March 2022 seemed barely believable. The programme from his funeral service was a painful reminder of the reality.

Credit: William West/AFP via Getty Images

Contributors

Tanya Aldred
Andy Arlidge
Mike Atherton
Sambit Bal
Jack Bannister
Greg Baum
Richie Benaud
Marcus Berkmann
Scyld Berry
Edward Bevan
Soumya Bhattacharya
Harsha Bhogle
Martin Blake
Paul Bolton
Max Bonnell
Richard Boock
Lawrence Booth
Daniel Brettig
Simon Briggs
Alex Brown
Craig Butcher
Mark Butcher
Alex Buzo
Don Cameron
Ken Casellas
Ian Chappell
Hugh Chevallier
Simon Cleaves
Adam Collins
Patrick Collins
Malcolm Conn
Paul Coupar
Mike Coward
John Crace
Robert Craddock

Edward Craig
Tony Cozier
Peter Deeley
Allan Donald
Rahul Dravid
Matthew Engel
Peter English
Melinda Farrell
Stephen Fay
Paton Fenton
David Foot
Neville Foulger
Warwick Franks
David Frith
Nigel Fuller
Stephen W. Gibbs
Andrew Gidley
John Gleeson
Nagraj Gollapudi
Trevor Grant
Gideon Haigh
Peter Hanlon
Ian Healy
Michael Henderson
Jim Higgs
Eric Hill
Robin Hobbs
Richard Hobson
Bob Holland
David Hopps
Jon Hotten
Nick Hoult
Nasser Hussain
Terry Jenner
Ian Jessup

Peter Johnson

Jacques Kallis

Simon Katich

Will Kendall

Jarrod Kimber

Malcolm Knox

Kate Laven

Alan Lee

Jonathan Liew

Tim de Lisle

Simon Lister

David Lloyd

Steven Lynch

Peter McIntyre

Adrian McGregor

John MacKinnon

Brian McMillan

Ashley Mallett

Neil Manthorp

Vic Marks

Norman De Mesquita

Andrew Miller

Alison Mitchell

Kevin Mitchell

Chris Moore

Patrick Murphy

Nick Newman

Daniel Norcross

Scott Oliver

Mark Pennell

Sam Perry

Ken Piesse

Geoff Piggott

Terry Power

Dilip Premachandran

Derek Pringle

Abdul Qadir

Andrew Ramsey

Yas Rana

Mark Ray

Ron Reed

Barry Richards

Peter Roebuck

Graham Russell

Dicky Rutnagur

Christian Ryan

Chloe Saltau

Rex Sellers

Patrick Smithers

Rob Smyth

Rob Steen

John Stern

Alec Stewart

Andrew Strauss

Pat Symes

John Thicknesse

Hashan Tillekeratne

Marcus Trescothick

Frank Tyson

Chaminda Vaas

Phil Walker

Shane Warne

David Warner

Paul Weaver

Danny Weidler

Cameron White

Richard Whitehead

John Woodcock

Bob Woolmer

Andy Zaltzman

Acknowledgments

A number of people were vital in bringing this book to publication and their contributions should not go unremarked. First, I should thank Shane Warne's former partner in crime, Ian Healy, for his heartfelt foreword. Katy McAdam, publisher of *Wisden* and Head of Yearbooks at Bloomsbury, commissioned the book, shepherded it through production, and was helpful in ways too numerous to mention. Christopher Lane, *Wisden*'s Consultant Publisher, has more experience and knowledge of the Almanack than anyone and proved a staunch ally. He made several significant suggestions that improved the final product enormously. John Stern, former editor of *Wisden Cricket Monthly* and *The Wisden Cricketer*, and Tim Hallissey, former Head of Sport at *The Times*, read my section introductions and made shrewd observations and improvements. Walter Gammie's fact-checking of those pieces was also greatly appreciated. Hugh Chevallier, co-editor of *Wisden*, took time out from his busy schedule to scan the magazine covers and cartoons. I should also thank Lawrence Booth, editor of *Wisden*, Jo Harman, editor of *Wisden Cricket Monthly*, plus Marion Brinton and Pete and Rhona Vandepeer.

Bibliography

Although the material in this book is extracted from various editions of *Wisden Cricketers' Almanack, Wisden Cricketers' Almanack Australia, Wisden Cricket Monthly, The Wisden Cricketer, Wisden Asia Cricket* and *The Nightwatchman*, a number of other books on Shane Warne were consulted and proved invaluable. They were:

No Spin: Shane Warne, my autobiography by Shane Warne with Mark Nicholas (Ebury Press, 2018)

On Warne by Gideon Haigh (Simon & Schuster, 2012)

Shane Warne: my autobiography by Shane Warne with Richard Hobson (Hodder & Stoughton, 2001)

Shane Warne: my illustrated career by Shane Warne with Richard Hobson (Cassell Illustrated, 2006)

Shane Warne: portrait of a flawed genius by Simon Wilde (John Murray, 2007)

Index